THE UNITED STATES OF
MURDER INC.

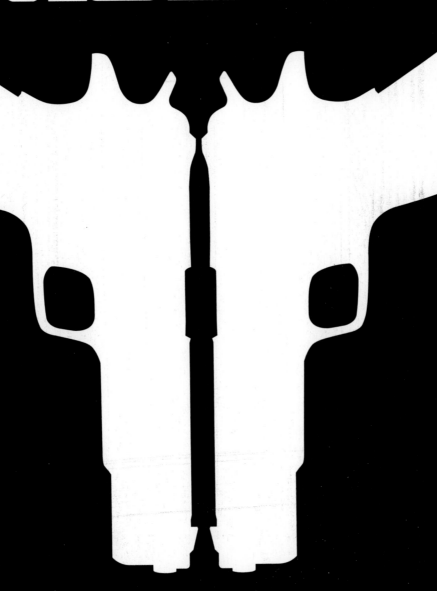

VOLUME ONE
TRUTH

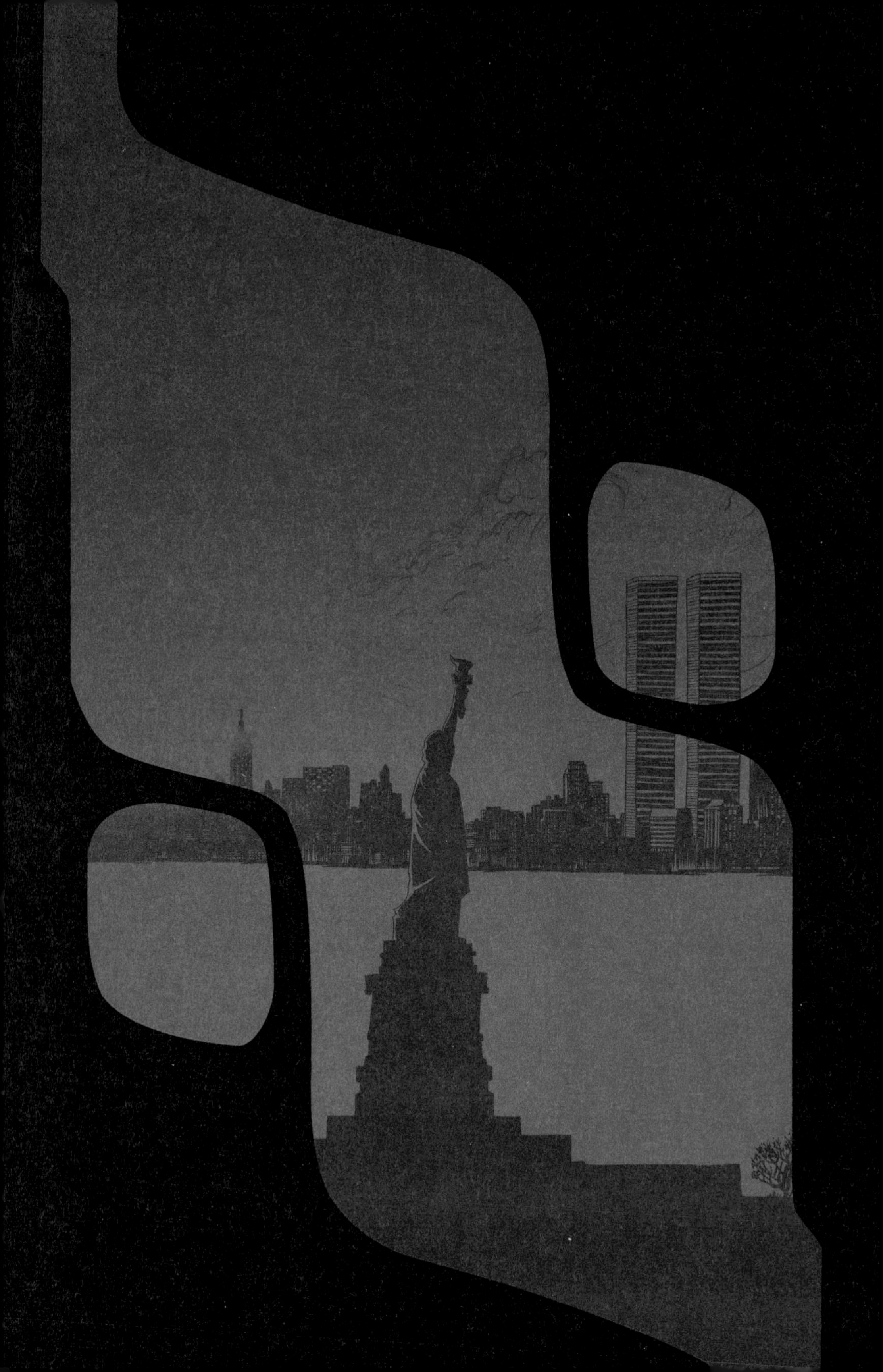

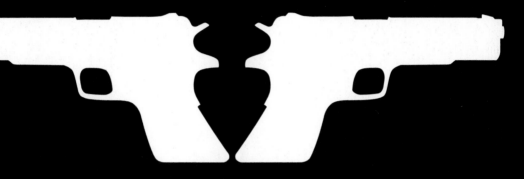

THE UNITED STATES OF MURDER INC.

VOLUME ONE
TRUTH

Created by
BRIAN MICHAEL BENDIS
& MICHAEL AVON OEMING

Colors: TAKI SOMA

Letters: CHRIS ELIOPOULOS

Series and collection cover art: MICHAEL AVON OEMING

Editing and Production: JENNIFER GRÜNWALD

THE UNITED STATES OF MURDER INC. VOLUME ONE: TRUTH

Originally published in single magazine form in THE UNITED STATES OF MURDER INC. 1-6. Copyright © 2016 Jinxworld, Inc. All Rights Reserved. THE UNITED ST
OF MURDER INC., its logo design, the Jinxworld logo, all characters, their distinctive likenesses and related elements featured in this publication are trademark
Jinxworld, Inc. The stories, characters and incidents featured in this publication are entirely fictional. DC Comics does not read or accept unsolicited submission
ideas, stories or artwork.

DC Comics, 2900 West Alameda Ave., Burbank, CA 91505
Printed by LSC Communications, Owensville, MO, USA. 9/7/18. First Printing.
ISBN: 978-1-4012-8746-7

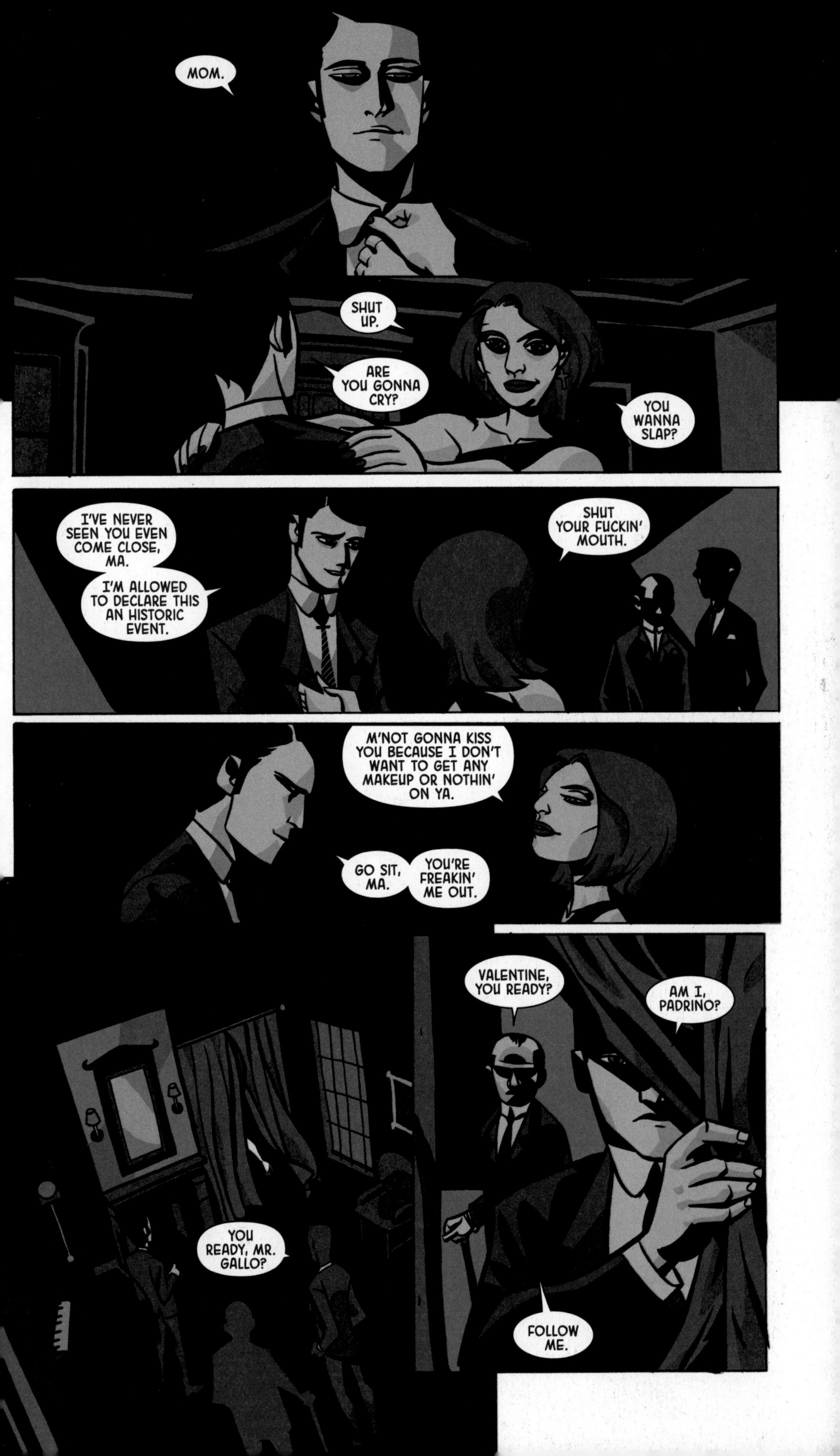
MOM.
SHUT UP.
ARE YOU GONNA CRY?
YOU WANNA SLAP?
I'VE NEVER SEEN YOU EVEN COME CLOSE, MA.
I'M ALLOWED TO DECLARE THIS AN HISTORIC EVENT.
SHUT YOUR FUCKIN' MOUTH.
M'NOT GONNA KISS YOU BECAUSE I DON'T WANT TO GET ANY MAKEUP OR NOTHIN' ON YA.
GO SIT, MA.
YOU'RE FREAKIN' ME OUT.
VALENTINE, YOU READY?
AM I, PADRINO?
YOU READY, MR. GALLO?
FOLLOW ME.

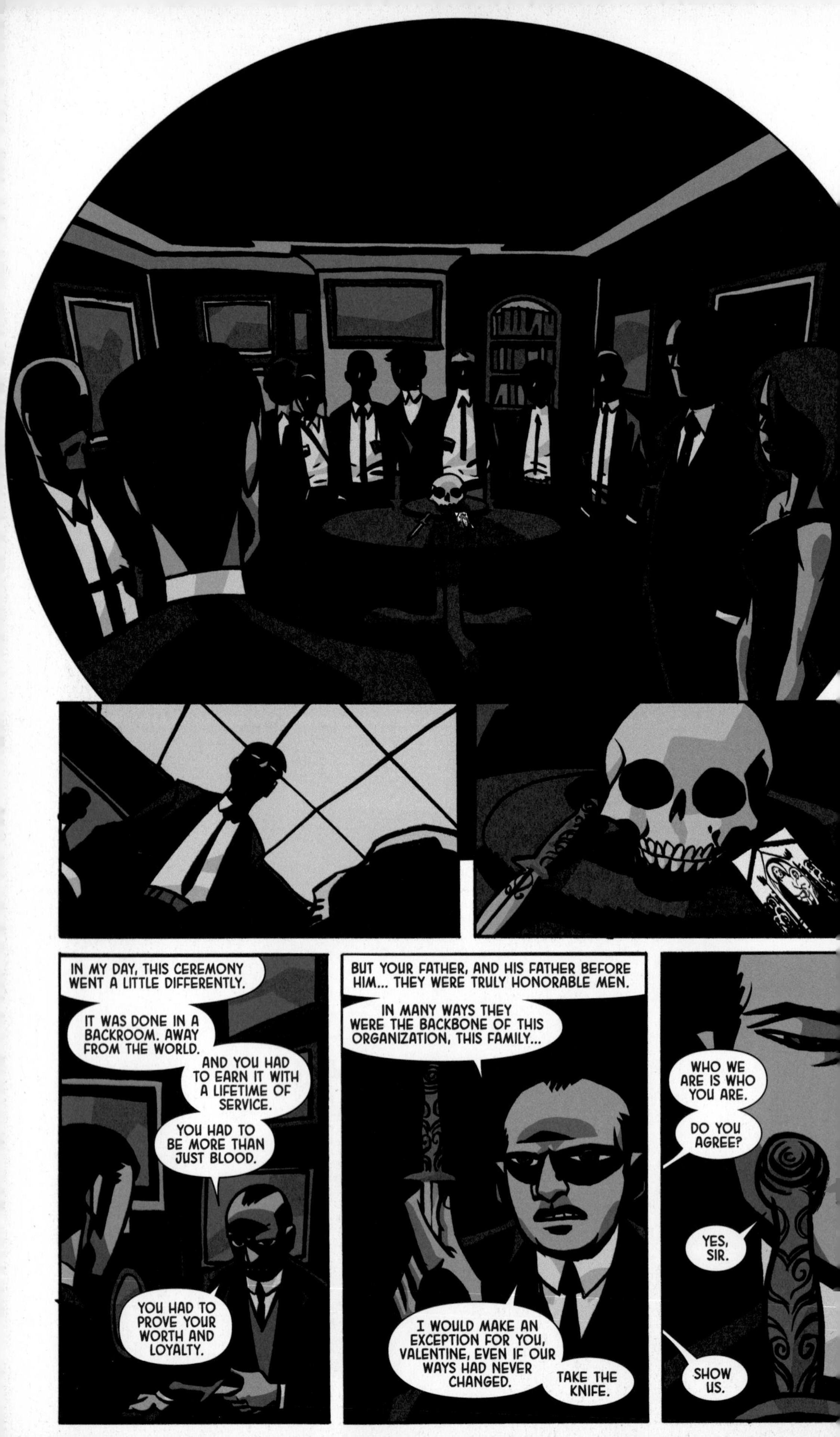
IN MY DAY, THIS CEREMONY WENT A LITTLE DIFFERENTLY.
IT WAS DONE IN A BACKROOM. AWAY FROM THE WORLD.
AND YOU HAD TO EARN IT WITH A LIFETIME OF SERVICE.
YOU HAD TO BE MORE THAN JUST BLOOD.
YOU HAD TO PROVE YOUR WORTH AND LOYALTY.
BUT YOUR FATHER, AND HIS FATHER BEFORE HIM... THEY WERE TRULY HONORABLE MEN.
IN MANY WAYS THEY WERE THE BACKBONE OF THIS ORGANIZATION, THIS FAMILY...
I WOULD MAKE AN EXCEPTION FOR YOU, VALENTINE, EVEN IF OUR WAYS HAD NEVER CHANGED.
TAKE THE KNIFE.
WHO WE ARE IS WHO YOU ARE.
DO YOU AGREE?
YES, SIR.
SHOW US.

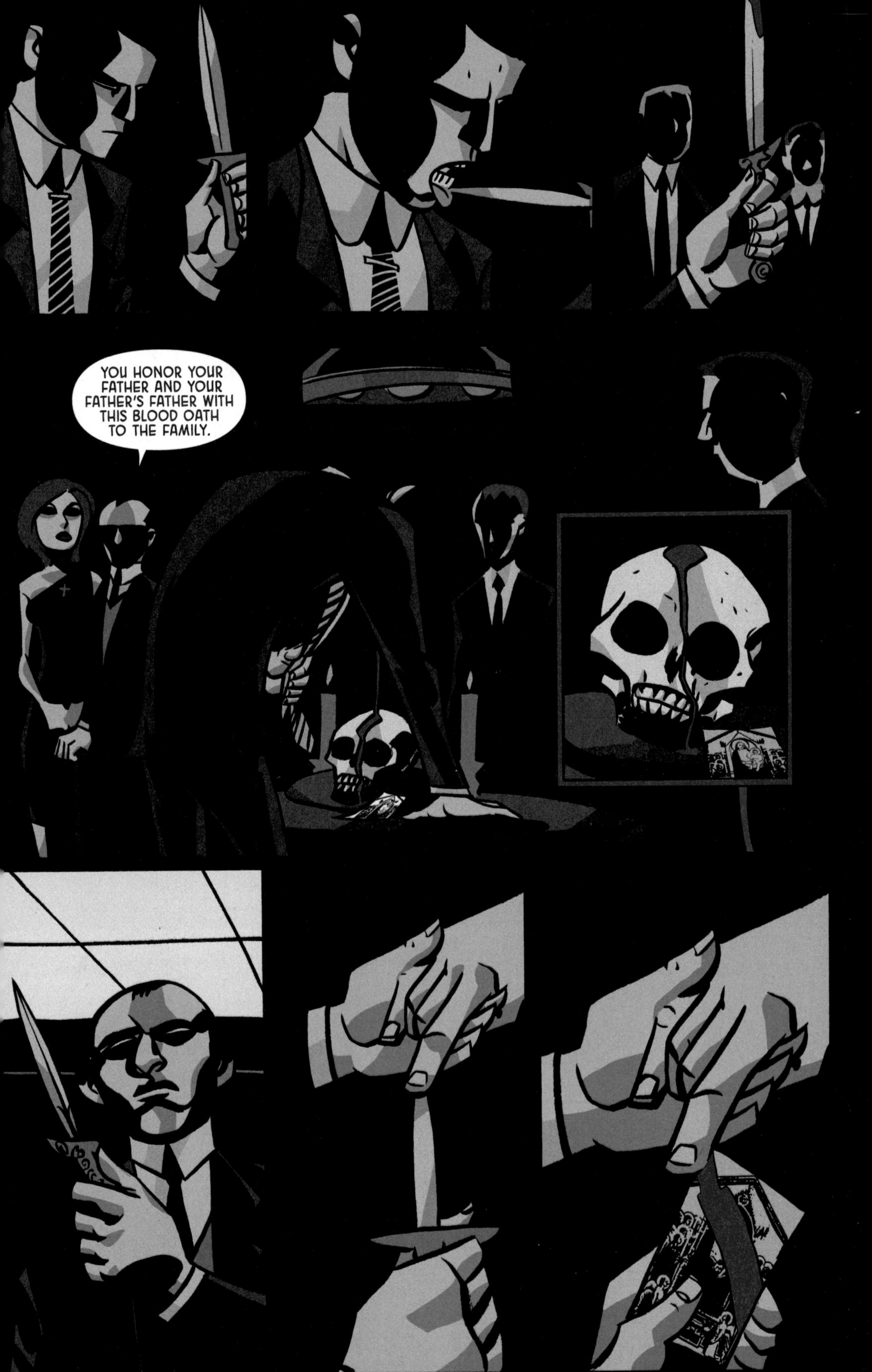
YOU HONOR YOUR FATHER AND YOUR FATHER'S FATHER WITH THIS BLOOD OATH TO THE FAMILY.

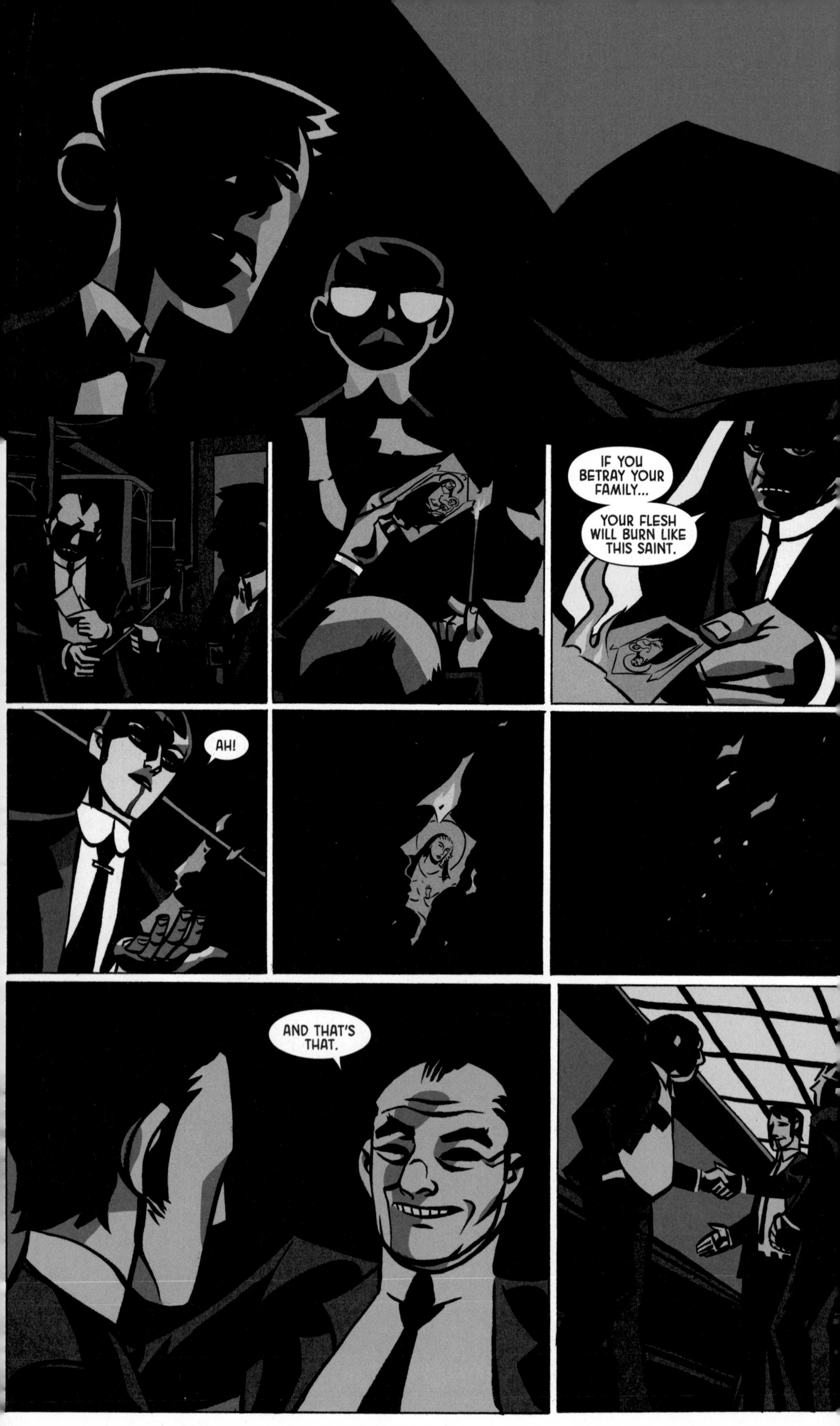
IF YOU BETRAY YOUR FAMILY...
YOUR FLESH WILL BURN LIKE THIS SAINT.
AH!
AND THAT'S THAT.

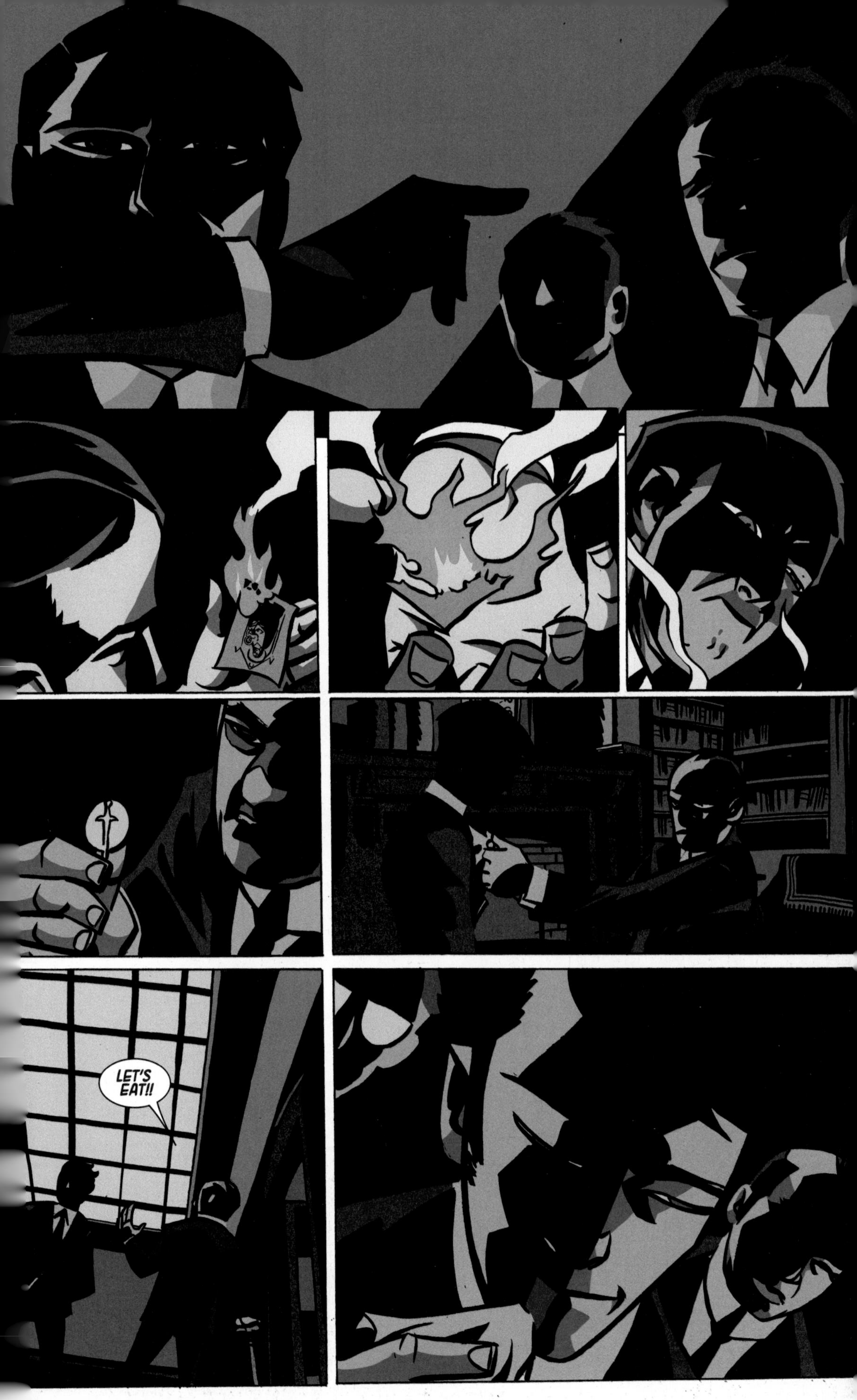
LET'S EAT!!

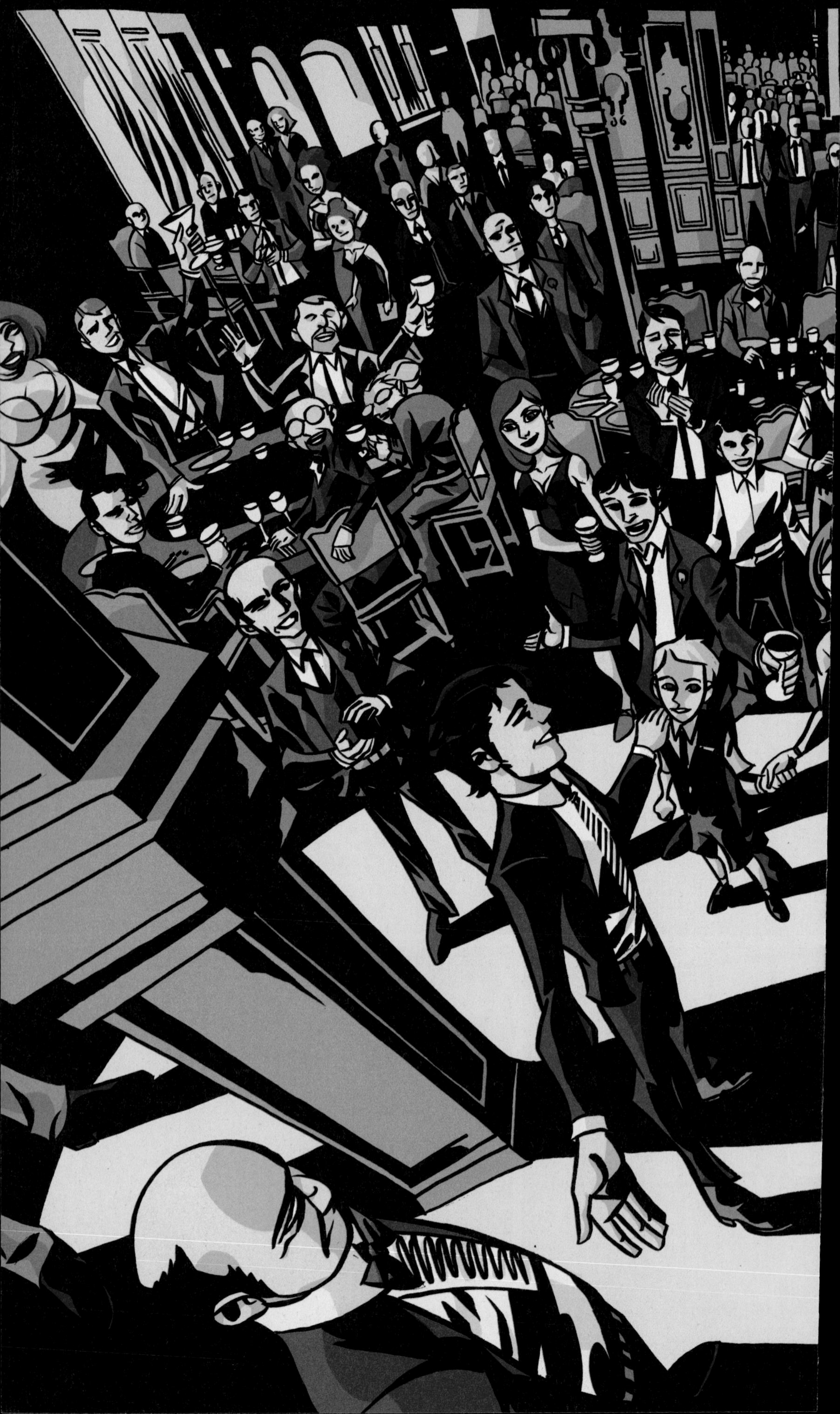

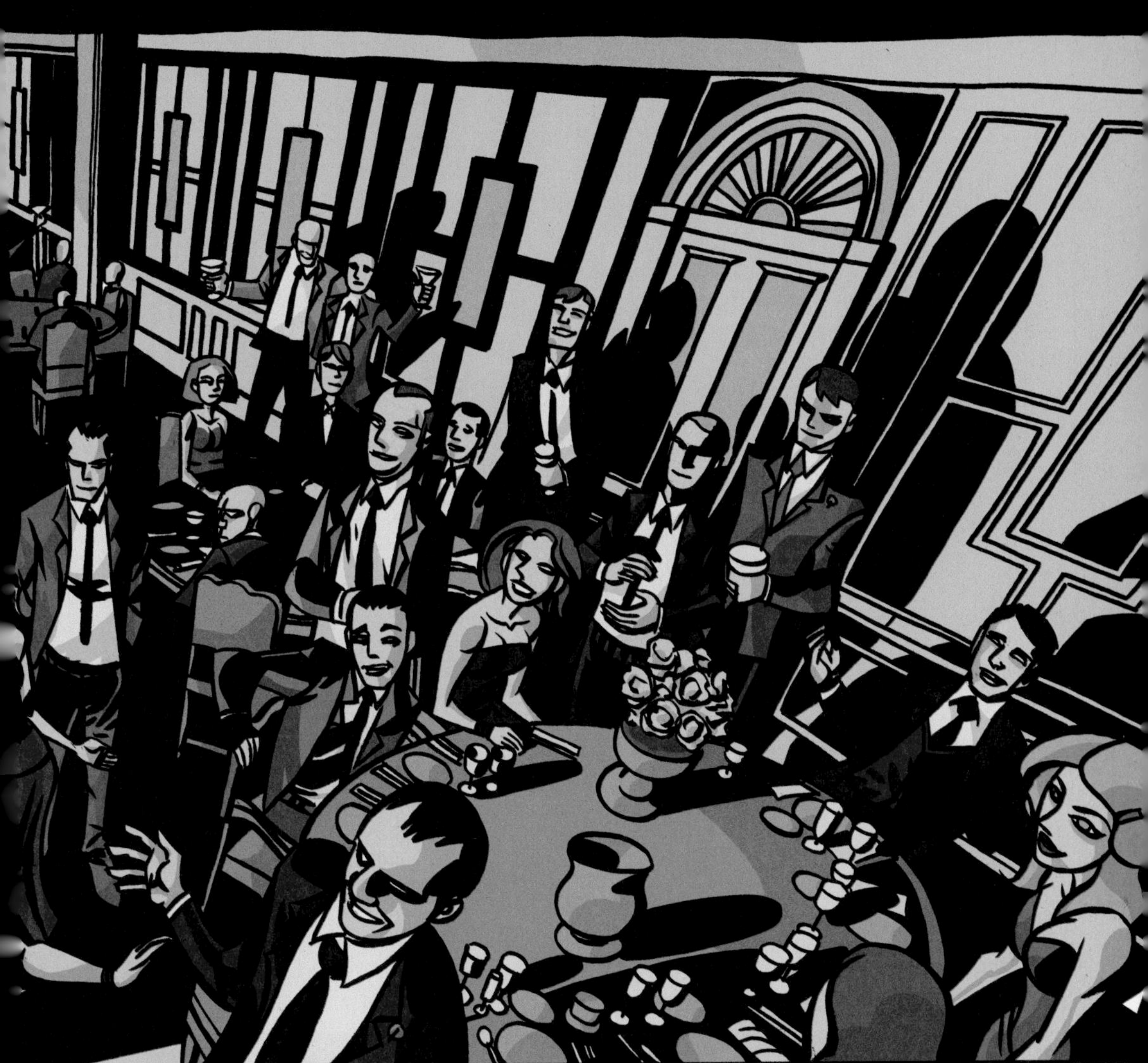

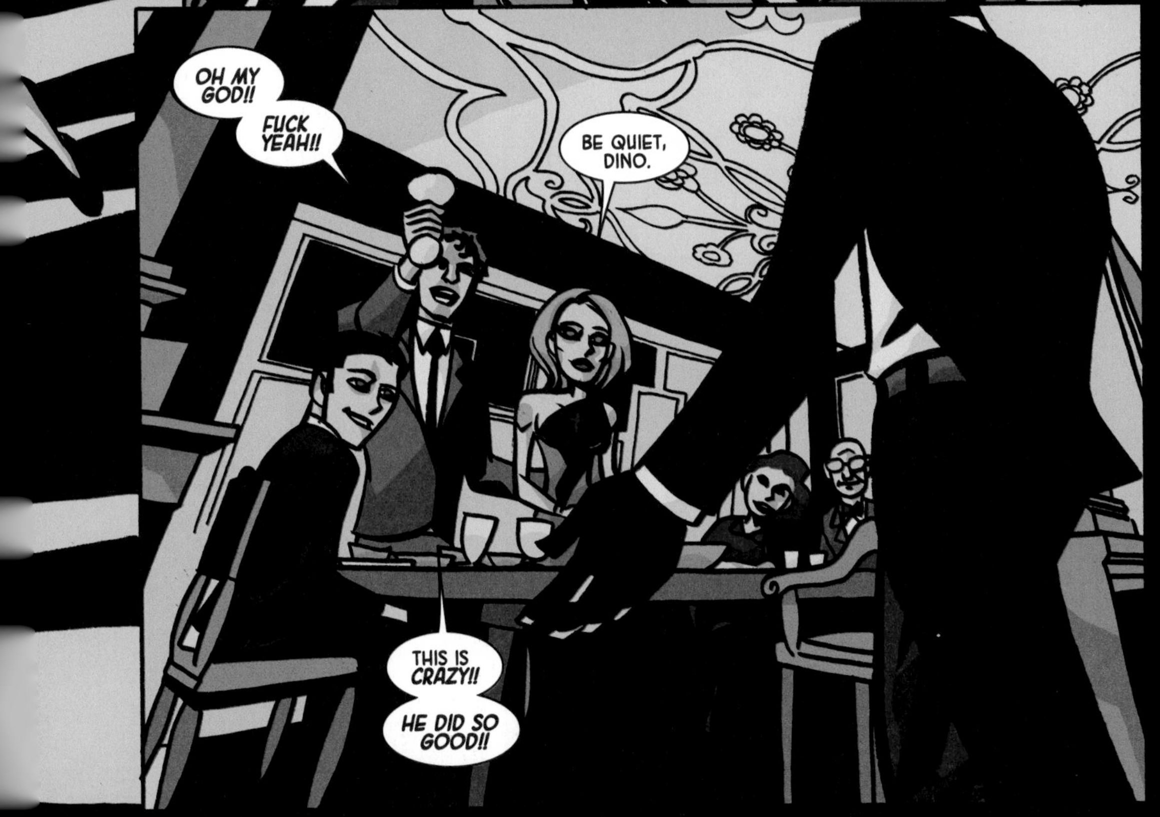
OH MY GOD!!
FUCK YEAH!!
BE QUIET, DINO.
THIS IS CRAZY!!
HE DID SO GOOD!!

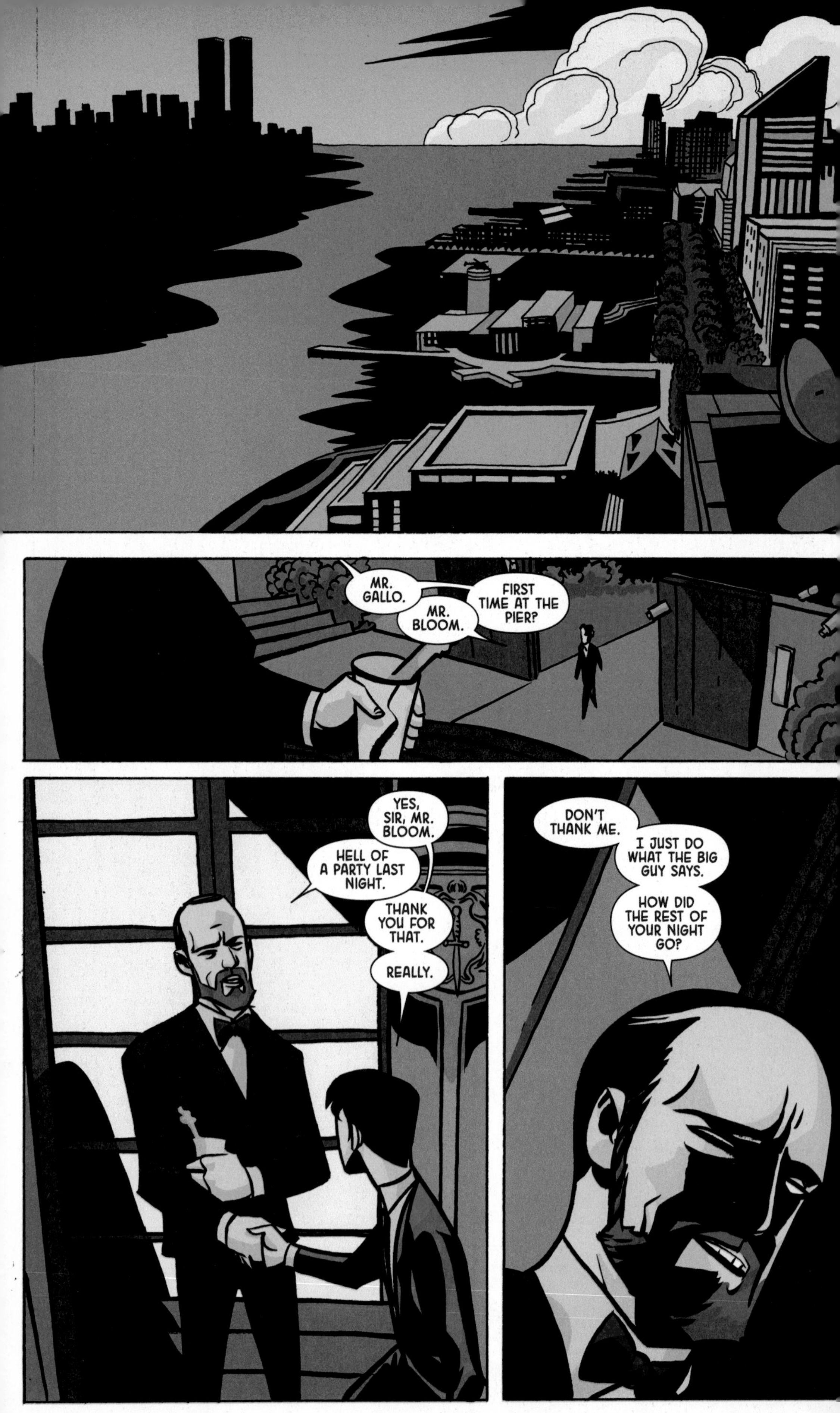

MR. GALLO.
MR. BLOOM.
FIRST TIME AT THE PIER?
YES, SIR, MR. BLOOM.
HELL OF A PARTY LAST NIGHT.
THANK YOU FOR THAT.
REALLY.
DON'T THANK ME.
I JUST DO WHAT THE BIG GUY SAYS.
HOW DID THE REST OF YOUR NIGHT GO?

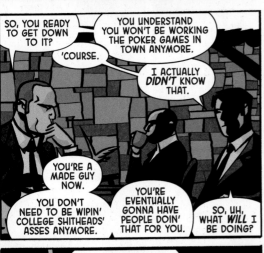

ALL RIGHT.

YOU CAN THANK HIM FOR THAT TOO.

HE'S WAITING FOR YOU.

VALENTINE.

MR. TUZZO.

SO, YOU READY TO GET DOWN TO IT?

YOU UNDERSTAND YOU WON'T BE WORKING THE POKER GAMES IN TOWN ANYMORE.

'COURSE.

I ACTUALLY *DIDN'T* KNOW THAT.

YOU'RE A MADE GUY NOW.

YOU DON'T NEED TO BE WIPIN' COLLEGE SHITHEADS' ASSES ANYMORE.

YOU'RE EVENTUALLY GONNA HAVE PEOPLE DOIN' THAT FOR YOU.

SO, UH, WHAT *WILL* I BE DOING?

TELL HIM.

TODAY YOU'RE GOING ON A LITTLE TRIP. AS A REPRESENTATIVE OF *OURS*.

OH.

YOU'RE GONNA GO TO D.C. AND DELIVER THIS TO A GUY.

D.C.?

WASHINGTON, D.C.?

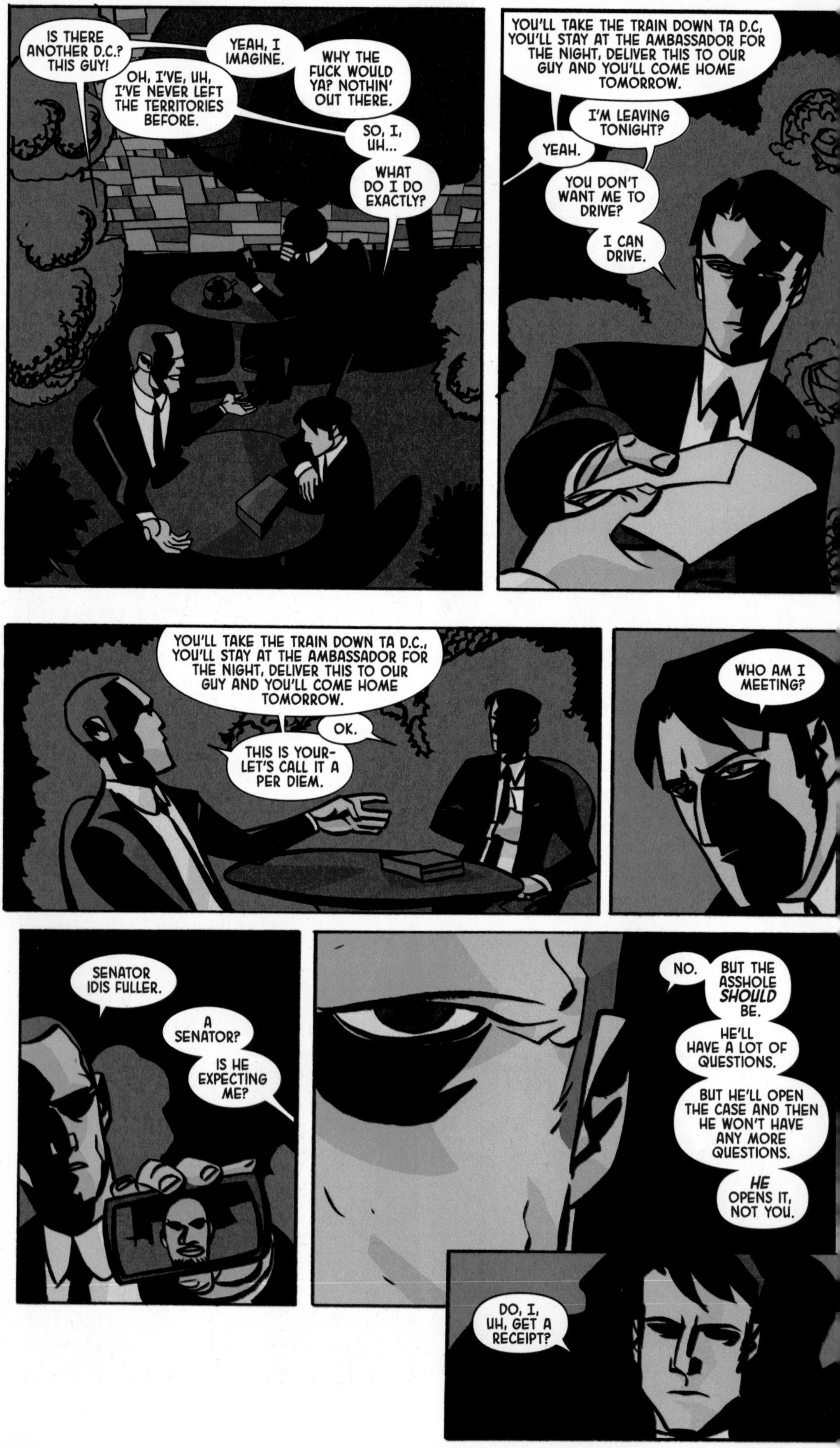
IS THERE ANOTHER D.C.? THIS GUY!
YEAH, I IMAGINE.
WHY THE FUCK WOULD YA? NOTHIN' OUT THERE.
OH, I'VE, UH, I'VE NEVER LEFT THE TERRITORIES BEFORE.
SO, I, UH...
WHAT DO I DO EXACTLY?
YOU'LL TAKE THE TRAIN DOWN TA D.C, YOU'LL STAY AT THE AMBASSADOR FOR THE NIGHT, DELIVER THIS TO OUR GUY AND YOU'LL COME HOME TOMORROW.
I'M LEAVING TONIGHT?
YEAH.
YOU DON'T WANT ME TO DRIVE?
I CAN DRIVE.
YOU'LL TAKE THE TRAIN DOWN TA D.C., YOU'LL STAY AT THE AMBASSADOR FOR THE NIGHT, DELIVER THIS TO OUR GUY AND YOU'LL COME HOME TOMORROW.
OK.
THIS IS YOUR- LET'S CALL IT A PER DIEM.
WHO AM I MEETING?
SENATOR IDIS FULLER.
A SENATOR?
IS HE EXPECTING ME?
NO.
BUT THE ASSHOLE *SHOULD* BE.
HE'LL HAVE A LOT OF QUESTIONS.
BUT HE'LL OPEN THE CASE AND THEN HE WON'T HAVE ANY MORE QUESTIONS.
HE OPENS IT, NOT YOU.
DO, I, UH, GET A RECEIPT?

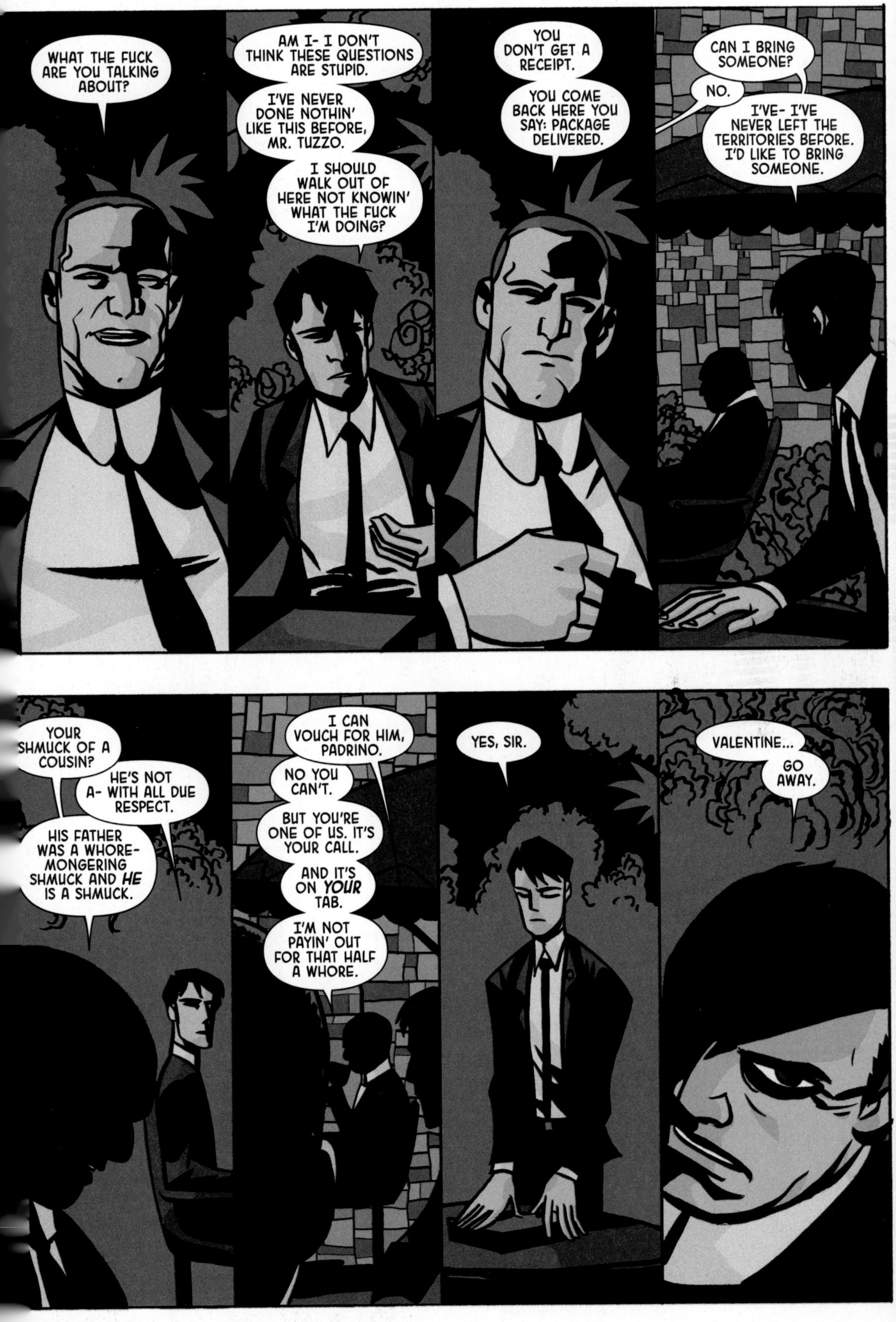
WHAT THE FUCK ARE YOU TALKING ABOUT?
AM I- I DON'T THINK THESE QUESTIONS ARE STUPID.
I'VE NEVER DONE NOTHIN' LIKE THIS BEFORE, MR. TUZZO.
I SHOULD WALK OUT OF HERE NOT KNOWIN' WHAT THE FUCK I'M DOING?
YOU DON'T GET A RECEIPT.
YOU COME BACK HERE YOU SAY: PACKAGE DELIVERED.
CAN I BRING SOMEONE?
NO.
I'VE- I'VE NEVER LEFT THE TERRITORIES BEFORE. I'D LIKE TO BRING SOMEONE.
YOUR SHMUCK OF A COUSIN?
HE'S NOT A- WITH ALL DUE RESPECT.
HIS FATHER WAS A WHORE-MONGERING SHMUCK AND *HE* IS A SHMUCK.
I CAN VOUCH FOR HIM, PADRINO.
NO YOU CAN'T.
BUT YOU'RE ONE OF US. IT'S YOUR CALL.
AND IT'S ON *YOUR* TAB.
I'M NOT PAYIN' OUT FOR THAT HALF A WHORE.
YES, SIR.
VALENTINE...
GO AWAY.

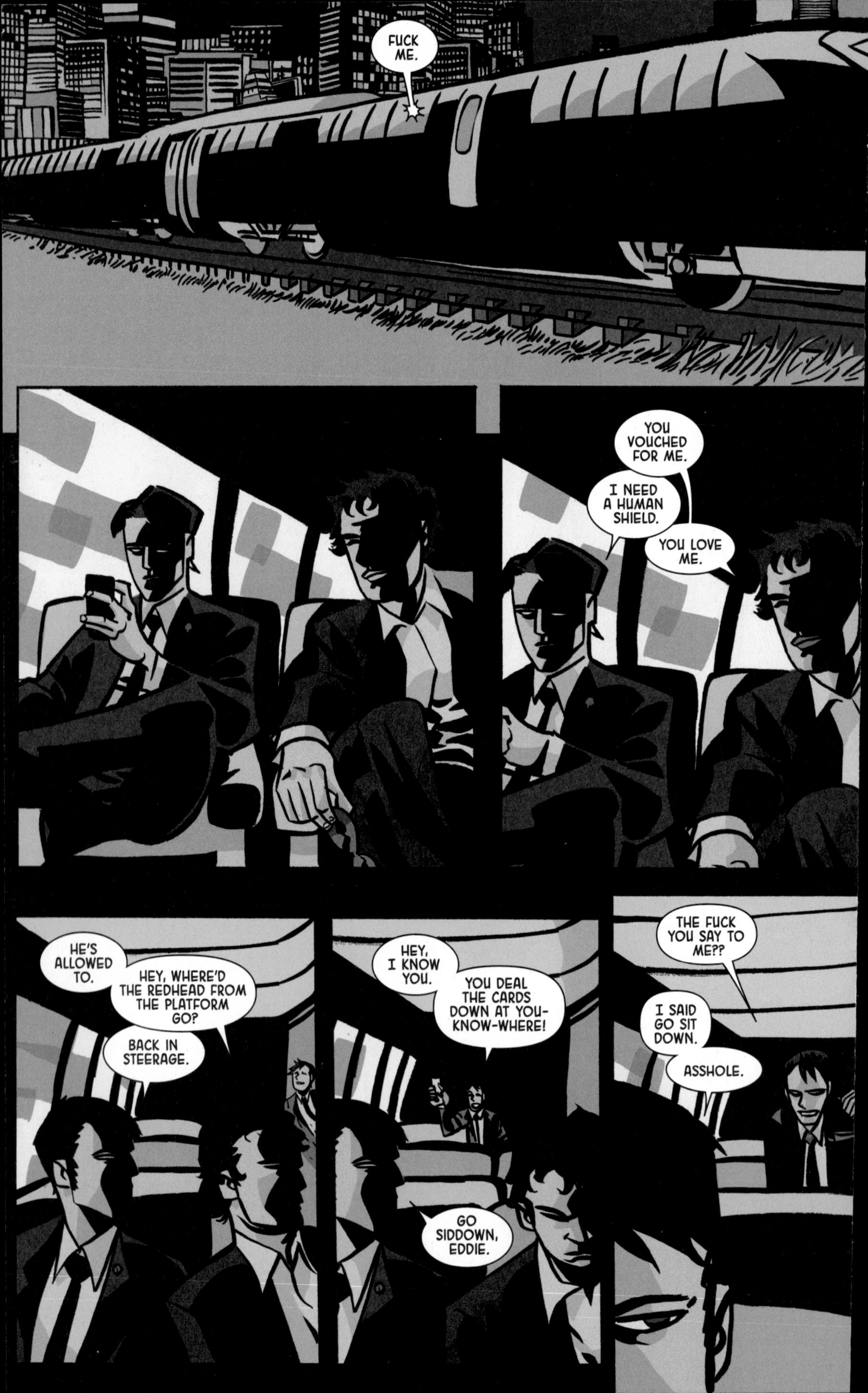
FUCK ME.
YOU VOUCHED FOR ME.
I NEED A HUMAN SHIELD.
YOU LOVE ME.
HE'S ALLOWED TO.
HEY, WHERE'D THE REDHEAD FROM THE PLATFORM GO?
BACK IN STEERAGE.
HEY, I KNOW YOU.
YOU DEAL THE CARDS DOWN AT YOU-KNOW-WHERE!
GO SIDDOWN, EDDIE.
THE FUCK YOU SAY TO ME??
I SAID GO SIT DOWN.
ASSHOLE.

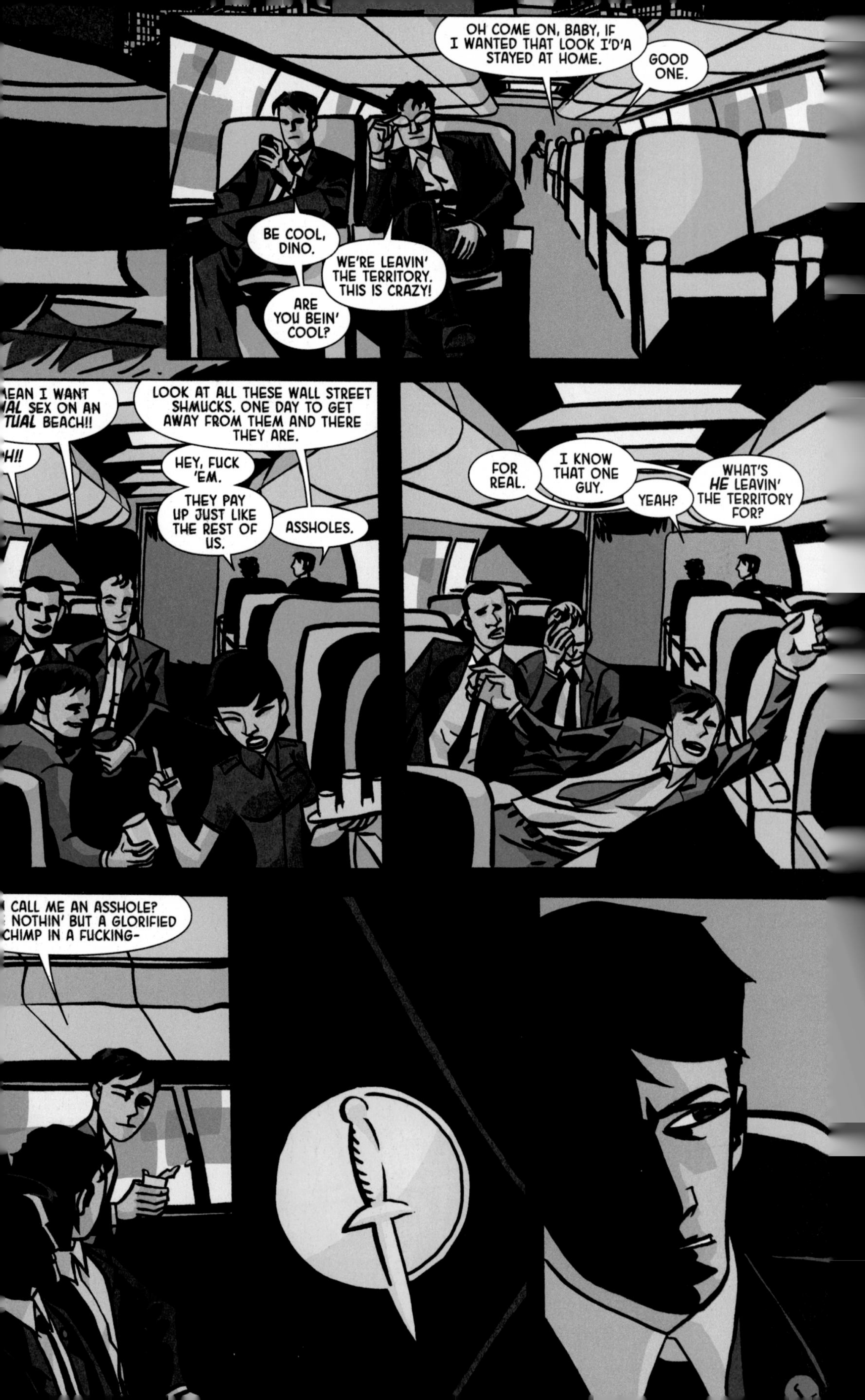
OH COME ON, BABY, IF I WANTED THAT LOOK I'D'A STAYED AT HOME.
GOOD ONE.
BE COOL, DINO.
WE'RE LEAVIN' THE TERRITORY. THIS IS CRAZY!
ARE YOU BEIN' COOL?
EAN I WANT AL SEX ON AN TUAL BEACH!!
LOOK AT ALL THESE WALL STREET SHMUCKS. ONE DAY TO GET AWAY FROM THEM AND THERE THEY ARE.
H!!
HEY, FUCK 'EM.
THEY PAY UP JUST LIKE THE REST OF US.
ASSHOLES.
FOR REAL.
I KNOW THAT ONE GUY.
YEAH?
WHAT'S HE LEAVIN' THE TERRITORY FOR?
CALL ME AN ASSHOLE? NOTHIN' BUT A GLORIFIED CHIMP IN A FUCKING-

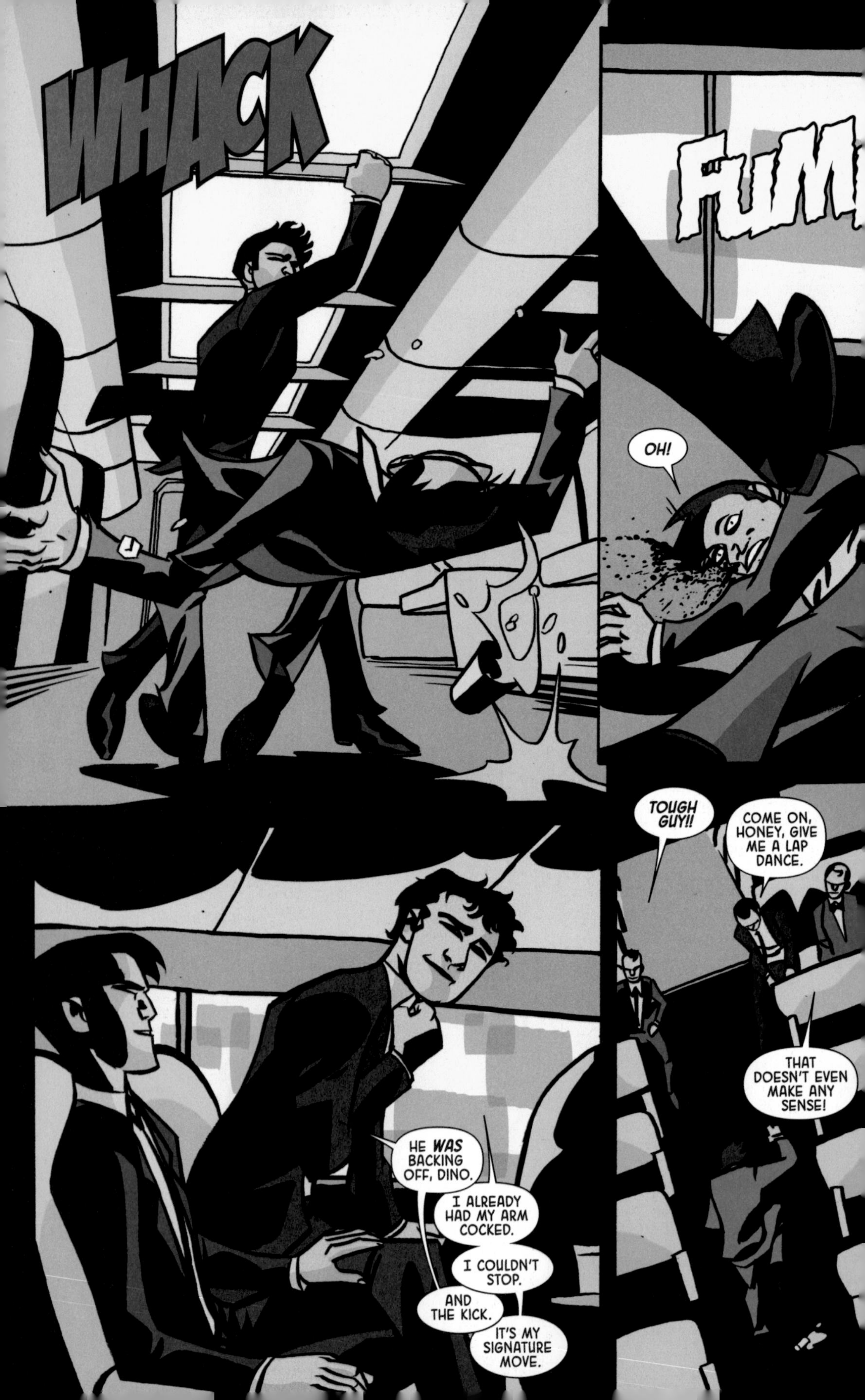
WHACK
FUM
OH!
TOUGH GUY!!
COME ON, HONEY, GIVE ME A LAP DANCE.
THAT DOESN'T EVEN MAKE ANY SENSE!
HE WAS BACKING OFF, DINO.
I ALREADY HAD MY ARM COCKED.
I COULDN'T STOP.
AND THE KICK.
IT'S MY SIGNATURE MOVE.

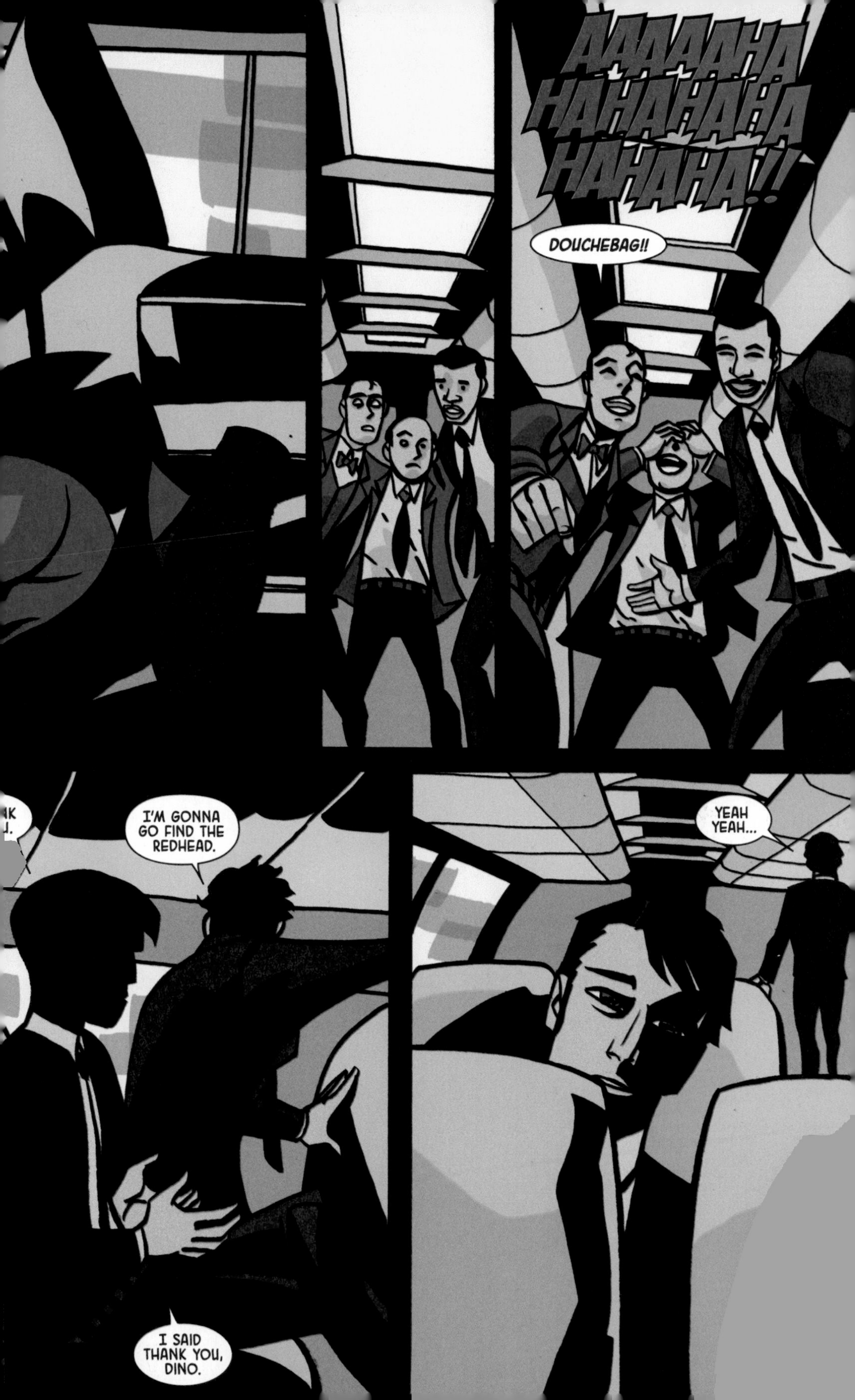
AAAAAHA HAHAHAHA HAHAHA!!
DOUCHEBAG!!
I'M GONNA GO FIND THE REDHEAD.
I SAID THANK YOU, DINO.
YEAH YEAH...

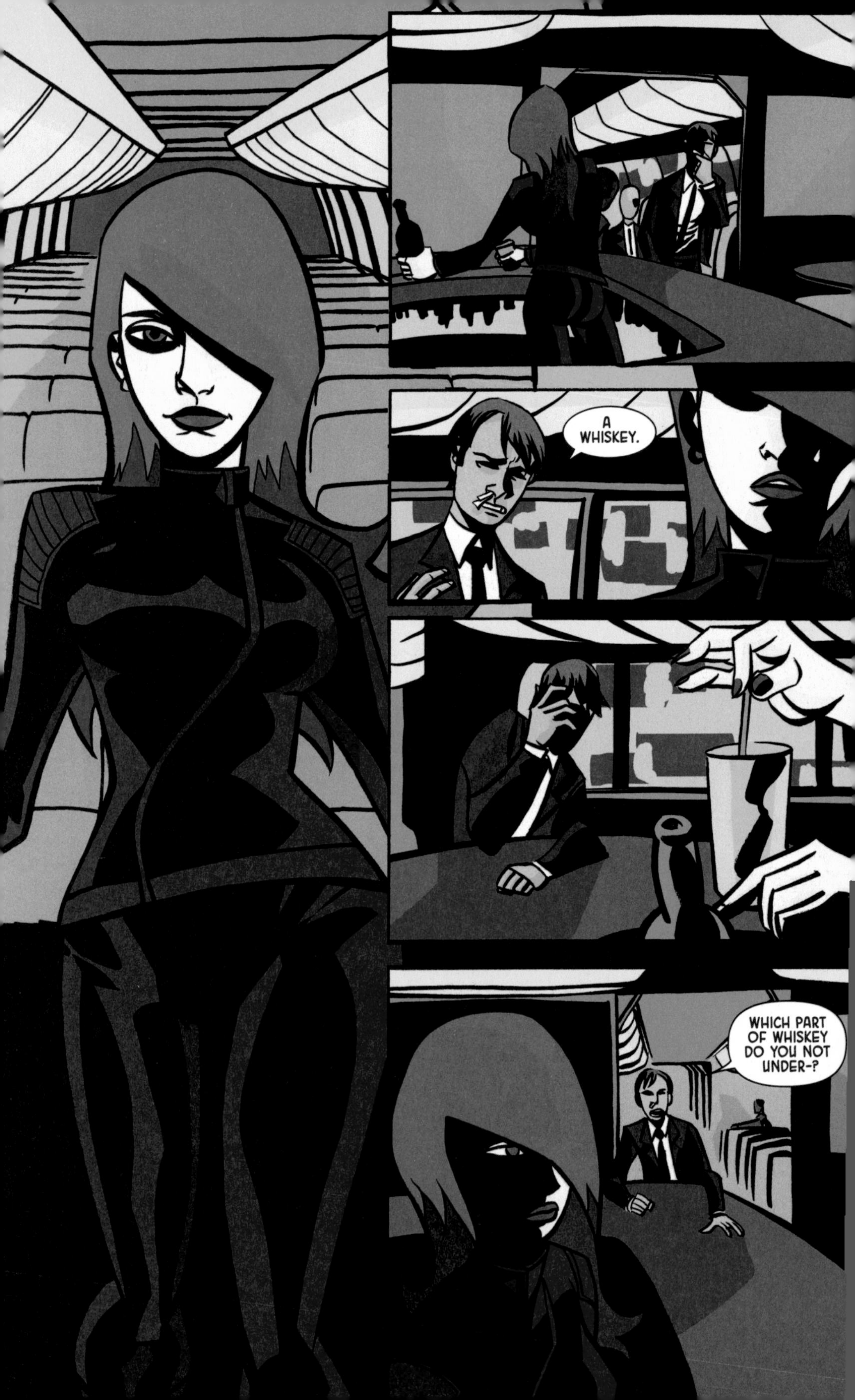
A WHISKEY.
WHICH PART OF WHISKEY DO YOU NOT UNDER-?

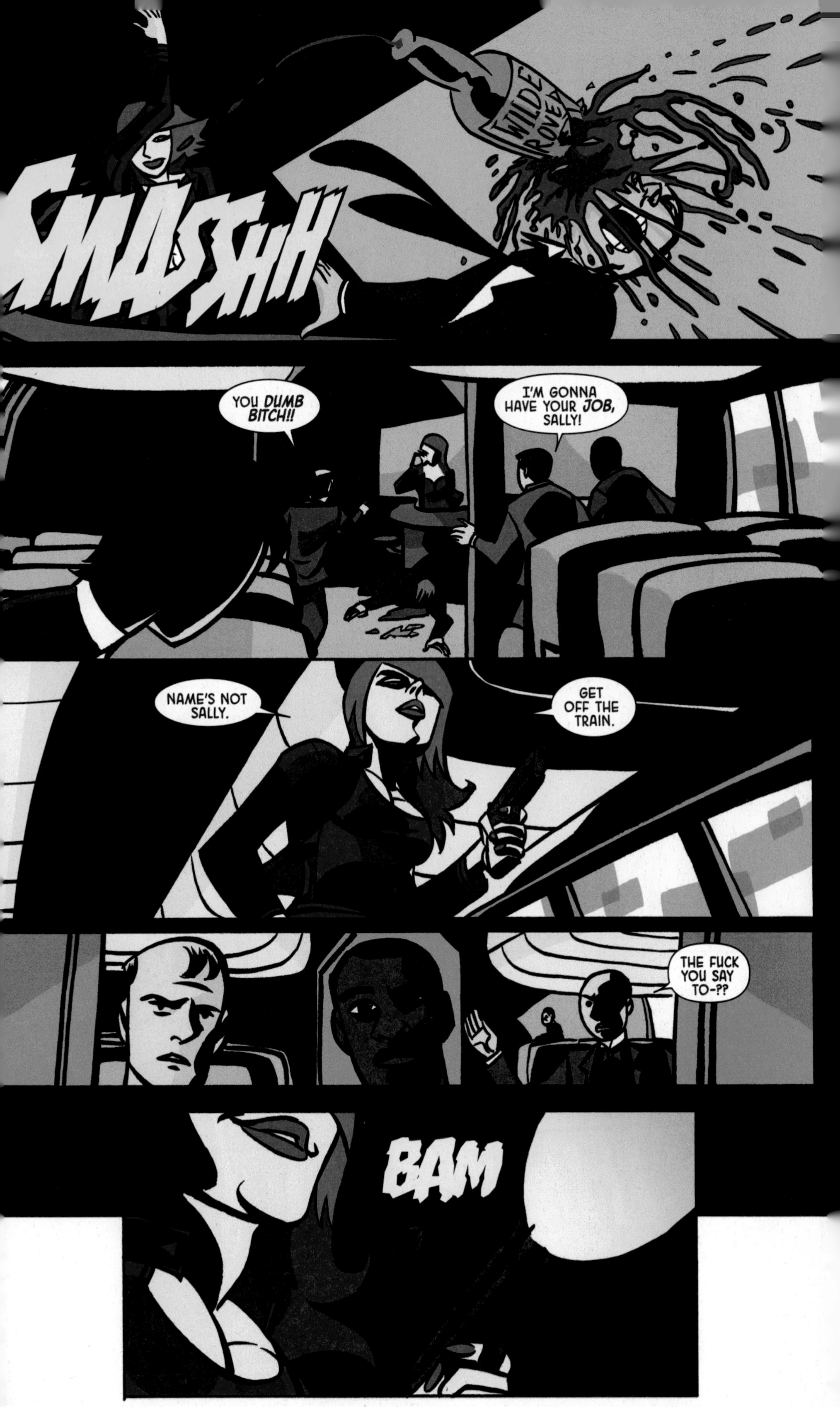
WILDE ONE
SMASHH
YOU DUMB BITCH!!
I'M GONNA HAVE YOUR JOB, SALLY!
NAME'S NOT SALLY.
GET OFF THE TRAIN.
THE FUCK YOU SAY TO-??
BAM

WHAT THE FUCK!??

WHO'S NEXT?

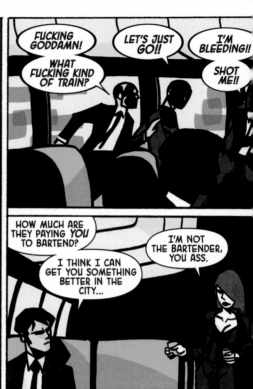

FUCKING GODDAMN!

WHAT FUCKING KIND OF TRAIN?

LET'S JUST GO!!

I'M BLEEDING!!

SHOT ME!!

HOW MUCH ARE THEY PAYING *YOU* TO BARTEND?

I THINK I CAN GET YOU SOMETHING BETTER IN THE CITY...

I'M NOT THE BARTENDER, YOU ASS.

HI, I'M—

VALENTINE. I *KNOW.*

I WENT TO SCHOOL WITH YOUR SISTER.

NO, THAT WASN'T YOU...

JESUS HELP ME.

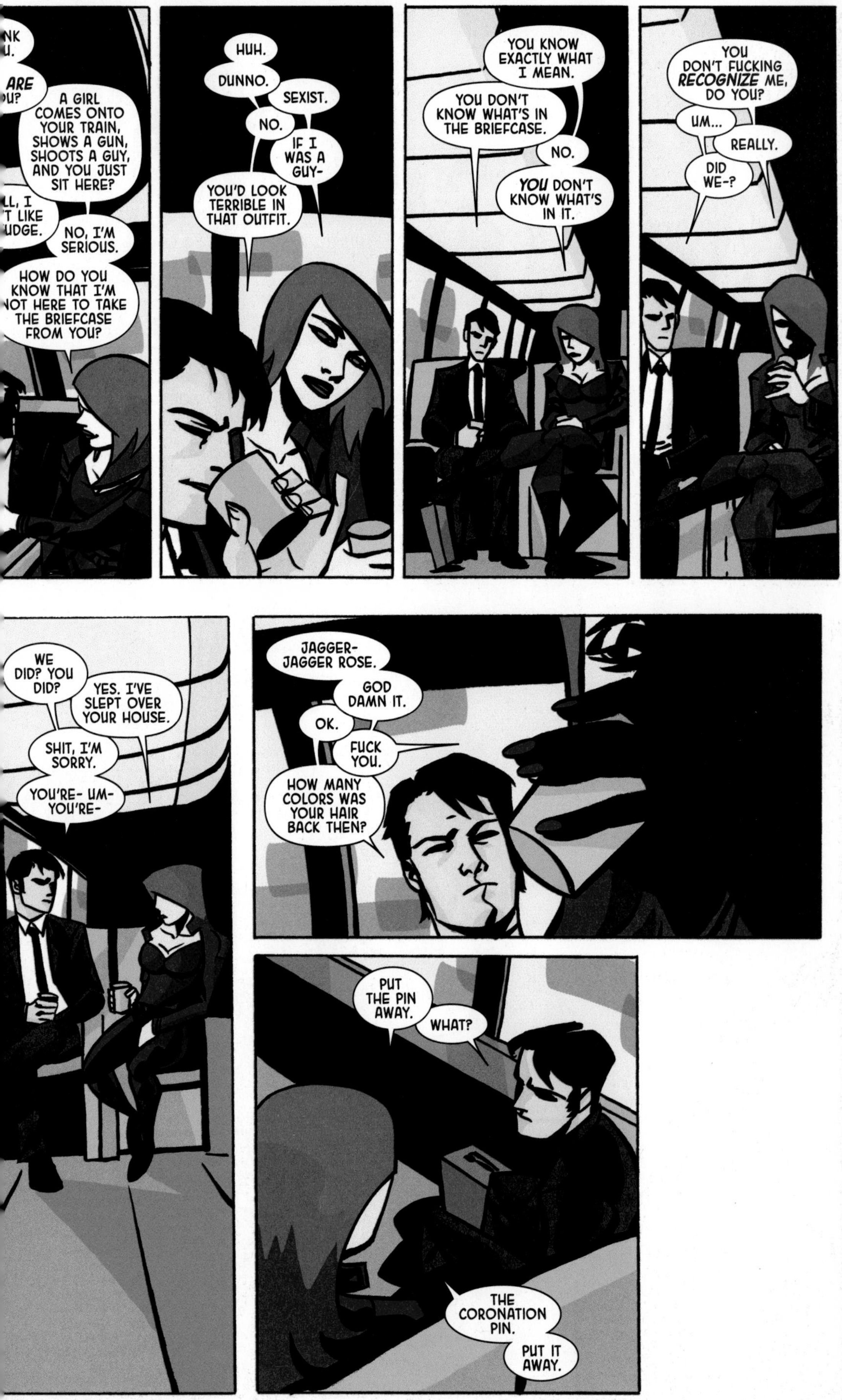

A GIRL COMES ONTO YOUR TRAIN, SHOWS A GUN, SHOOTS A GUY, AND YOU JUST SIT HERE?
NO, I'M SERIOUS.
HOW DO YOU KNOW THAT I'M NOT HERE TO TAKE THE BRIEFCASE FROM YOU?
HUH.
DUNNO.
SEXIST.
NO.
IF I WAS A GUY-
YOU'D LOOK TERRIBLE IN THAT OUTFIT.
YOU KNOW EXACTLY WHAT I MEAN.
YOU DON'T KNOW WHAT'S IN THE BRIEFCASE.
NO.
YOU DON'T KNOW WHAT'S IN IT.
YOU DON'T FUCKING RECOGNIZE ME, DO YOU?
UM...
REALLY.
DID WE-?
WE DID? YOU DID?
YES. I'VE SLEPT OVER YOUR HOUSE.
SHIT, I'M SORRY.
YOU'RE- UM- YOU'RE-
JAGGER- JAGGER ROSE.
GOD DAMN IT.
OK.
FUCK YOU.
HOW MANY COLORS WAS YOUR HAIR BACK THEN?
PUT THE PIN AWAY.
WHAT?
THE CORONATION PIN.
PUT IT AWAY.

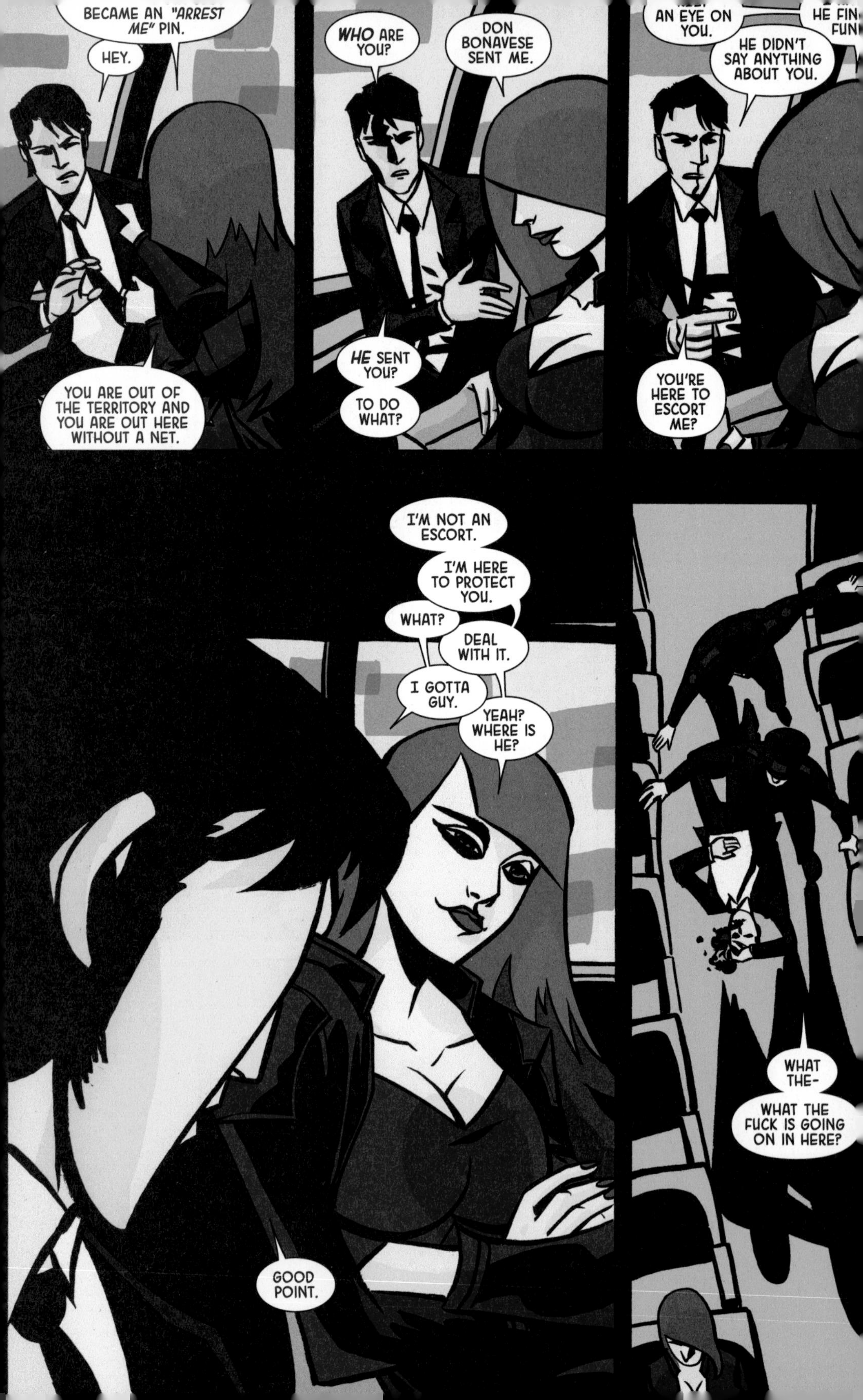
BECAME AN "ARREST ME" PIN.
HEY.
YOU ARE OUT OF THE TERRITORY AND YOU ARE OUT HERE WITHOUT A NET.
WHO ARE YOU?
DON BONAVESE SENT ME.
HE SENT YOU?
TO DO WHAT?
AN EYE ON YOU.
HE DIDN'T SAY ANYTHING ABOUT YOU.
YOU'RE HERE TO ESCORT ME?
I'M NOT AN ESCORT.
I'M HERE TO PROTECT YOU.
WHAT?
DEAL WITH IT.
I GOTTA GUY.
YEAH? WHERE IS HE?
GOOD POINT.
WHAT THE-
WHAT THE FUCK IS GOING ON IN HERE?

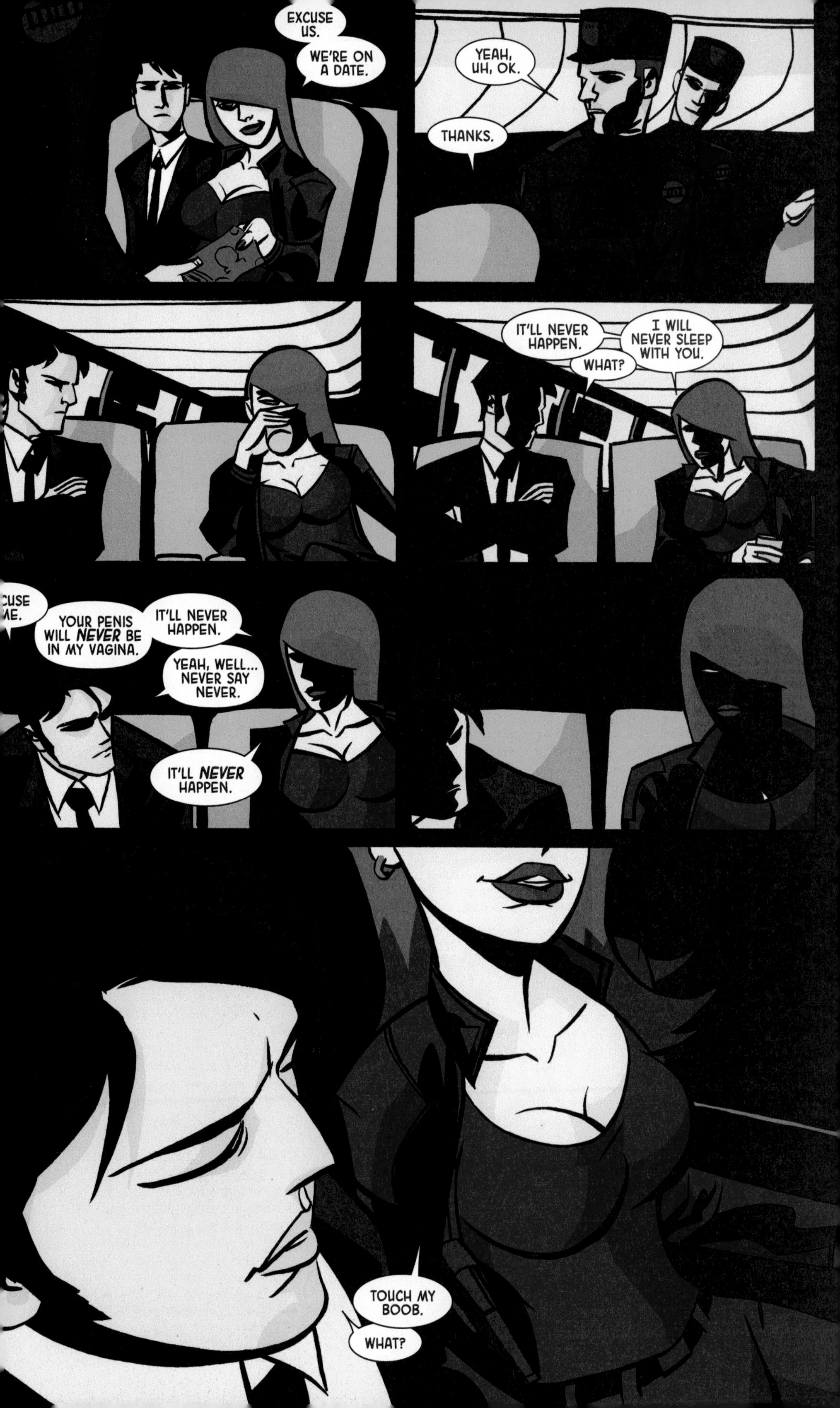
EXCUSE US.
WE'RE ON A DATE.
YEAH, UH, OK.
THANKS.
IT'LL NEVER HAPPEN.
I WILL NEVER SLEEP WITH YOU.
WHAT?
CUSE ME.
YOUR PENIS WILL NEVER BE IN MY VAGINA.
IT'LL NEVER HAPPEN.
YEAH, WELL... NEVER SAY NEVER.
IT'LL NEVER HAPPEN.
TOUCH MY BOOB.
WHAT?

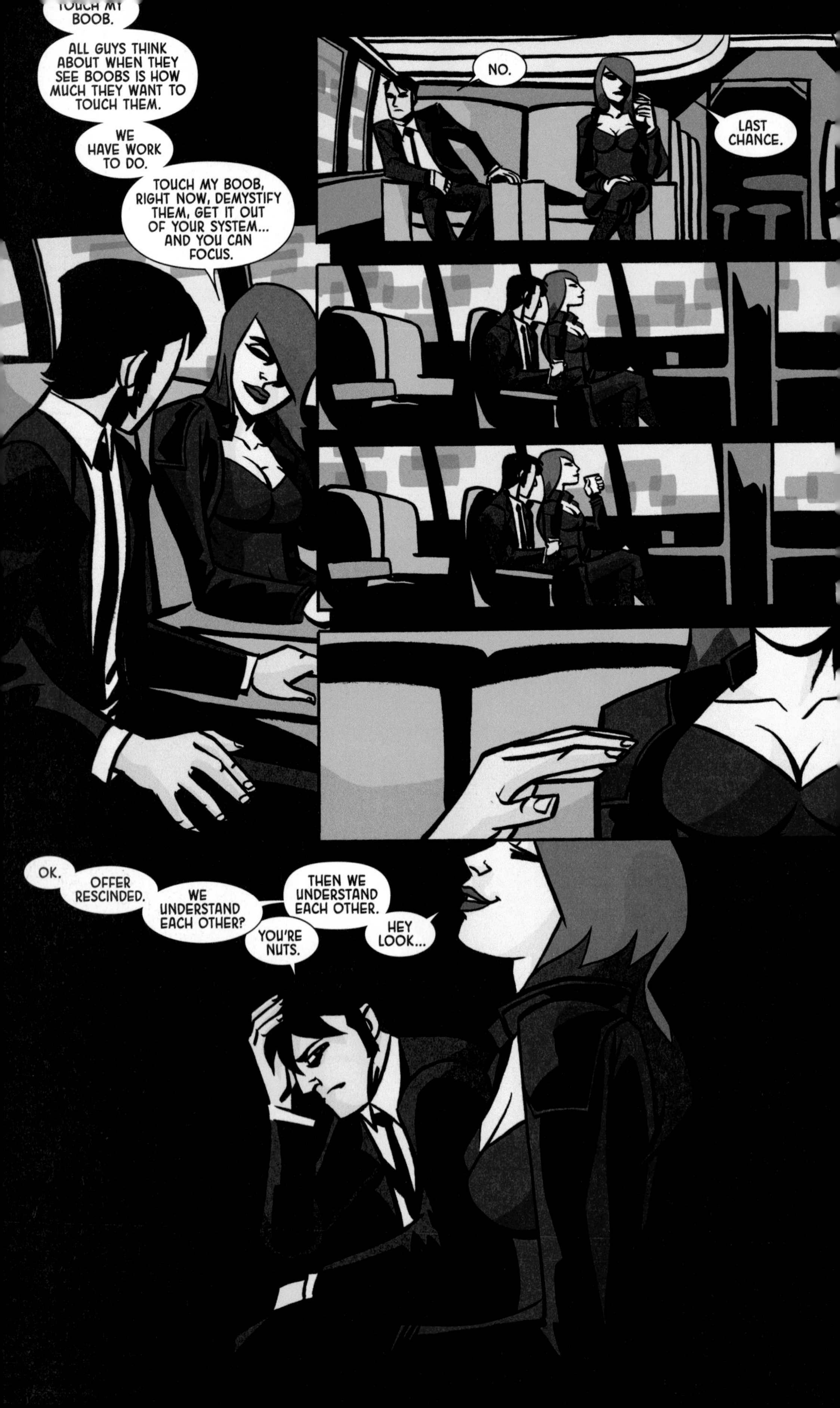
BOOB.
ALL GUYS THINK ABOUT WHEN THEY SEE BOOBS IS HOW MUCH THEY WANT TO TOUCH THEM.
WE HAVE WORK TO DO.
TOUCH MY BOOB, RIGHT NOW, DEMYSTIFY THEM, GET IT OUT OF YOUR SYSTEM... AND YOU CAN FOCUS.
NO.
LAST CHANCE.
OK.
OFFER RESCINDED.
WE UNDERSTAND EACH OTHER?
YOU'RE NUTS.
THEN WE UNDERSTAND EACH OTHER.
HEY LOOK...

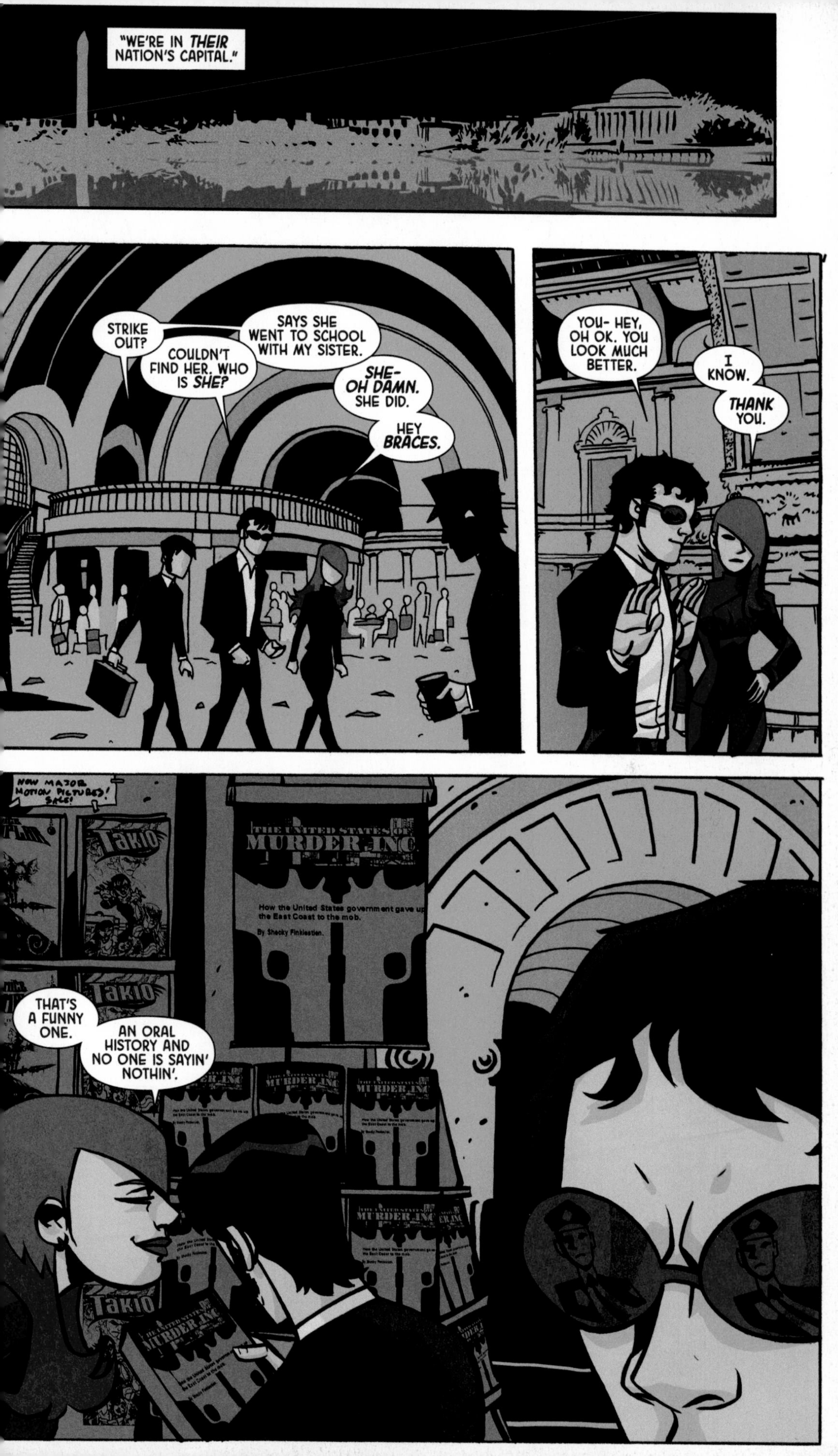

"WE'RE IN THEIR NATION'S CAPITAL."
STRIKE OUT?
COULDN'T FIND HER. WHO IS SHE?
SAYS SHE WENT TO SCHOOL WITH MY SISTER.
SHE- OH DAMN. SHE DID.
HEY BRACES.
YOU- HEY, OH OK. YOU LOOK MUCH BETTER.
I KNOW.
THANK YOU.
NOW MAJOR MOTION PICTURES! SALE!
TAKIO
THE UNITED STATES OF MURDER INC
How the United States government gave up the East Coast to the mob.
By Shecky Finkiestien.
THAT'S A FUNNY ONE.
AN ORAL HISTORY AND NO ONE IS SAYIN' NOTHIN'.

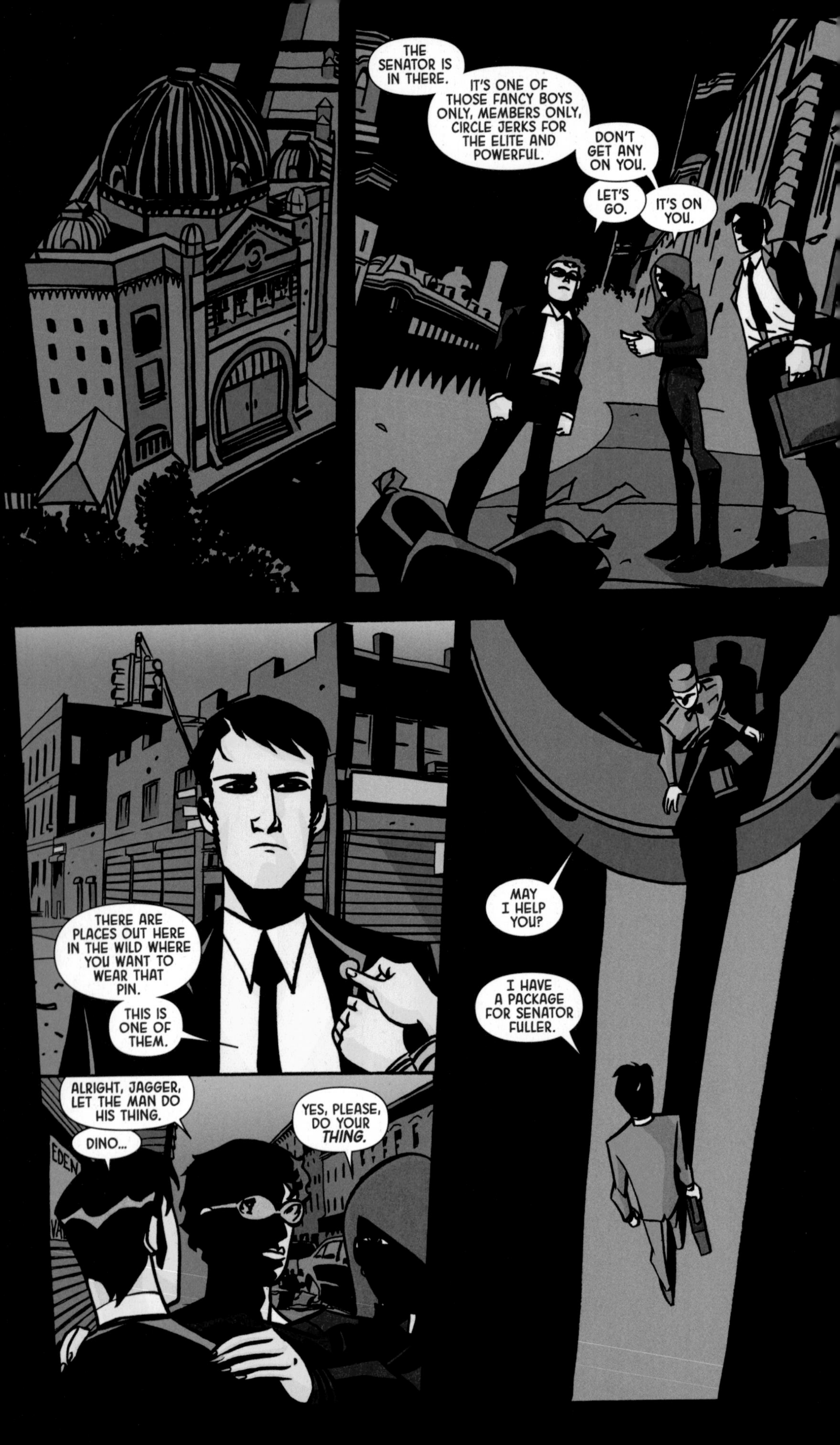
THE SENATOR IS IN THERE.
IT'S ONE OF THOSE FANCY BOYS ONLY, MEMBERS ONLY, CIRCLE JERKS FOR THE ELITE AND POWERFUL.
DON'T GET ANY ON YOU.
LET'S GO.
IT'S ON YOU.
THERE ARE PLACES OUT HERE IN THE WILD WHERE YOU WANT TO WEAR THAT PIN.
THIS IS ONE OF THEM.
ALRIGHT, JAGGER, LET THE MAN DO HIS THING.
DINO...
YES, PLEASE, DO YOUR *THING.*
EDEN
MAY I HELP YOU?
I HAVE A PACKAGE FOR SENATOR FULLER.

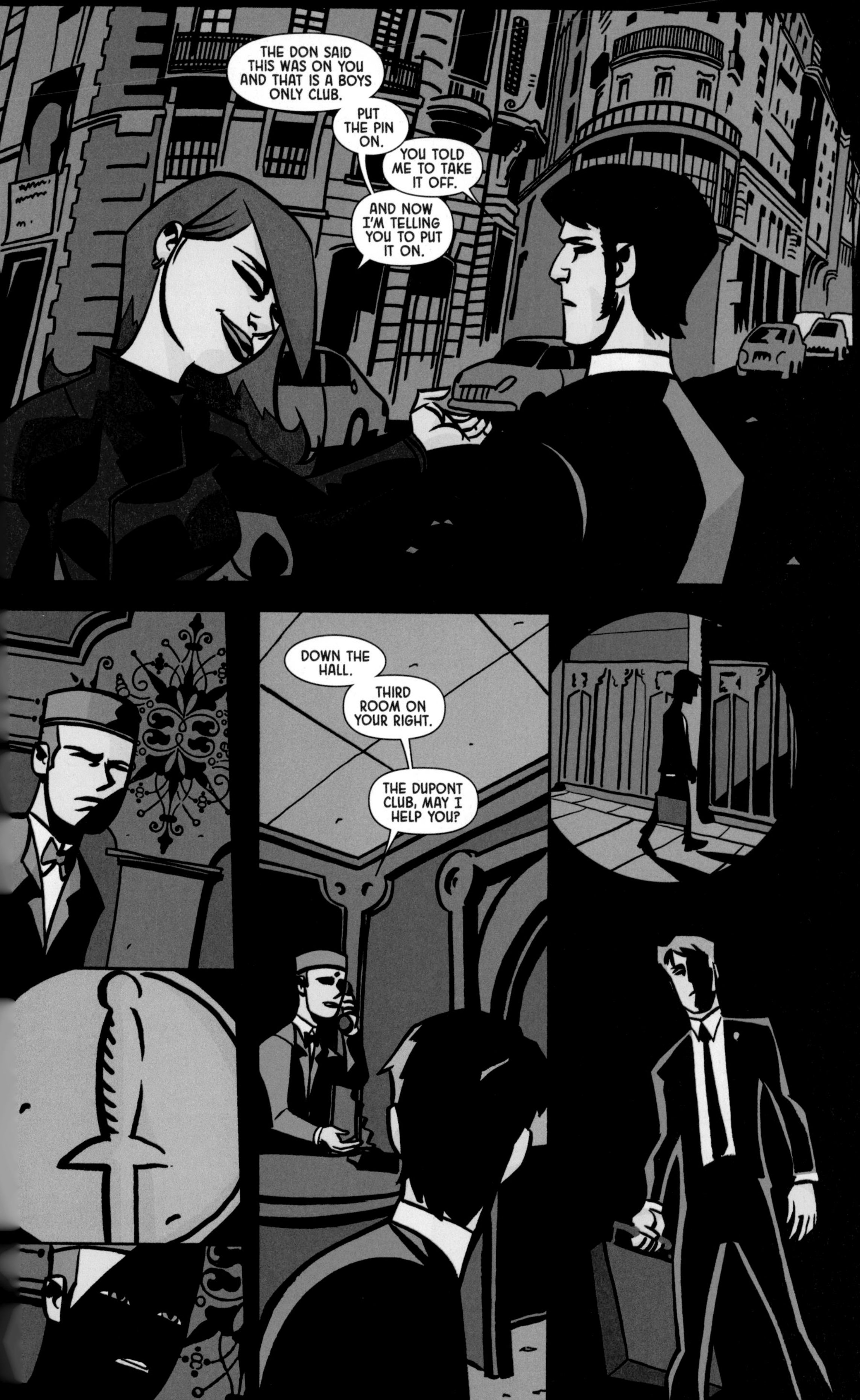
THE DON SAID THIS WAS ON YOU AND THAT IS A BOYS ONLY CLUB.
PUT THE PIN ON.
YOU TOLD ME TO TAKE IT OFF.
AND NOW I'M TELLING YOU TO PUT IT ON.
DOWN THE HALL.
THIRD ROOM ON YOUR RIGHT.
THE DUPONT CLUB, MAY I HELP YOU?

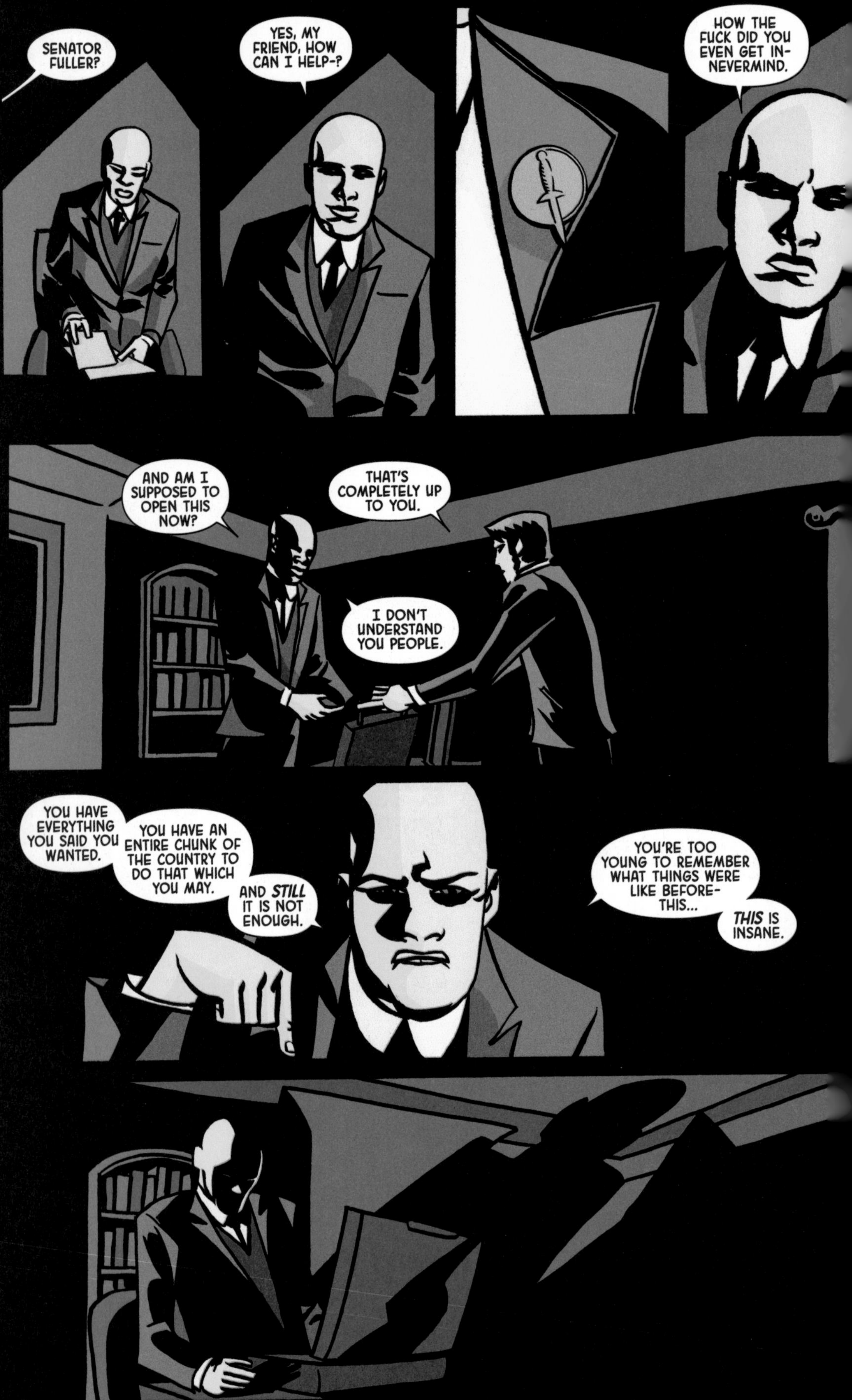
SENATOR FULLER?
YES, MY FRIEND, HOW CAN I HELP-?
HOW THE FUCK DID YOU EVEN GET IN- NEVERMIND.
AND AM I SUPPOSED TO OPEN THIS NOW?
THAT'S COMPLETELY UP TO YOU.
I DON'T UNDERSTAND YOU PEOPLE.
YOU HAVE EVERYTHING YOU SAID YOU WANTED.
YOU HAVE AN ENTIRE CHUNK OF THE COUNTRY TO DO THAT WHICH YOU MAY.
AND *STILL* IT IS NOT ENOUGH.
YOU'RE TOO YOUNG TO REMEMBER WHAT THINGS WERE LIKE BEFORE- THIS...
THIS IS INSANE.

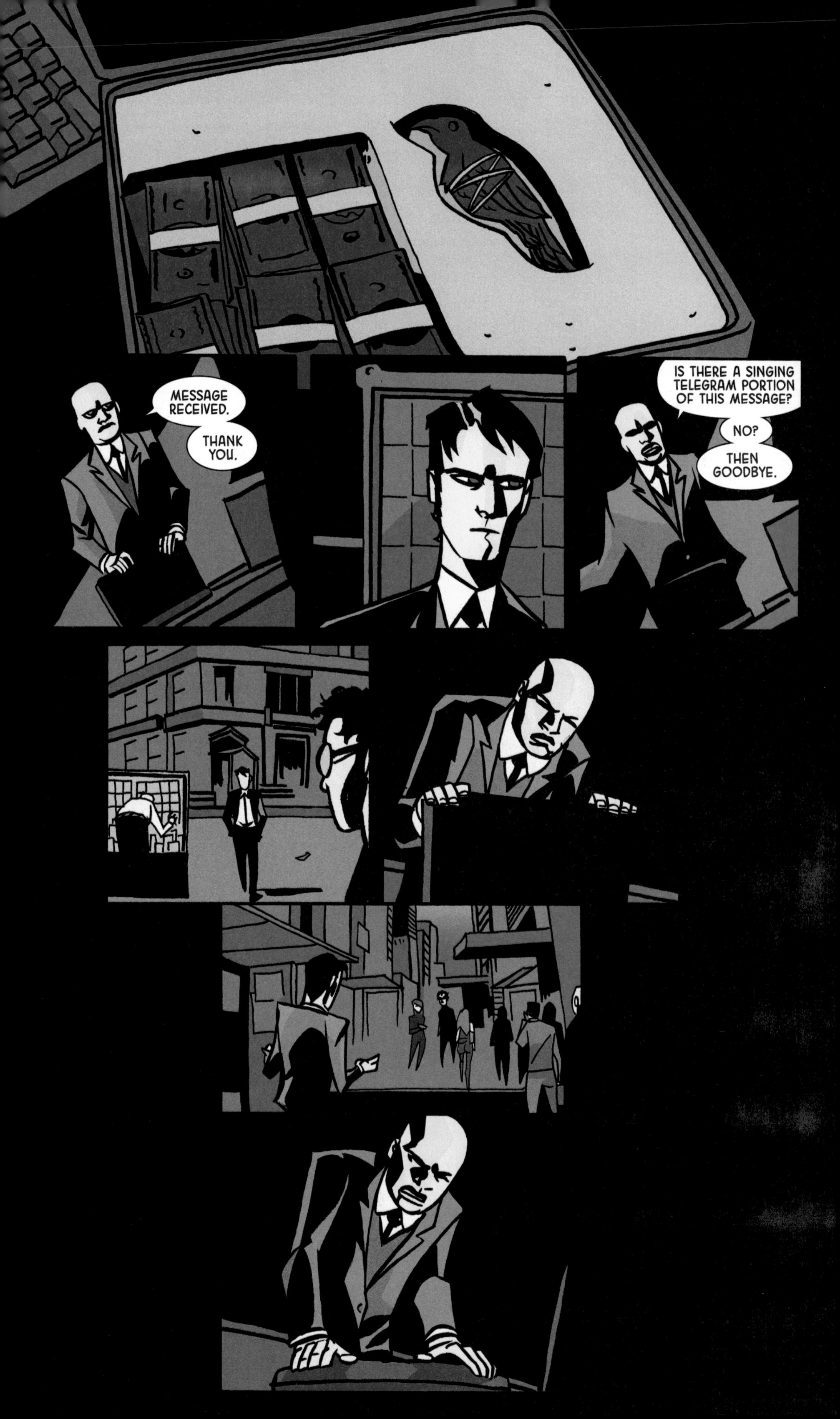
MESSAGE RECEIVED.
THANK YOU.
IS THERE A SINGING TELEGRAM PORTION OF THIS MESSAGE?
NO?
THEN GOODBYE.

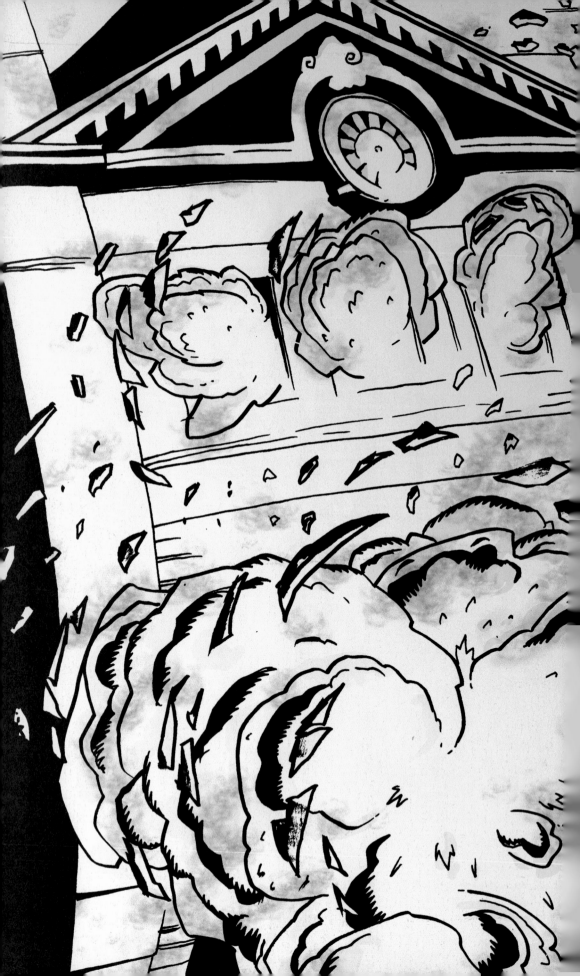

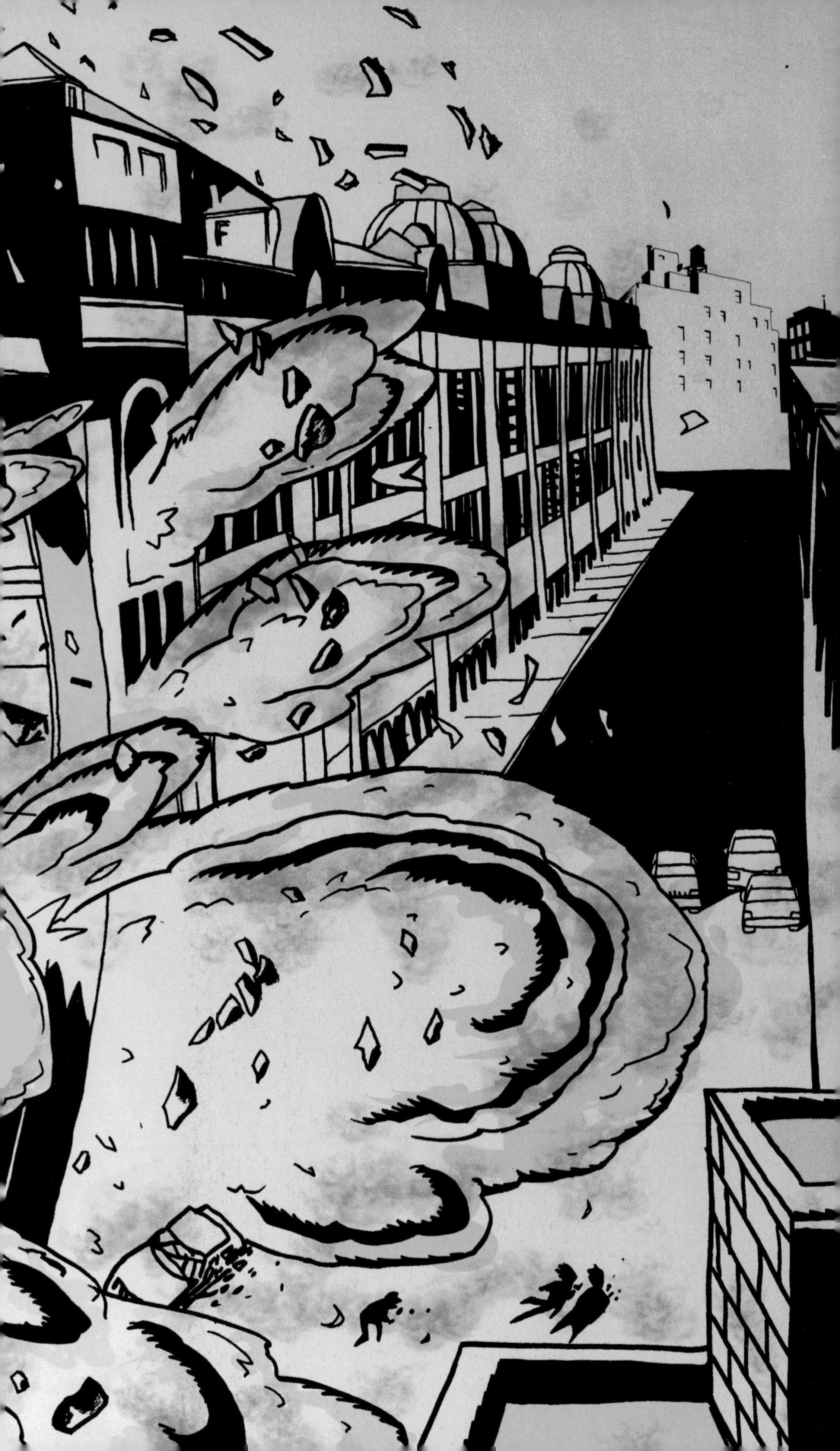
F

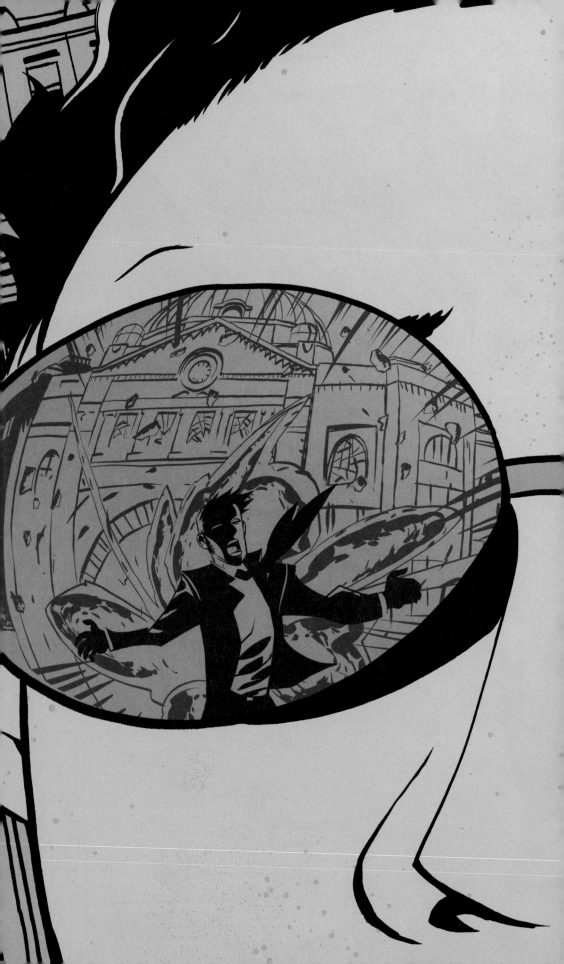

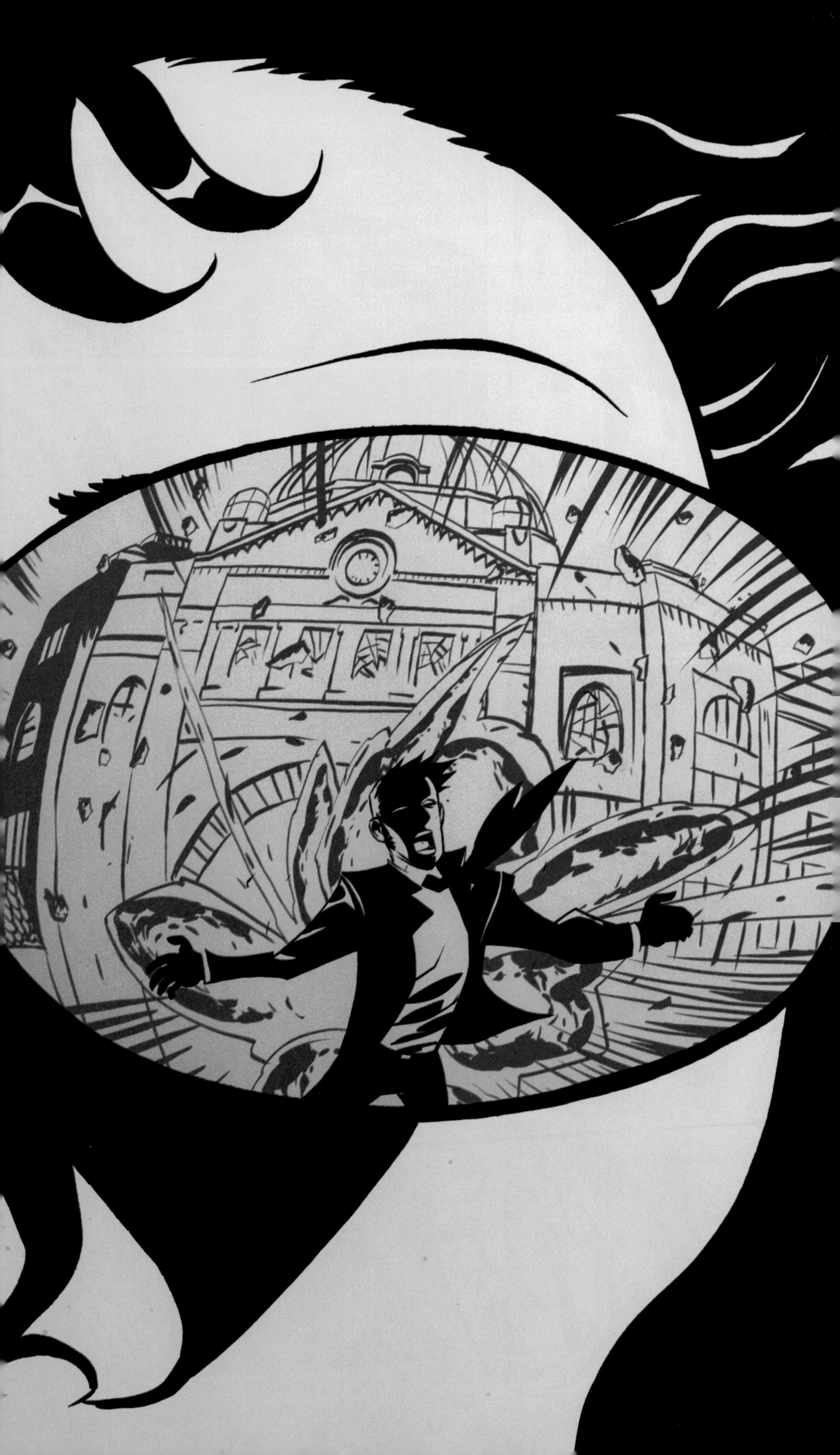

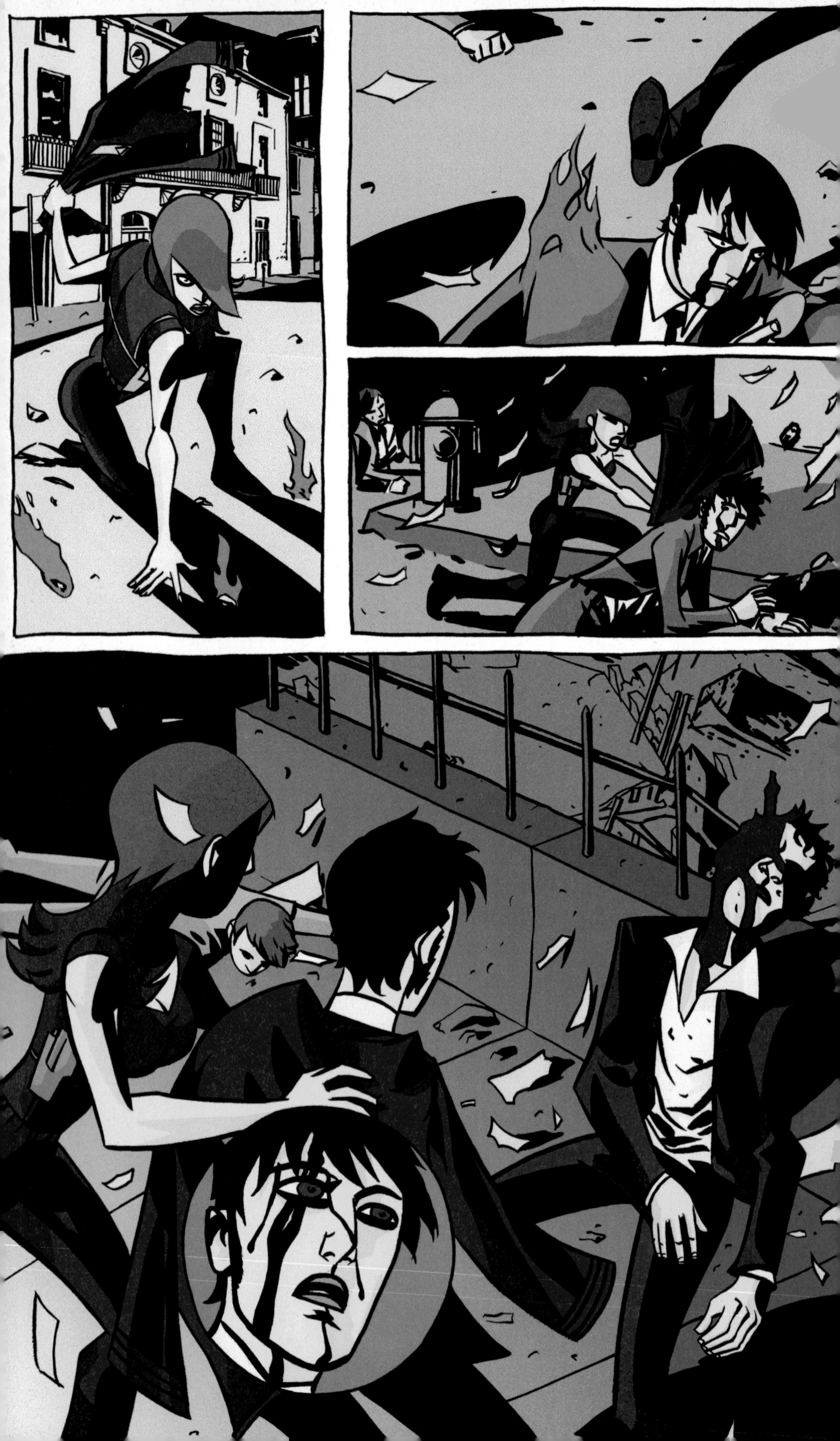

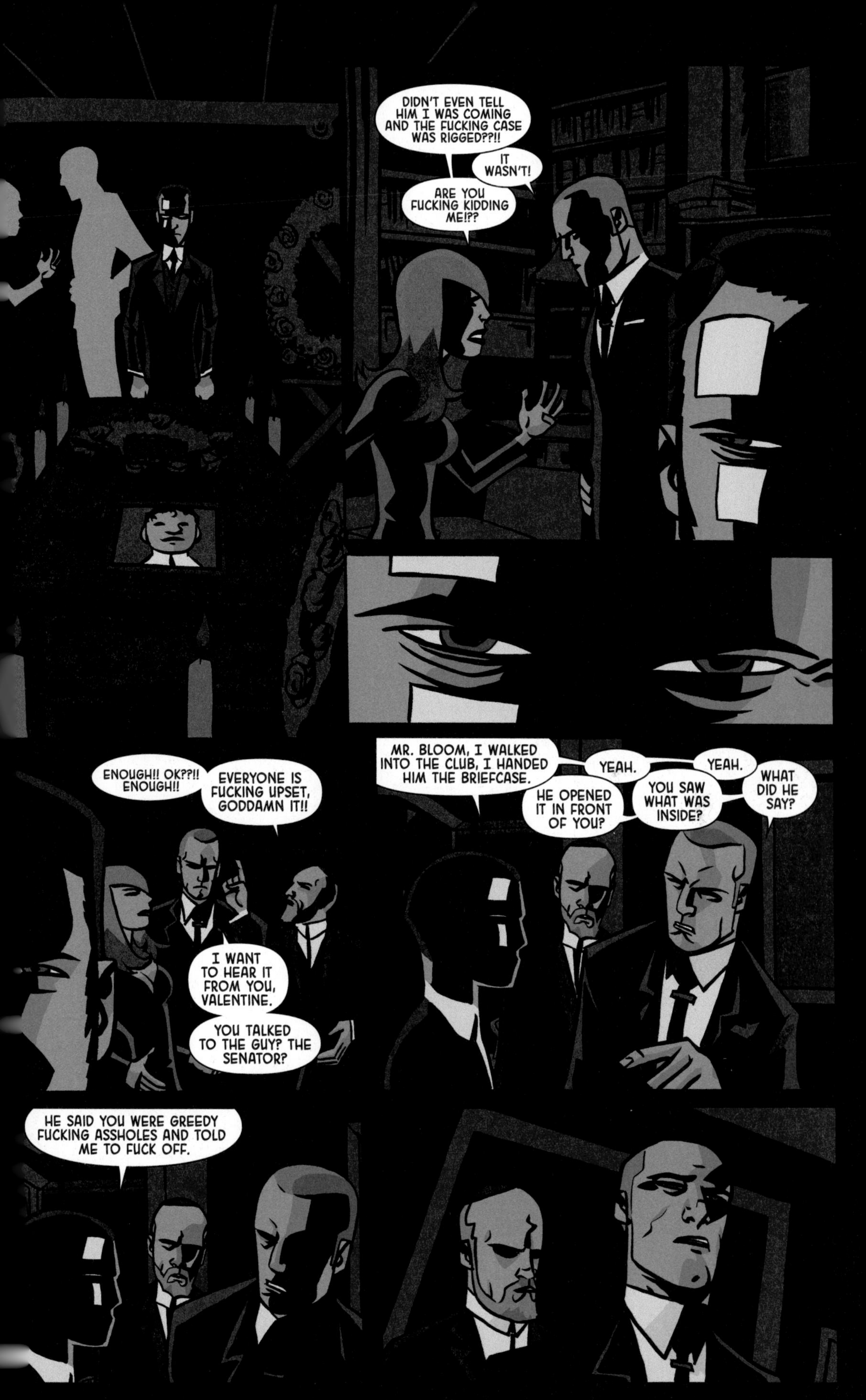
DIDN'T EVEN TELL HIM I WAS COMING AND THE FUCKING CASE WAS RIGGED??!!
IT WASN'T!
ARE YOU FUCKING KIDDING ME!??
ENOUGH!! OK??!! ENOUGH!!
EVERYONE IS FUCKING UPSET, GODDAMN IT!!
I WANT TO HEAR IT FROM YOU, VALENTINE.
YOU TALKED TO THE GUY? THE SENATOR?
MR. BLOOM, I WALKED INTO THE CLUB, I HANDED HIM THE BRIEFCASE.
YEAH.
HE OPENED IT IN FRONT OF YOU?
YEAH.
YOU SAW WHAT WAS INSIDE?
WHAT DID HE SAY?
HE SAID YOU WERE GREEDY FUCKING ASSHOLES AND TOLD ME TO FUCK OFF.

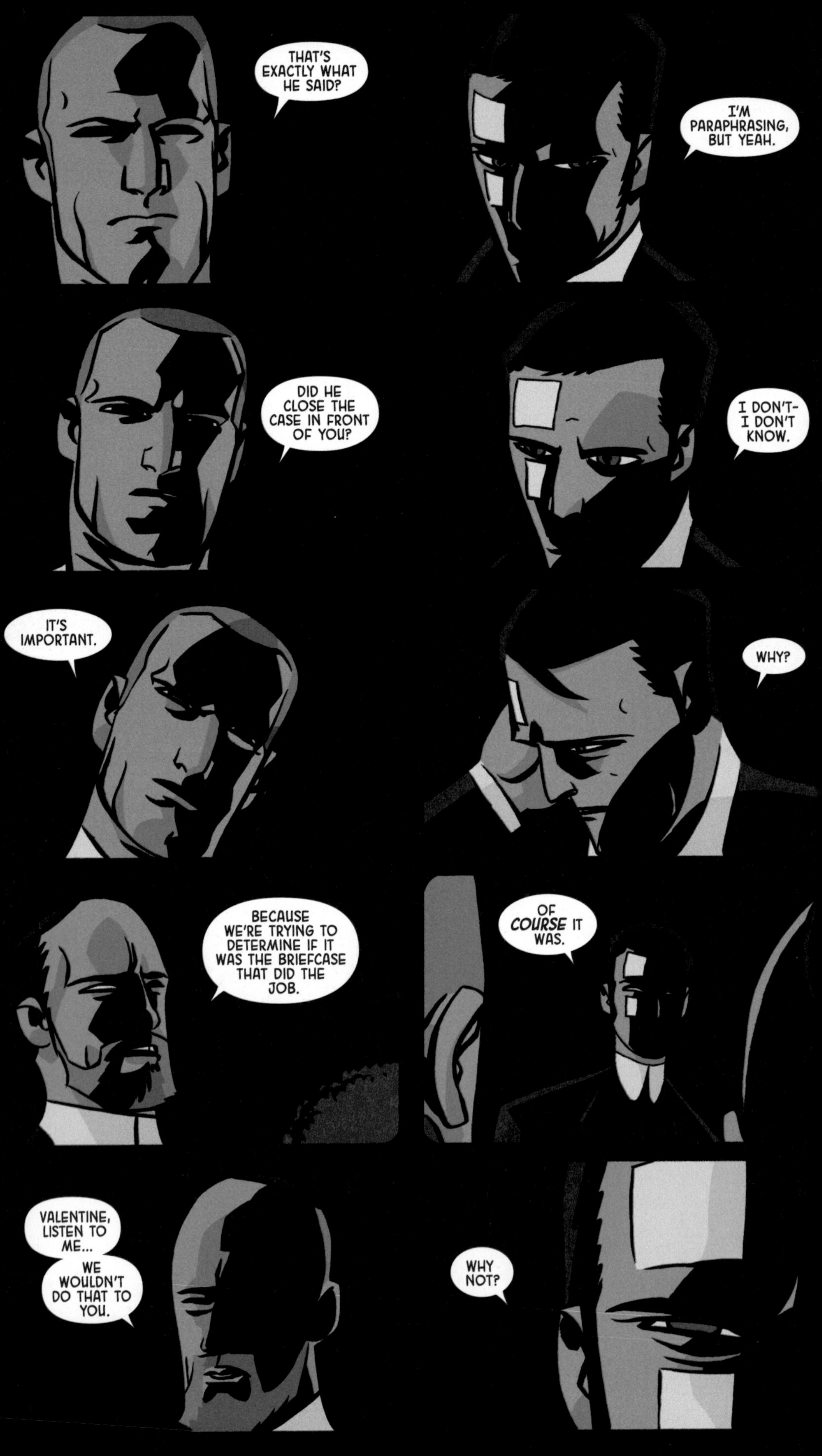
THAT'S EXACTLY WHAT HE SAID?
I'M PARAPHRASING, BUT YEAH.
DID HE CLOSE THE CASE IN FRONT OF YOU?
I DON'T- I DON'T KNOW.
IT'S IMPORTANT.
WHY?
BECAUSE WE'RE TRYING TO DETERMINE IF IT WAS THE BRIEFCASE THAT DID THE JOB.
OF *COURSE* IT WAS.
VALENTINE, LISTEN TO ME...
WE WOULDN'T DO THAT TO YOU.
WHY NOT?

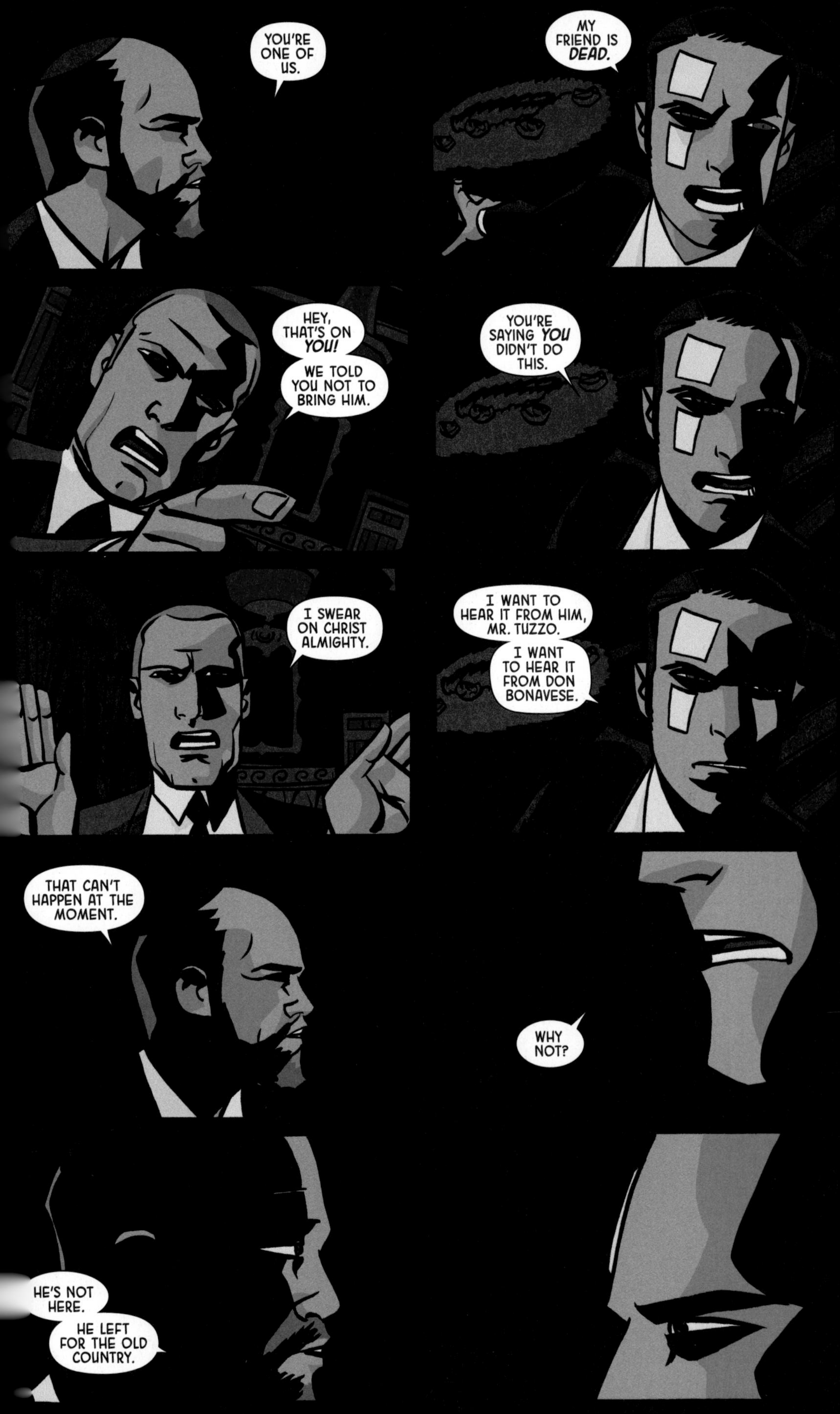
YOU'RE ONE OF US.
MY FRIEND IS DEAD.
HEY, THAT'S ON YOU!
WE TOLD YOU NOT TO BRING HIM.
YOU'RE SAYING YOU DIDN'T DO THIS.
I SWEAR ON CHRIST ALMIGHTY.
I WANT TO HEAR IT FROM HIM, MR. TUZZO.
I WANT TO HEAR IT FROM DON BONAVESE.
THAT CAN'T HAPPEN AT THE MOMENT.
WHY NOT?
HE'S NOT HERE.
HE LEFT FOR THE OLD COUNTRY.

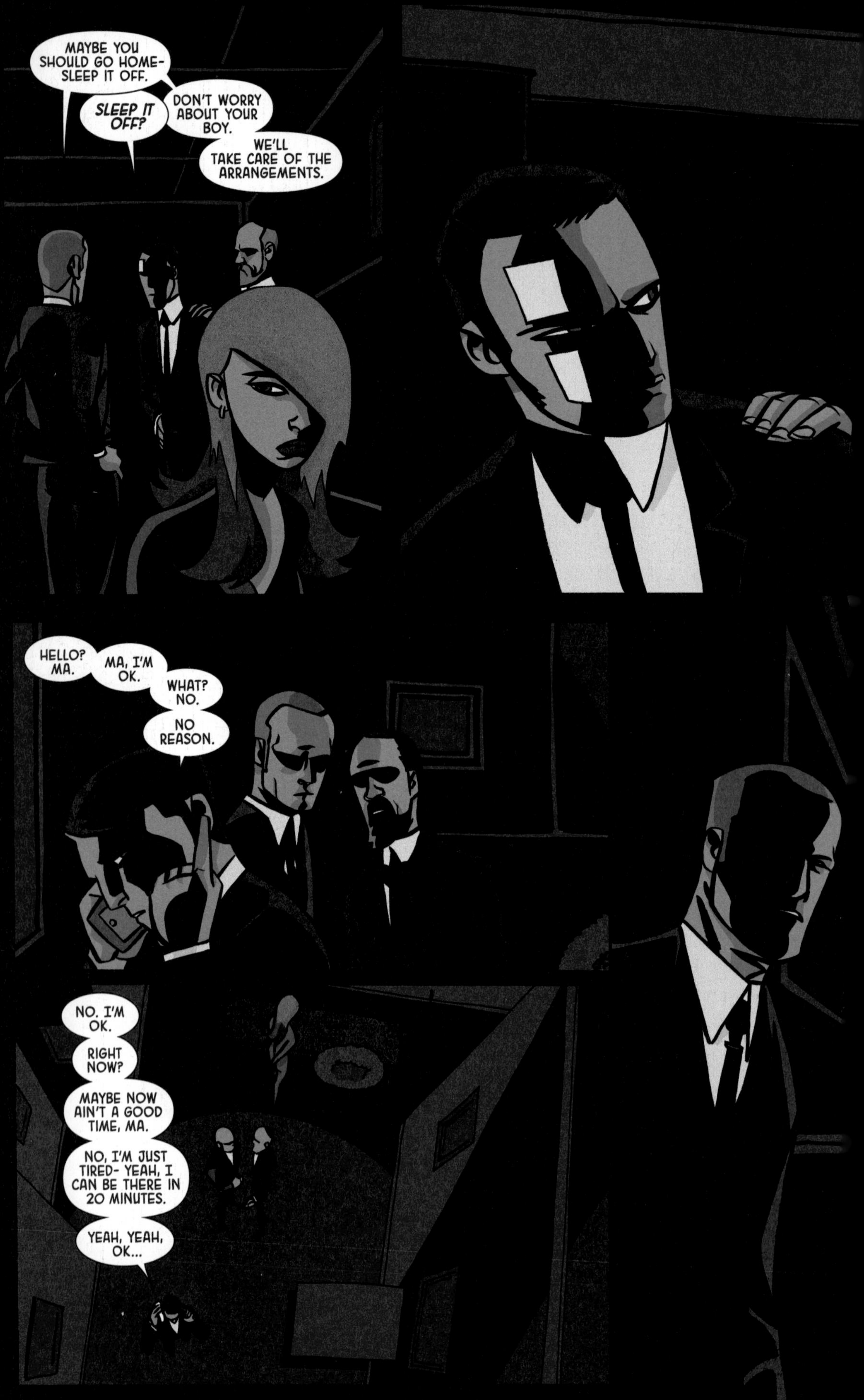
MAYBE YOU SHOULD GO HOME- SLEEP IT OFF.
SLEEP IT OFF?
DON'T WORRY ABOUT YOUR BOY.
WE'LL TAKE CARE OF THE ARRANGEMENTS.
HELLO? MA.
MA, I'M OK.
WHAT? NO.
NO REASON.
NO. I'M OK.
RIGHT NOW?
MAYBE NOW AIN'T A GOOD TIME, MA.
NO, I'M JUST TIRED- YEAH, I CAN BE THERE IN 20 MINUTES.
YEAH, YEAH, OK...

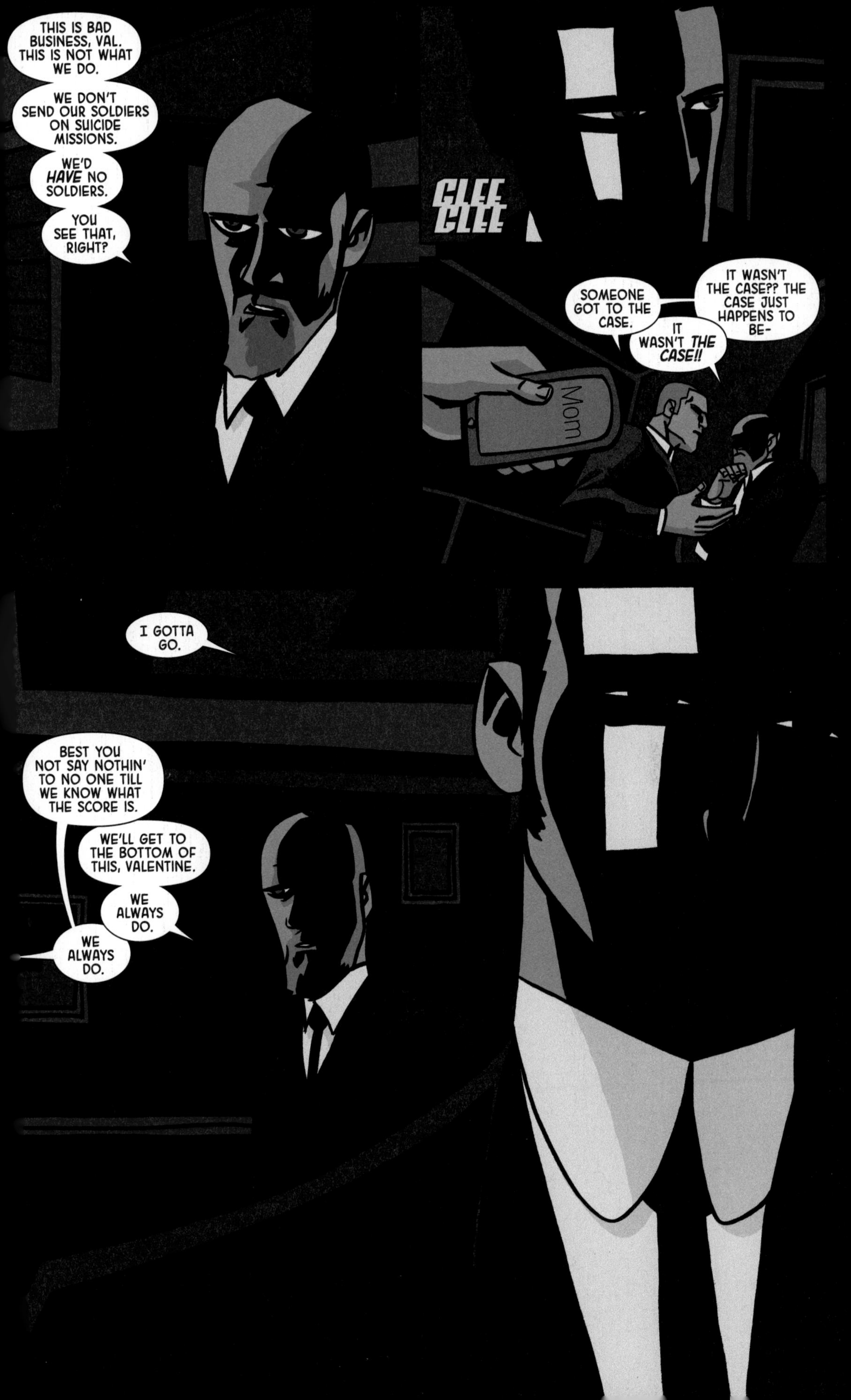
THIS IS BAD BUSINESS, VAL. THIS IS NOT WHAT WE DO.
WE DON'T SEND OUR SOLDIERS ON SUICIDE MISSIONS.
WE'D *HAVE* NO SOLDIERS.
YOU SEE THAT, RIGHT?
CLEE CLEE
SOMEONE GOT TO THE CASE.
IT WASN'T THE CASE?? THE CASE JUST HAPPENS TO BE-
IT WASN'T *THE CASE!!*
Mom
I GOTTA GO.
BEST YOU NOT SAY NOTHIN' TO NO ONE TILL WE KNOW WHAT THE SCORE IS.
WE'LL GET TO THE BOTTOM OF THIS, VALENTINE.
WE ALWAYS DO.
WE ALWAYS DO.

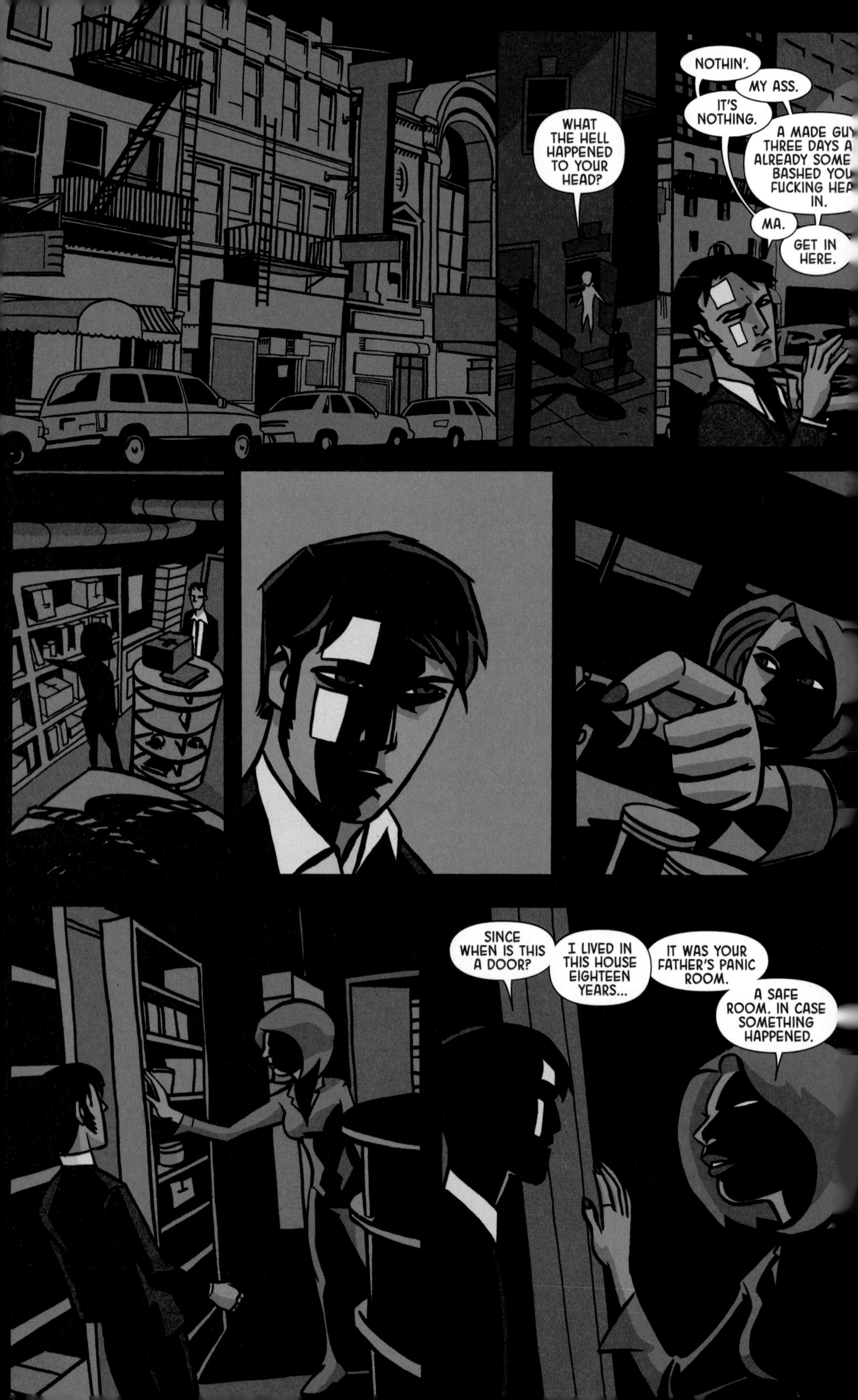
WHAT THE HELL HAPPENED TO YOUR HEAD?
NOTHIN'.
MY ASS.
IT'S NOTHING.
A MADE GUY THREE DAYS A ALREADY SOME BASHED YOU FUCKING HEA IN.
MA.
GET IN HERE.
SINCE WHEN IS THIS A DOOR?
I LIVED IN THIS HOUSE EIGHTEEN YEARS...
IT WAS YOUR FATHER'S PANIC ROOM.
A SAFE ROOM. IN CASE SOMETHING HAPPENED.

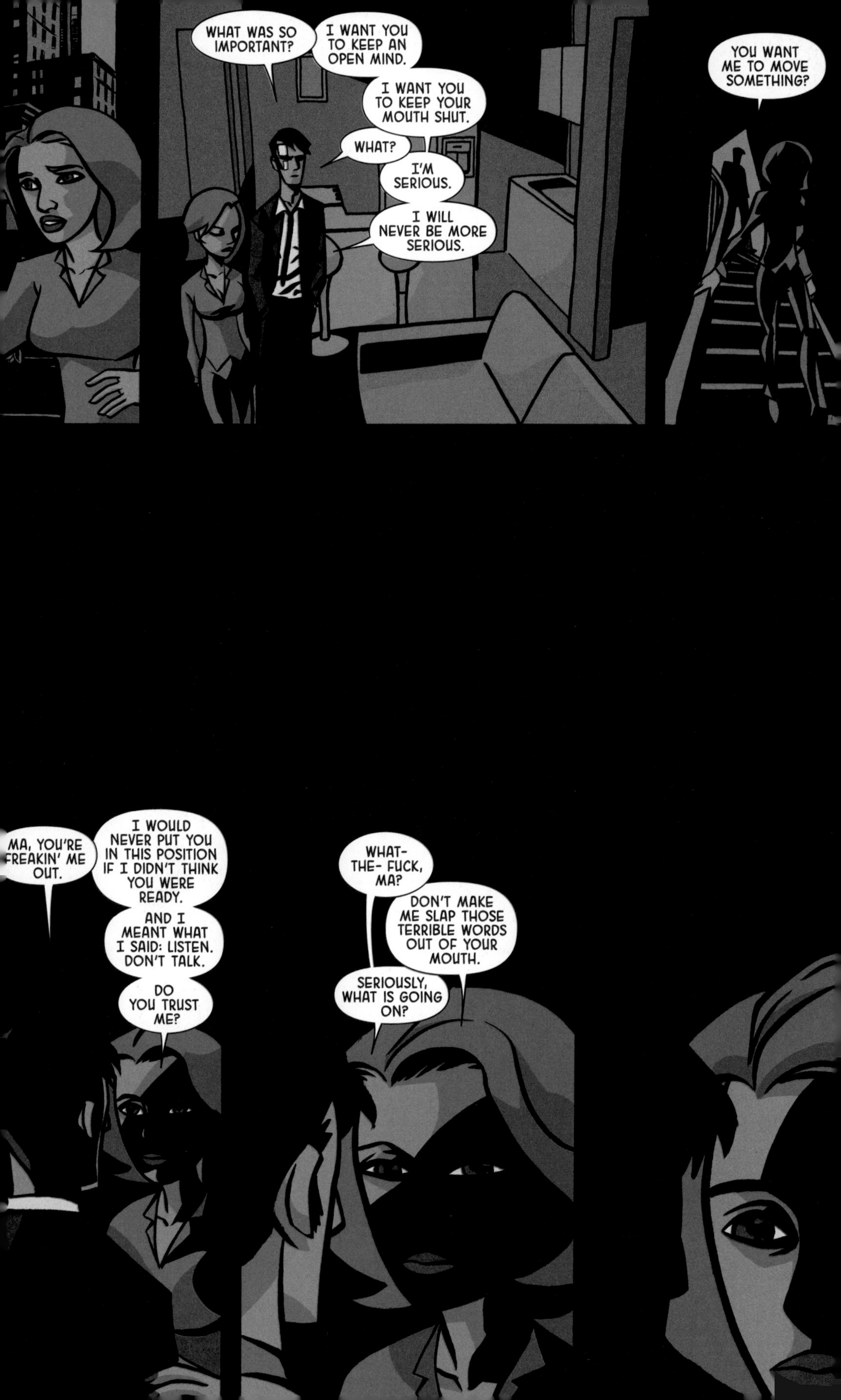
WHAT WAS SO IMPORTANT?
I WANT YOU TO KEEP AN OPEN MIND.
I WANT YOU TO KEEP YOUR MOUTH SHUT.
WHAT?
I'M SERIOUS.
I WILL NEVER BE MORE SERIOUS.
YOU WANT ME TO MOVE SOMETHING?
MA, YOU'RE FREAKIN' ME OUT.
I WOULD NEVER PUT YOU IN THIS POSITION IF I DIDN'T THINK YOU WERE READY.
AND I MEANT WHAT I SAID: LISTEN. DON'T TALK.
DO YOU TRUST ME?
WHAT-THE- FUCK, MA?
DON'T MAKE ME SLAP THOSE TERRIBLE WORDS OUT OF YOUR MOUTH.
SERIOUSLY, WHAT IS GOING ON?

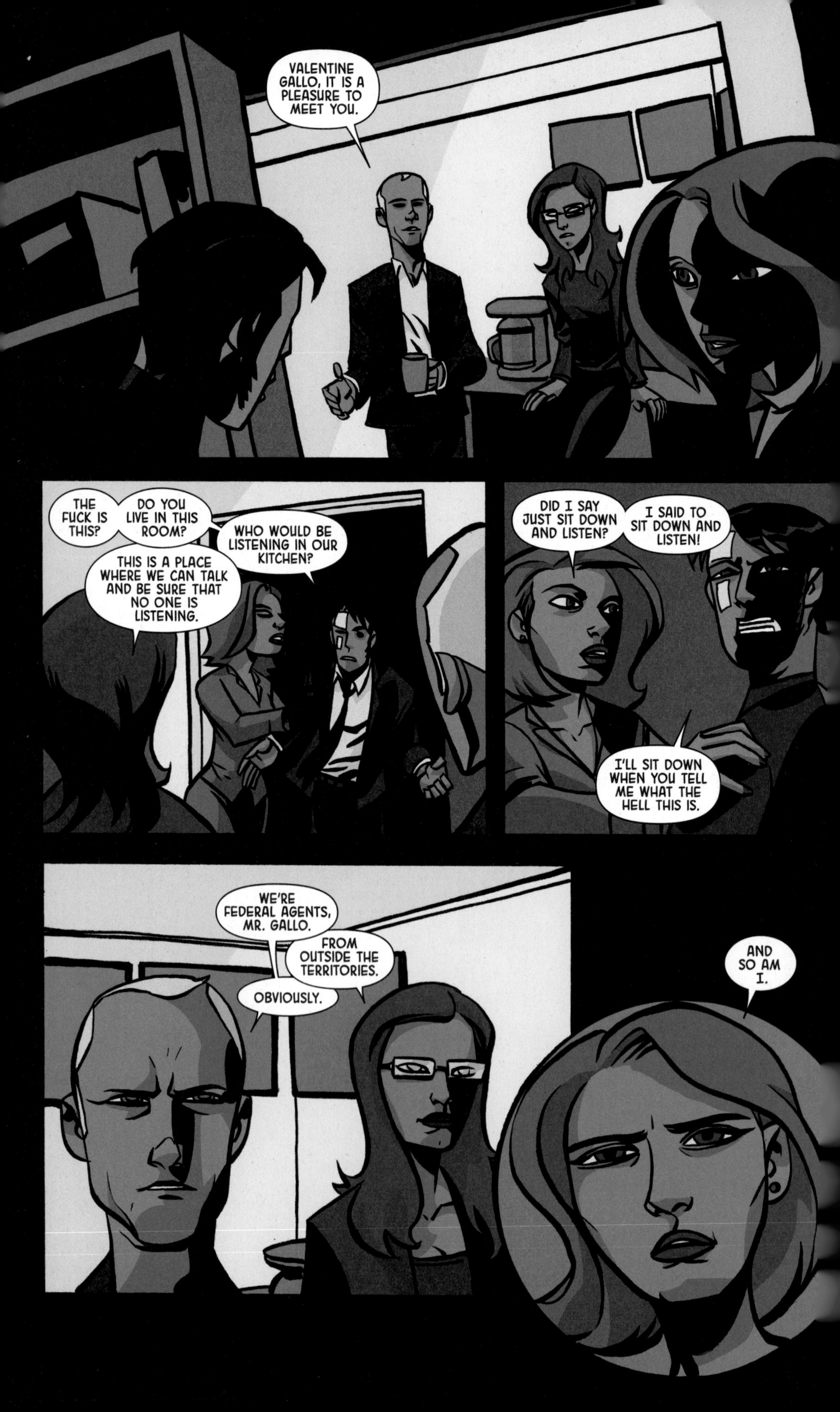
VALENTINE GALLO, IT IS A PLEASURE TO MEET YOU.
THE FUCK IS THIS?
DO YOU LIVE IN THIS ROOM?
THIS IS A PLACE WHERE WE CAN TALK AND BE SURE THAT NO ONE IS LISTENING.
WHO WOULD BE LISTENING IN OUR KITCHEN?
DID I SAY JUST SIT DOWN AND LISTEN?
I SAID TO SIT DOWN AND LISTEN!
I'LL SIT DOWN WHEN YOU TELL ME WHAT THE HELL THIS IS.
WE'RE FEDERAL AGENTS, MR. GALLO.
FROM OUTSIDE THE TERRITORIES.
OBVIOUSLY.
AND SO AM I.

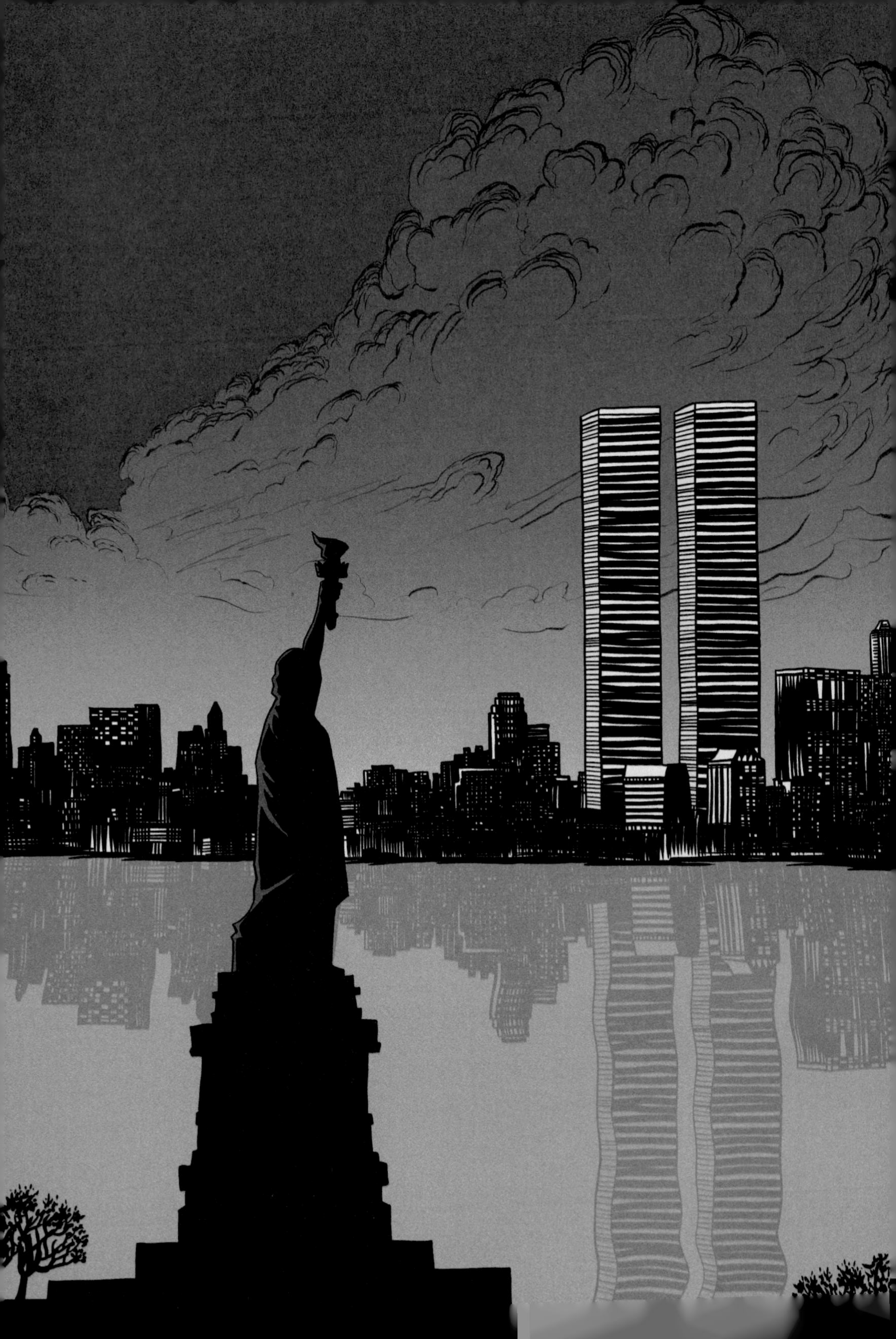

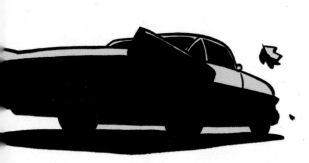

GHT ON TIME.

JIMMY, YOU REALLY GONNA ACT LIKE THIS AIN'T NO BIG DEAL?

IT AIN'T.

THE HELL'S THE MATTER WITH YOU?

WE'VE DONE THIS SHIT FIFTY TIMES.

YOU REALLY DON'T THINK THIS IS DIFFERENT?

NO.

IT IS WHAT IT IS.

ONE GUY FUCKED UP.

ANOTHER GUY PAYS US TO TAKE CARE OF SAID FUCKUP.

THE END.

CLIK CLAK

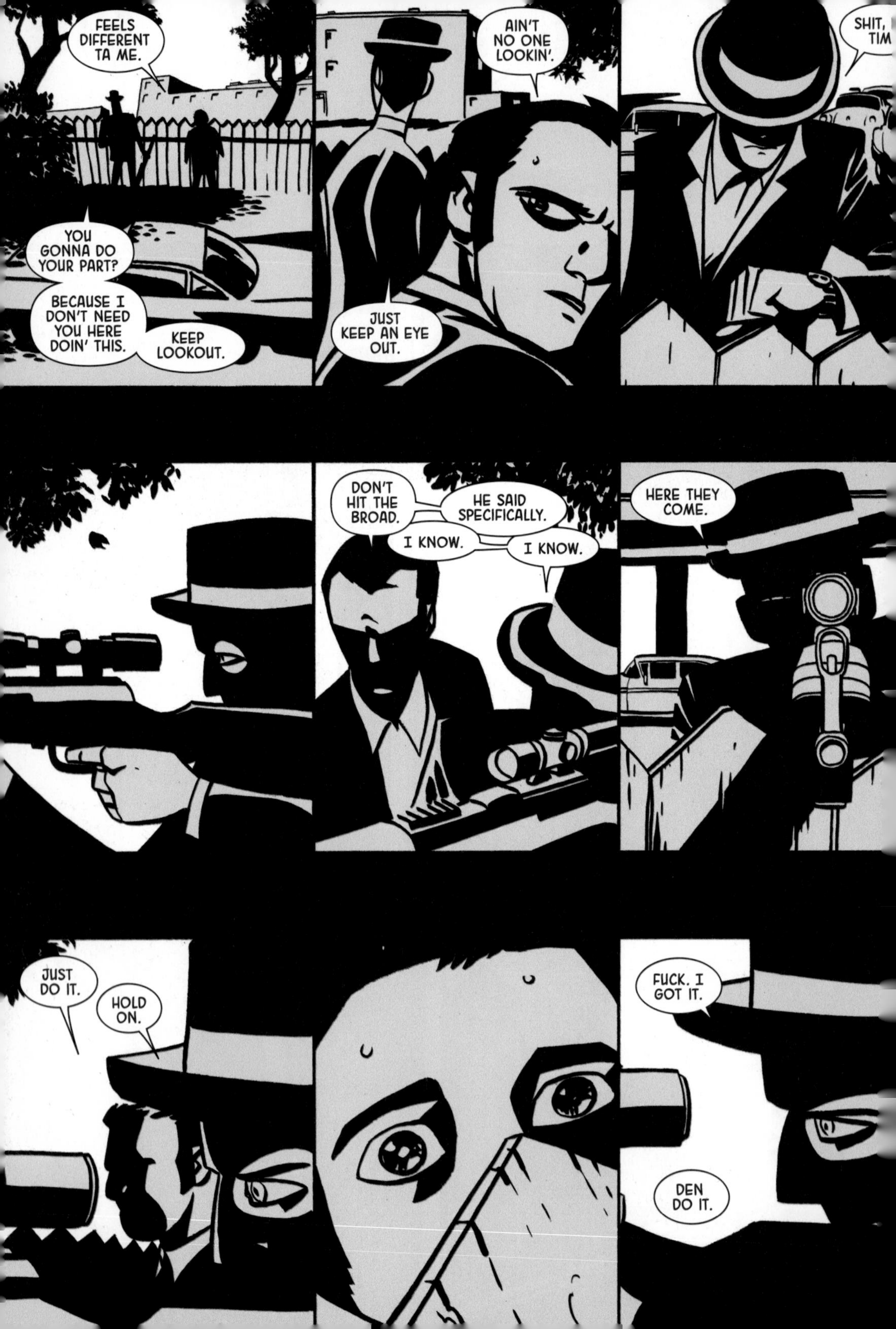
FEELS DIFFERENT TA ME.
YOU GONNA DO YOUR PART?
BECAUSE I DON'T NEED YOU HERE DOIN' THIS.
KEEP LOOKOUT.
AIN'T NO ONE LOOKIN'.
JUST KEEP AN EYE OUT.
SHIT, TIM
DON'T HIT THE BROAD.
HE SAID SPECIFICALLY.
I KNOW.
I KNOW.
HERE THEY COME.
JUST DO IT.
HOLD ON.
FUCK. I GOT IT.
DEN DO IT.

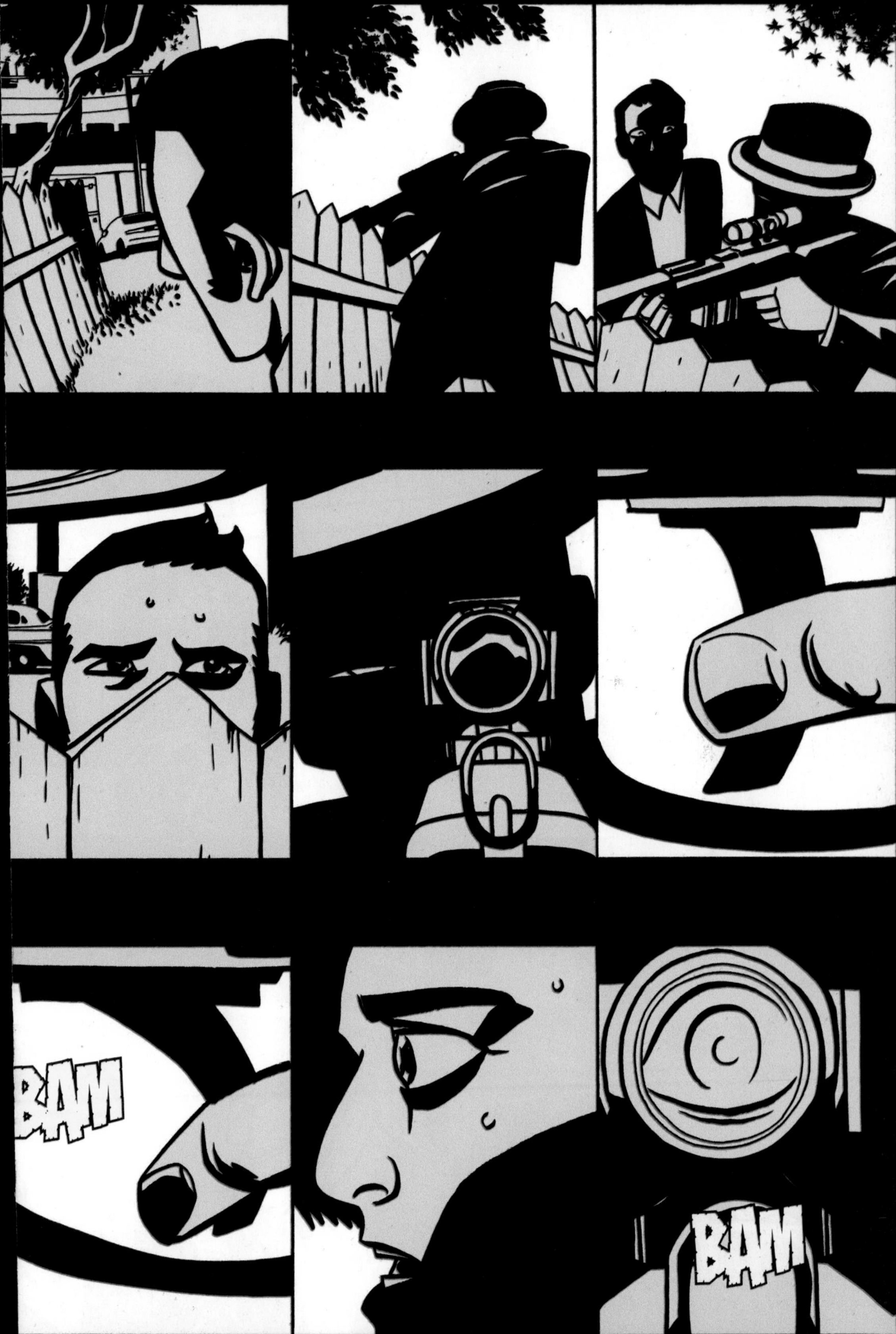
BAM
BAM

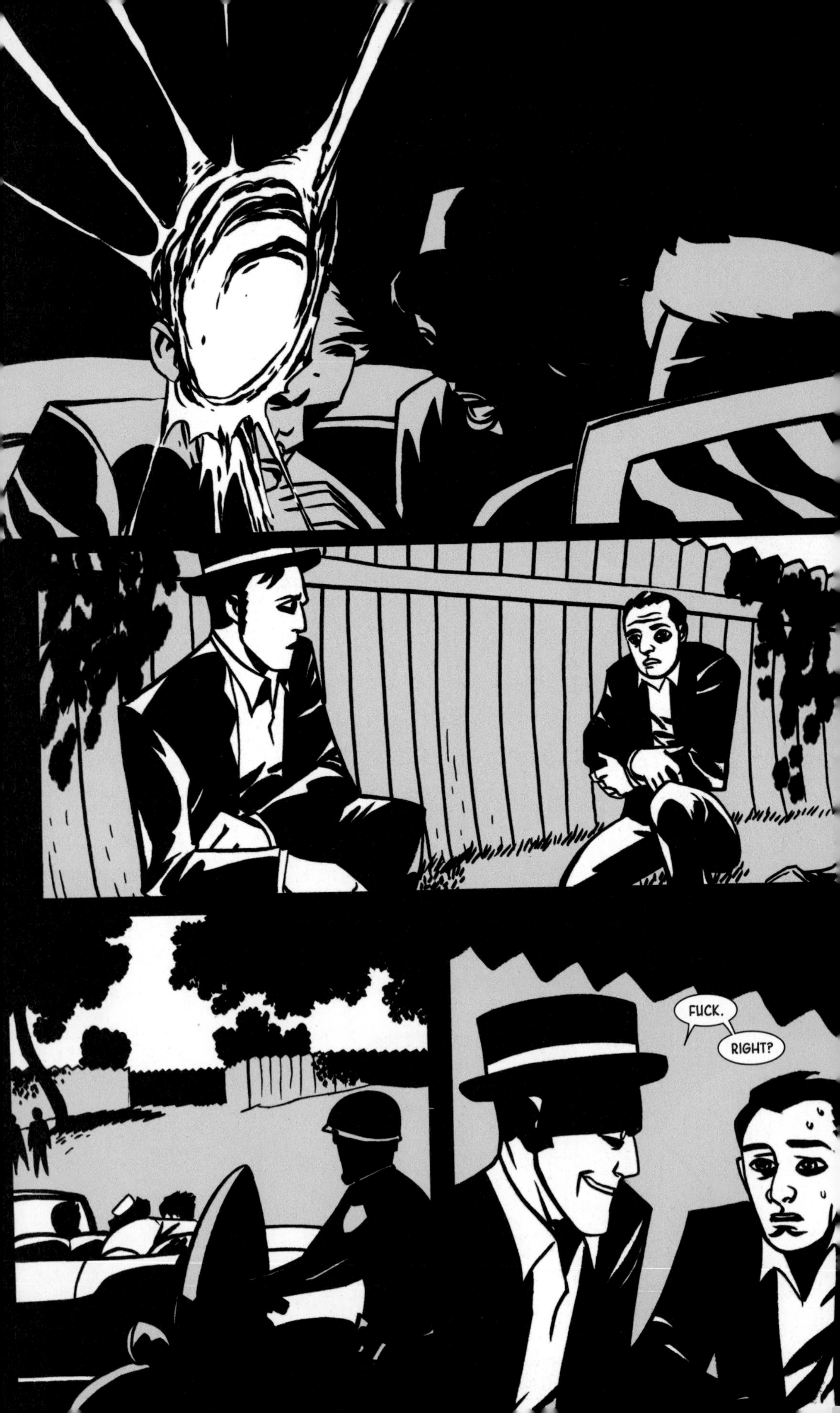
FUCK.
RIGHT?

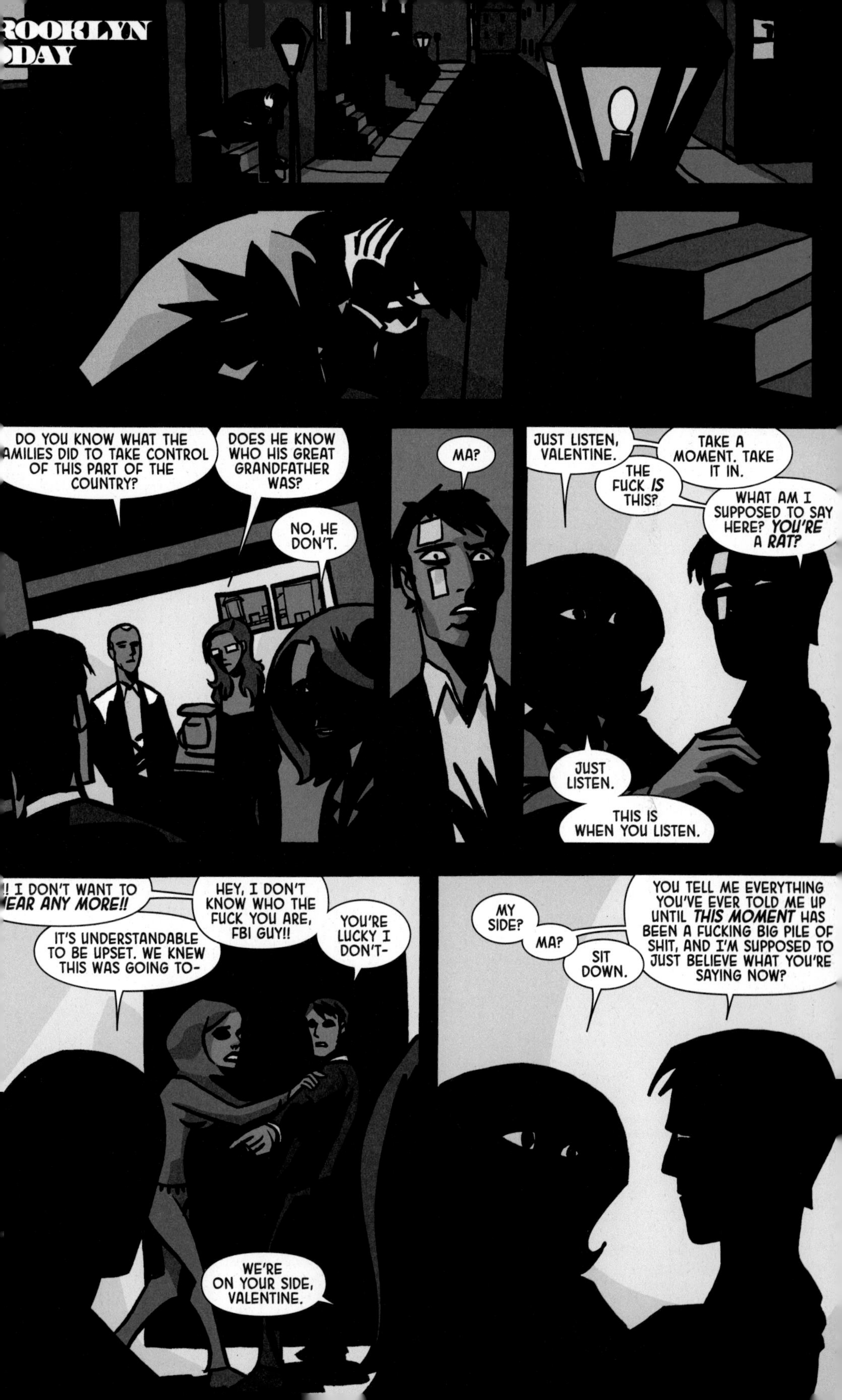
ROOKLYN
DAY
DO YOU KNOW WHAT THE AMILIES DID TO TAKE CONTROL OF THIS PART OF THE COUNTRY?
DOES HE KNOW WHO HIS GREAT GRANDFATHER WAS?
NO, HE DON'T.
MA?
JUST LISTEN, VALENTINE.
TAKE A MOMENT. TAKE IT IN.
THE FUCK *IS* THIS?
WHAT AM I SUPPOSED TO SAY HERE? *YOU'RE* A *RAT?*
JUST LISTEN.
THIS IS WHEN YOU LISTEN.
! I DON'T WANT TO *EAR ANY MORE!!*
HEY, I DON'T KNOW WHO THE FUCK YOU ARE, FBI GUY!!
IT'S UNDERSTANDABLE TO BE UPSET. WE KNEW THIS WAS GOING TO-
YOU'RE LUCKY I DON'T-
WE'RE ON YOUR SIDE, VALENTINE.
MY SIDE?
MA?
SIT DOWN.
YOU TELL ME EVERYTHING YOU'VE EVER TOLD ME UP UNTIL *THIS MOMENT* HAS BEEN A FUCKING BIG PILE OF SHIT, AND I'M SUPPOSED TO JUST BELIEVE WHAT YOU'RE SAYING NOW?

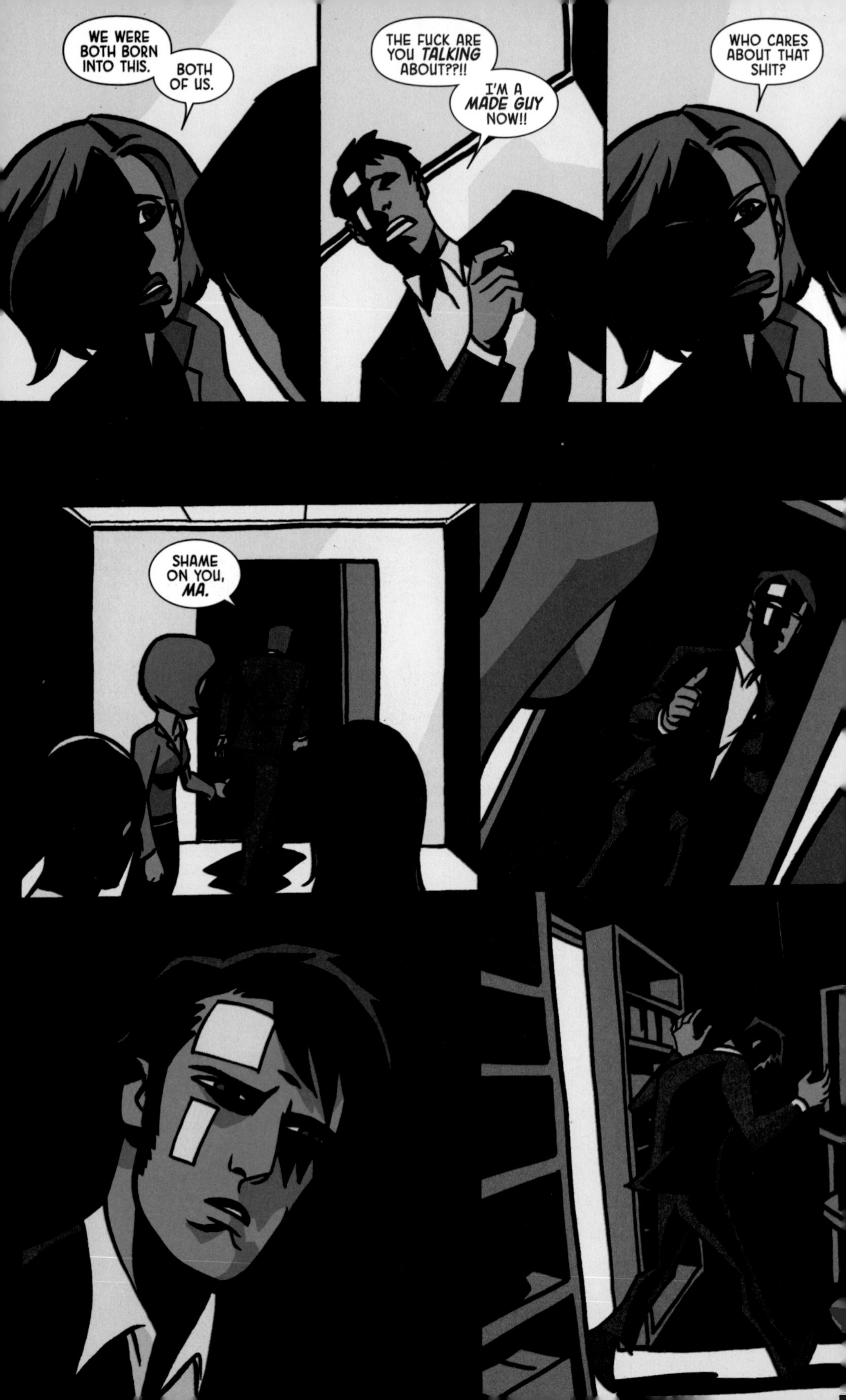
WE WERE BOTH BORN INTO THIS.
BOTH OF US.
THE FUCK ARE YOU *TALKING* ABOUT??!!
I'M A *MADE GUY* NOW!!
WHO CARES ABOUT THAT SHIT?
SHAME ON YOU, *MA.*

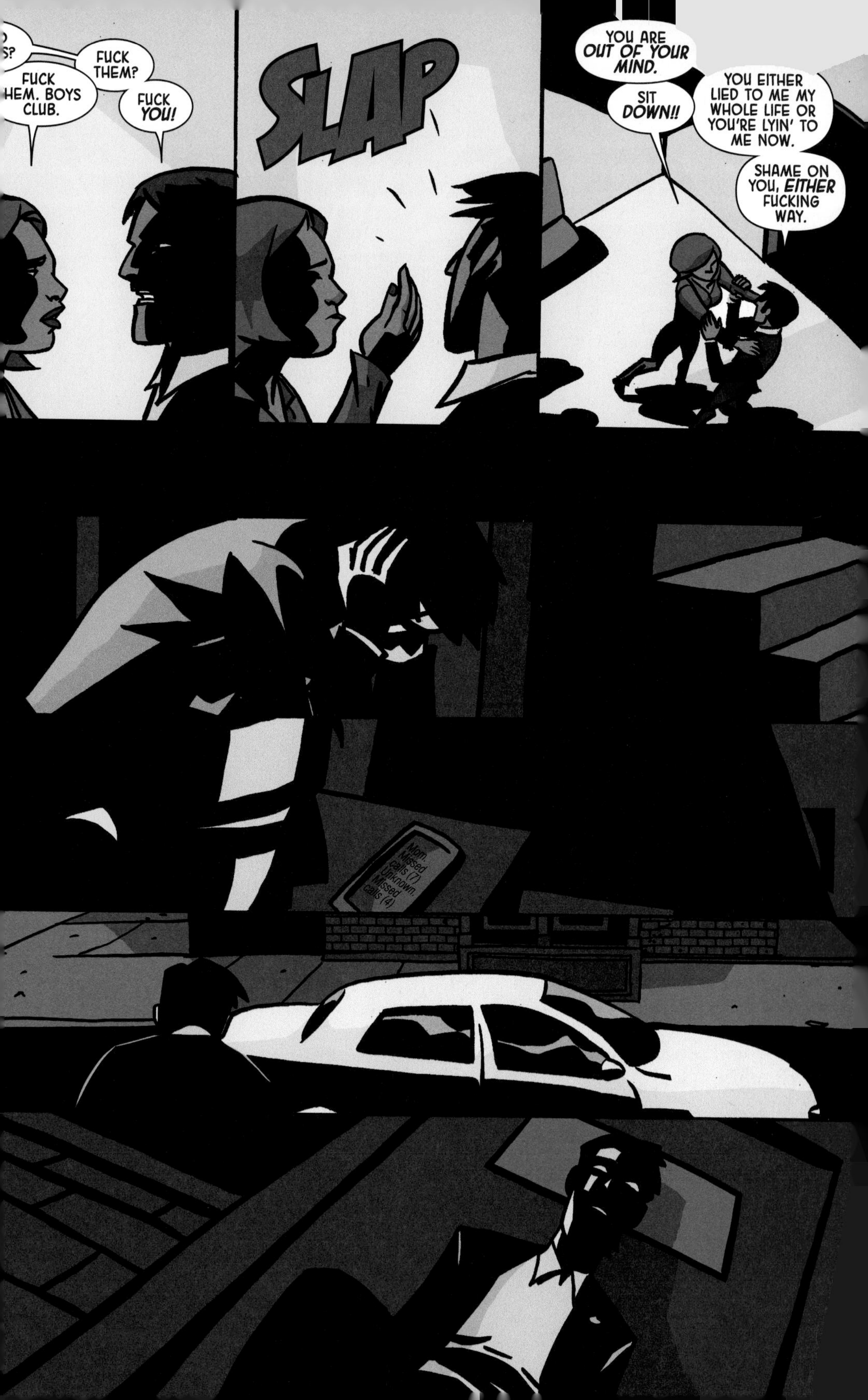
FUCK HEM. BOYS CLUB.
FUCK THEM?
FUCK YOU!
SLAP
YOU ARE OUT OF YOUR MIND.
SIT DOWN!!
YOU EITHER LIED TO ME MY WHOLE LIFE OR YOU'RE LYIN' TO ME NOW.
SHAME ON YOU, EITHER FUCKING WAY.
Mom. Missed calls (7) Unknown. Missed calls (4)

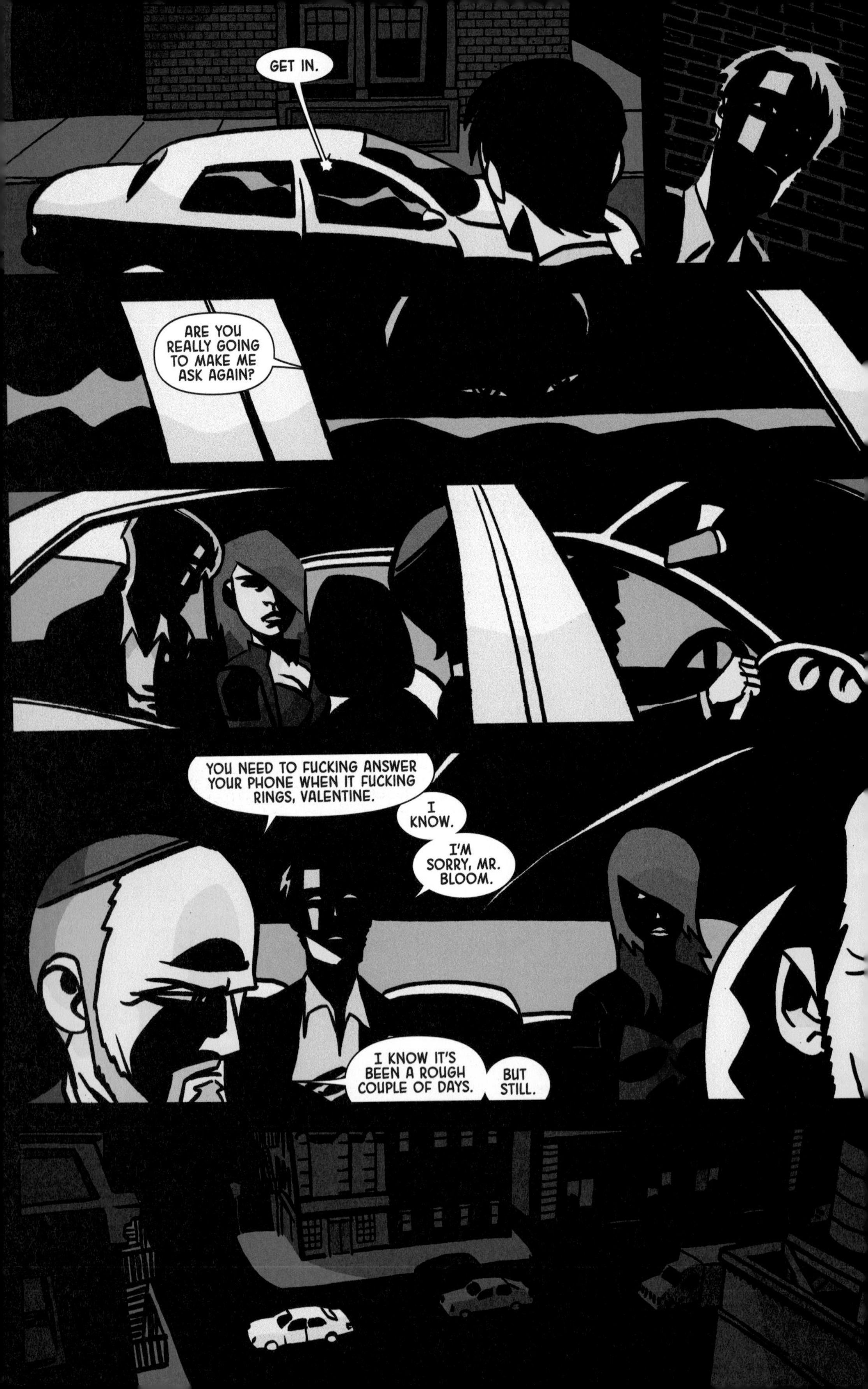
GET IN.
ARE YOU REALLY GOING TO MAKE ME ASK AGAIN?
YOU NEED TO FUCKING ANSWER YOUR PHONE WHEN IT FUCKING RINGS, VALENTINE.
I KNOW.
I'M SORRY, MR. BLOOM.
I KNOW IT'S BEEN A ROUGH COUPLE OF DAYS.
BUT STILL.

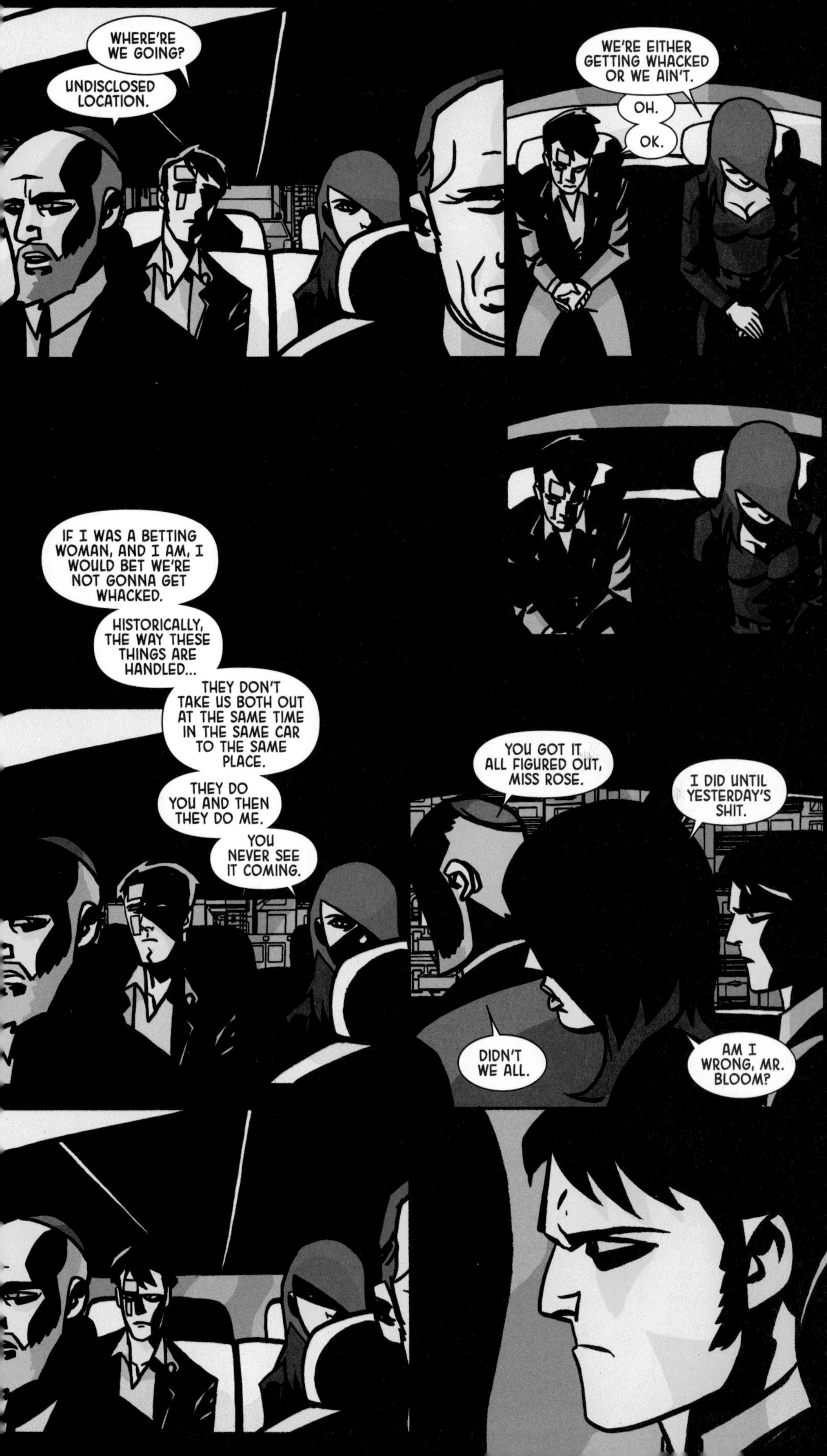
WHERE'RE WE GOING?
UNDISCLOSED LOCATION.
WE'RE EITHER GETTING WHACKED OR WE AIN'T.
OH.
OK.
IF I WAS A BETTING WOMAN, AND I AM, I WOULD BET WE'RE NOT GONNA GET WHACKED.
HISTORICALLY, THE WAY THESE THINGS ARE HANDLED...
THEY DON'T TAKE US BOTH OUT AT THE SAME TIME IN THE SAME CAR TO THE SAME PLACE.
THEY DO YOU AND THEN THEY DO ME.
YOU NEVER SEE IT COMING.
YOU GOT IT ALL FIGURED OUT, MISS ROSE.
I DID UNTIL YESTERDAY'S SHIT.
DIDN'T WE ALL.
AM I WRONG, MR. BLOOM?

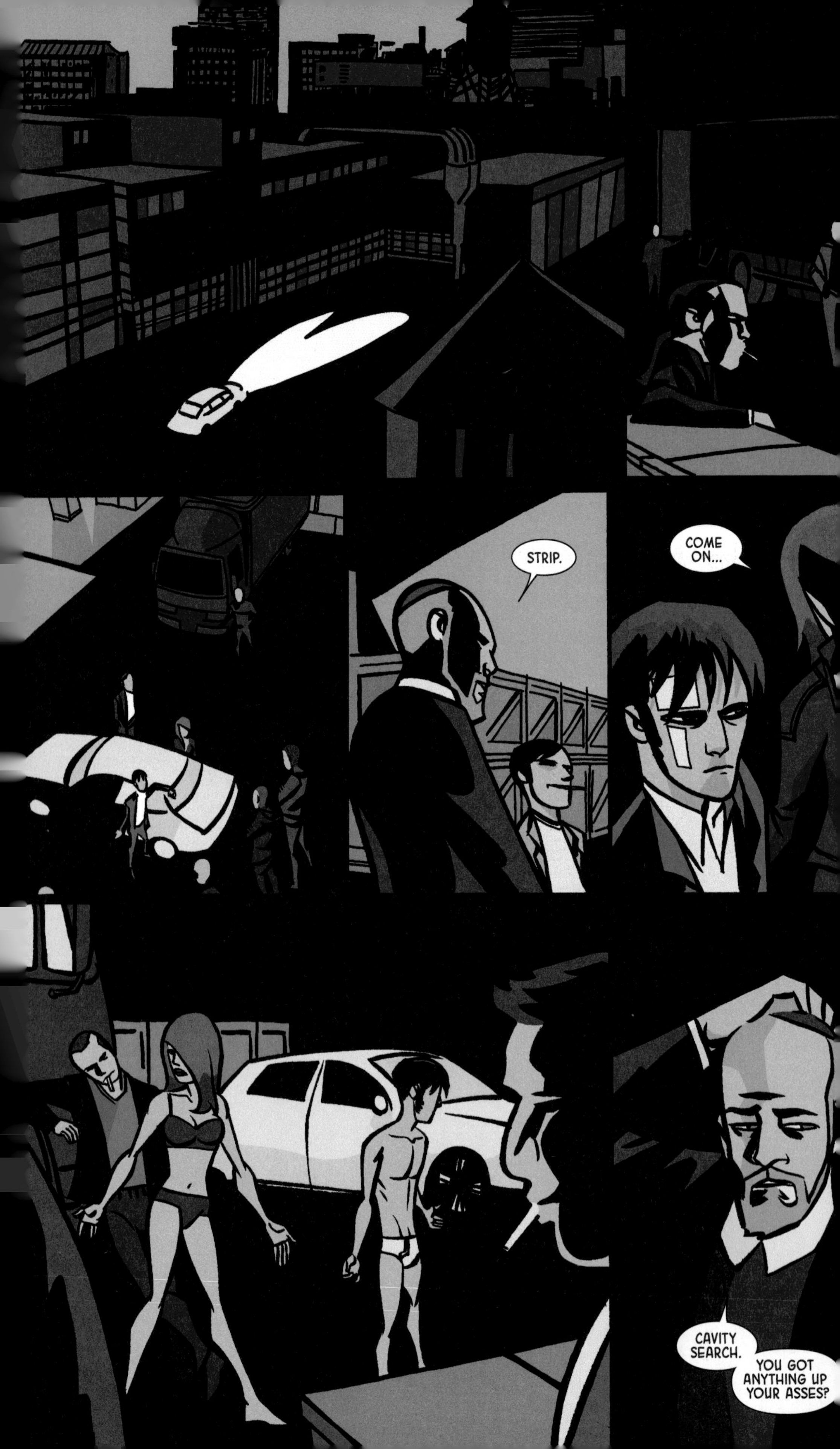
STRIP.
COME ON...
CAVITY SEARCH.
YOU GOT ANYTHING UP YOUR ASSES?

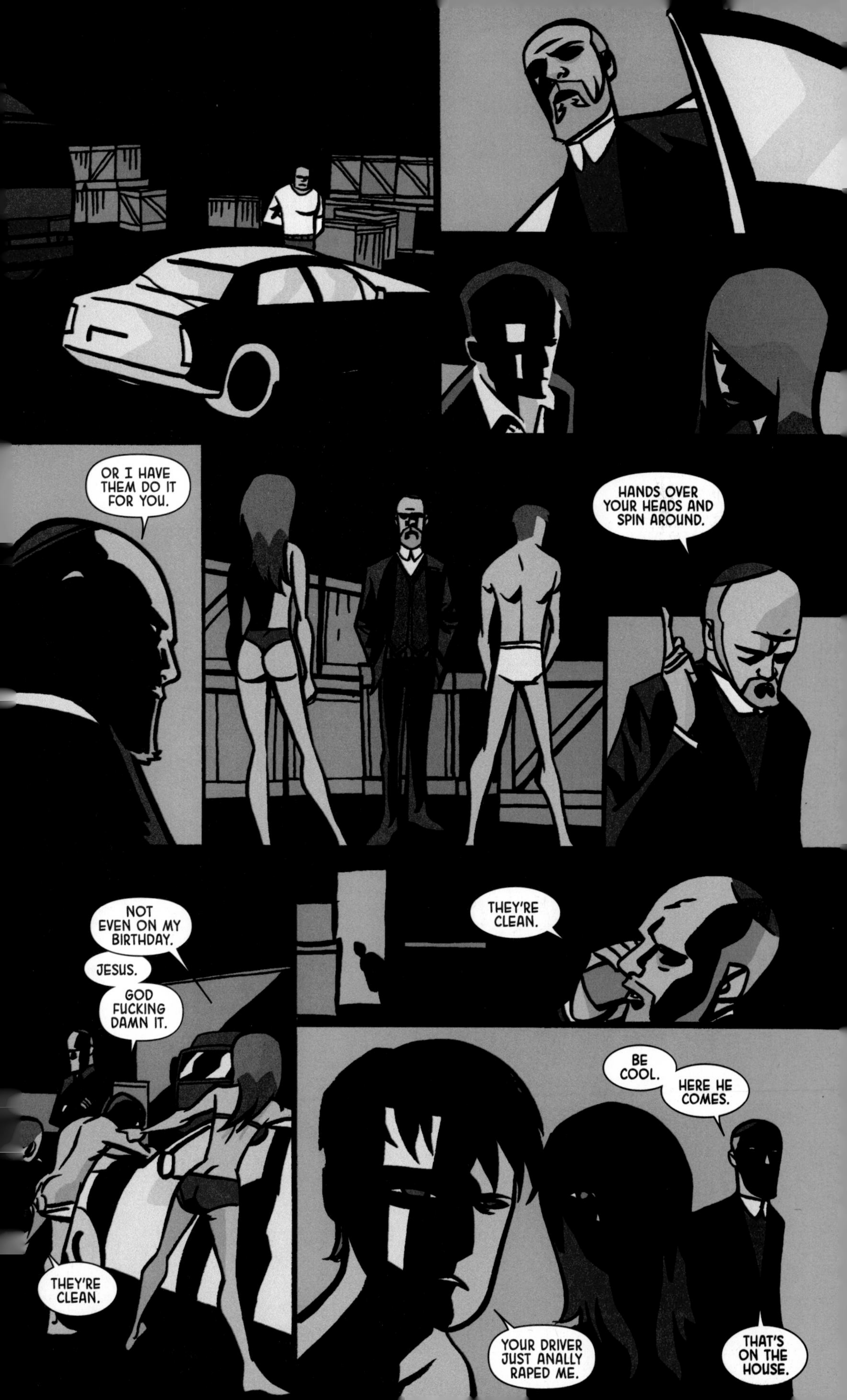
OR I HAVE THEM DO IT FOR YOU.
HANDS OVER YOUR HEADS AND SPIN AROUND.
NOT EVEN ON MY BIRTHDAY.
JESUS.
GOD FUCKING DAMN IT.
THEY'RE CLEAN.
THEY'RE CLEAN.
BE COOL.
HERE HE COMES.
YOUR DRIVER JUST ANALLY RAPED ME.
THAT'S ON THE HOUSE.

MY APOLOGIES TO BOTH OF YOU TWO.

DON BONAVESE.

THEY SAID YOU LEFT THE COUNTRY.

I HAD. ON HOLIDAY. A SCHEDULED TRIP UNRELATED TO YOU OR THIS MESS.

I CAME BACK BECAUSE I KNOW MY ABSENCE MUST HAVE CAUSED BOTH OF YOU A GREAT DEAL OF SUSPICION AND DOUBT.

POOR VALENTINE, YOU'VE BEEN A MADE GUY ALL OF TWO DAYS AND THIS IS WHAT YOU GET.

BUT WE HAD TO BE SURE YOU TWO WERE CLEAN.

I THINK YOU CAN UNDERSTAND THIS FROM MY POINT OF VIEW.

I WANT TO DEAL WITH THIS PERSONALLY, AS A MAN, BUT THIS IS SUDDENLY A VERY DANGEROUS AND UNPLEASANT SITUATION.

GET DRESSED.

THIS WASHINGTON, D.C., INCIDENT COULD CAUSE A WAR BETWEEN THE FAMILIES.

AND WHO KNOWS WHAT THE FEDS WILL TRY BECAUSE OF IT.

AND I DIDN'T WANT EITHER OF YOU TO HAVE ANY DOUBT... I DID NOT SEND YOU TO WASHINGTON TO KILL. I SENT YOU WITH A MESSAGE OF INTIMIDATION.

NOTHING MORE.

JAGGER HAS BEEN RUNNING SUCH ERRANDS FOR ME FOR YEARS.

SHE KNOWS.

I HAVE NO PROBLEM GIVING KILL ORDERS MYSELF.

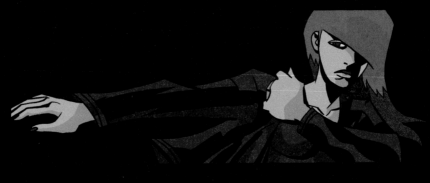

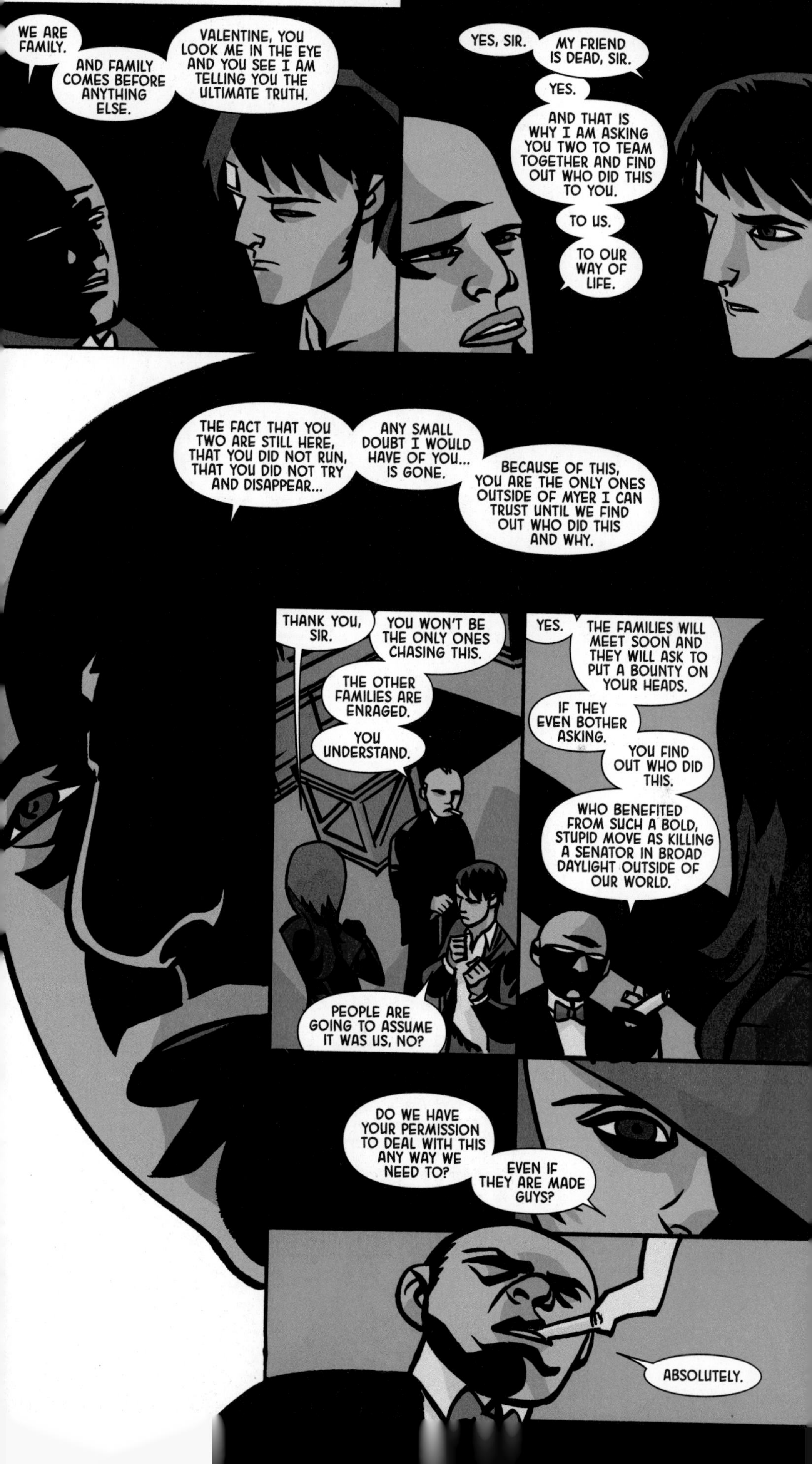
WE ARE FAMILY.
AND FAMILY COMES BEFORE ANYTHING ELSE.
VALENTINE, YOU LOOK ME IN THE EYE AND YOU SEE I AM TELLING YOU THE ULTIMATE TRUTH.
YES, SIR.
MY FRIEND IS DEAD, SIR.
YES.
AND THAT IS WHY I AM ASKING YOU TWO TO TEAM TOGETHER AND FIND OUT WHO DID THIS TO YOU.
TO US.
TO OUR WAY OF LIFE.
THE FACT THAT YOU TWO ARE STILL HERE, THAT YOU DID NOT RUN, THAT YOU DID NOT TRY AND DISAPPEAR...
ANY SMALL DOUBT I WOULD HAVE OF YOU... IS GONE.
BECAUSE OF THIS, YOU ARE THE ONLY ONES OUTSIDE OF MYER I CAN TRUST UNTIL WE FIND OUT WHO DID THIS AND WHY.
THANK YOU, SIR.
YOU WON'T BE THE ONLY ONES CHASING THIS.
THE OTHER FAMILIES ARE ENRAGED.
YOU UNDERSTAND.
PEOPLE ARE GOING TO ASSUME IT WAS US, NO?
YES.
THE FAMILIES WILL MEET SOON AND THEY WILL ASK TO PUT A BOUNTY ON YOUR HEADS.
IF THEY EVEN BOTHER ASKING.
YOU FIND OUT WHO DID THIS.
WHO BENEFITED FROM SUCH A BOLD, STUPID MOVE AS KILLING A SENATOR IN BROAD DAYLIGHT OUTSIDE OF OUR WORLD.
DO WE HAVE YOUR PERMISSION TO DEAL WITH THIS ANY WAY WE NEED TO?
EVEN IF THEY ARE MADE GUYS?
ABSOLUTELY.

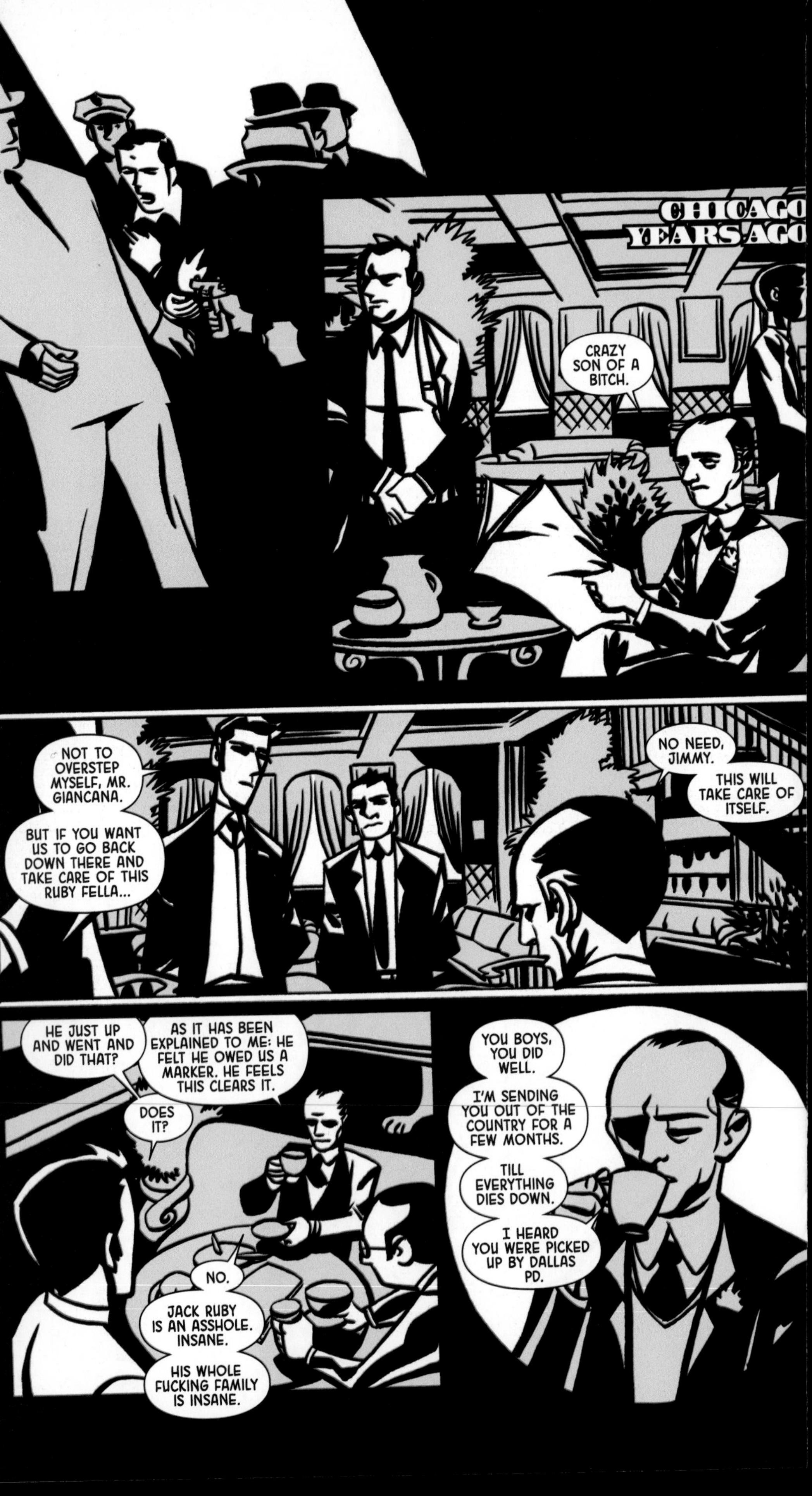
CHICAGO
YEARS AGO
CRAZY SON OF A BITCH.
NOT TO OVERSTEP MYSELF, MR. GIANCANA.
BUT IF YOU WANT US TO GO BACK DOWN THERE AND TAKE CARE OF THIS RUBY FELLA...
NO NEED, JIMMY.
THIS WILL TAKE CARE OF ITSELF.
HE JUST UP AND WENT AND DID THAT?
AS IT HAS BEEN EXPLAINED TO ME: HE FELT HE OWED US A MARKER. HE FEELS THIS CLEARS IT.
DOES IT?
NO.
JACK RUBY IS AN ASSHOLE. INSANE.
HIS WHOLE FUCKING FAMILY IS INSANE.
YOU BOYS, YOU DID WELL.
I'M SENDING YOU OUT OF THE COUNTRY FOR A FEW MONTHS.
TILL EVERYTHING DIES DOWN.
I HEARD YOU WERE PICKED UP BY DALLAS PD.

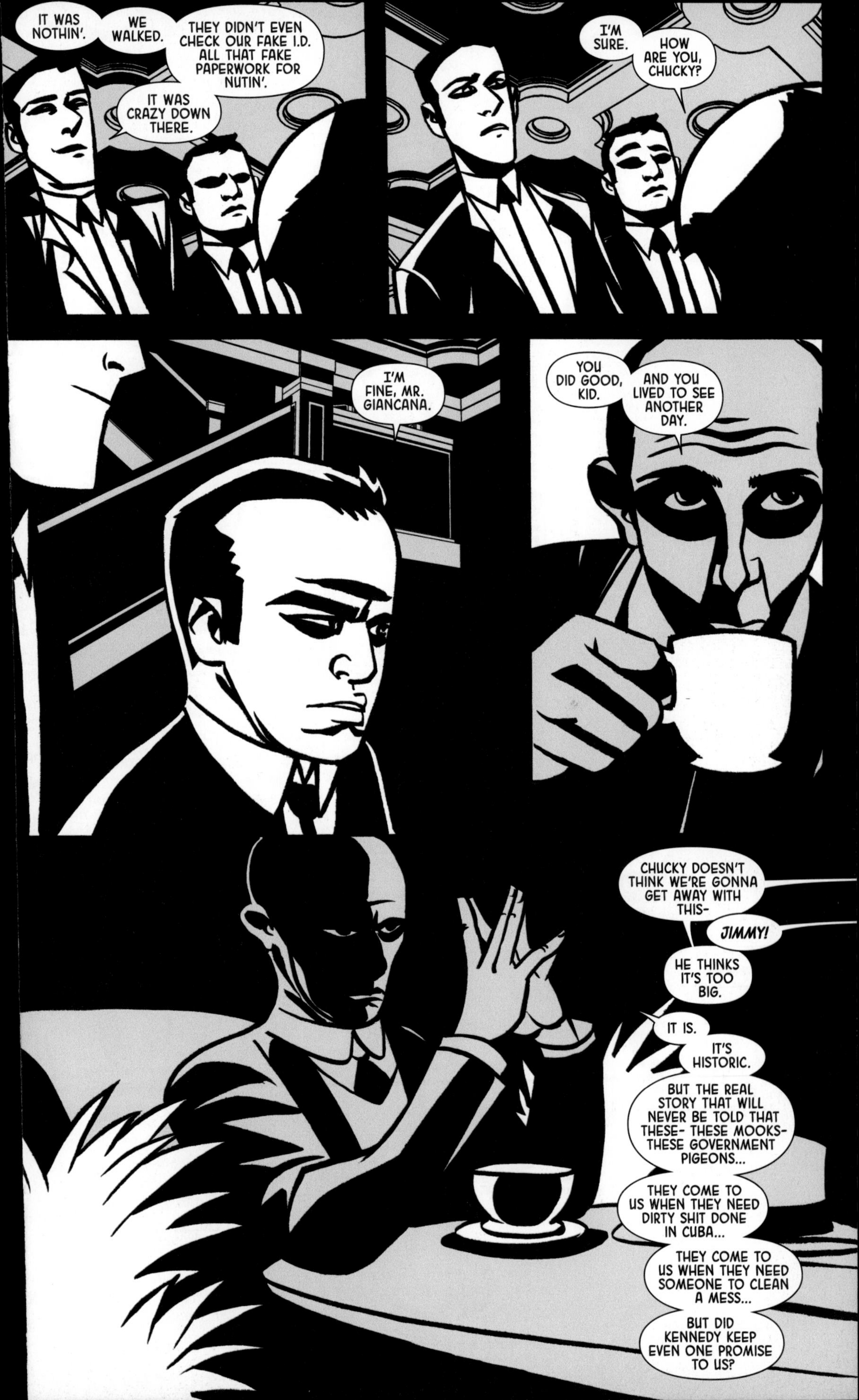
IT WAS NOTHIN'.
WE WALKED.
THEY DIDN'T EVEN CHECK OUR FAKE I.D. ALL THAT FAKE PAPERWORK FOR NUTIN'.
IT WAS CRAZY DOWN THERE.
I'M SURE.
HOW ARE YOU, CHUCKY?
I'M FINE, MR. GIANCANA.
YOU DID GOOD, KID.
AND YOU LIVED TO SEE ANOTHER DAY.
CHUCKY DOESN'T THINK WE'RE GONNA GET AWAY WITH THIS-
JIMMY!
HE THINKS IT'S TOO BIG.
IT IS.
IT'S HISTORIC.
BUT THE REAL STORY THAT WILL NEVER BE TOLD THAT THESE- THESE MOOKS- THESE GOVERNMENT PIGEONS...
THEY COME TO US WHEN THEY NEED DIRTY SHIT DONE IN CUBA...
THEY COME TO US WHEN THEY NEED SOMEONE TO CLEAN A MESS...
BUT DID KENNEDY KEEP EVEN ONE PROMISE TO US?

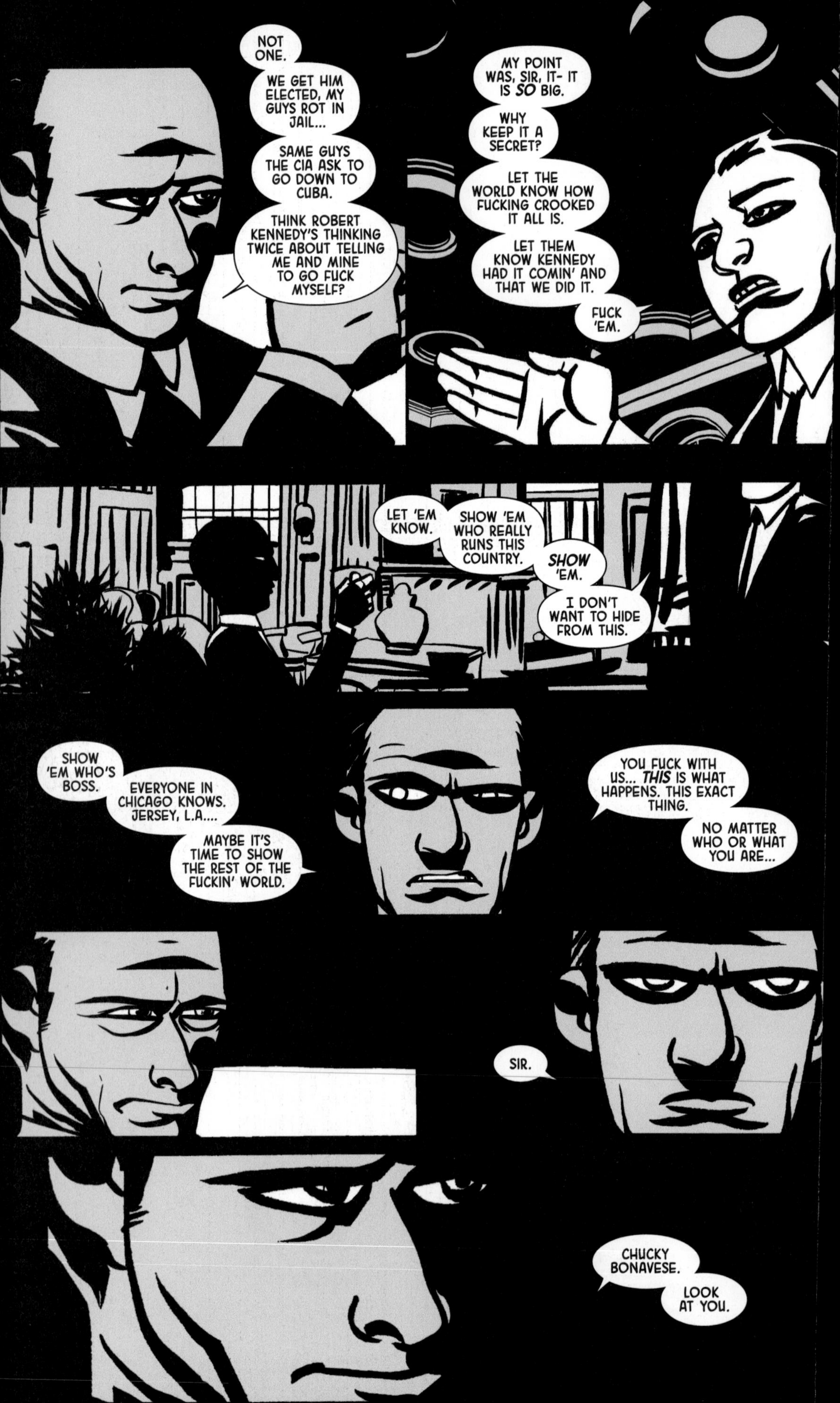
NOT ONE.
WE GET HIM ELECTED, MY GUYS ROT IN JAIL...
SAME GUYS THE CIA ASK TO GO DOWN TO CUBA.
THINK ROBERT KENNEDY'S THINKING TWICE ABOUT TELLING ME AND MINE TO GO FUCK MYSELF?
MY POINT WAS, SIR, IT- IT IS SO BIG.
WHY KEEP IT A SECRET?
LET THE WORLD KNOW HOW FUCKING CROOKED IT ALL IS.
LET THEM KNOW KENNEDY HAD IT COMIN' AND THAT WE DID IT.
FUCK 'EM.
LET 'EM KNOW.
SHOW 'EM WHO REALLY RUNS THIS COUNTRY.
SHOW 'EM.
I DON'T WANT TO HIDE FROM THIS.
SHOW 'EM WHO'S BOSS.
EVERYONE IN CHICAGO KNOWS. JERSEY, L.A....
MAYBE IT'S TIME TO SHOW THE REST OF THE FUCKIN' WORLD.
YOU FUCK WITH US... THIS IS WHAT HAPPENS. THIS EXACT THING.
NO MATTER WHO OR WHAT YOU ARE...
SIR.
CHUCKY BONAVESE.
LOOK AT YOU.

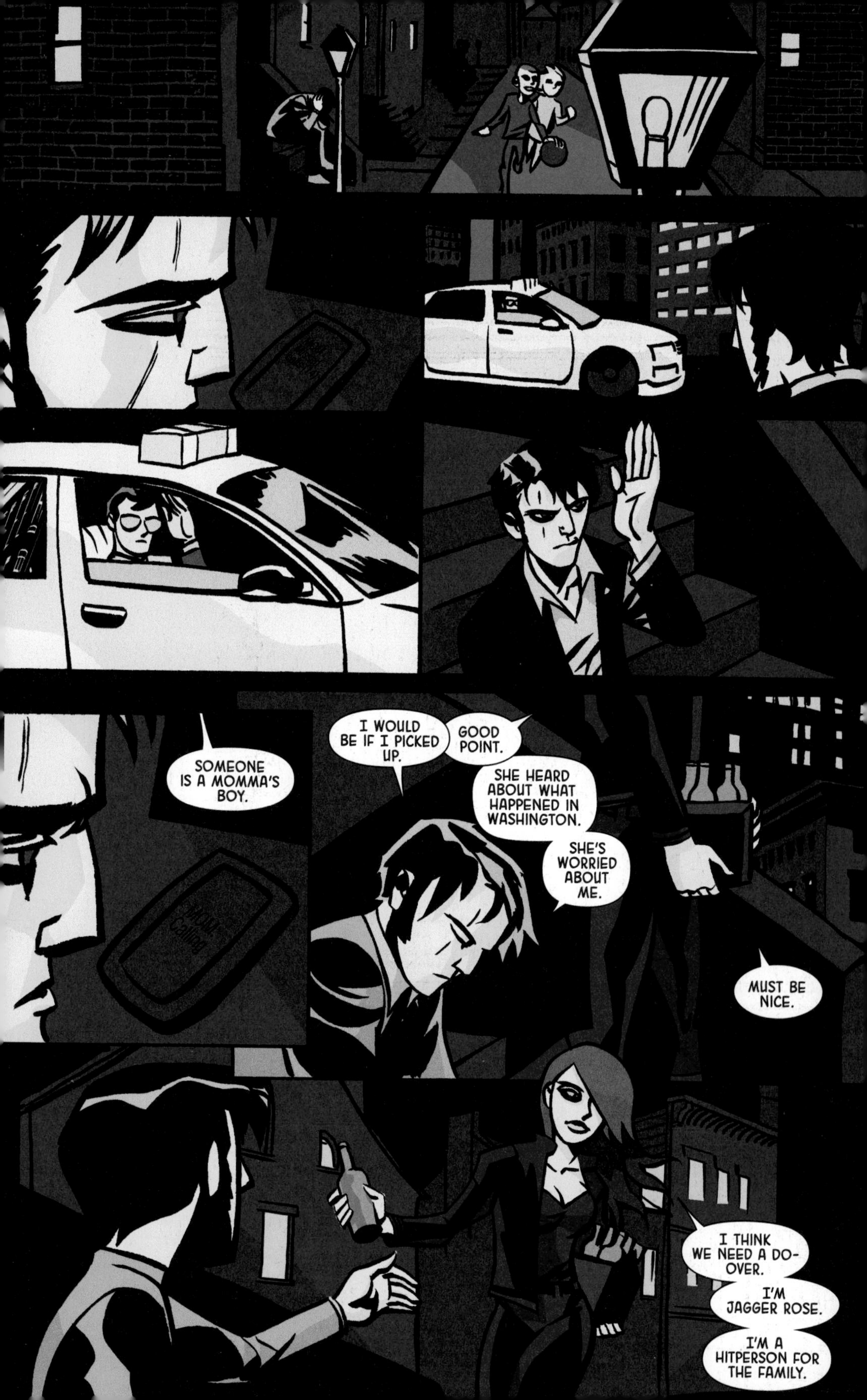
SOMEONE IS A MOMMA'S BOY.
I WOULD BE IF I PICKED UP.
GOOD POINT.
SHE HEARD ABOUT WHAT HAPPENED IN WASHINGTON.
SHE'S WORRIED ABOUT ME.
MUST BE NICE.
I THINK WE NEED A DO-OVER.
I'M JAGGER ROSE.
I'M A HITPERSON FOR THE FAMILY.

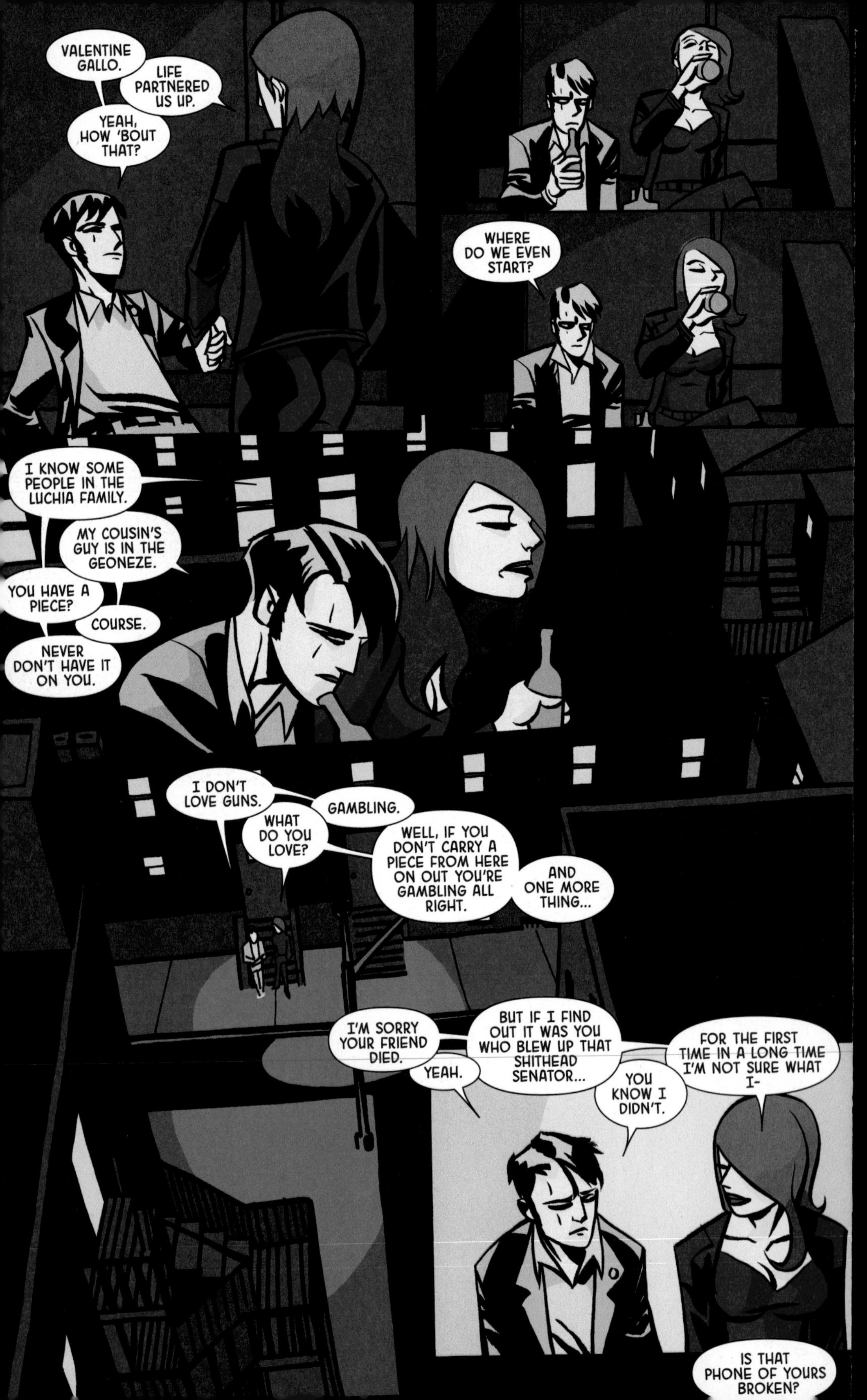
VALENTINE GALLO.
LIFE PARTNERED US UP.
YEAH, HOW 'BOUT THAT?
WHERE DO WE EVEN START?
I KNOW SOME PEOPLE IN THE LUCHIA FAMILY.
MY COUSIN'S GUY IS IN THE GEONEZE.
YOU HAVE A PIECE?
COURSE.
NEVER DON'T HAVE IT ON YOU.
I DON'T LOVE GUNS.
WHAT DO YOU LOVE?
GAMBLING.
WELL, IF YOU DON'T CARRY A PIECE FROM HERE ON OUT YOU'RE GAMBLING ALL RIGHT.
AND ONE MORE THING...
I'M SORRY YOUR FRIEND DIED.
YEAH.
BUT IF I FIND OUT IT WAS YOU WHO BLEW UP THAT SHITHEAD SENATOR...
YOU KNOW I DIDN'T.
FOR THE FIRST TIME IN A LONG TIME I'M NOT SURE WHAT I-
IS THAT PHONE OF YOURS BROKEN?

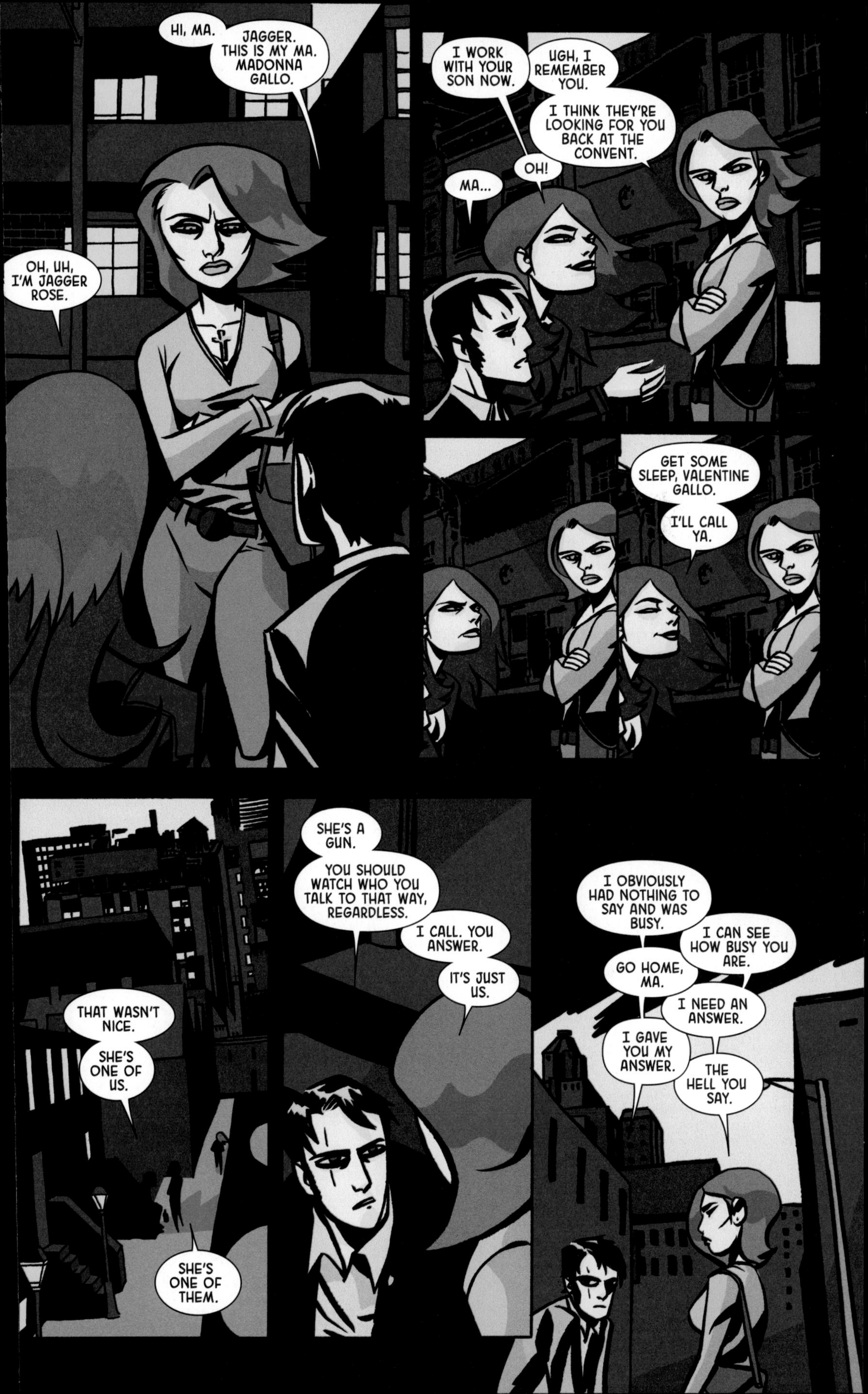
HI, MA.
JAGGER. THIS IS MY MA. MADONNA GALLO.
OH, UH, I'M JAGGER ROSE.
I WORK WITH YOUR SON NOW.
UGH, I REMEMBER YOU.
I THINK THEY'RE LOOKING FOR YOU BACK AT THE CONVENT.
OH!
MA...
GET SOME SLEEP, VALENTINE GALLO.
I'LL CALL YA.
THAT WASN'T NICE.
SHE'S ONE OF US.
SHE'S ONE OF THEM.
SHE'S A GUN.
YOU SHOULD WATCH WHO YOU TALK TO THAT WAY, REGARDLESS.
I CALL. YOU ANSWER.
IT'S JUST US.
I OBVIOUSLY HAD NOTHING TO SAY AND WAS BUSY.
I CAN SEE HOW BUSY YOU ARE.
GO HOME, MA.
I NEED AN ANSWER.
I GAVE YOU MY ANSWER.
THE HELL YOU SAY.

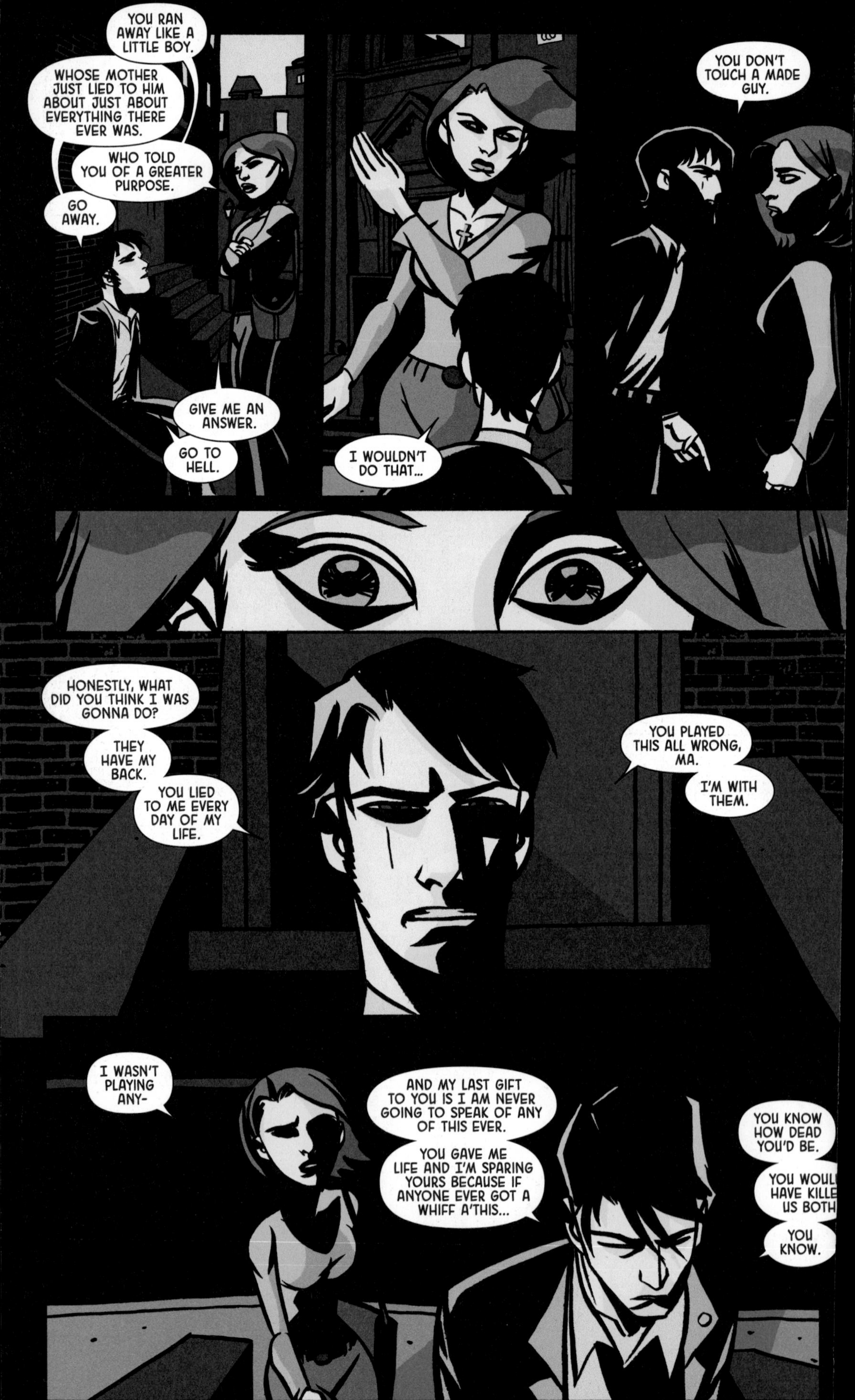
YOU RAN AWAY LIKE A LITTLE BOY.
WHOSE MOTHER JUST LIED TO HIM ABOUT JUST ABOUT EVERYTHING THERE EVER WAS.
WHO TOLD YOU OF A GREATER PURPOSE.
GO AWAY.
GIVE ME AN ANSWER.
GO TO HELL.
I WOULDN'T DO THAT...
YOU DON'T TOUCH A MADE GUY.
HONESTLY, WHAT DID YOU THINK I WAS GONNA DO?
THEY HAVE MY BACK.
YOU LIED TO ME EVERY DAY OF MY LIFE.
YOU PLAYED THIS ALL WRONG, MA.
I'M WITH THEM.
I WASN'T PLAYING ANY-
AND MY LAST GIFT TO YOU IS I AM NEVER GOING TO SPEAK OF ANY OF THIS EVER.
YOU GAVE ME LIFE AND I'M SPARING YOURS BECAUSE IF ANYONE EVER GOT A WHIFF A'THIS...
YOU KNOW HOW DEAD YOU'D BE.
YOU KNOW.

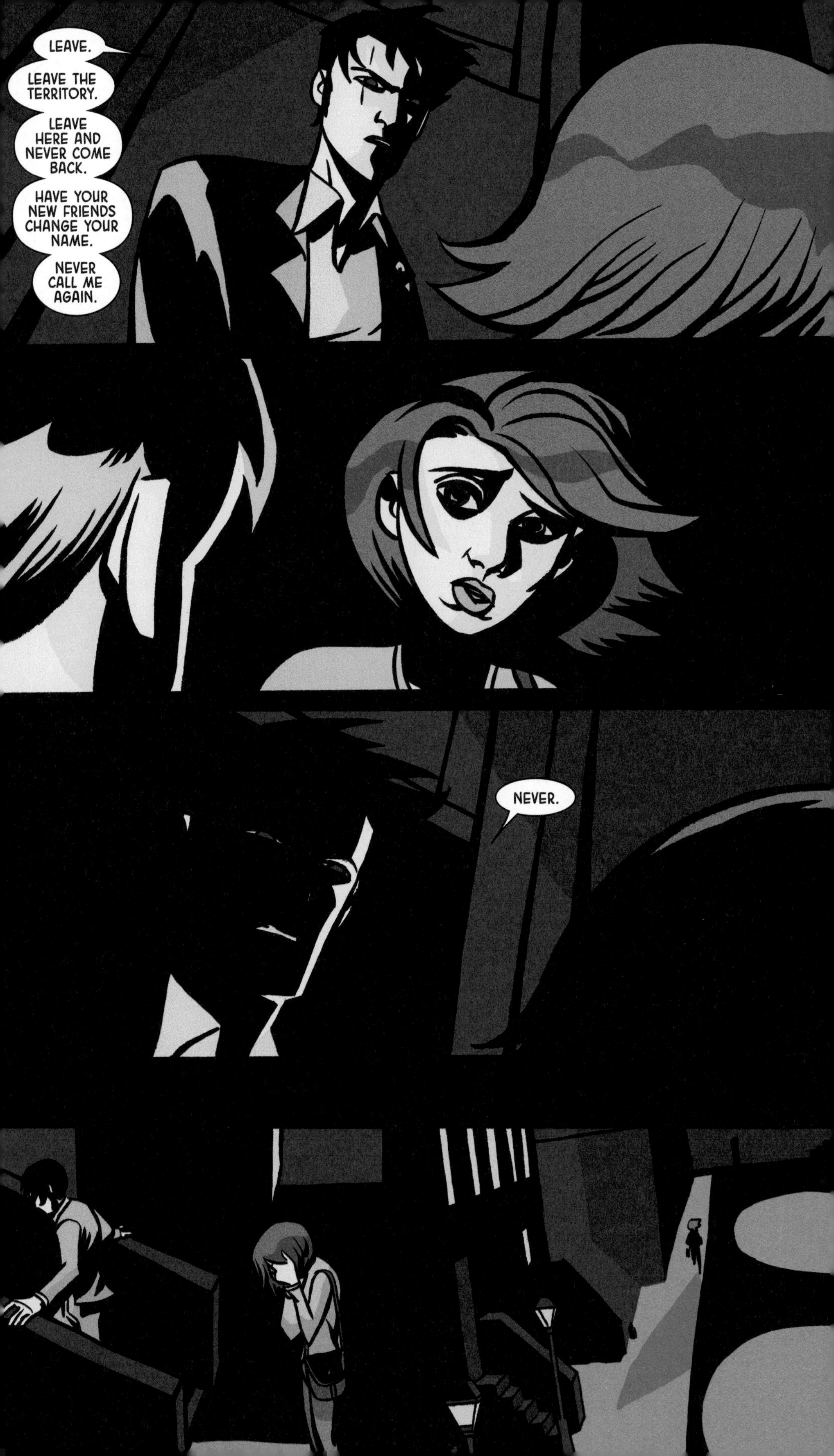
LEAVE.
LEAVE THE TERRITORY.
LEAVE HERE AND NEVER COME BACK.
HAVE YOUR NEW FRIENDS CHANGE YOUR NAME.
NEVER CALL ME AGAIN.
NEVER.

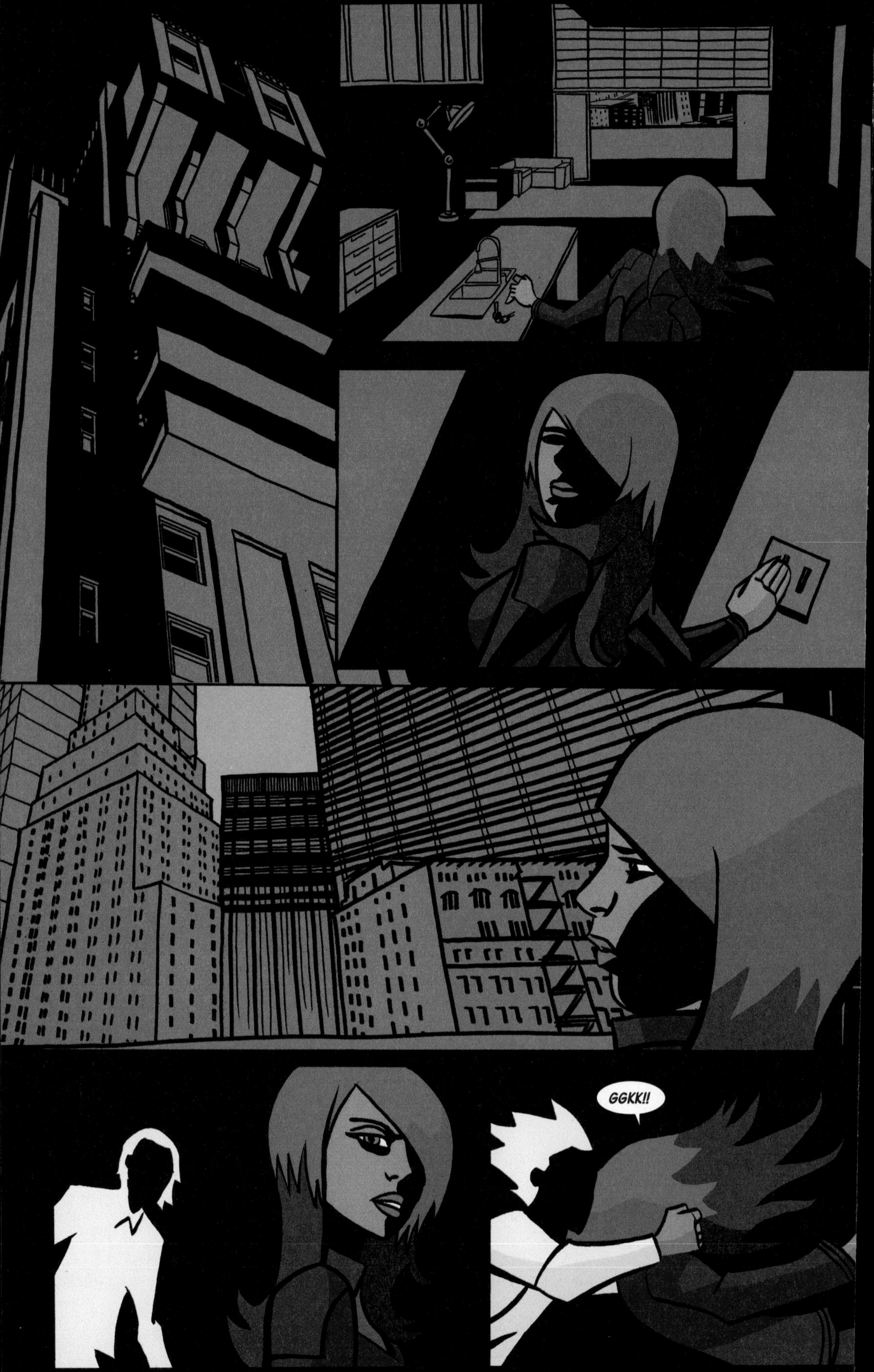
GGKK!!

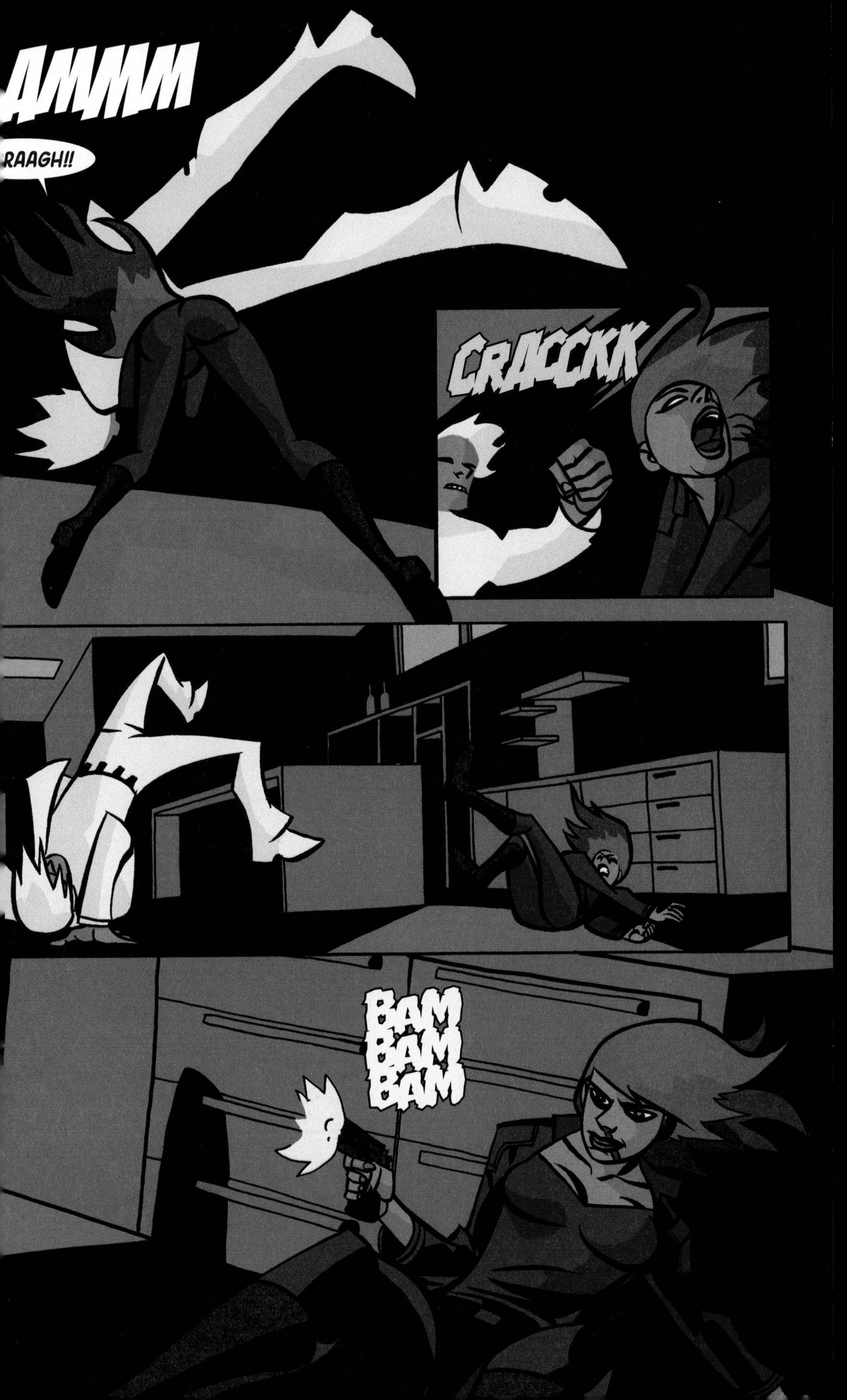
AMMM
RAAGH!!
CRACCKK
BAM
BAM
BAM

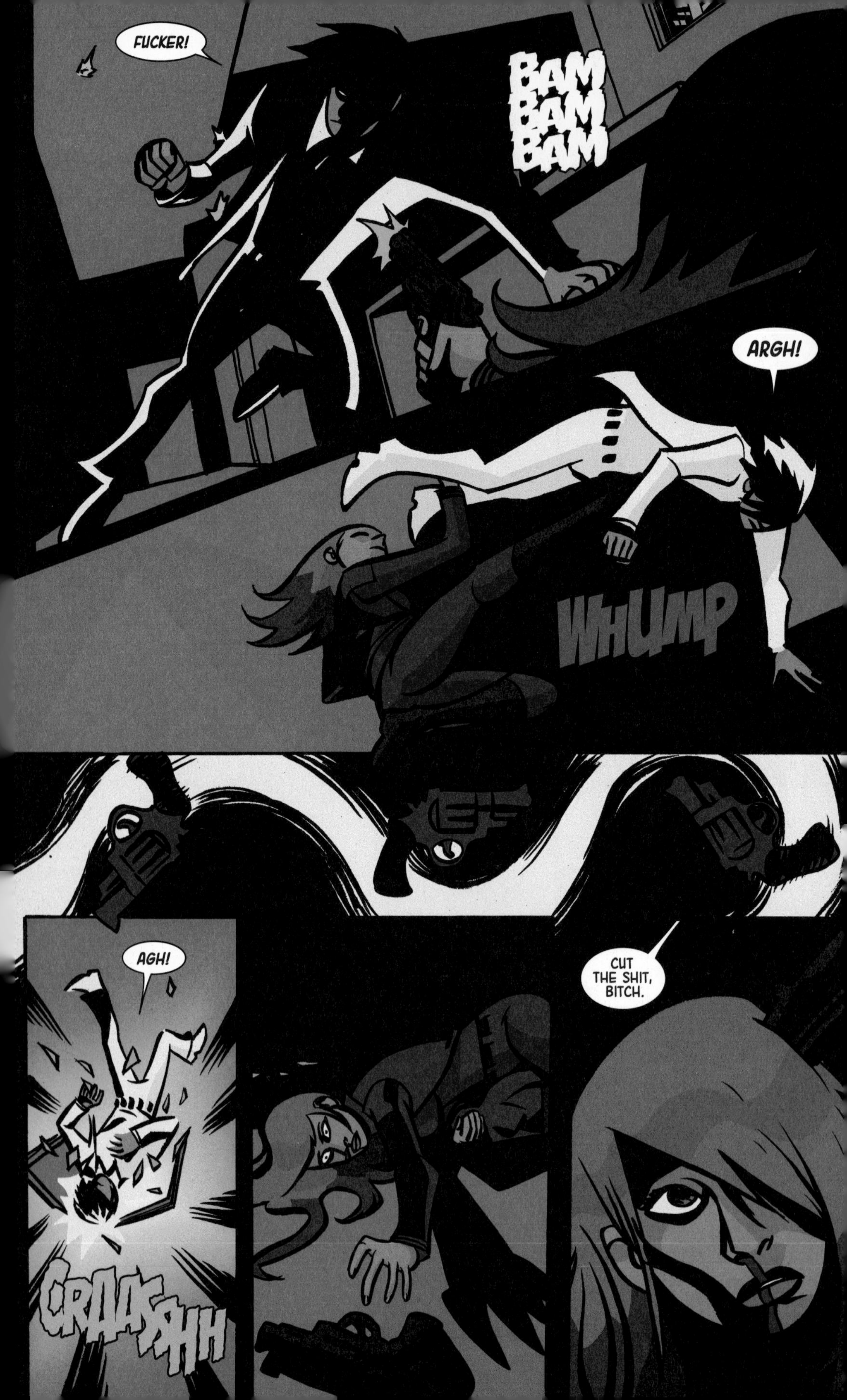
FUCKER!
BAM BAM BAM
ARGH!
WHUMP
AGH!
CRAASHH
CUT THE SHIT, BITCH.

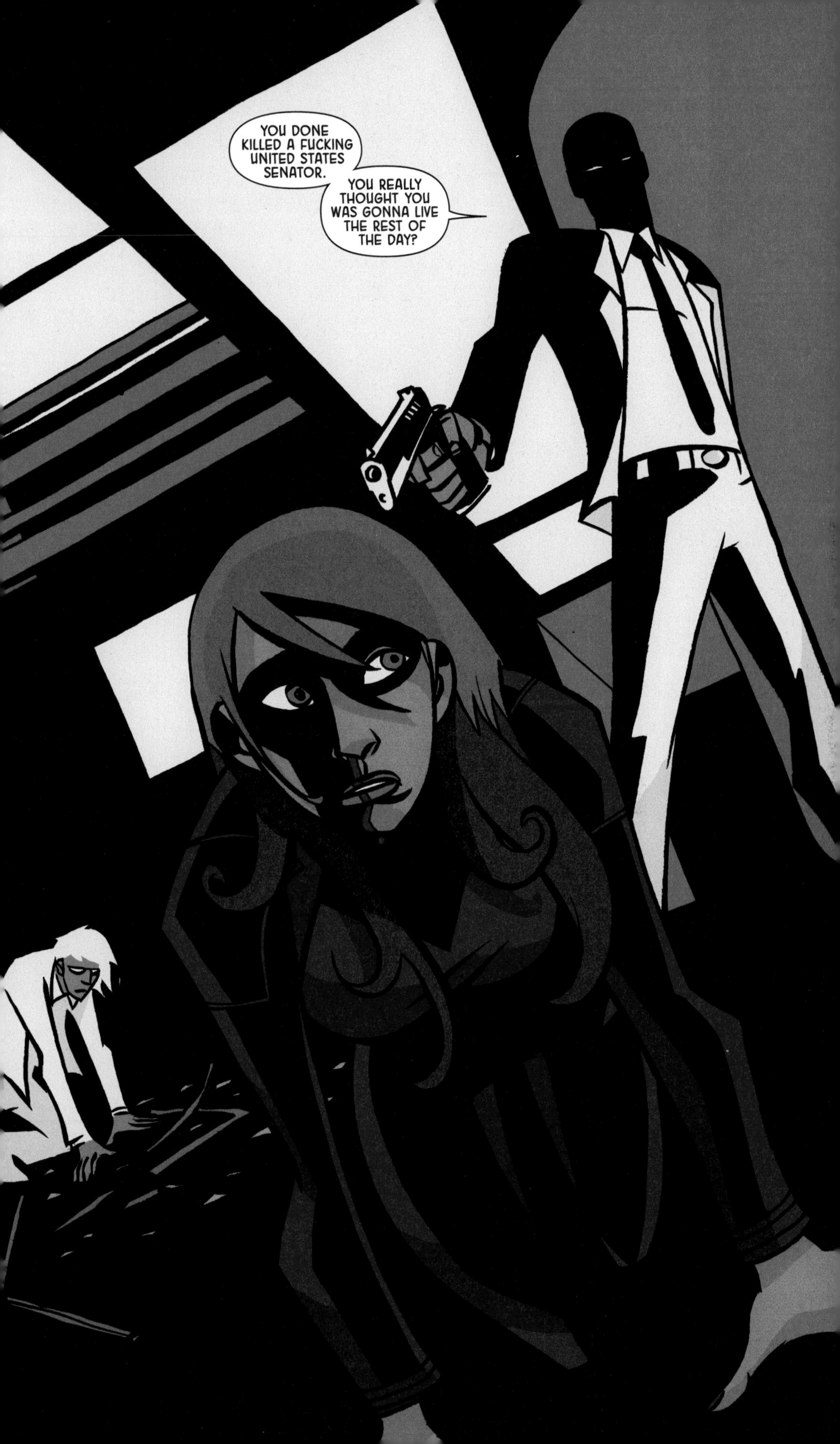
YOU DONE KILLED A FUCKING UNITED STATES SENATOR.
YOU REALLY THOUGHT YOU WAS GONNA LIVE THE REST OF THE DAY?

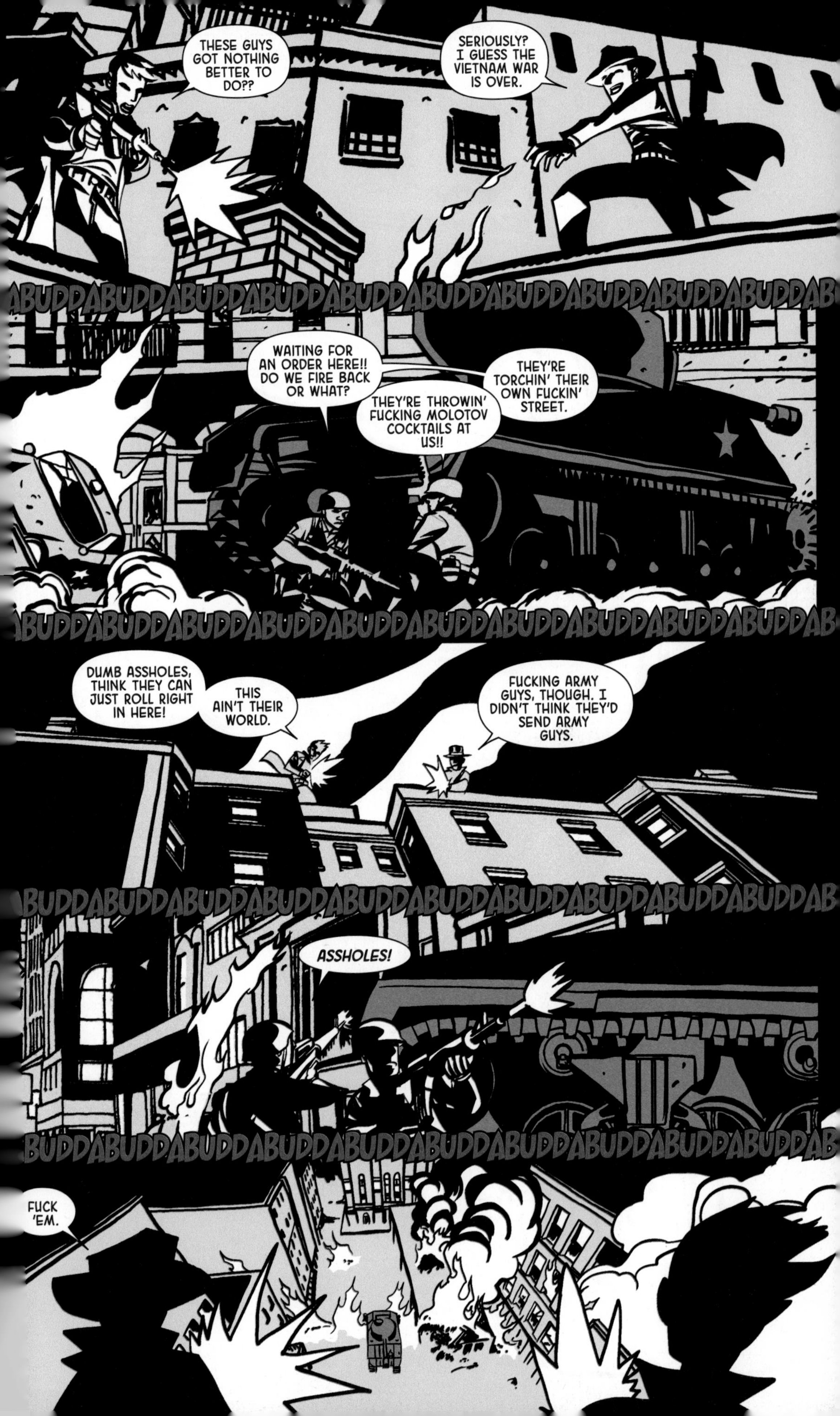
THESE GUYS GOT NOTHING BETTER TO DO??
SERIOUSLY? I GUESS THE VIETNAM WAR IS OVER.
ABUDDABUDDABUDDABUDDABUDDABUDDABUDDABUDDABUDDAB
WAITING FOR AN ORDER HERE!! DO WE FIRE BACK OR WHAT?
THEY'RE TORCHIN' THEIR OWN FUCKIN' STREET.
THEY'RE THROWIN' FUCKING MOLOTOV COCKTAILS AT US!!
ABUDDABUDDABUDDABUDDABUDDABUDDABUDDABUDDABUDDAB
DUMB ASSHOLES, THINK THEY CAN JUST ROLL RIGHT IN HERE!
THIS AIN'T THEIR WORLD.
FUCKING ARMY GUYS, THOUGH. I DIDN'T THINK THEY'D SEND ARMY GUYS.
ABUDDABUDDABUDDABUDDABUDDABUDDABUDDABUDDABUDDAB
ASSHOLES!
ABUDDABUDDABUDDABUDDABUDDABUDDABUDDABUDDABUDDAB
FUCK 'EM.

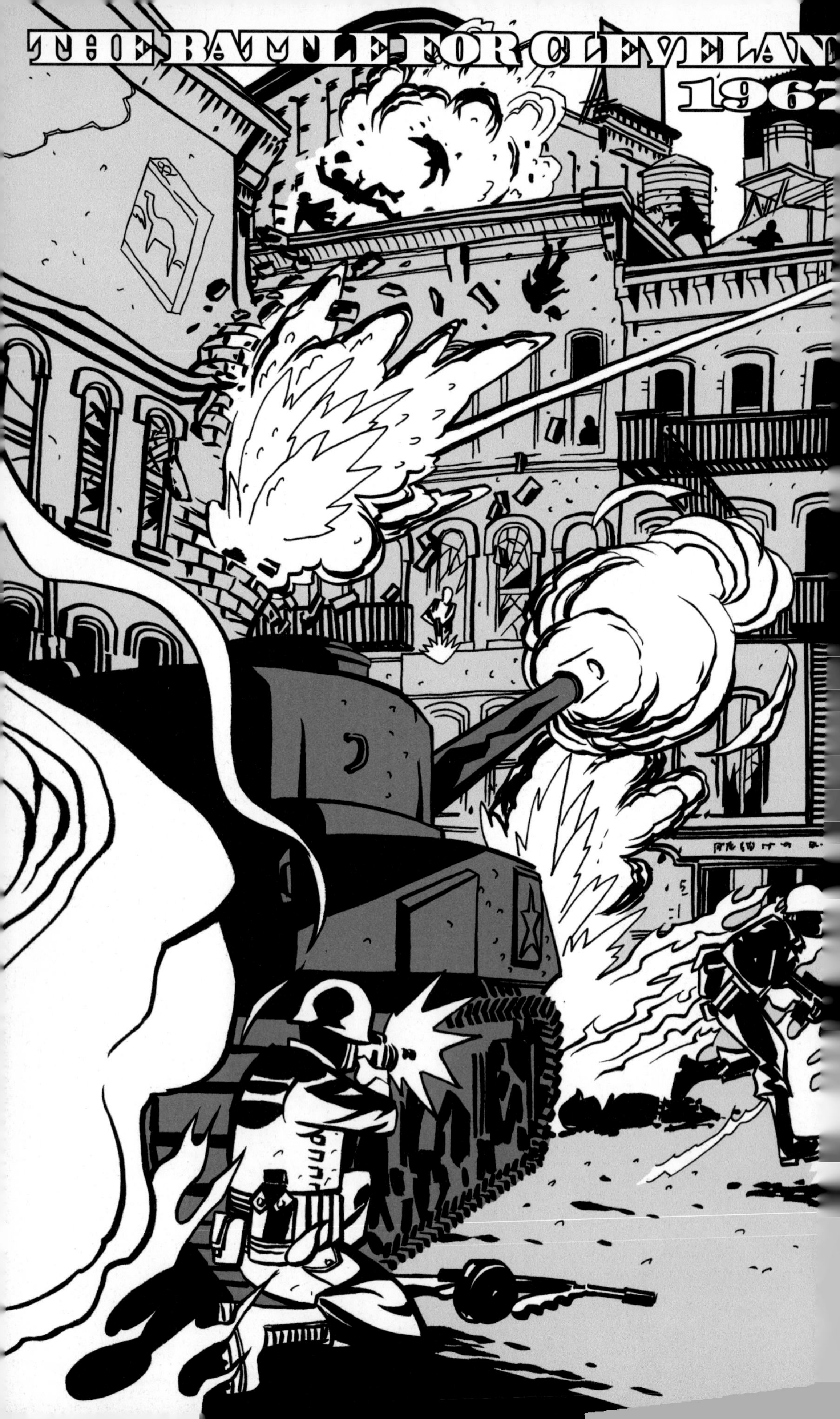
THE BATTLE FOR CLEVELAN
196

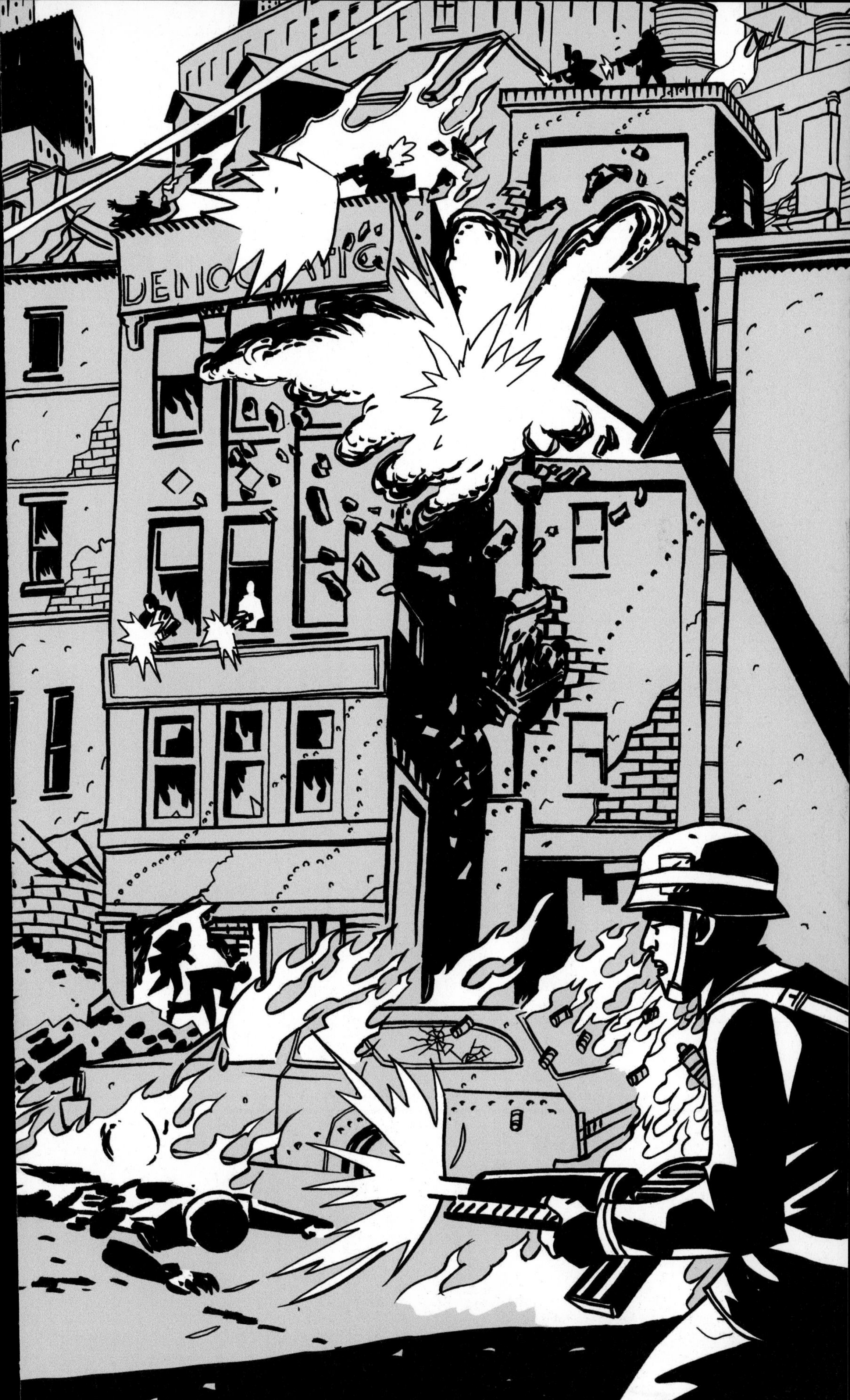

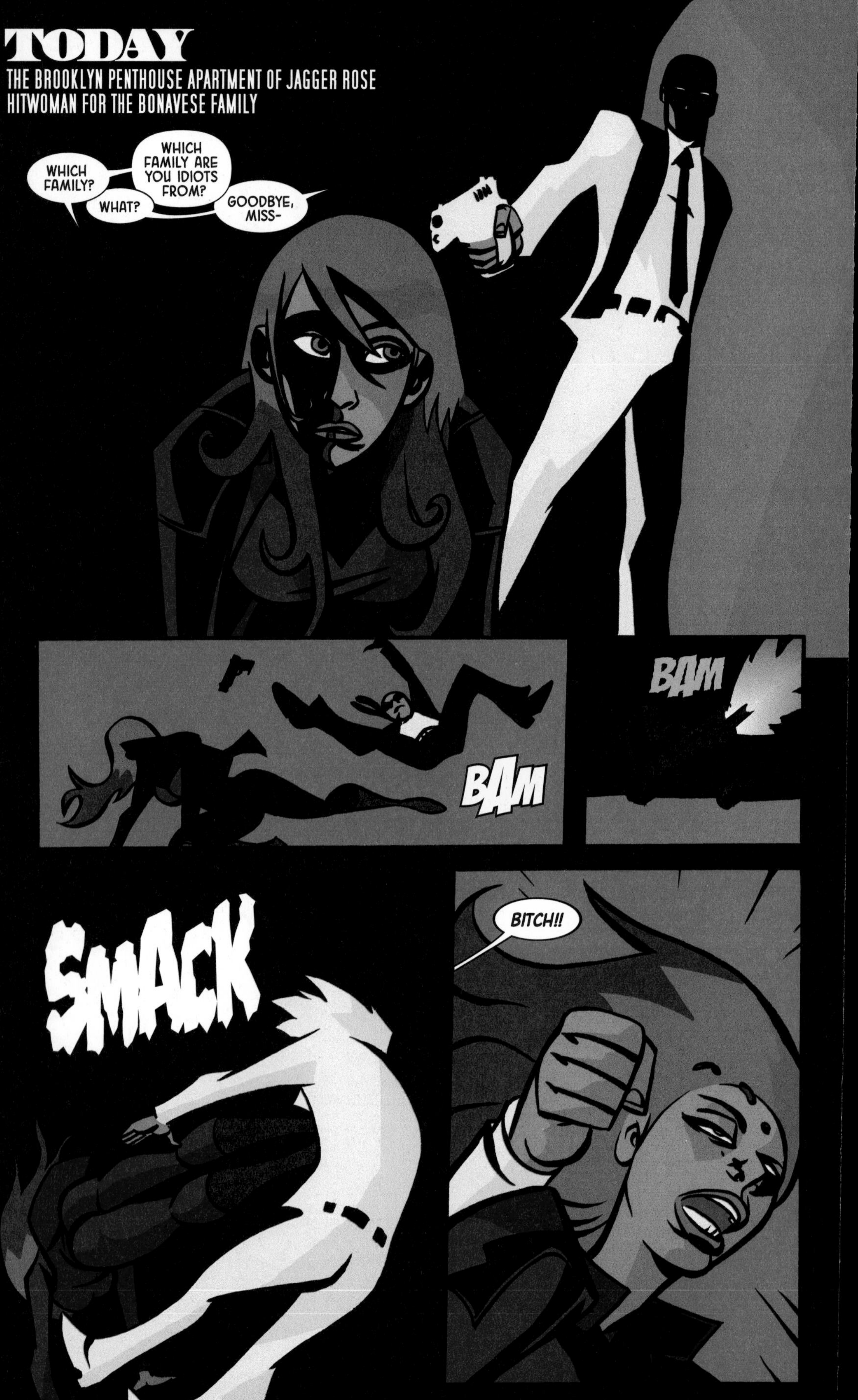
TODAY
THE BROOKLYN PENTHOUSE APARTMENT OF JAGGER ROSE
HITWOMAN FOR THE BONAVESE FAMILY
WHICH FAMILY?
WHICH FAMILY ARE YOU IDIOTS FROM?
WHAT?
GOODBYE, MISS-
BAM
BAM
SMACK
BITCH!!

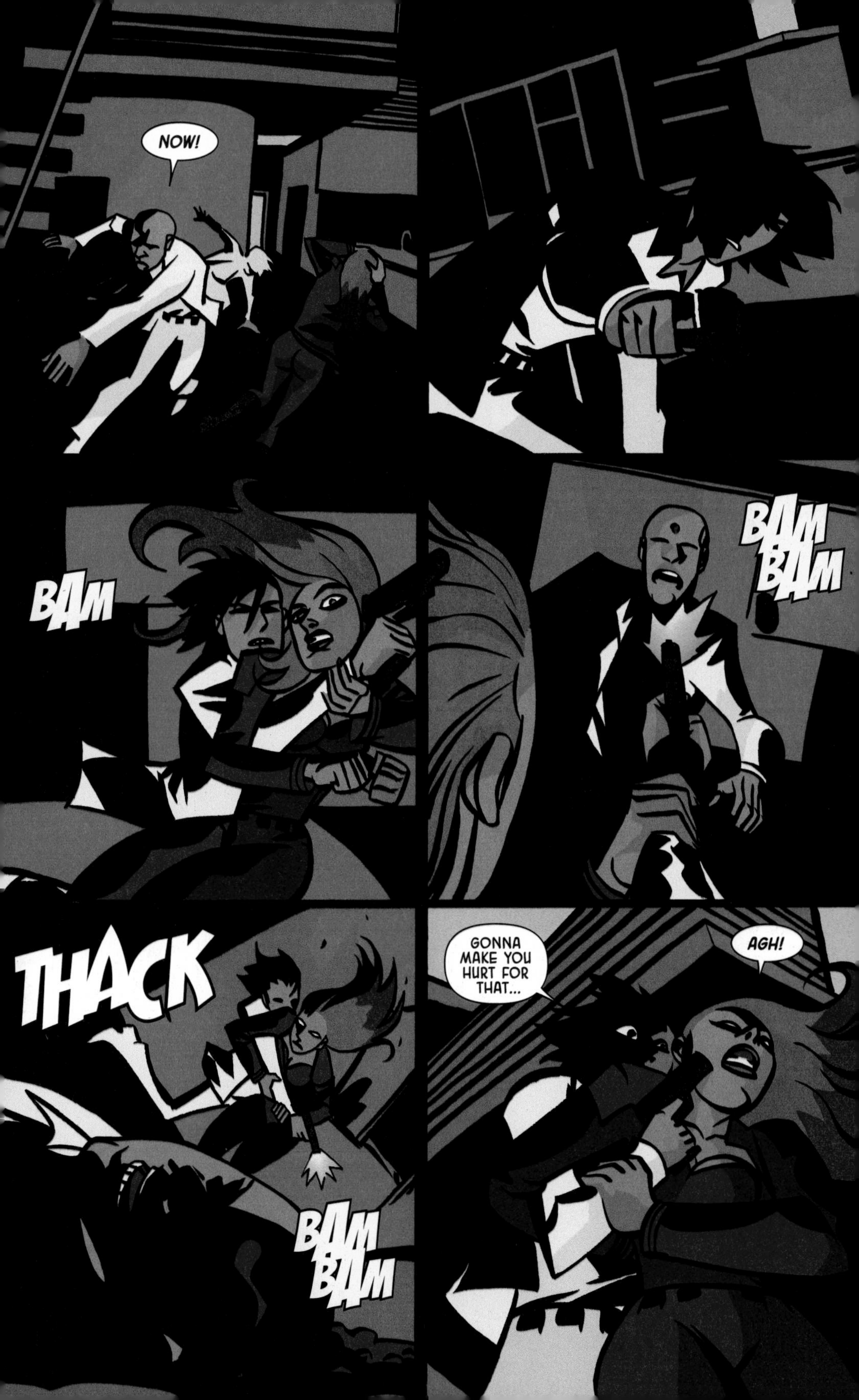
NOW!
BAM
BAM
BAM
THACK
BAM
BAM
GONNA MAKE YOU HURT FOR THAT...
AGH!

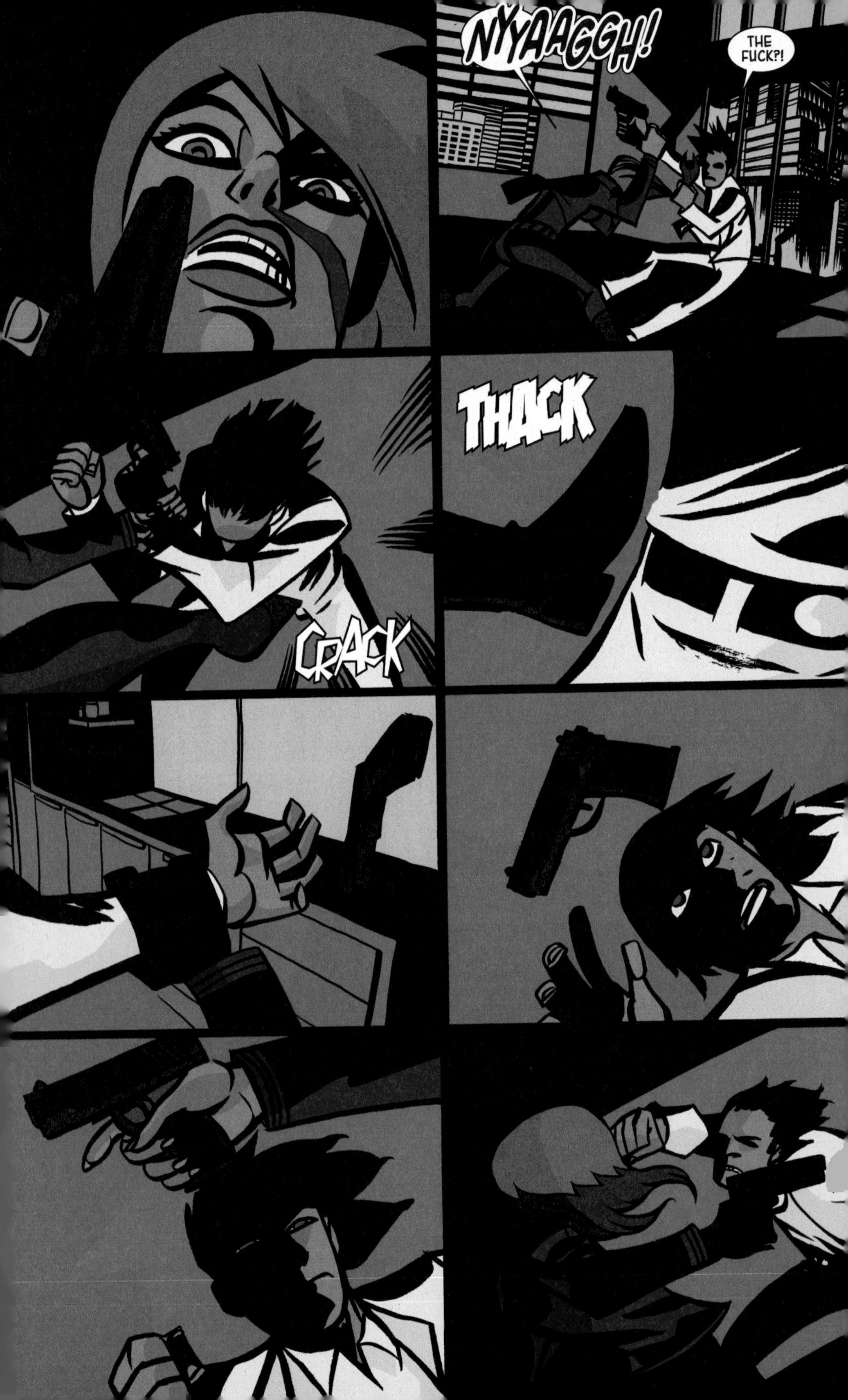
NYYAAGGH!
THE FUCK?!
CRACK
THACK

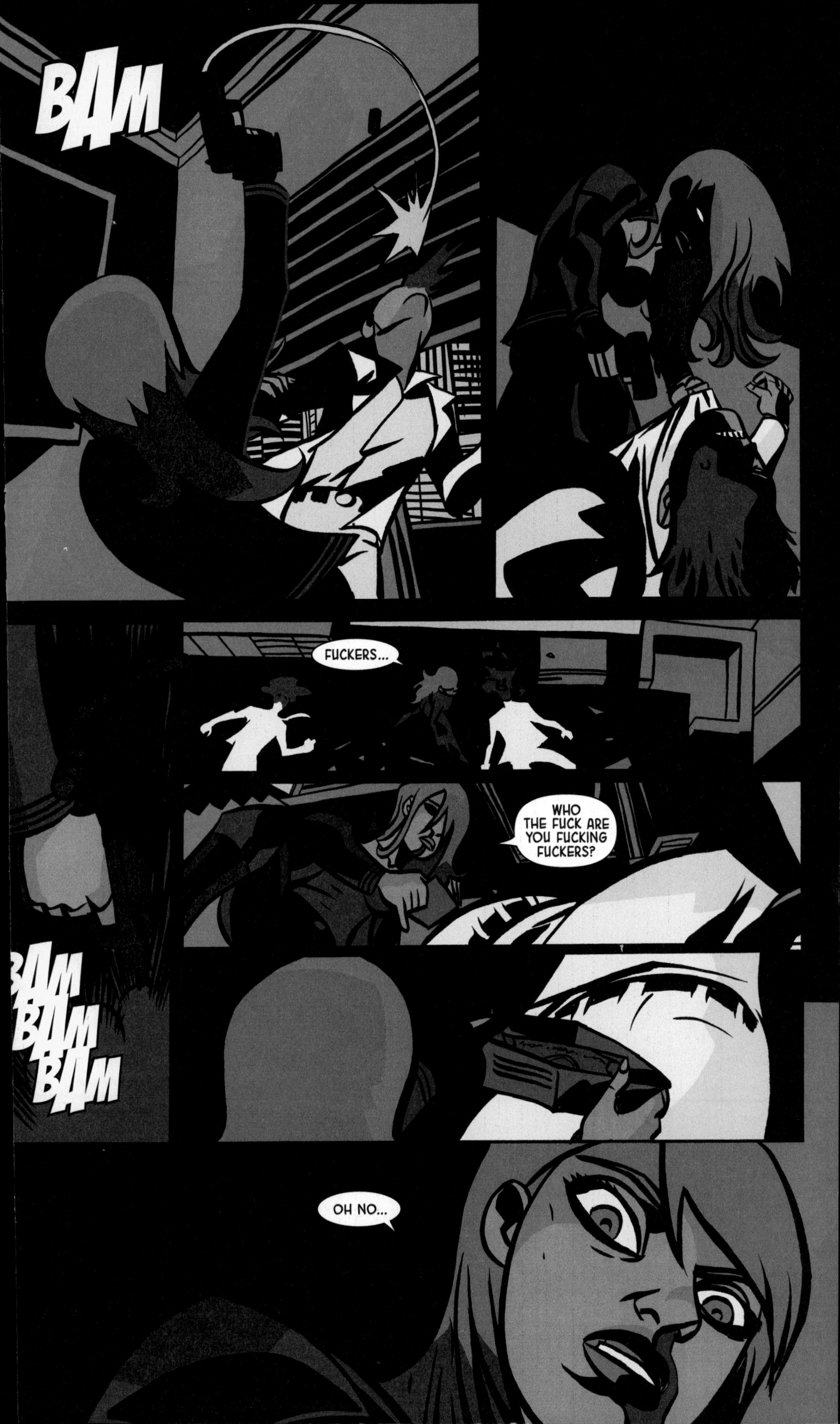
BAM
FUCKERS...
WHO THE FUCK ARE YOU FUCKING FUCKERS?
BAM BAM BAM
OH NO...

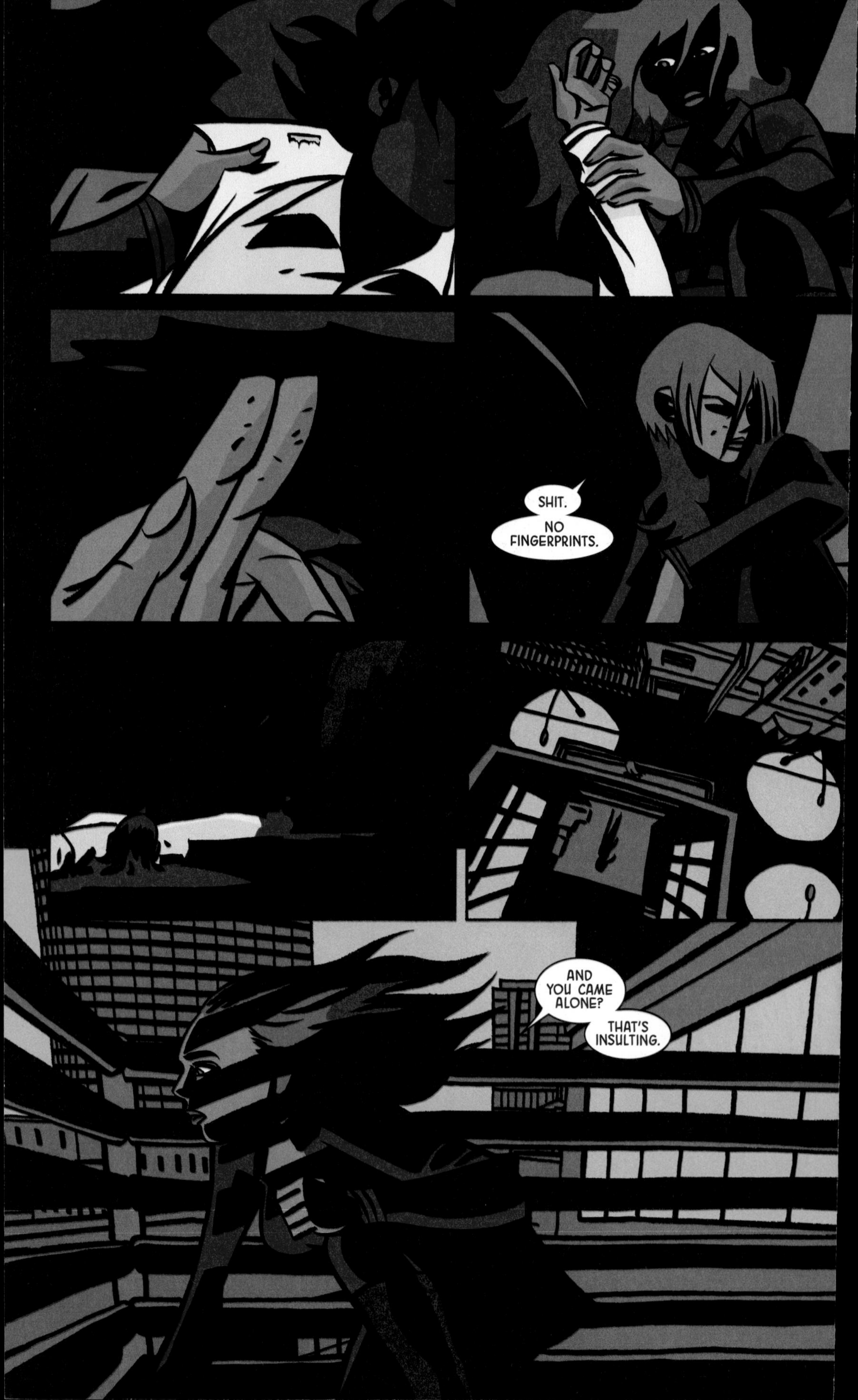
SHIT.
NO FINGERPRINTS.
AND YOU CAME ALONE?
THAT'S INSULTING.

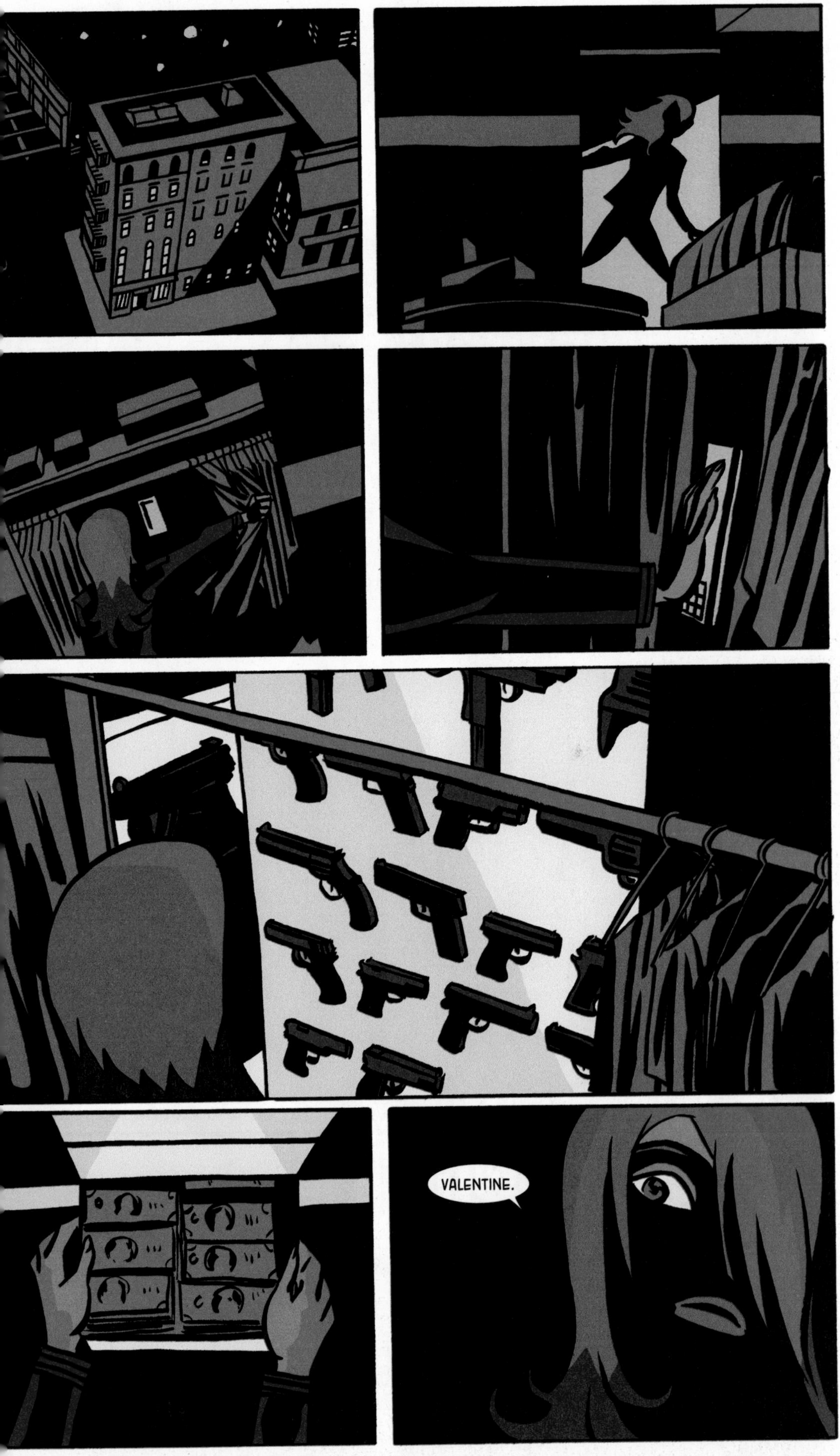
VALENTINE.

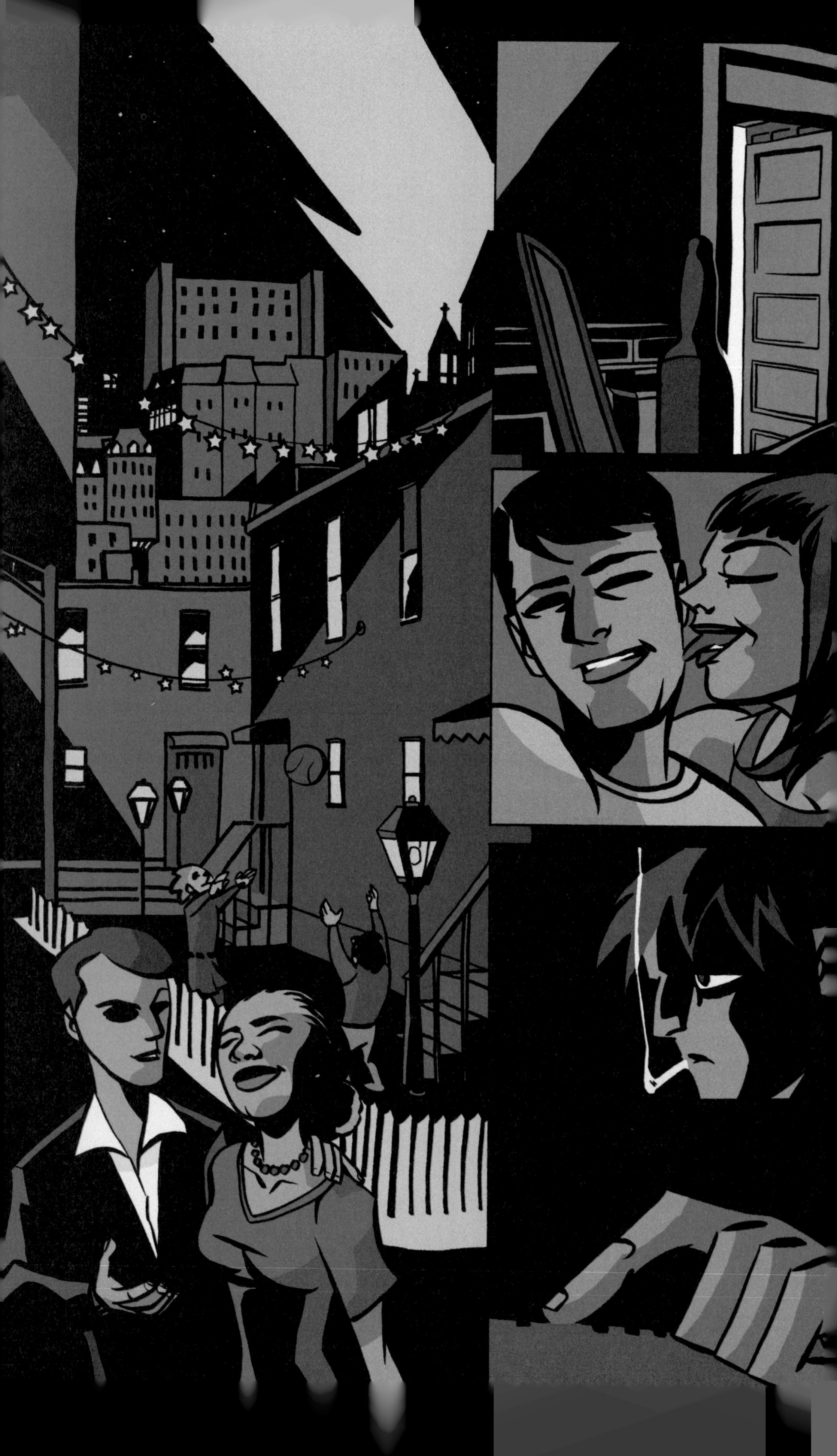

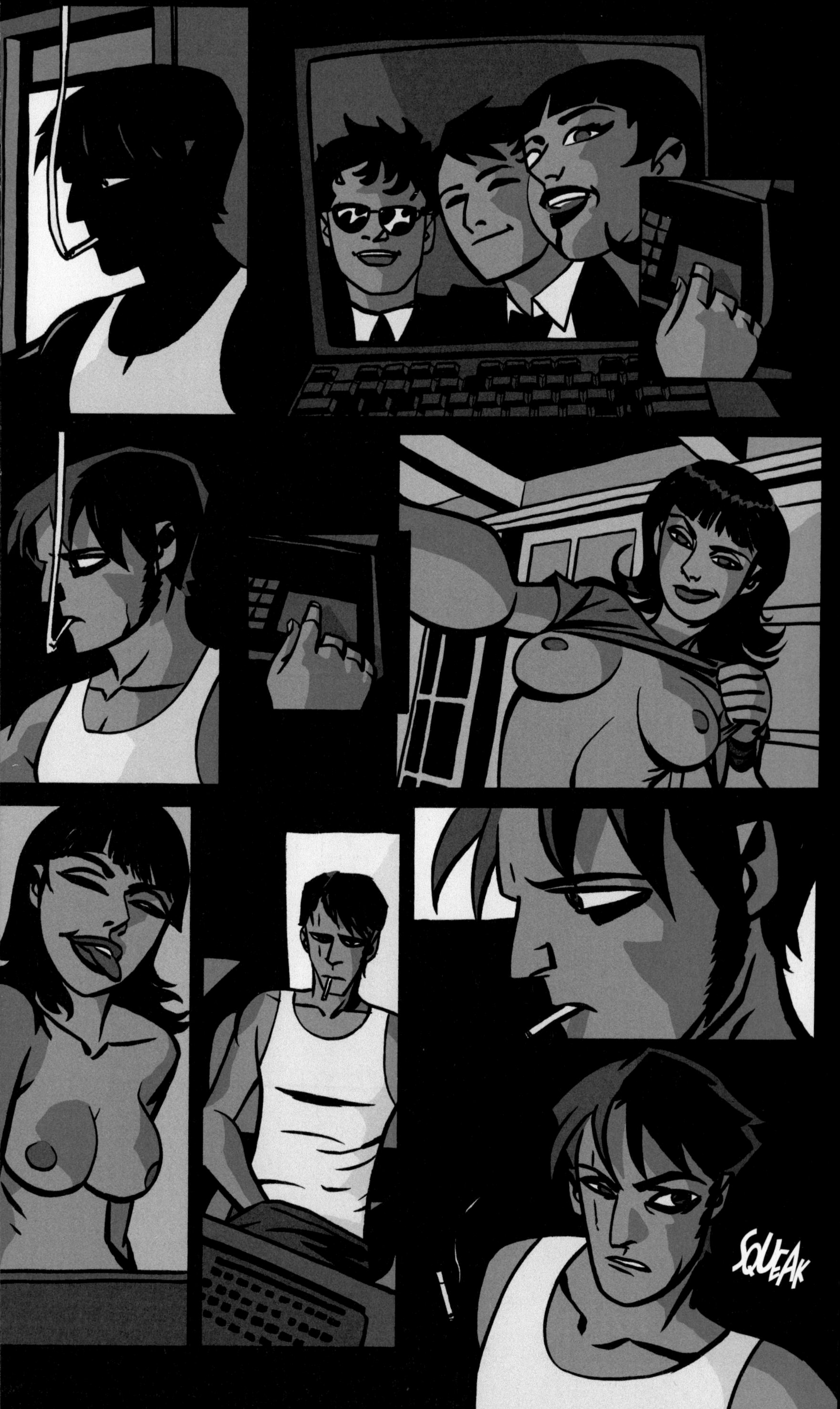
SQUEAK

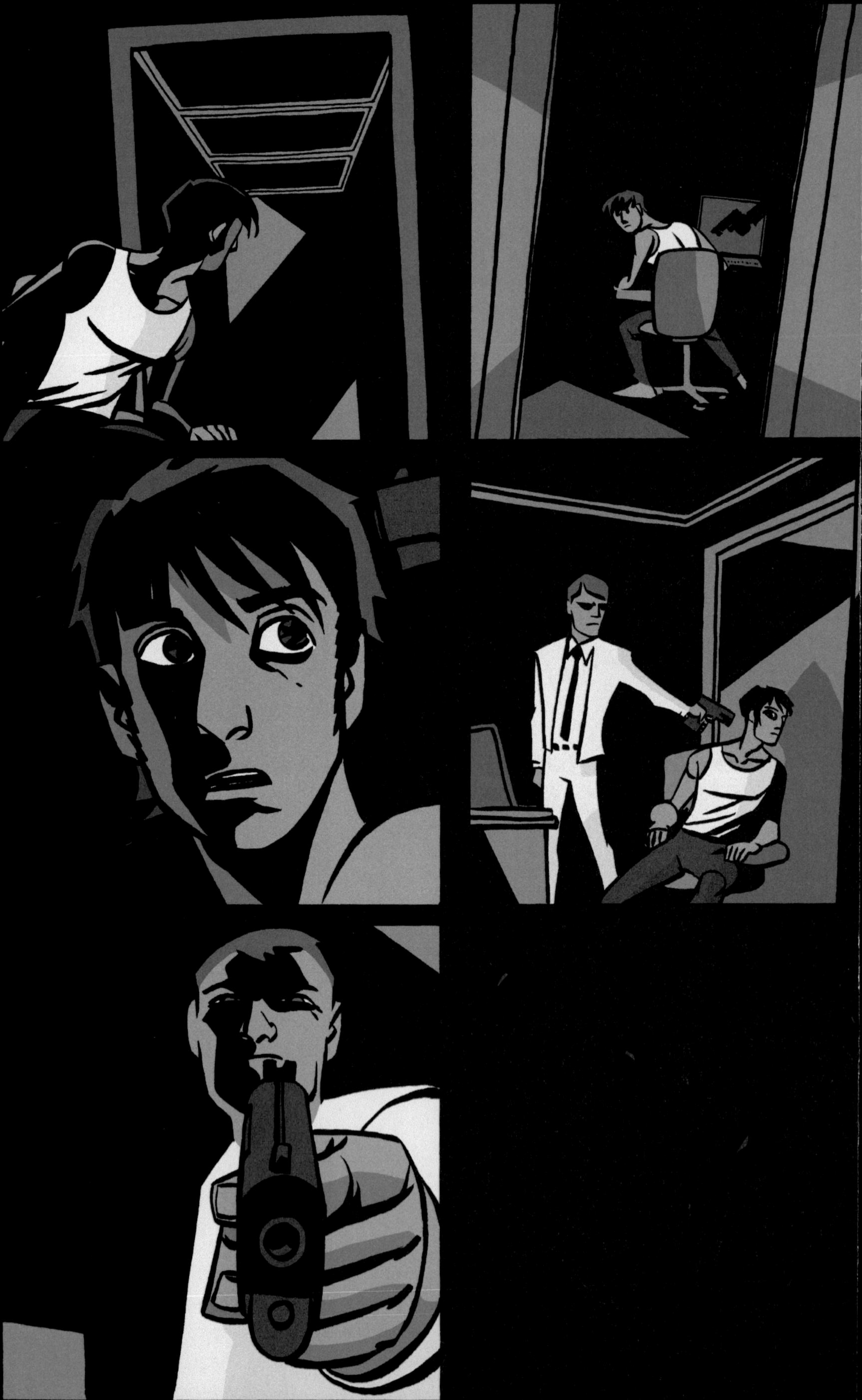

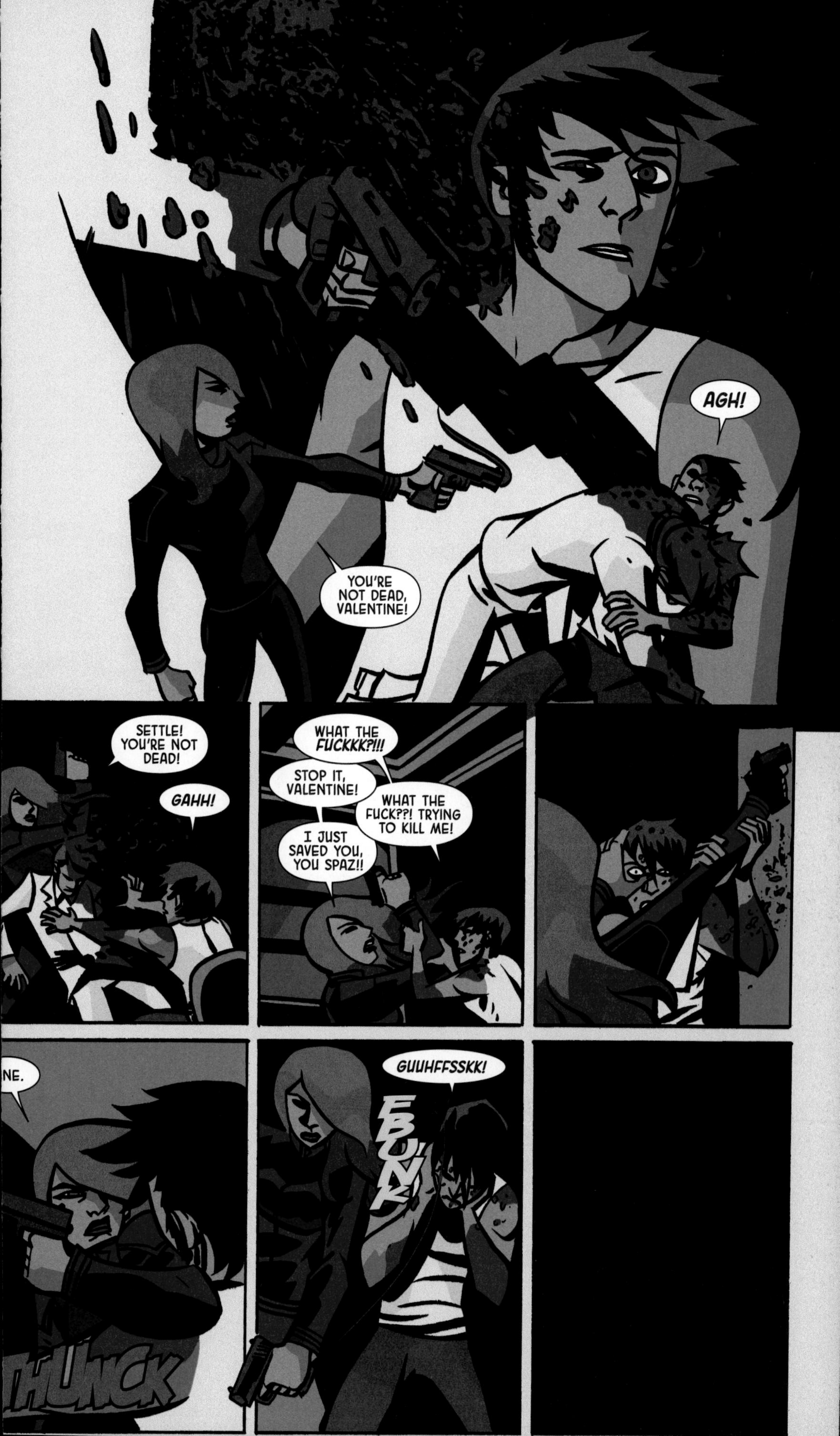
AGH!
YOU'RE NOT DEAD, VALENTINE!
SETTLE! YOU'RE NOT DEAD!
GAHH!
WHAT THE FUCKKK?!!!
STOP IT, VALENTINE!
WHAT THE FUCK??! TRYING TO KILL ME!
I JUST SAVED YOU, YOU SPAZ!!
NE.
THUNCK
GUUHFFSSKK!
FBUNK

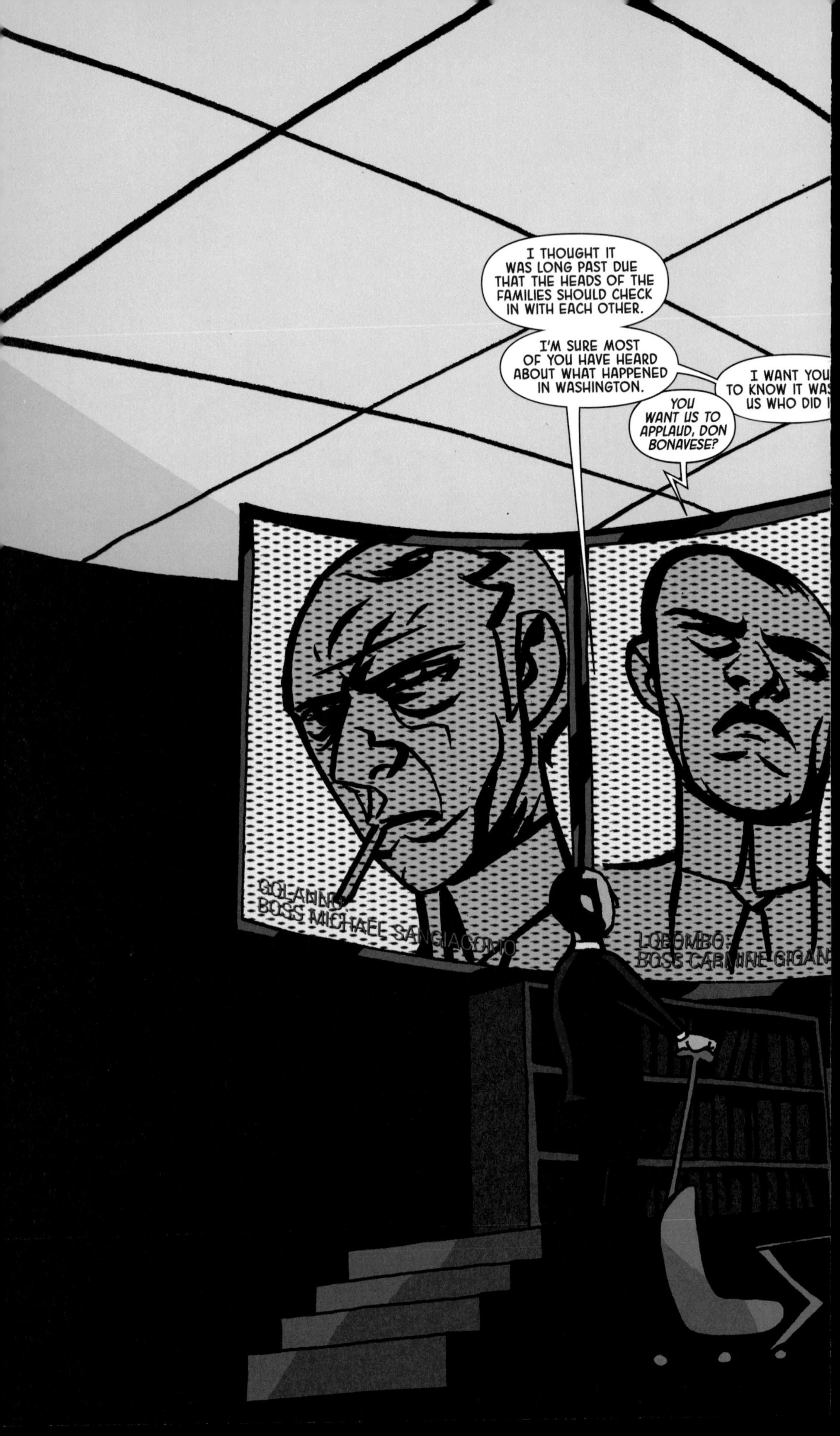
I THOUGHT IT WAS LONG PAST DUE THAT THE HEADS OF THE FAMILIES SHOULD CHECK IN WITH EACH OTHER.
I'M SURE MOST OF YOU HAVE HEARD ABOUT WHAT HAPPENED IN WASHINGTON.
I WANT YOU TO KNOW IT WAS US WHO DID
YOU WANT US TO APPLAUD, DON BONAVESE?
GOLANNO: BOSS MICHAEL SANGIACOMO
LOBOMBO: BOSS CARMINE

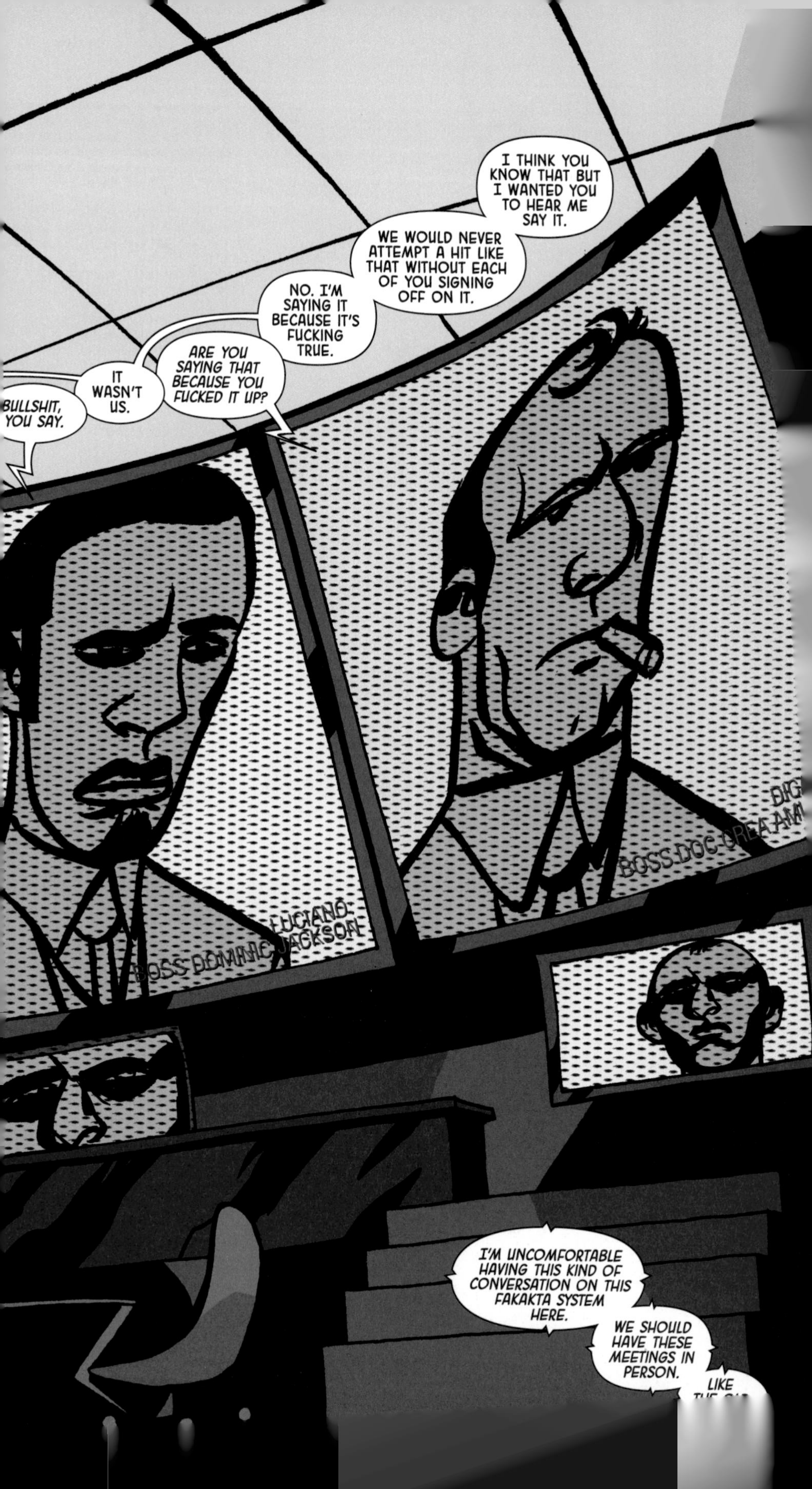
BULLSHIT, YOU SAY.
IT WASN'T US.
ARE YOU SAYING THAT BECAUSE YOU FUCKED IT UP?
NO. I'M SAYING IT BECAUSE IT'S FUCKING TRUE.
WE WOULD NEVER ATTEMPT A HIT LIKE THAT WITHOUT EACH OF YOU SIGNING OFF ON IT.
I THINK YOU KNOW THAT BUT I WANTED YOU TO HEAR ME SAY IT.
LUCIANO JACKSON
I'M UNCOMFORTABLE HAVING THIS KIND OF CONVERSATION ON THIS FAKAKTA SYSTEM HERE.
WE SHOULD HAVE THESE MEETINGS IN PERSON.
LIKE

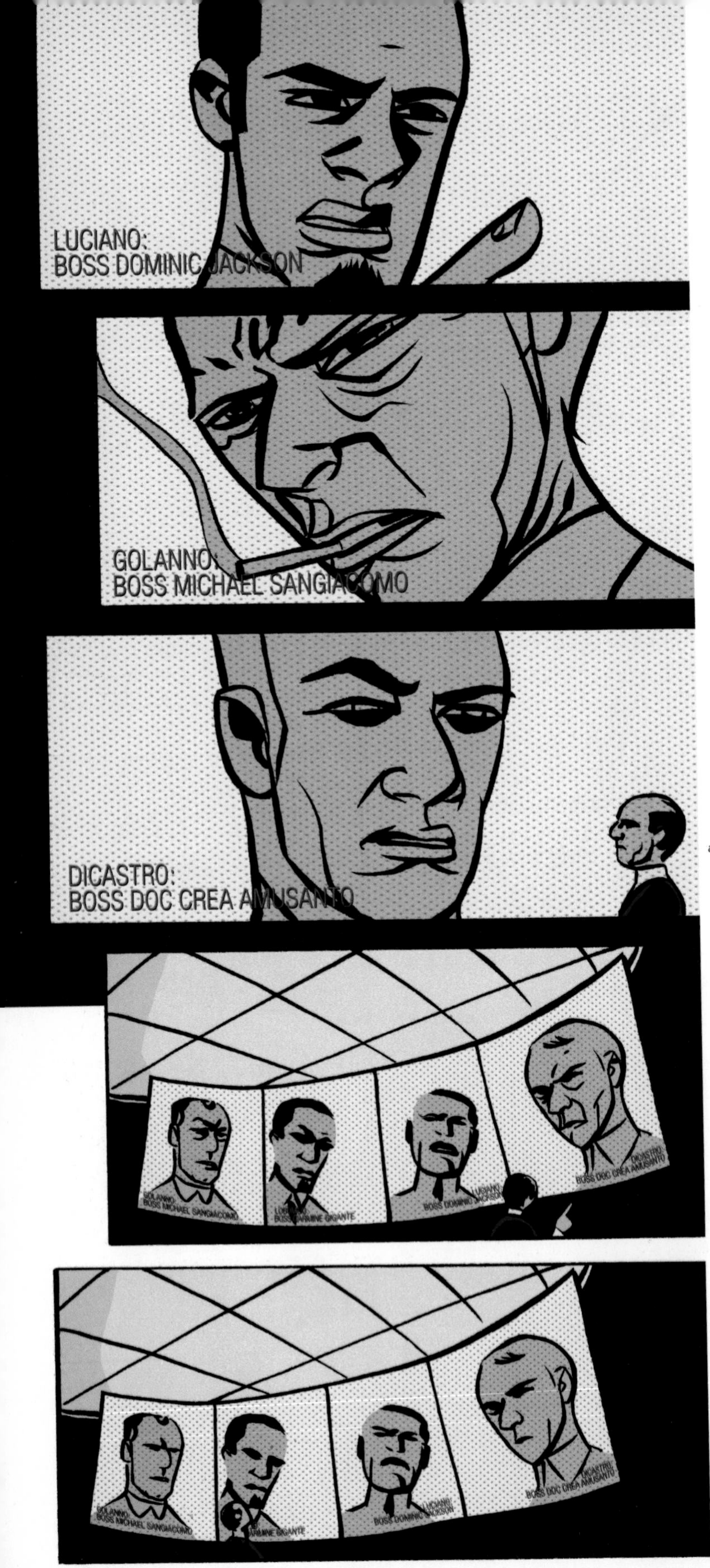
LUCIANO:
BOSS DOMINIC JACKSON
GOLANNO:
BOSS MICHAEL SANGIACOMO
DICASTRO:
BOSS DOC CREA AMUSANTO

DOMINIC JACKSON
Oh yes.

The days where you old fucks got
together and whacked each other

MICHAEL SANGIACOMO
We'd get together and build what
you are sitting on, you piece
of shit.

DON CREA
This is a closed-circuit system
No one can see or hear us but u

MICHAEL SANGIACOMO
Says you.

DON BONAVESE
I am hoping to
quickly clear the air among
us and if any of you know why
and how this happened...

CARMINE GIGANTE
You think it was one of us??!!

DON BONAVESE
It wasn't me or my people
but it was someone.

MICHAEL SANGIACOMO
Maybe the guy you sent fucked it
a top hat. Heard it was a kid.

DON BONAVESE
I promise you... I'm looking at
it from all angles.

DOMINIC JACKSON
Wasn't my guys. I can tell you th

CARMINE GIGANTE
I don't send my guys out of my
territory and this is exactly fuc
why.

DON CREA
You're going to have Feds up yo
ass, Bonavese. You gave them an ex

MICHAEL SANGIACOMO
They're going to be up all our
asses and it's on you as far a
I'm concerned.

DON BONAVESE
I was hoping to keep this civi

MICHAEL SANGIACOMO
And I was hoping you wouldn't pu
in this fucking position.

DOMINIC JACKSON
Yo, man, it wasn't him that di
this. He said it wasn't him- i
wasn't him. We have to take ea
other on each other's word.

MICHAEL SANGIACOMO
If he'd leave our ways well th
fuck alone and stay to his pa
of the beach, he wouldn't hav
no reason to be sending his
guys to Washington in the fir
fucking place. This is how w
lost Cleveland.

DON CREA
Again, with fucking Clevelan

MICHAEL SANGIACOMO
Yes. Yes, again with fucking Clev

Those who don't know their his
and all that shit...

Do you know the amount
of money we left on the tab
when we gave up Cleveland??

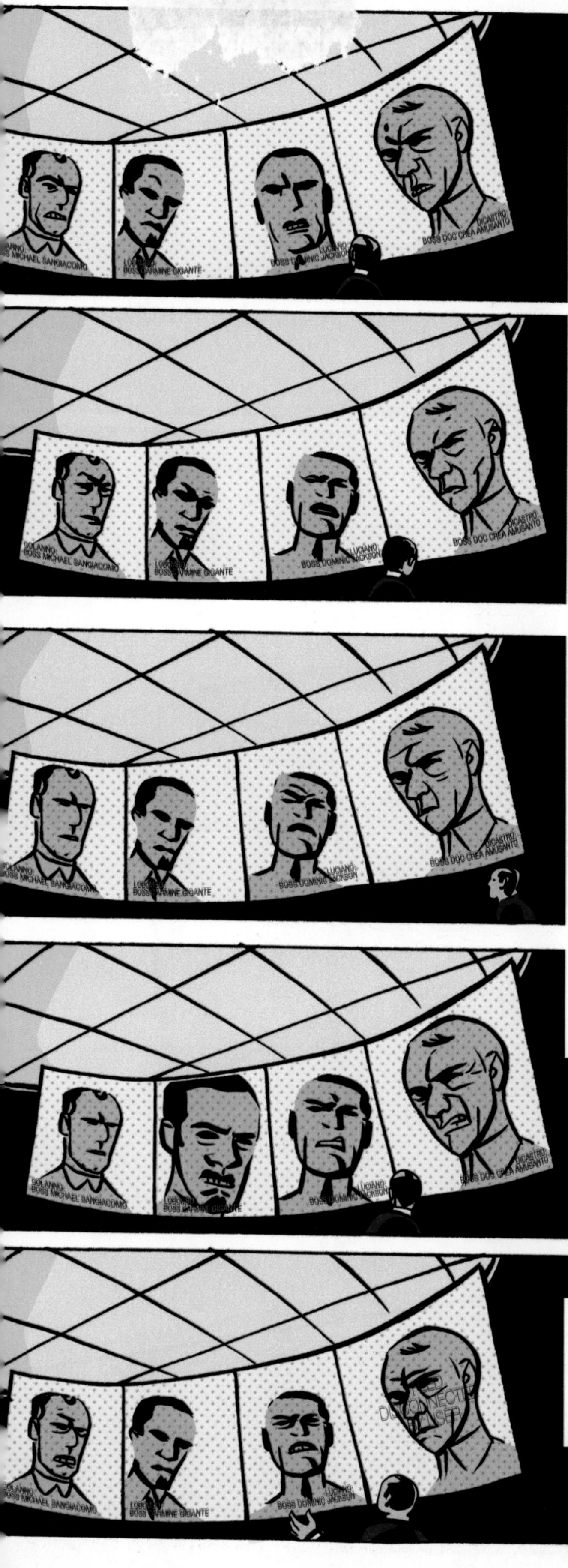

DOMINIC JACKSON
It's Cleveland... so, I'm guessing over two hundred dollars.

CARMINE GIGANTE
Don Bonavese wants to hear it from us and I want him to hear it from me... it wasn't us.

DON BONAVESE
Thank you, Don Gigante.

MICHAEL SANGIACOMO
Of course, if any of you fucked a donkey this bad, the fuck you'd tell any of us.

CARMINE GIGANTE
True.

MICHAEL SANGIACOMO
And if you fucked it on purpose then-

CARMINE GIGANTE
You'd be able to tell. I have a terrible poker face.

DOMINIC JACKSON
Anyone else think Sangiacomo is being extra fucking rude today? Why don't you calm your old ass down and keep it civil.

MICHAEL SANGIACOMO
Fuck me then. I guess I'm- I'm old school. That means you don't whack United States senators and you don't talk about whacking United States senators on a fucking TV. You want to talk to me? You come fucking see me.

DOMINIC JACKSON
Yeah, let's all fly out to Vegas and listen to father time rip us a new one.

DON CREA
You're taking care of this, I assume, Don Bonevese?

DON BONAVESE
Of course. I just want to keep everything aboveboard among us.

DOMINIC JACKSON
You'll keep us posted on all this...

DON BONAVESE
And if any of you hear anything...

CARMINE GIGANTE
You know, the old man was right about one thing...

DON BONAVESE
What's that, Carmine?

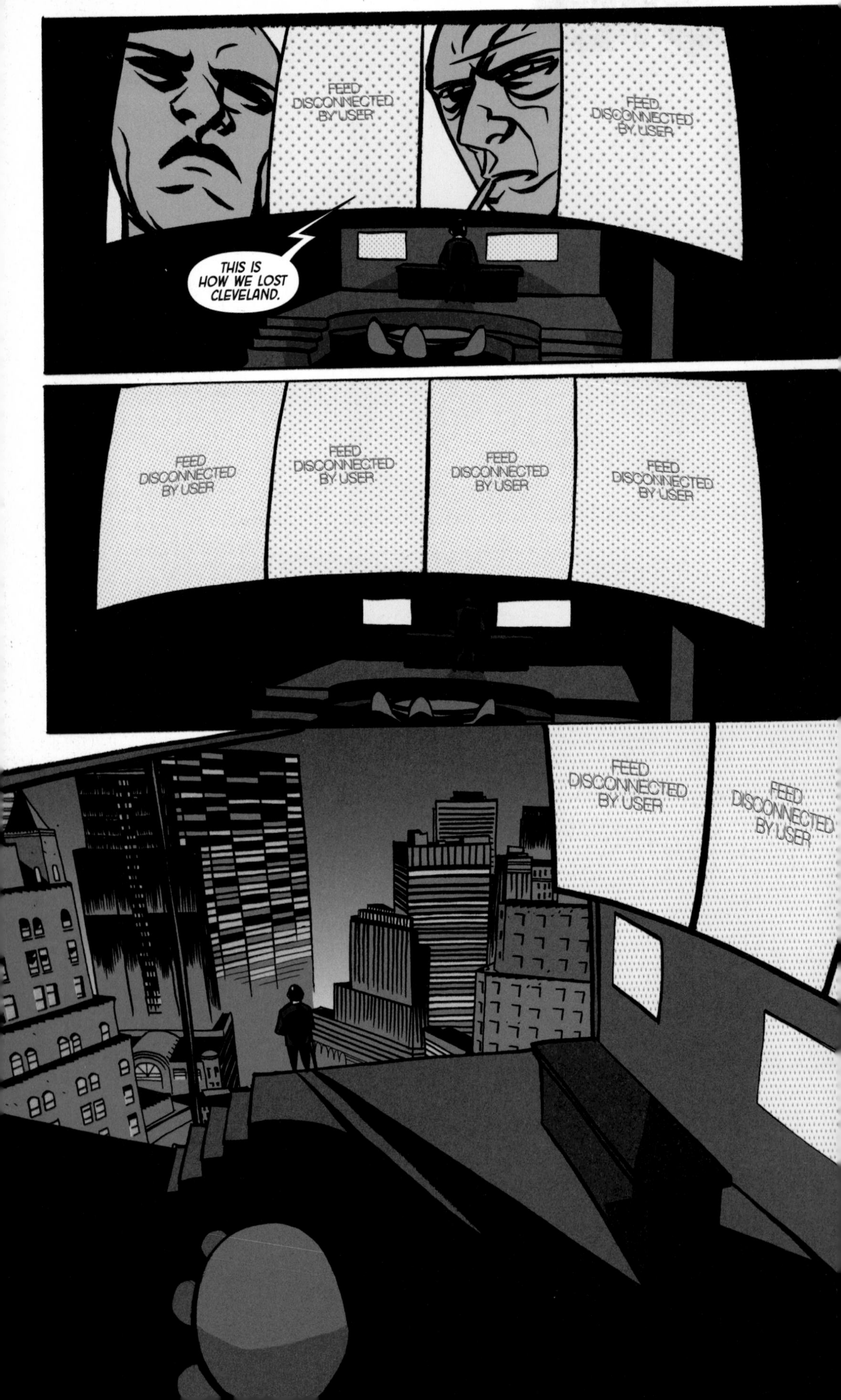
FEED DISCONNECTED BY USER
FEED DISCONNECTED BY USER
THIS IS HOW WE LOST CLEVELAND.
FEED DISCONNECTED BY USER
FEED DISCONNECTED BY USER
FEED DISCONNECTED BY USER
FEED DISCONNECTED BY USER
FEED DISCONNECTED BY USER
FEED DISCONNECTED BY USER

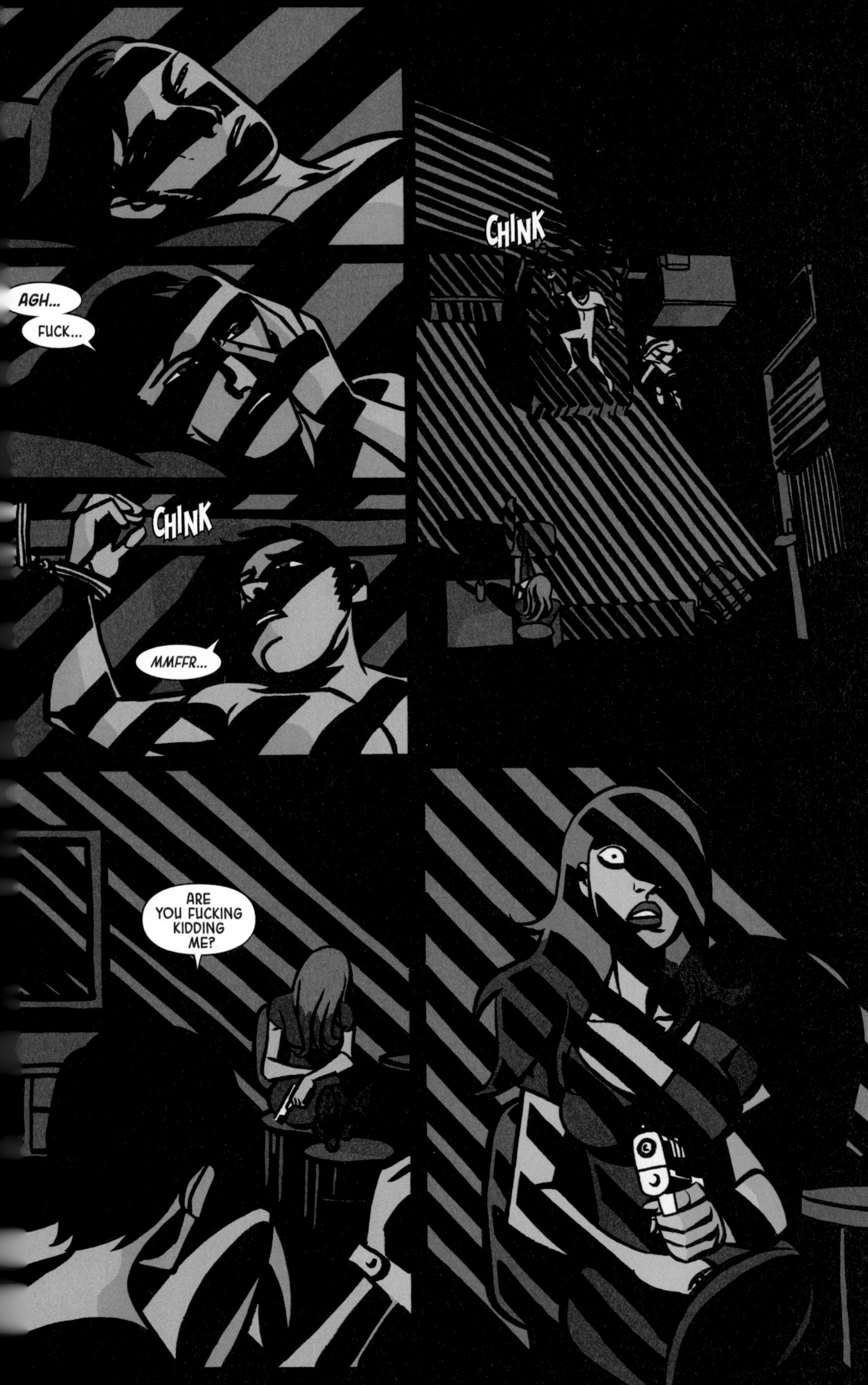
AGH...
FUCK...
CHINK
MMFFR...
CHINK
ARE YOU FUCKING KIDDING ME?

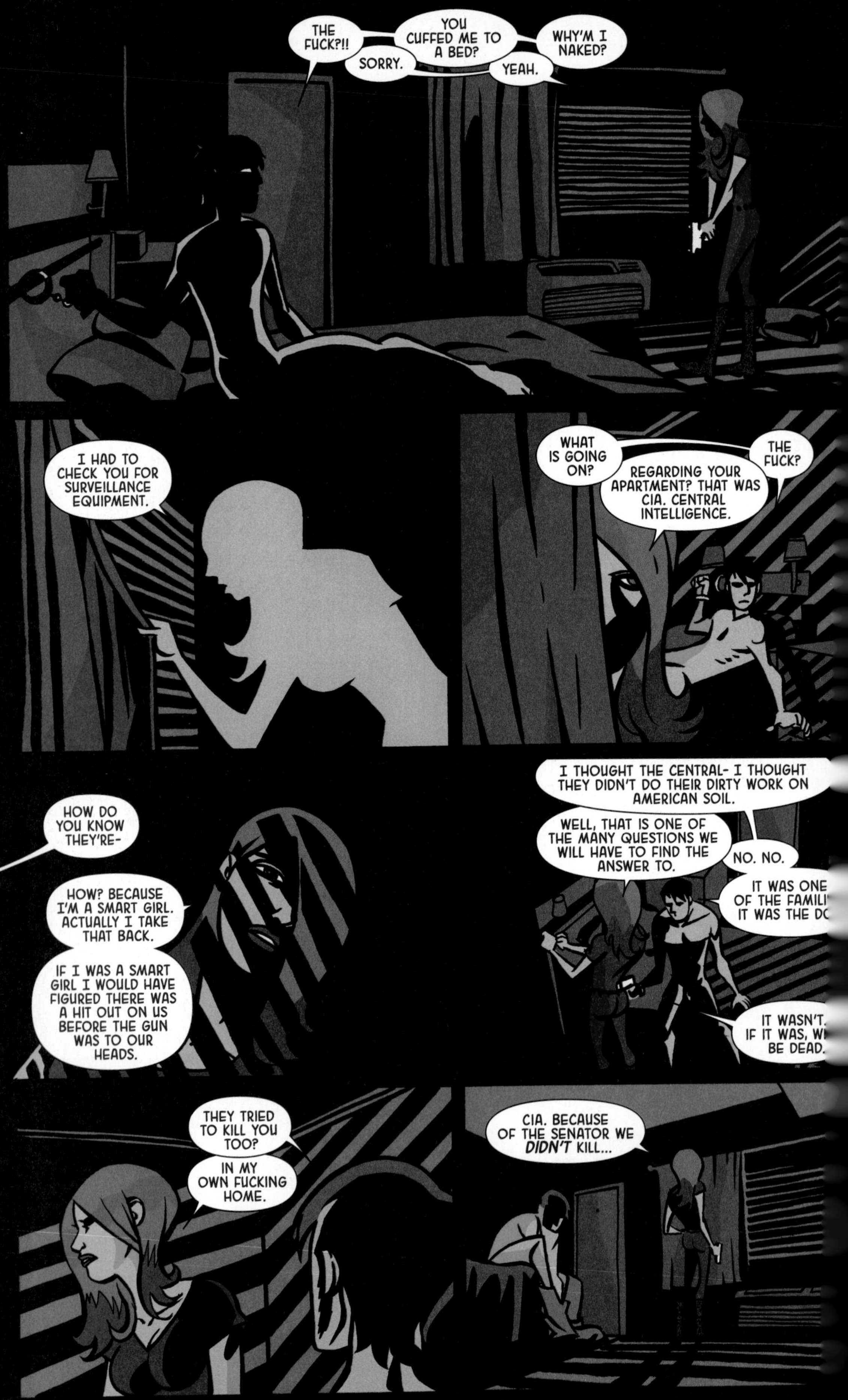
THE FUCK?!!
YOU CUFFED ME TO A BED?
WHY'M I NAKED?
SORRY.
YEAH.
I HAD TO CHECK YOU FOR SURVEILLANCE EQUIPMENT.
WHAT IS GOING ON?
THE FUCK?
REGARDING YOUR APARTMENT? THAT WAS CIA. CENTRAL INTELLIGENCE.
HOW DO YOU KNOW THEY'RE-
HOW? BECAUSE I'M A SMART GIRL. ACTUALLY I TAKE THAT BACK.
IF I WAS A SMART GIRL I WOULD HAVE FIGURED THERE WAS A HIT OUT ON US BEFORE THE GUN WAS TO OUR HEADS.
I THOUGHT THE CENTRAL- I THOUGHT THEY DIDN'T DO THEIR DIRTY WORK ON AMERICAN SOIL.
WELL, THAT IS ONE OF THE MANY QUESTIONS WE WILL HAVE TO FIND THE ANSWER TO.
NO. NO.
IT WASN'T.
THEY TRIED TO KILL YOU TOO?
IN MY OWN FUCKING HOME.
CIA. BECAUSE OF THE SENATOR WE *DIDN'T* KILL...

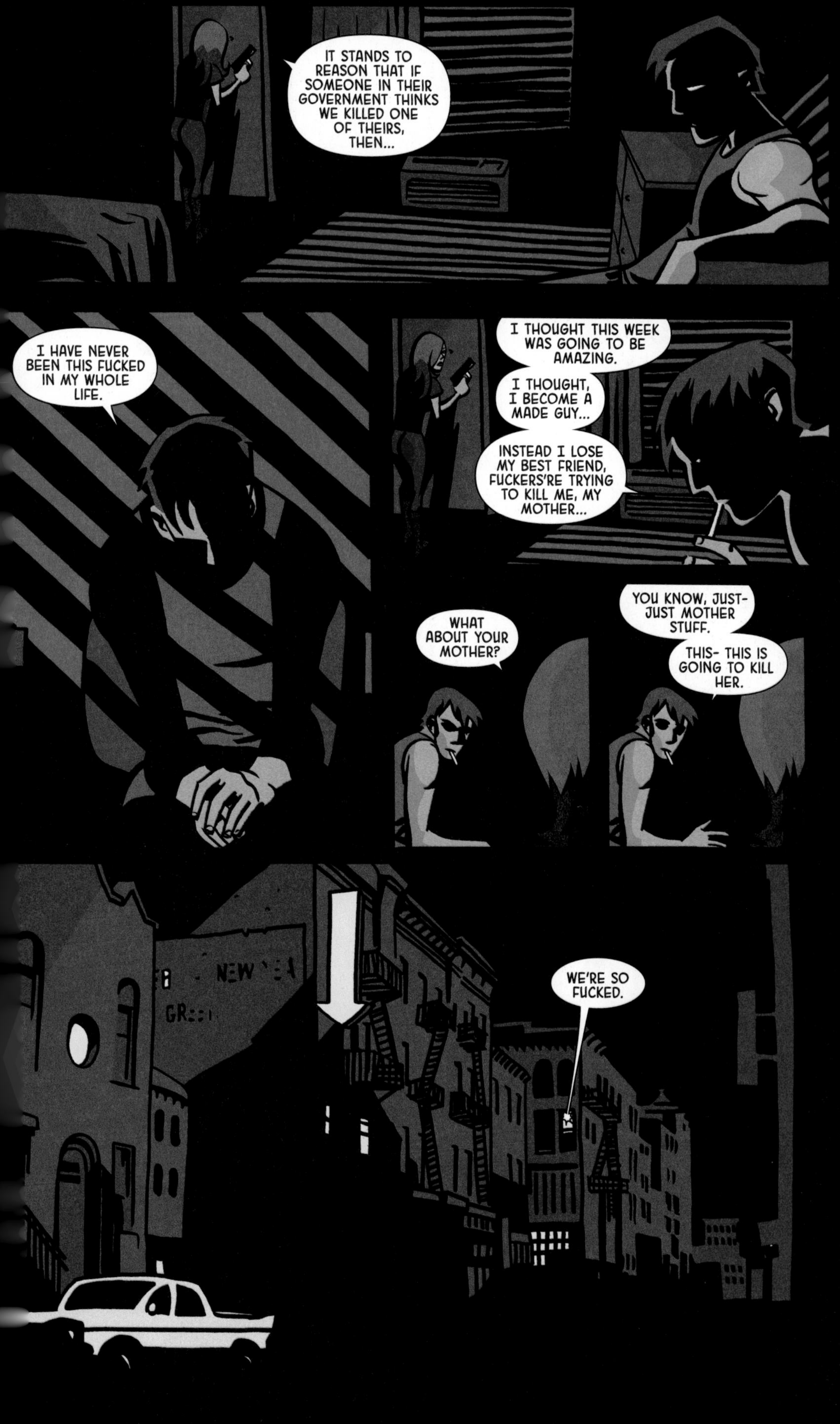
IT STANDS TO REASON THAT IF SOMEONE IN THEIR GOVERNMENT THINKS WE KILLED ONE OF THEIRS, THEN...
I HAVE NEVER BEEN THIS FUCKED IN MY WHOLE LIFE.
I THOUGHT THIS WEEK WAS GOING TO BE AMAZING.
I THOUGHT, I BECOME A MADE GUY...
INSTEAD I LOSE MY BEST FRIEND, FUCKERS'RE TRYING TO KILL ME, MY MOTHER...
WHAT ABOUT YOUR MOTHER?
YOU KNOW, JUST- JUST MOTHER STUFF.
THIS- THIS IS GOING TO KILL HER.
NEW
WE'RE SO FUCKED.

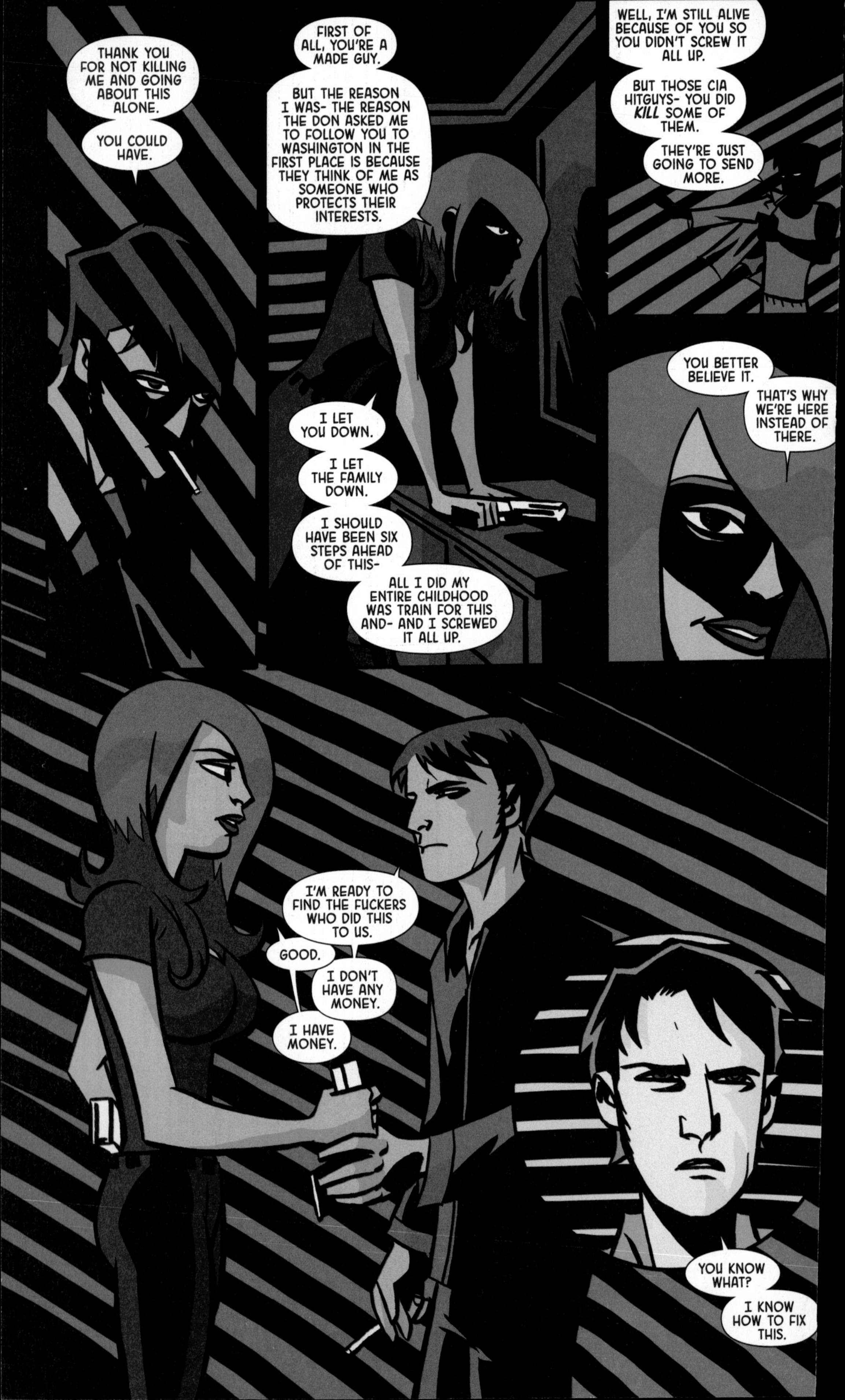
THANK YOU FOR NOT KILLING ME AND GOING ABOUT THIS ALONE.
YOU COULD HAVE.
FIRST OF ALL, YOU'RE A MADE GUY.
BUT THE REASON I WAS- THE REASON THE DON ASKED ME TO FOLLOW YOU TO WASHINGTON IN THE FIRST PLACE IS BECAUSE THEY THINK OF ME AS SOMEONE WHO PROTECTS THEIR INTERESTS.
I LET YOU DOWN.
I LET THE FAMILY DOWN.
I SHOULD HAVE BEEN SIX STEPS AHEAD OF THIS-
ALL I DID MY ENTIRE CHILDHOOD WAS TRAIN FOR THIS AND- AND I SCREWED IT ALL UP.
WELL, I'M STILL ALIVE BECAUSE OF YOU SO YOU DIDN'T SCREW IT ALL UP.
BUT THOSE CIA HITGUYS- YOU DID *KILL* SOME OF THEM.
THEY'RE JUST GOING TO SEND MORE.
YOU BETTER BELIEVE IT.
THAT'S WHY WE'RE HERE INSTEAD OF THERE.
I'M READY TO FIND THE FUCKERS WHO DID THIS TO US.
GOOD.
I DON'T HAVE ANY MONEY.
I HAVE MONEY.
YOU KNOW WHAT?
I KNOW HOW TO FIX THIS.

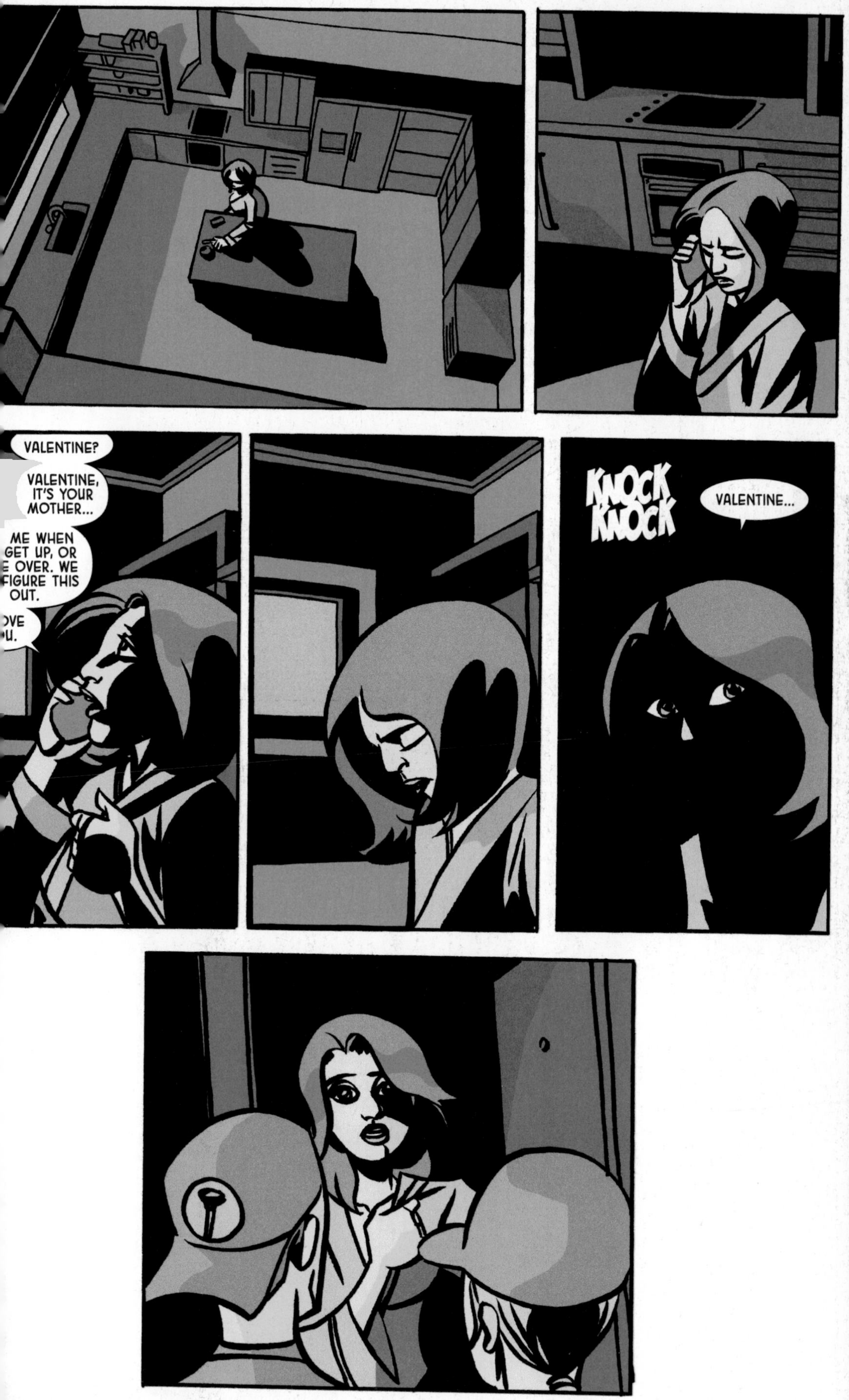
VALENTINE?
VALENTINE, IT'S YOUR MOTHER...
ME WHEN GET UP, OR E OVER. WE FIGURE THIS OUT.
OVE U.
KNOCK KNOCK
VALENTINE...

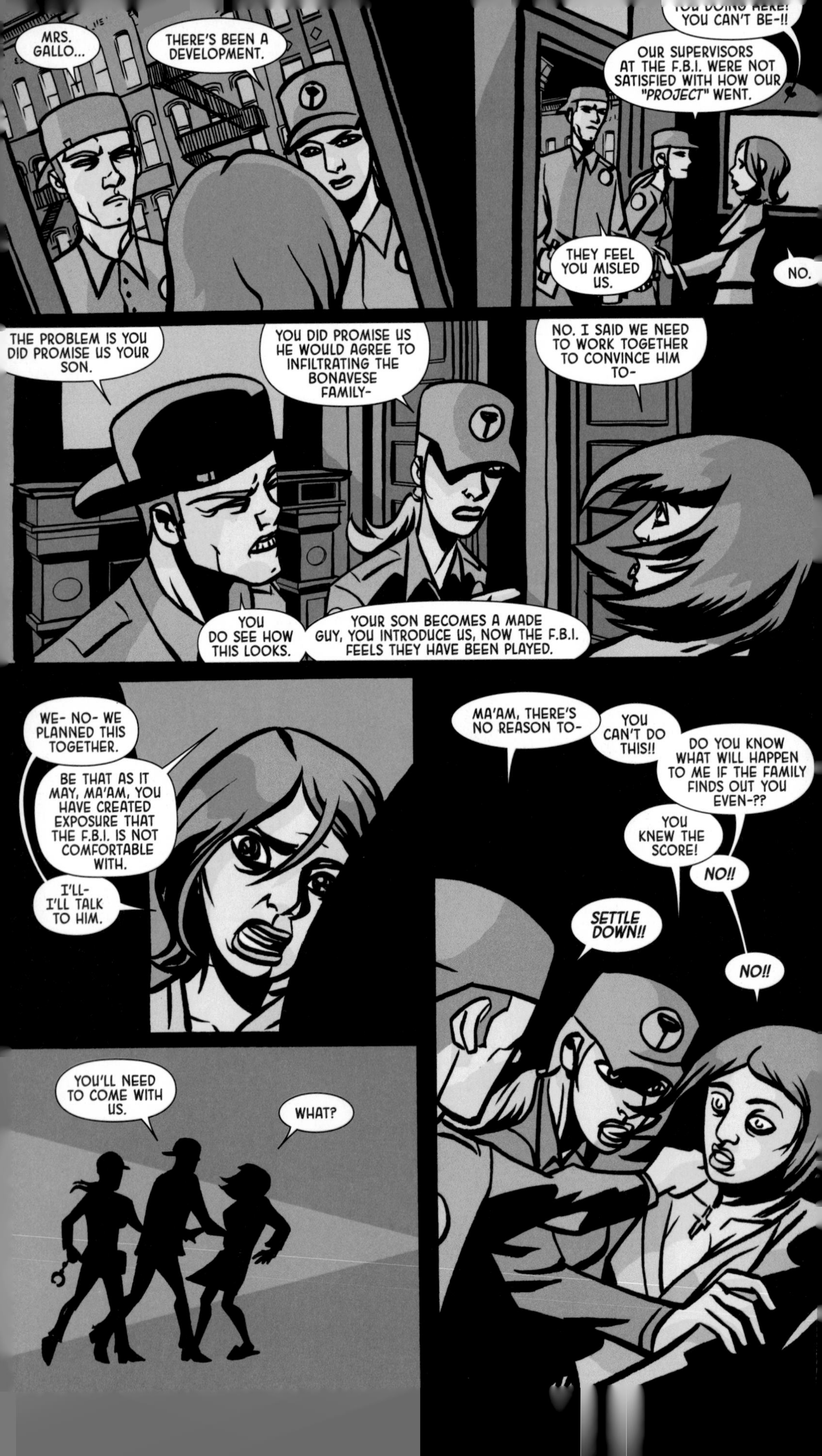

MRS. GALLO...
THERE'S BEEN A DEVELOPMENT.
YOU CAN'T BE-!!
OUR SUPERVISORS AT THE F.B.I. WERE NOT SATISFIED WITH HOW OUR "PROJECT" WENT.
THEY FEEL YOU MISLED US.
NO.
THE PROBLEM IS YOU DID PROMISE US YOUR SON.
YOU DID PROMISE US HE WOULD AGREE TO INFILTRATING THE BONAVESE FAMILY-
NO. I SAID WE NEED TO WORK TOGETHER TO CONVINCE HIM TO-
YOU DO SEE HOW THIS LOOKS.
YOUR SON BECOMES A MADE GUY, YOU INTRODUCE US, NOW THE F.B.I. FEELS THEY HAVE BEEN PLAYED.
WE- NO- WE PLANNED THIS TOGETHER.
BE THAT AS IT MAY, MA'AM, YOU HAVE CREATED EXPOSURE THAT THE F.B.I. IS NOT COMFORTABLE WITH.
I'LL- I'LL TALK TO HIM.
YOU'LL NEED TO COME WITH US.
WHAT?
MA'AM, THERE'S NO REASON TO-
YOU CAN'T DO THIS!!
DO YOU KNOW WHAT WILL HAPPEN TO ME IF THE FAMILY FINDS OUT YOU EVEN-??
YOU KNEW THE SCORE!
NO!!
SETTLE DOWN!!
NO!!

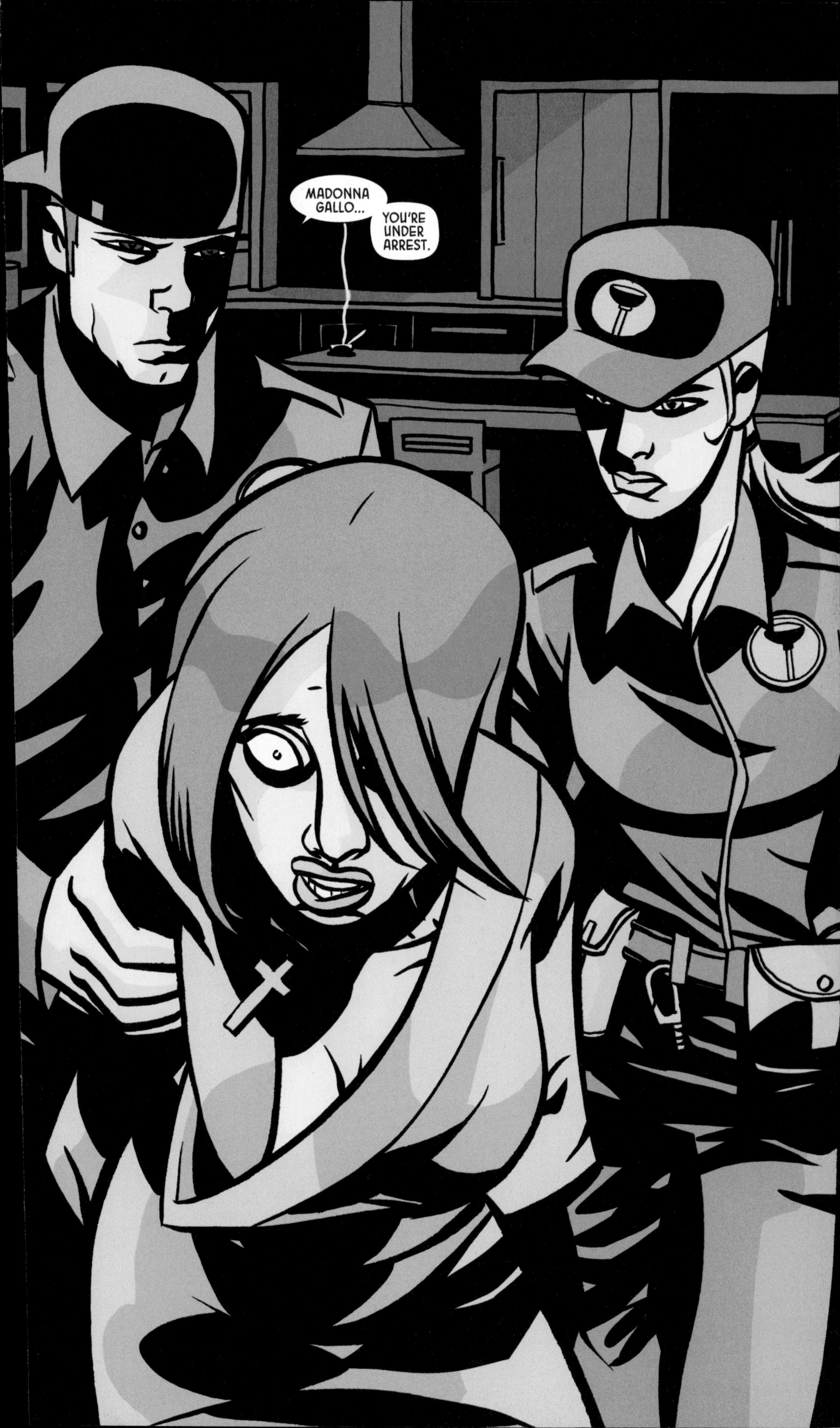
MADONNA GALLO...
YOU'RE UNDER ARREST.

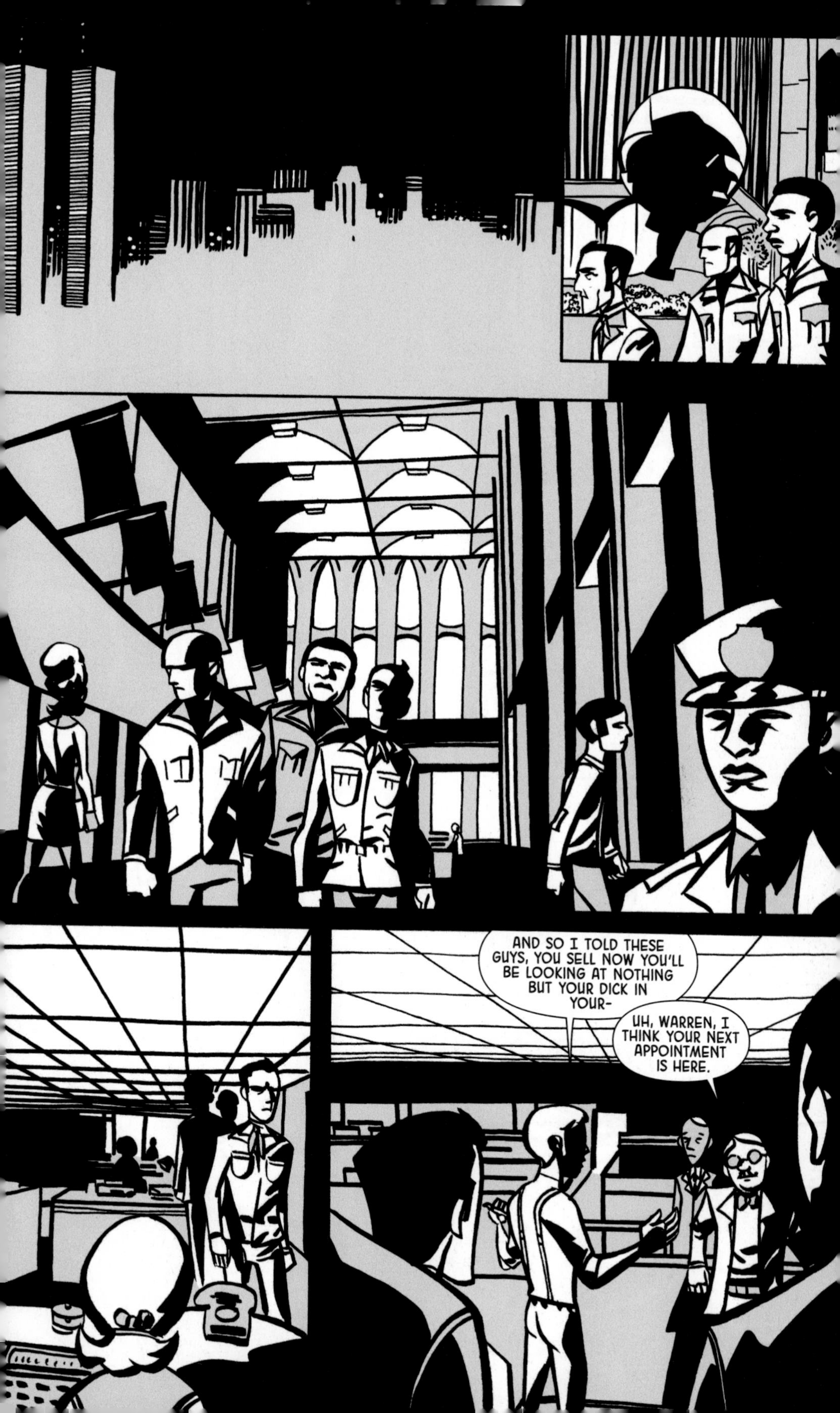
AND SO I TOLD THESE GUYS, YOU SELL NOW YOU'LL BE LOOKING AT NOTHING BUT YOUR DICK IN YOUR-
UH, WARREN, I THINK YOUR NEXT APPOINTMENT IS HERE.

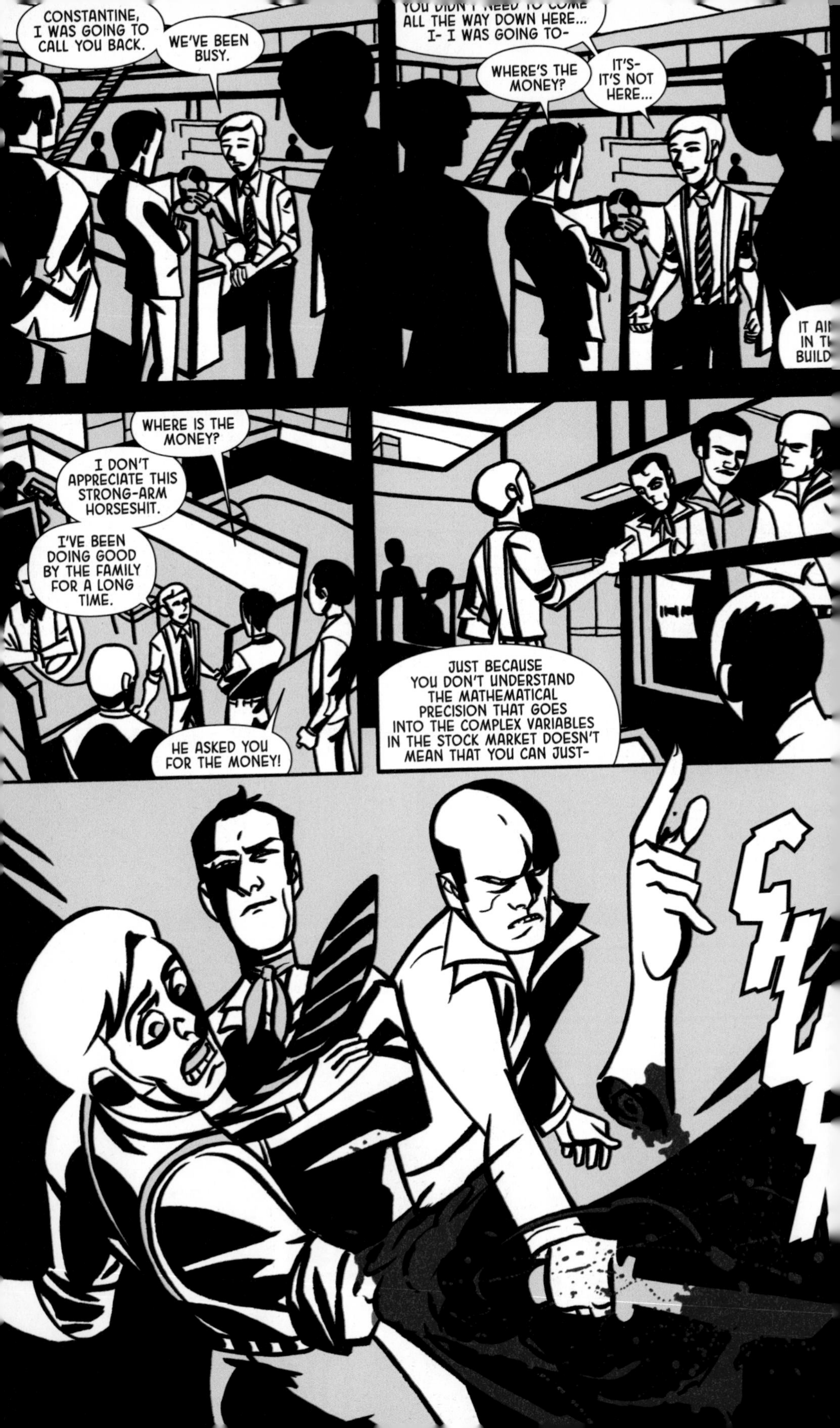
CONSTANTINE, I WAS GOING TO CALL YOU BACK.
WE'VE BEEN BUSY.
ALL THE WAY DOWN HERE... I- I WAS GOING TO-
WHERE'S THE MONEY?
IT'S- IT'S NOT HERE...
WHERE IS THE MONEY?
I DON'T APPRECIATE THIS STRONG-ARM HORSESHIT.
I'VE BEEN DOING GOOD BY THE FAMILY FOR A LONG TIME.
HE ASKED YOU FOR THE MONEY!
JUST BECAUSE YOU DON'T UNDERSTAND THE MATHEMATICAL PRECISION THAT GOES INTO THE COMPLEX VARIABLES IN THE STOCK MARKET DOESN'T MEAN THAT YOU CAN JUST-

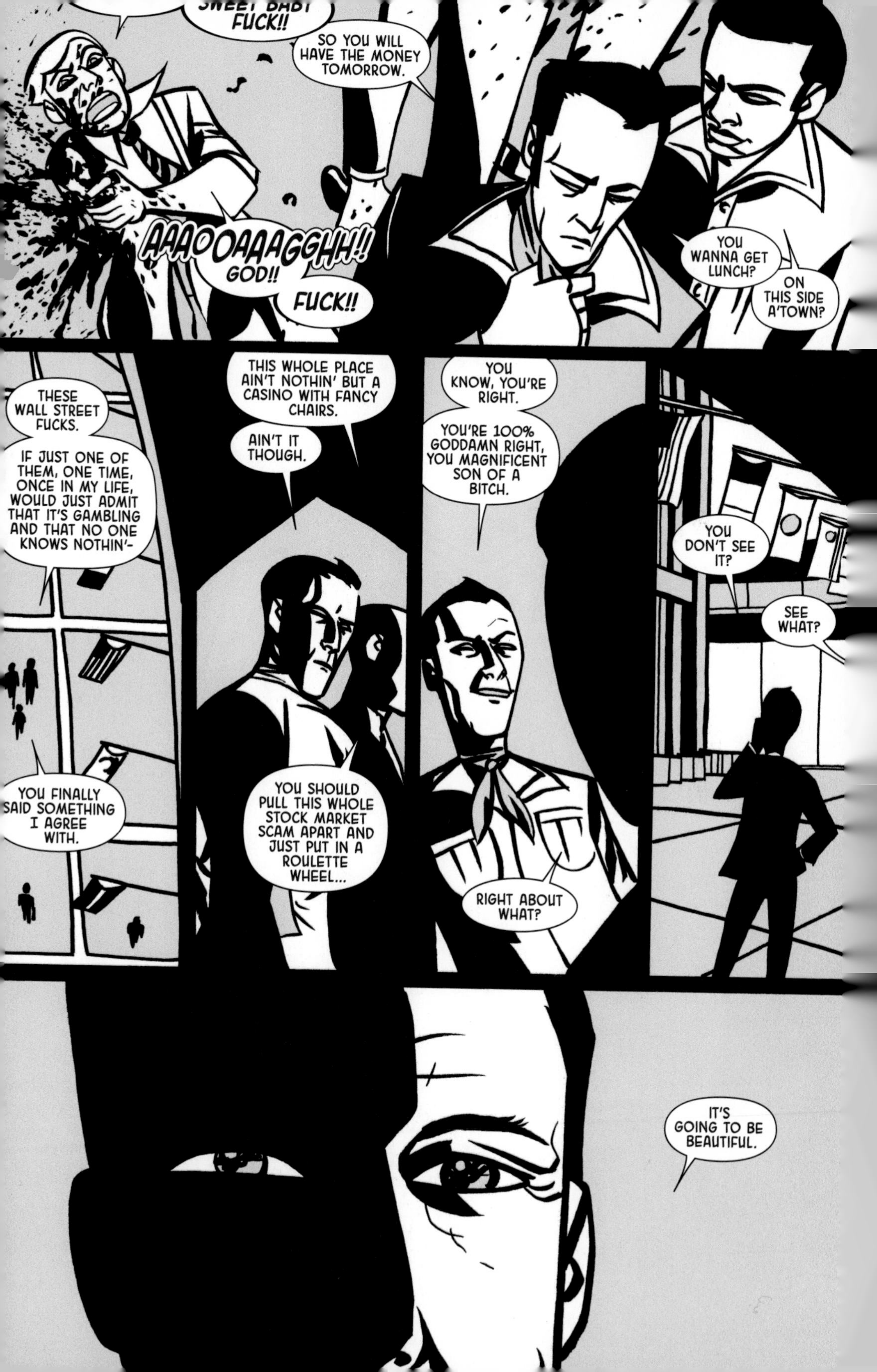
SWEET BABY FUCK!!
SO YOU WILL HAVE THE MONEY TOMORROW.
AAAOOAAAGGHH!! GOD!!
FUCK!!
YOU WANNA GET LUNCH?
ON THIS SIDE A'TOWN?
THESE WALL STREET FUCKS.
IF JUST ONE OF THEM, ONE TIME, ONCE IN MY LIFE, WOULD JUST ADMIT THAT IT'S GAMBLING AND THAT NO ONE KNOWS NOTHIN'-
YOU FINALLY SAID SOMETHING I AGREE WITH.
THIS WHOLE PLACE AIN'T NOTHIN' BUT A CASINO WITH FANCY CHAIRS.
AIN'T IT THOUGH.
YOU SHOULD PULL THIS WHOLE STOCK MARKET SCAM APART AND JUST PUT IN A ROULETTE WHEEL...
YOU KNOW, YOU'RE RIGHT.
YOU'RE 100% GODDAMN RIGHT, YOU MAGNIFICENT SON OF A BITCH.
RIGHT ABOUT WHAT?
YOU DON'T SEE IT?
SEE WHAT?
IT'S GOING TO BE BEAUTIFUL.

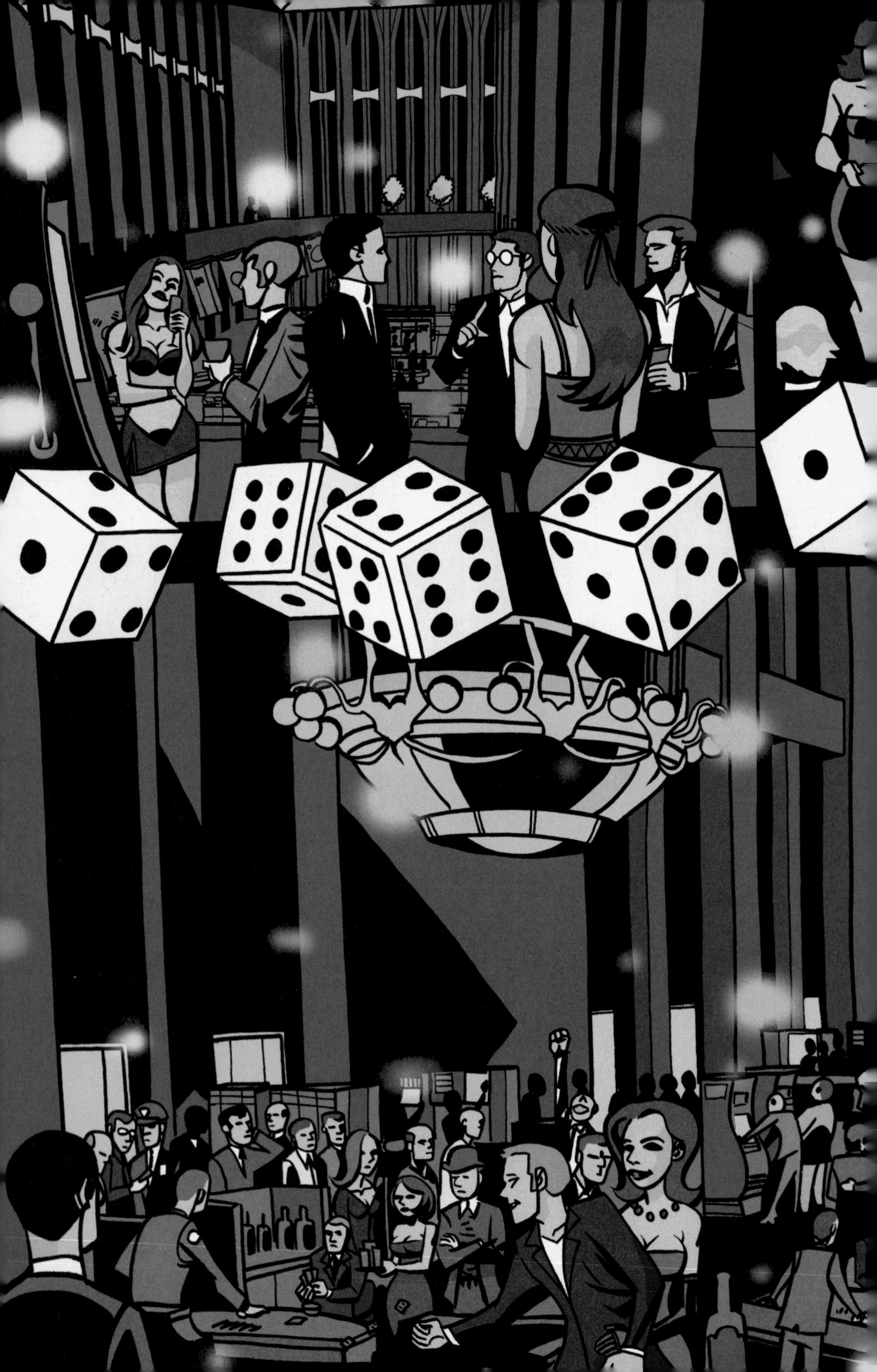

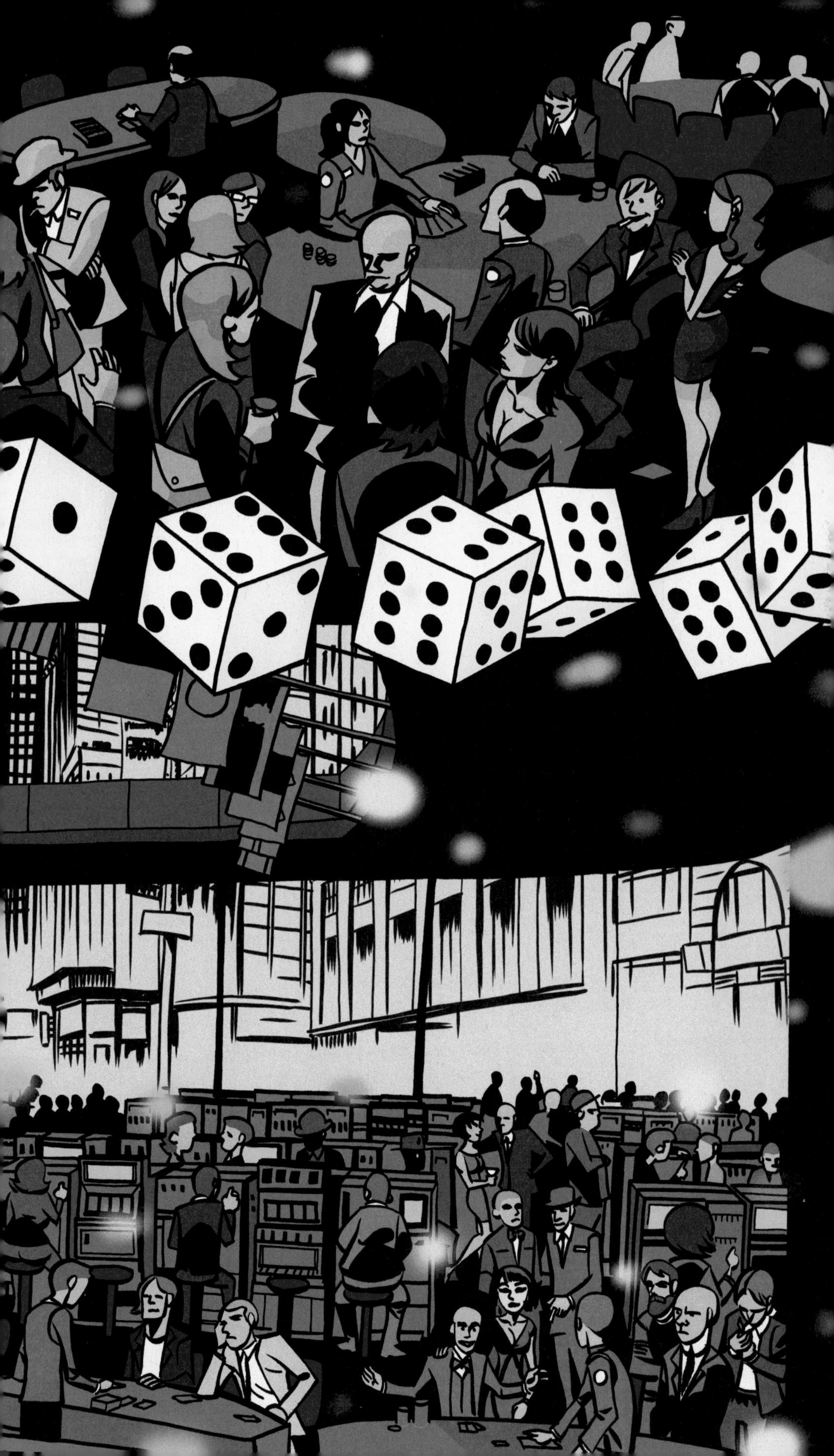

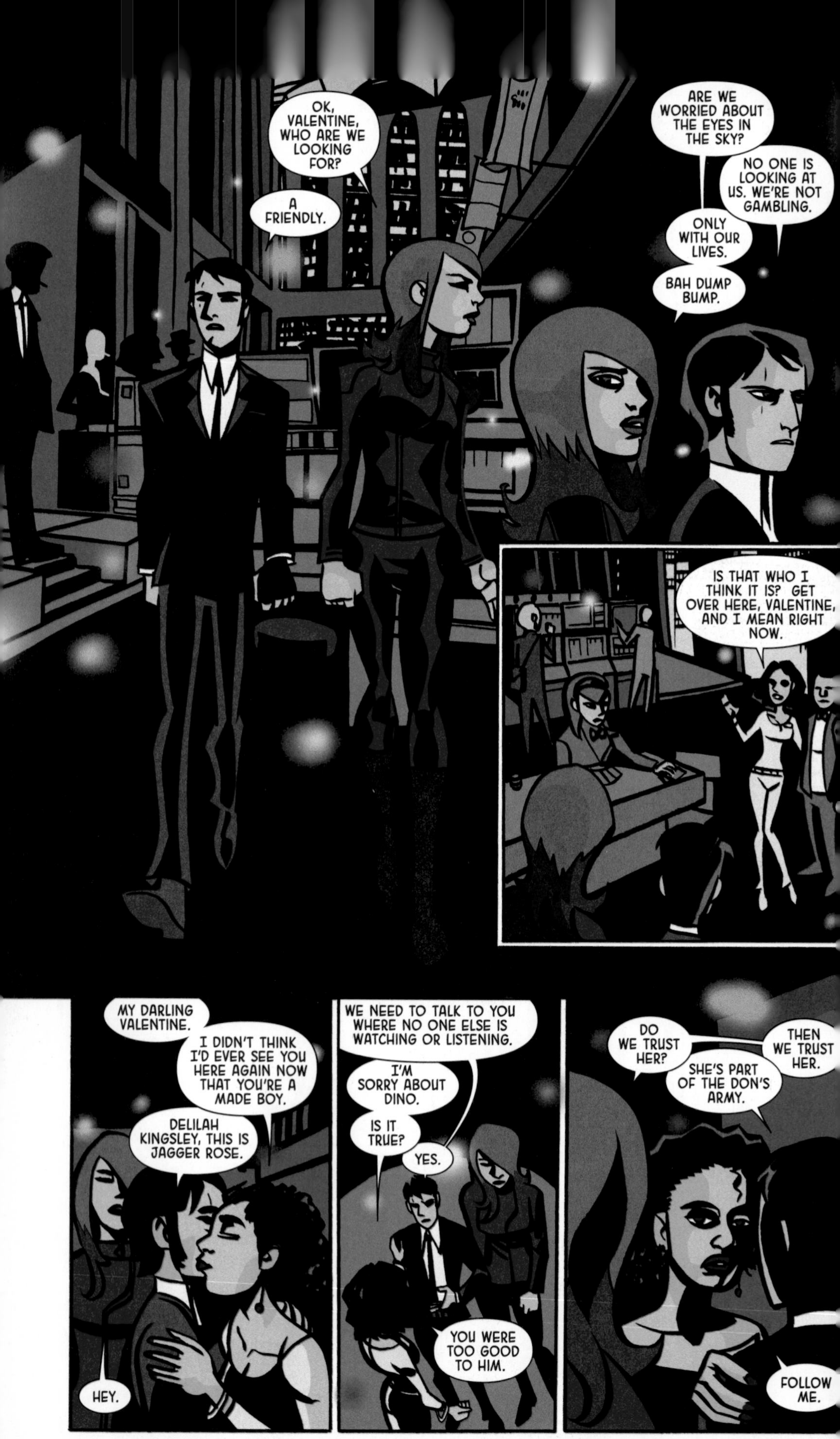

OK, VALENTINE, WHO ARE WE LOOKING FOR?
A FRIENDLY.
ARE WE WORRIED ABOUT THE EYES IN THE SKY?
NO ONE IS LOOKING AT US. WE'RE NOT GAMBLING.
ONLY WITH OUR LIVES.
BAH DUMP BUMP.
IS THAT WHO I THINK IT IS? GET OVER HERE, VALENTINE, AND I MEAN RIGHT NOW.
MY DARLING VALENTINE.
I DIDN'T THINK I'D EVER SEE YOU HERE AGAIN NOW THAT YOU'RE A MADE BOY.
DELILAH KINGSLEY, THIS IS JAGGER ROSE.
HEY.
WE NEED TO TALK TO YOU WHERE NO ONE ELSE IS WATCHING OR LISTENING.
I'M SORRY ABOUT DINO.
IS IT TRUE?
YES.
YOU WERE TOO GOOD TO HIM.
DO WE TRUST HER?
THEN WE TRUST HER.
SHE'S PART OF THE DON'S ARMY.
FOLLOW ME.

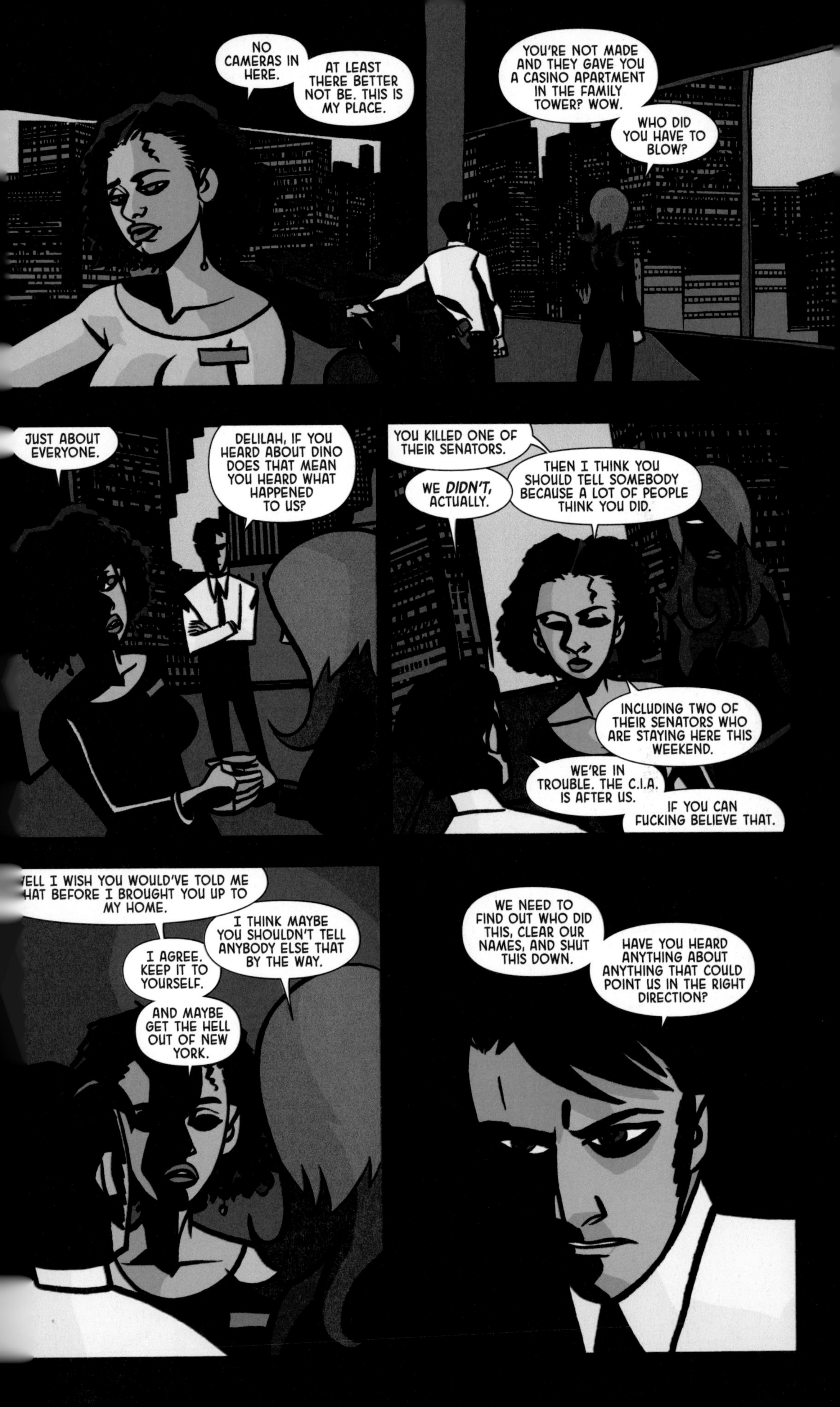

NO CAMERAS IN HERE.
AT LEAST THERE BETTER NOT BE. THIS IS MY PLACE.
YOU'RE NOT MADE AND THEY GAVE YOU A CASINO APARTMENT IN THE FAMILY TOWER? WOW.
WHO DID YOU HAVE TO BLOW?
JUST ABOUT EVERYONE.
DELILAH, IF YOU HEARD ABOUT DINO DOES THAT MEAN YOU HEARD WHAT HAPPENED TO US?
YOU KILLED ONE OF THEIR SENATORS.
WE *DIDN'T,* ACTUALLY.
THEN I THINK YOU SHOULD TELL SOMEBODY BECAUSE A LOT OF PEOPLE THINK YOU DID.
INCLUDING TWO OF THEIR SENATORS WHO ARE STAYING HERE THIS WEEKEND.
WE'RE IN TROUBLE. THE C.I.A. IS AFTER US.
IF YOU CAN FUCKING BELIEVE THAT.
WELL I WISH YOU WOULD'VE TOLD ME THAT BEFORE I BROUGHT YOU UP TO MY HOME.
I THINK MAYBE YOU SHOULDN'T TELL ANYBODY ELSE THAT BY THE WAY.
I AGREE. KEEP IT TO YOURSELF.
AND MAYBE GET THE HELL OUT OF NEW YORK.
WE NEED TO FIND OUT WHO DID THIS, CLEAR OUR NAMES, AND SHUT THIS DOWN.
HAVE YOU HEARD ANYTHING ABOUT ANYTHING THAT COULD POINT US IN THE RIGHT DIRECTION?

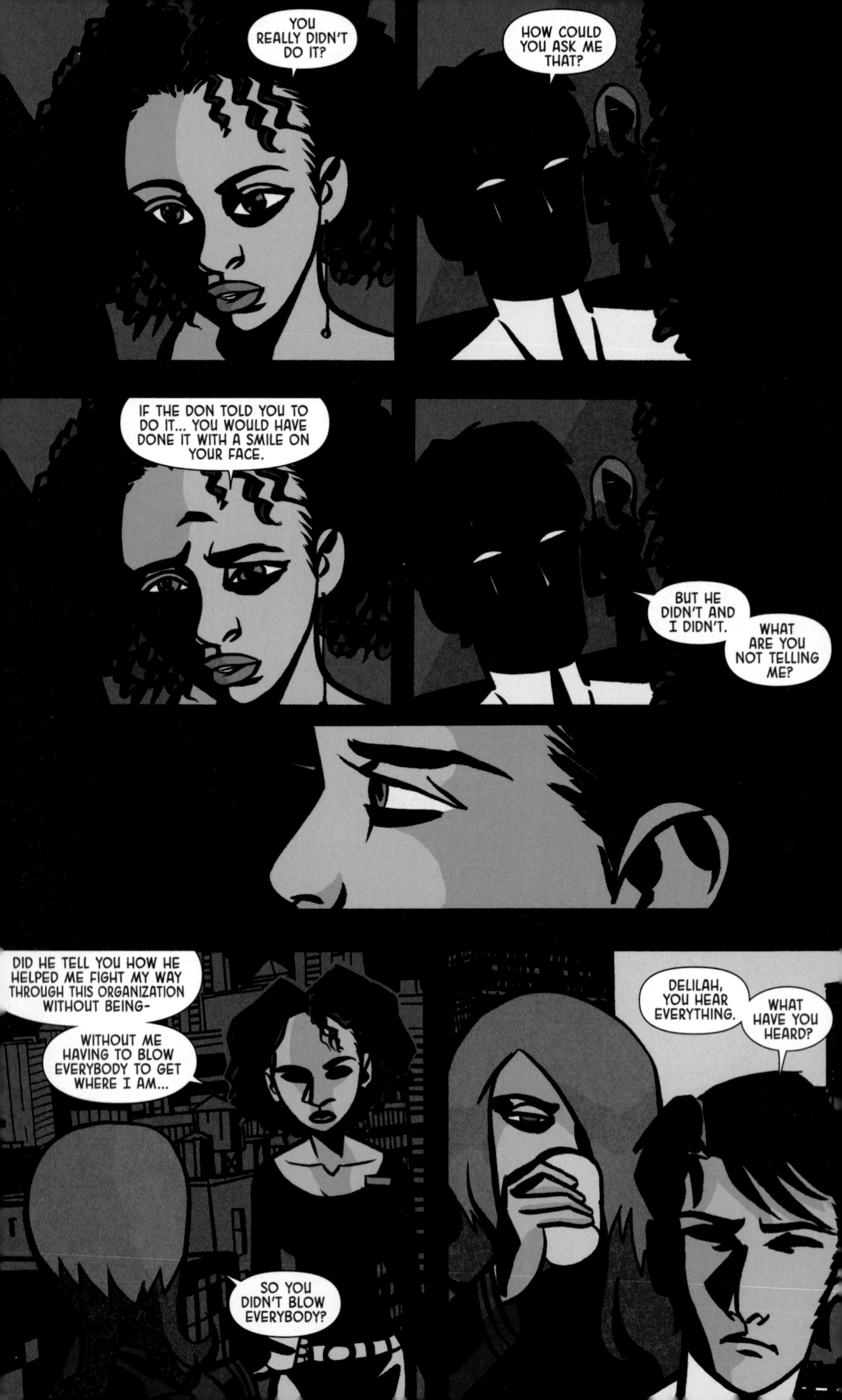
YOU REALLY DIDN'T DO IT?
HOW COULD YOU ASK ME THAT?
IF THE DON TOLD YOU TO DO IT... YOU WOULD HAVE DONE IT WITH A SMILE ON YOUR FACE.
BUT HE DIDN'T AND I DIDN'T.
WHAT ARE YOU NOT TELLING ME?
DID HE TELL YOU HOW HE HELPED ME FIGHT MY WAY THROUGH THIS ORGANIZATION WITHOUT BEING-
WITHOUT ME HAVING TO BLOW EVERYBODY TO GET WHERE I AM...
SO YOU DIDN'T BLOW EVERYBODY?
DELILAH, YOU HEAR EVERYTHING.
WHAT HAVE YOU HEARD?

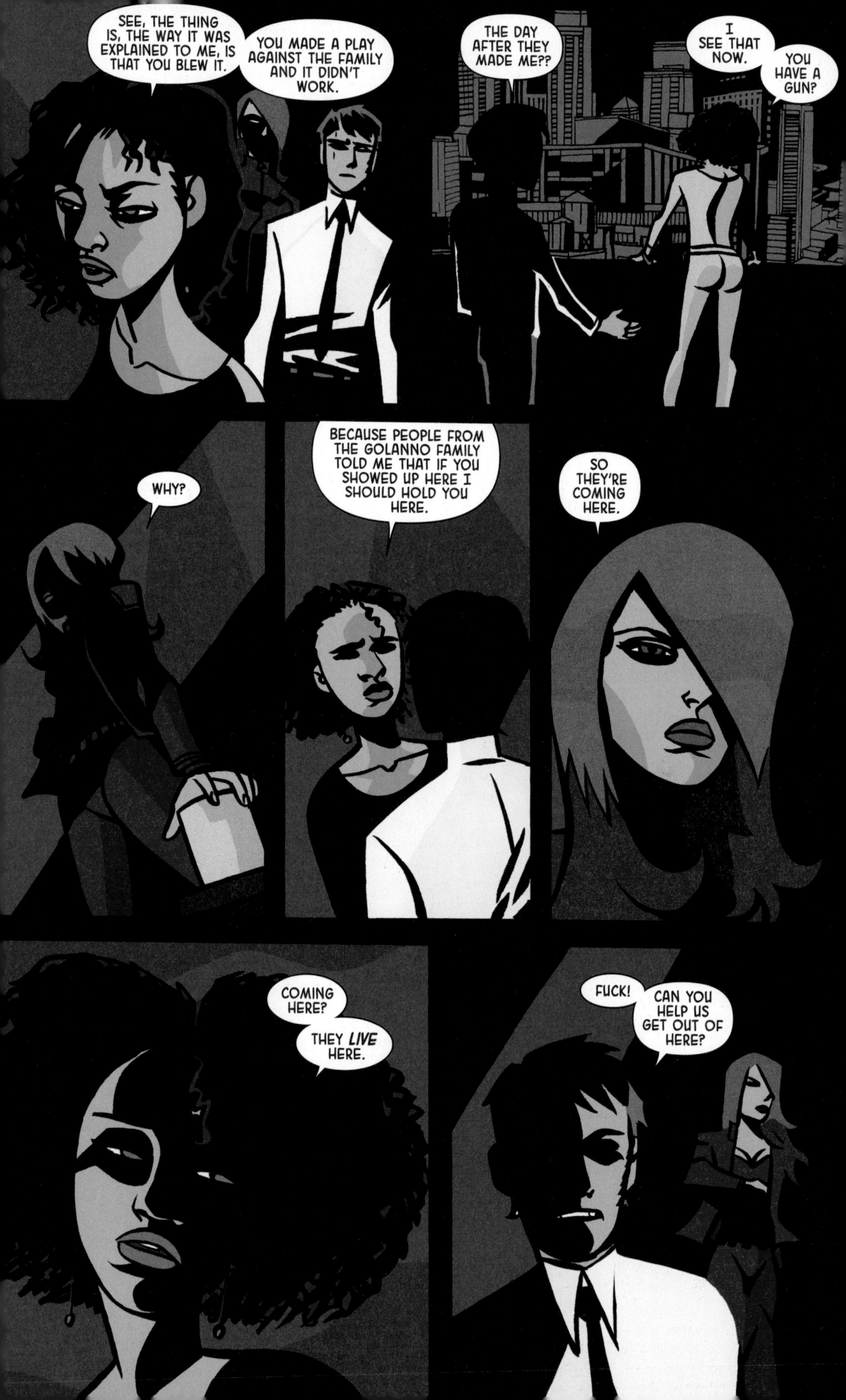
SEE, THE THING IS, THE WAY IT WAS EXPLAINED TO ME, IS THAT YOU BLEW IT.
YOU MADE A PLAY AGAINST THE FAMILY AND IT DIDN'T WORK.
THE DAY AFTER THEY MADE ME??
I SEE THAT NOW.
YOU HAVE A GUN?
WHY?
BECAUSE PEOPLE FROM THE GOLANNO FAMILY TOLD ME THAT IF YOU SHOWED UP HERE I SHOULD HOLD YOU HERE.
SO THEY'RE COMING HERE.
COMING HERE?
THEY *LIVE* HERE.
FUCK!
CAN YOU HELP US GET OUT OF HERE?

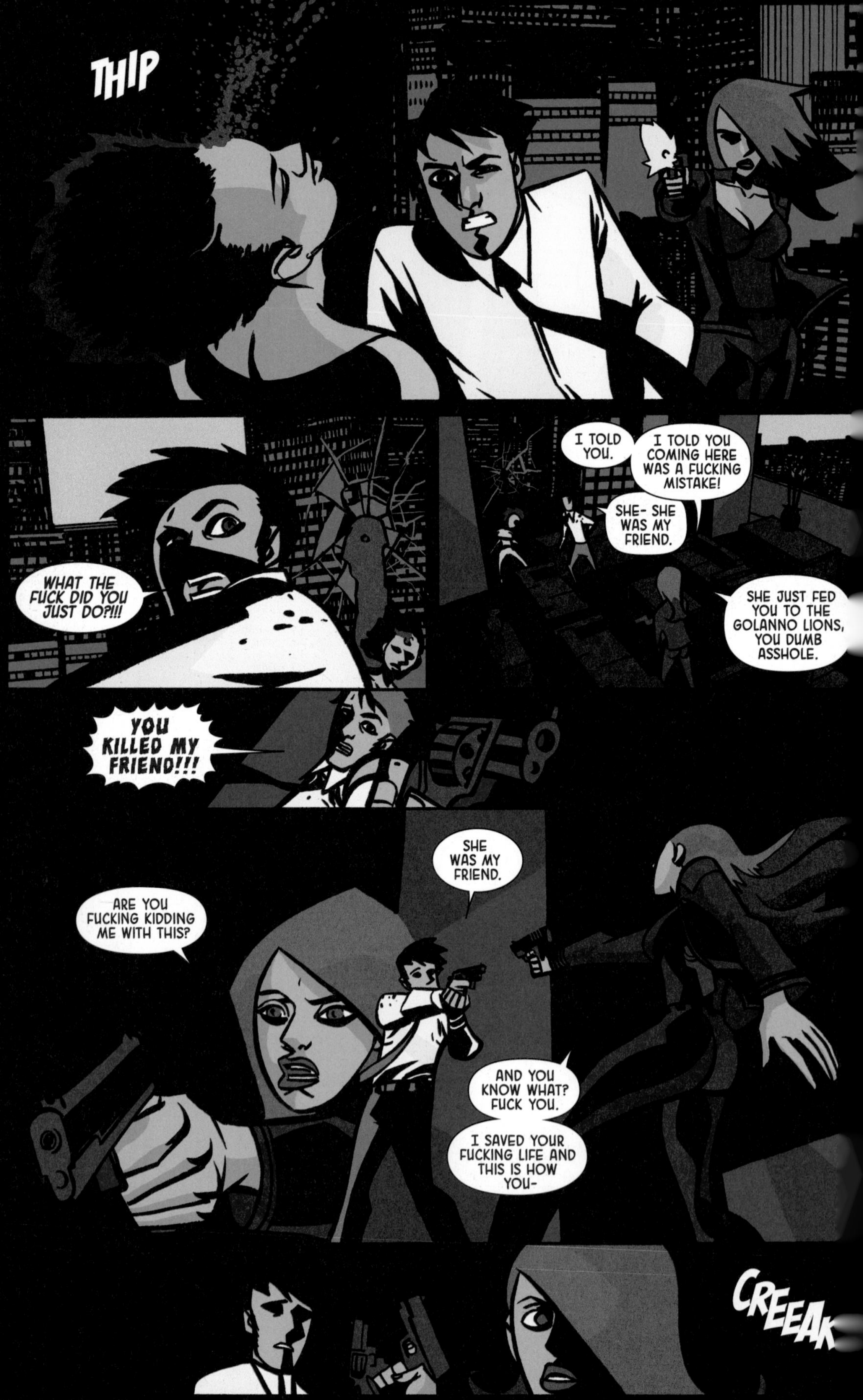
THIP
WHAT THE FUCK DID YOU JUST DO?!!!
I TOLD YOU.
I TOLD YOU COMING HERE WAS A FUCKING MISTAKE!
SHE- SHE WAS MY FRIEND.
SHE JUST FED YOU TO THE GOLANNO LIONS, YOU DUMB ASSHOLE.
YOU KILLED MY FRIEND!!!
SHE WAS MY FRIEND.
ARE YOU FUCKING KIDDING ME WITH THIS?
AND YOU KNOW WHAT? FUCK YOU.
I SAVED YOUR FUCKING LIFE AND THIS IS HOW YOU-
CREEAK

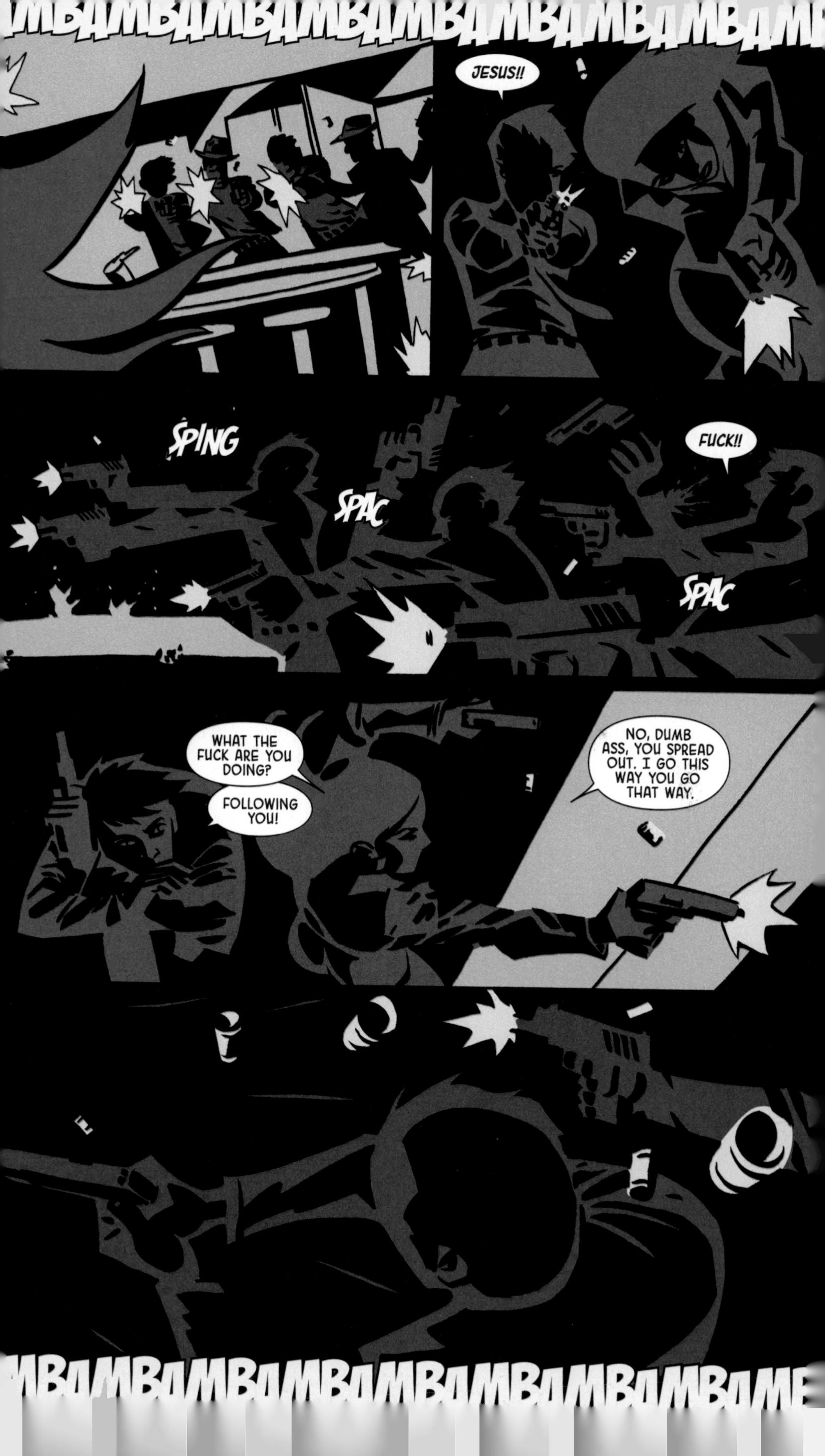
MBAMBAMBAMBAMBAMBAMBAMBAMBAM
JESUS!!
SPING
SPAC
FUCK!!
SPAC
WHAT THE FUCK ARE YOU DOING?
FOLLOWING YOU!
NO, DUMB ASS, YOU SPREAD OUT. I GO THIS WAY YOU GO THAT WAY.
MBAMBAMBAMBAMBAMBAMBAMBAM

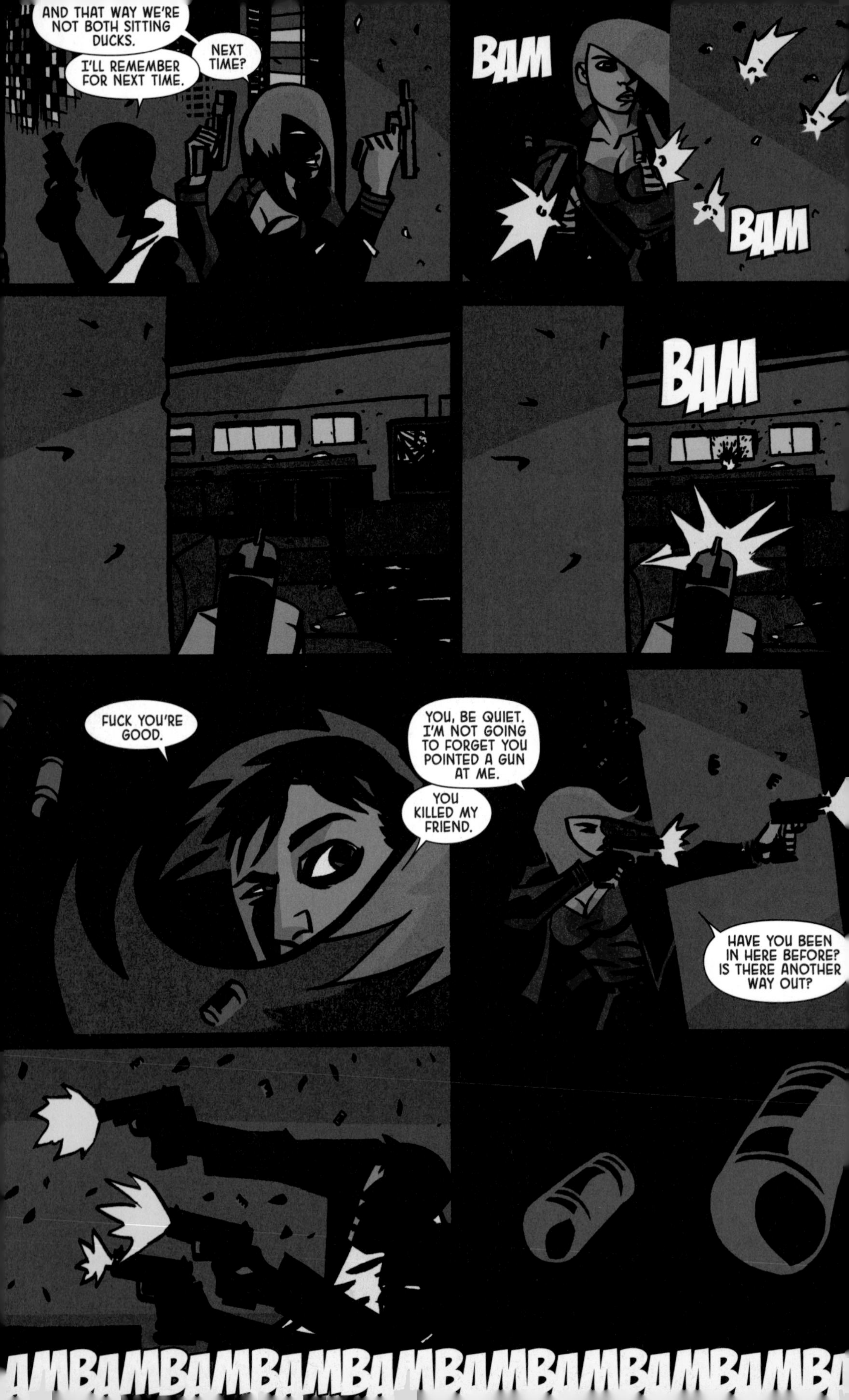
AND THAT WAY WE'RE NOT BOTH SITTING DUCKS.
NEXT TIME?
I'LL REMEMBER FOR NEXT TIME.
BAM
BAM
BAM
FUCK YOU'RE GOOD.
YOU, BE QUIET. I'M NOT GOING TO FORGET YOU POINTED A GUN AT ME.
YOU KILLED MY FRIEND.
HAVE YOU BEEN IN HERE BEFORE? IS THERE ANOTHER WAY OUT?
AMBAMBAMBAMBAMBAMBAMBAMBAMBAMBA

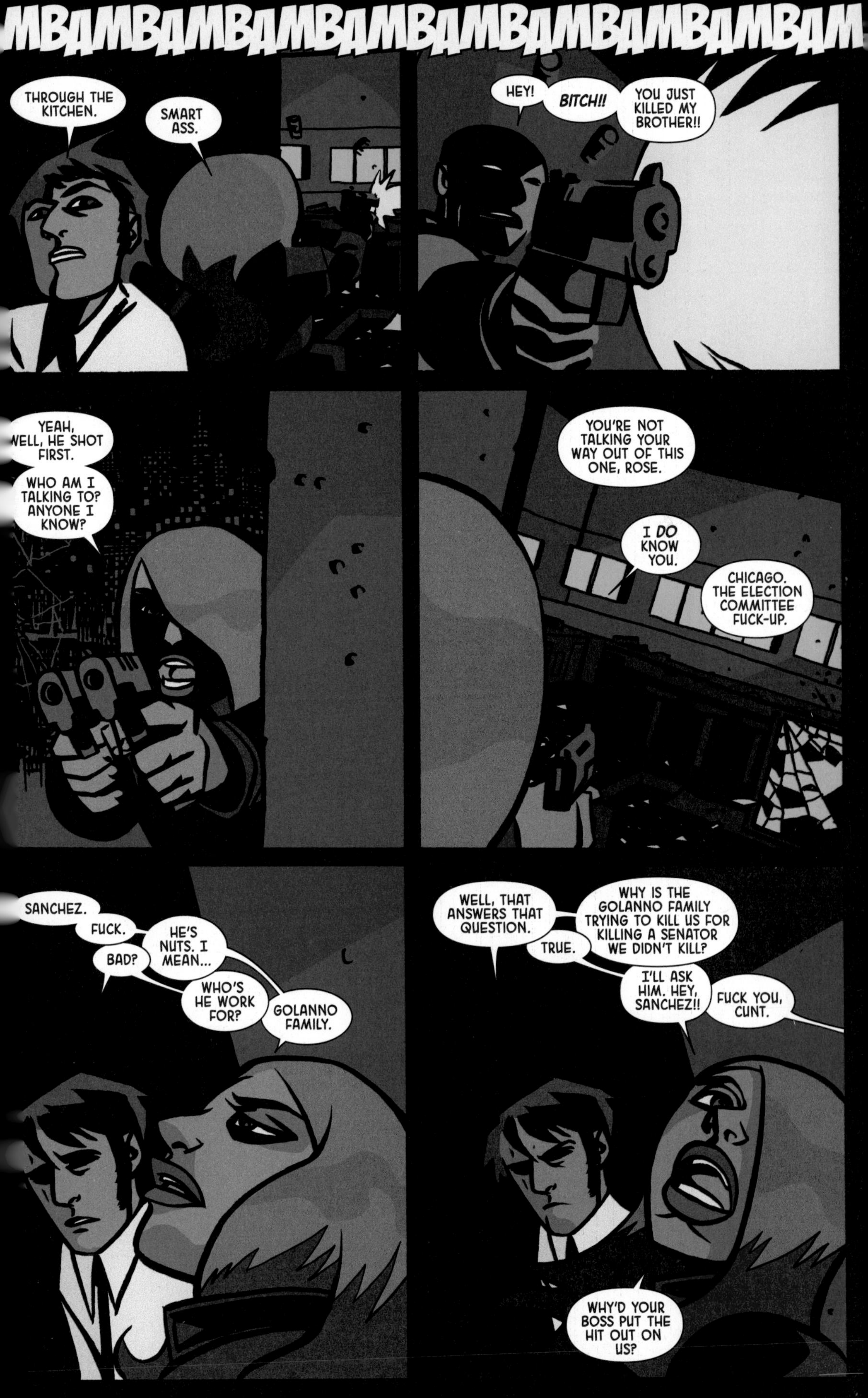
MBAMBAMBAMBAMBAMBAMBAMBAMBAMBAM
THROUGH THE KITCHEN.
SMART ASS.
HEY!
BITCH!!
YOU JUST KILLED MY BROTHER!!
YEAH, WELL, HE SHOT FIRST.
WHO AM I TALKING TO? ANYONE I KNOW?
YOU'RE NOT TALKING YOUR WAY OUT OF THIS ONE, ROSE.
I DO KNOW YOU.
CHICAGO. THE ELECTION COMMITTEE FUCK-UP.
SANCHEZ.
FUCK.
BAD?
HE'S NUTS. I MEAN...
WHO'S HE WORK FOR?
GOLANNO FAMILY.
WELL, THAT ANSWERS THAT QUESTION.
WHY IS THE GOLANNO FAMILY TRYING TO KILL US FOR KILLING A SENATOR WE DIDN'T KILL?
TRUE.
I'LL ASK HIM. HEY, SANCHEZ!!
FUCK YOU, CUNT.
WHY'D YOUR BOSS PUT THE HIT OUT ON US?

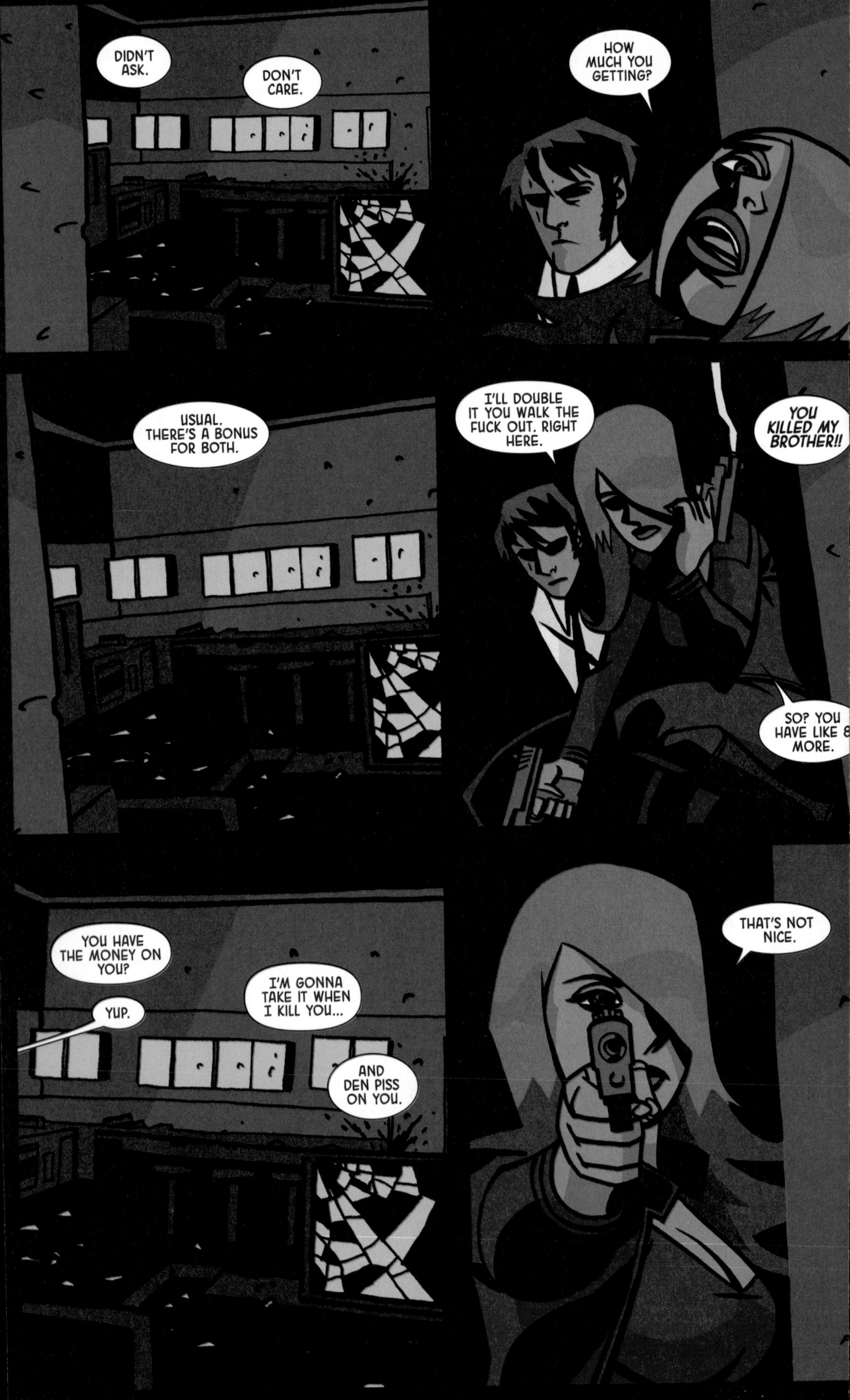

DIDN'T ASK.
DON'T CARE.
HOW MUCH YOU GETTING?
USUAL. THERE'S A BONUS FOR BOTH.
I'LL DOUBLE IT YOU WALK THE FUCK OUT. RIGHT HERE.
YOU KILLED MY BROTHER!!
SO? YOU HAVE LIKE 8 MORE.
YOU HAVE THE MONEY ON YOU?
YUP.
I'M GONNA TAKE IT WHEN I KILL YOU...
AND DEN PISS ON YOU.
THAT'S NOT NICE.

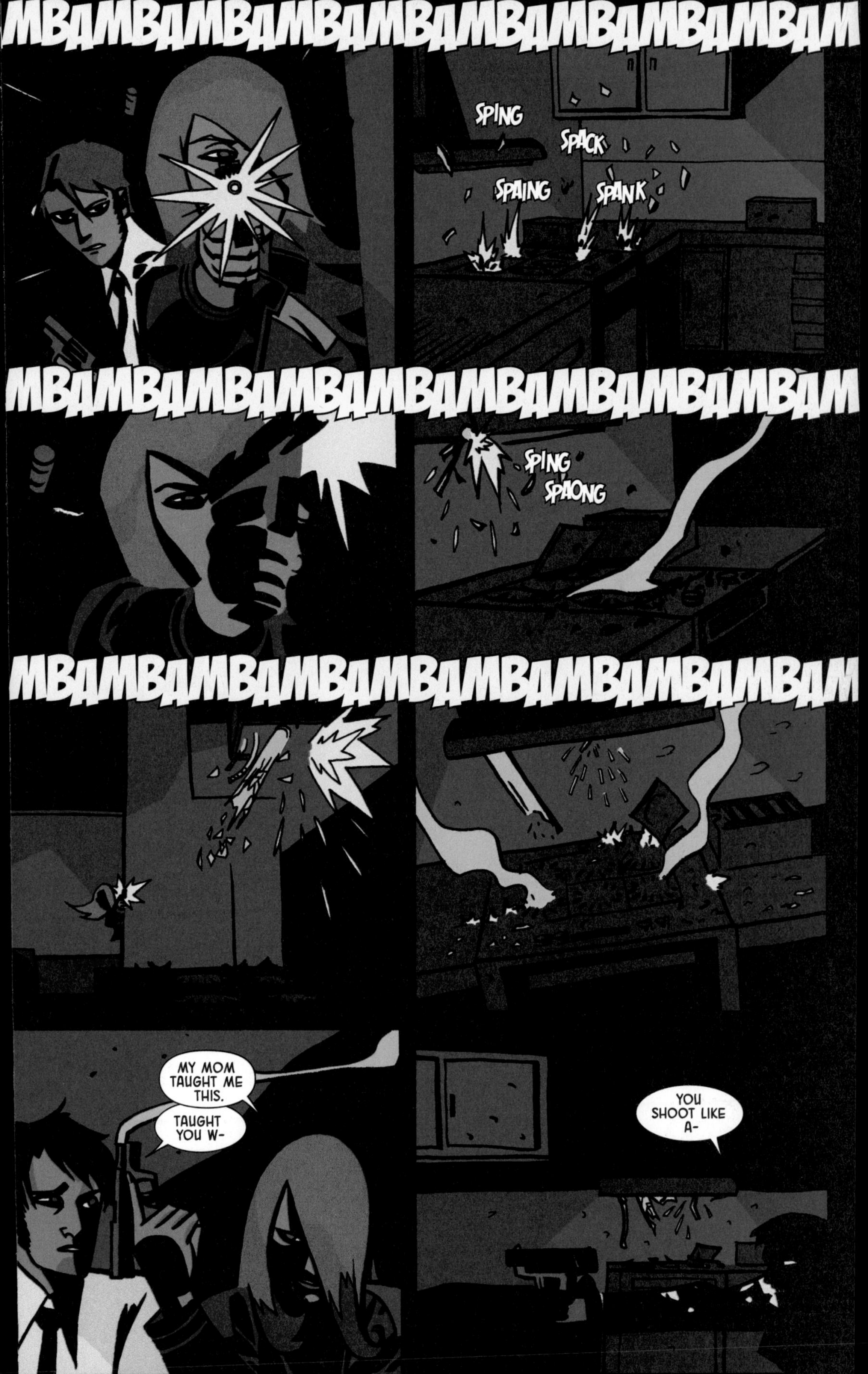
MBAMBAMBAMBAMBAMBAMBAMBAMBAMBAM
SPING
SPACK
SPAING
SPANK
MBAMBAMBAMBAMBAMBAMBAMBAMBAMBAM
SPING
SPAONG
MBAMBAMBAMBAMBAMBAMBAMBAMBAMBAM
MY MOM TAUGHT ME THIS.
TAUGHT YOU W-
YOU SHOOT LIKE A-

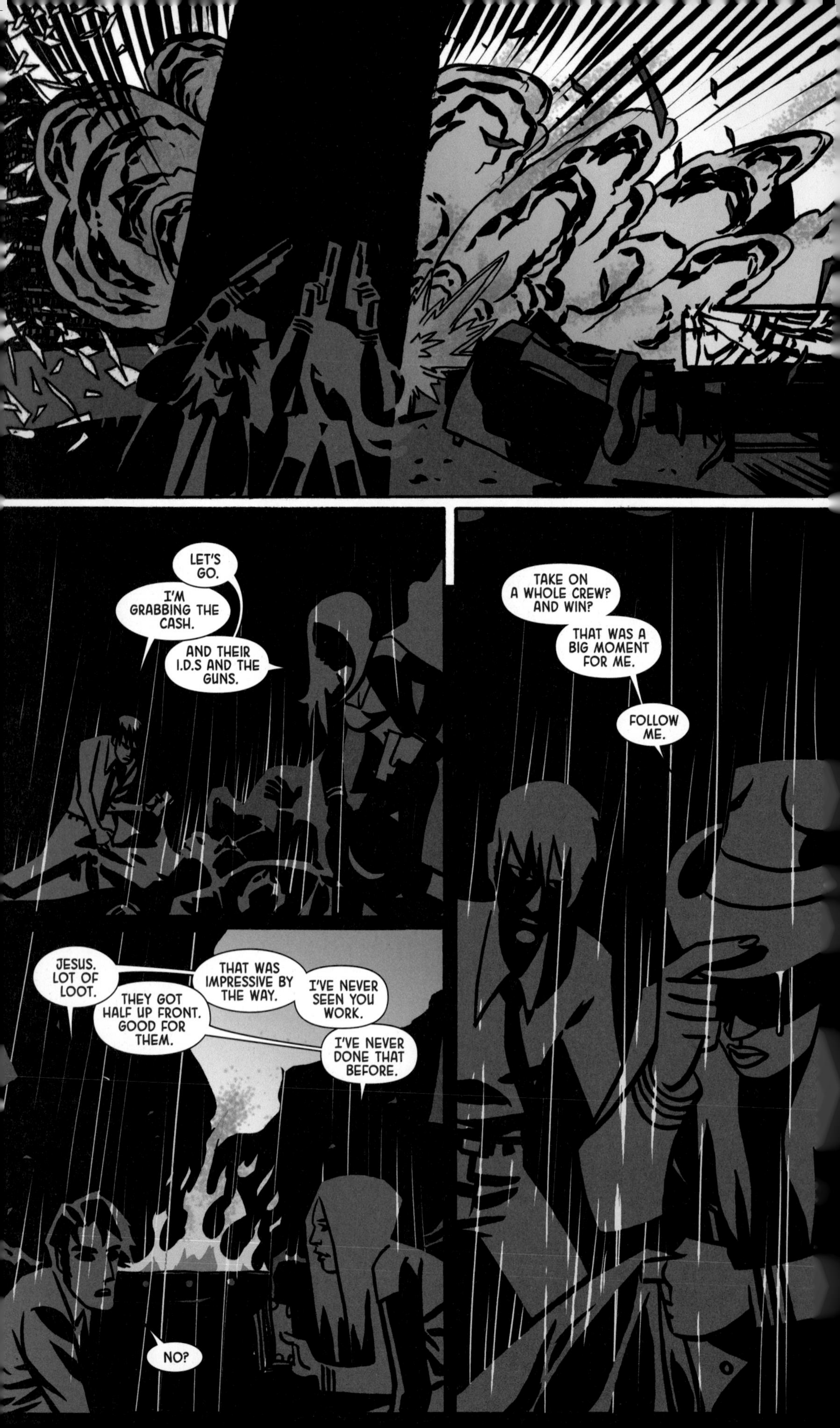

LET'S GO.
I'M GRABBING THE CASH.
AND THEIR I.D.S AND THE GUNS.
JESUS. LOT OF LOOT.
THEY GOT HALF UP FRONT. GOOD FOR THEM.
THAT WAS IMPRESSIVE BY THE WAY.
I'VE NEVER SEEN YOU WORK.
I'VE NEVER DONE THAT BEFORE.
NO?
TAKE ON A WHOLE CREW? AND WIN?
THAT WAS A BIG MOMENT FOR ME.
FOLLOW ME.

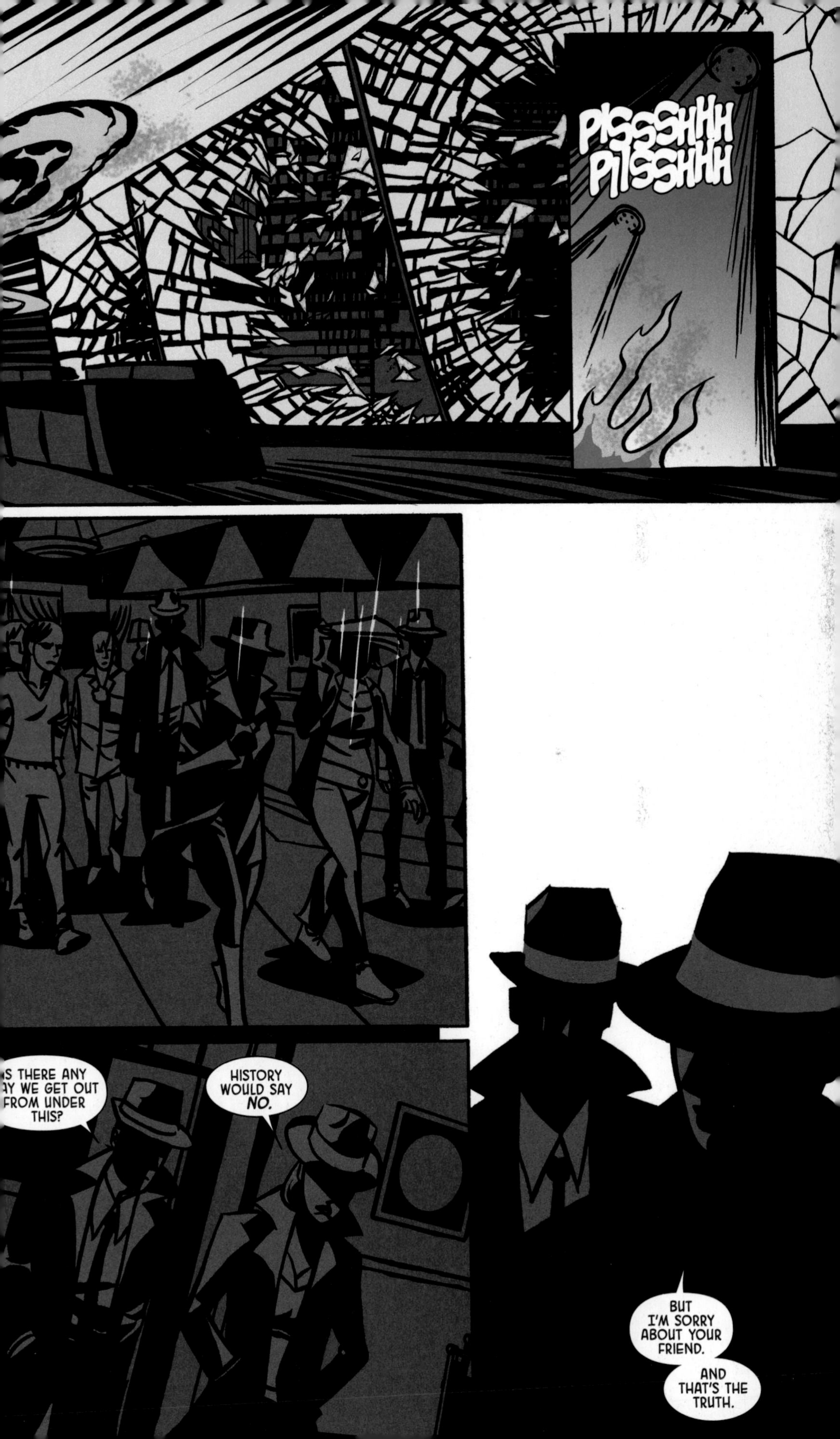
PISSSHHH PIISSHHH
S THERE ANY AY WE GET OUT FROM UNDER THIS?
HISTORY WOULD SAY NO.
BUT I'M SORRY ABOUT YOUR FRIEND.
AND THAT'S THE TRUTH.

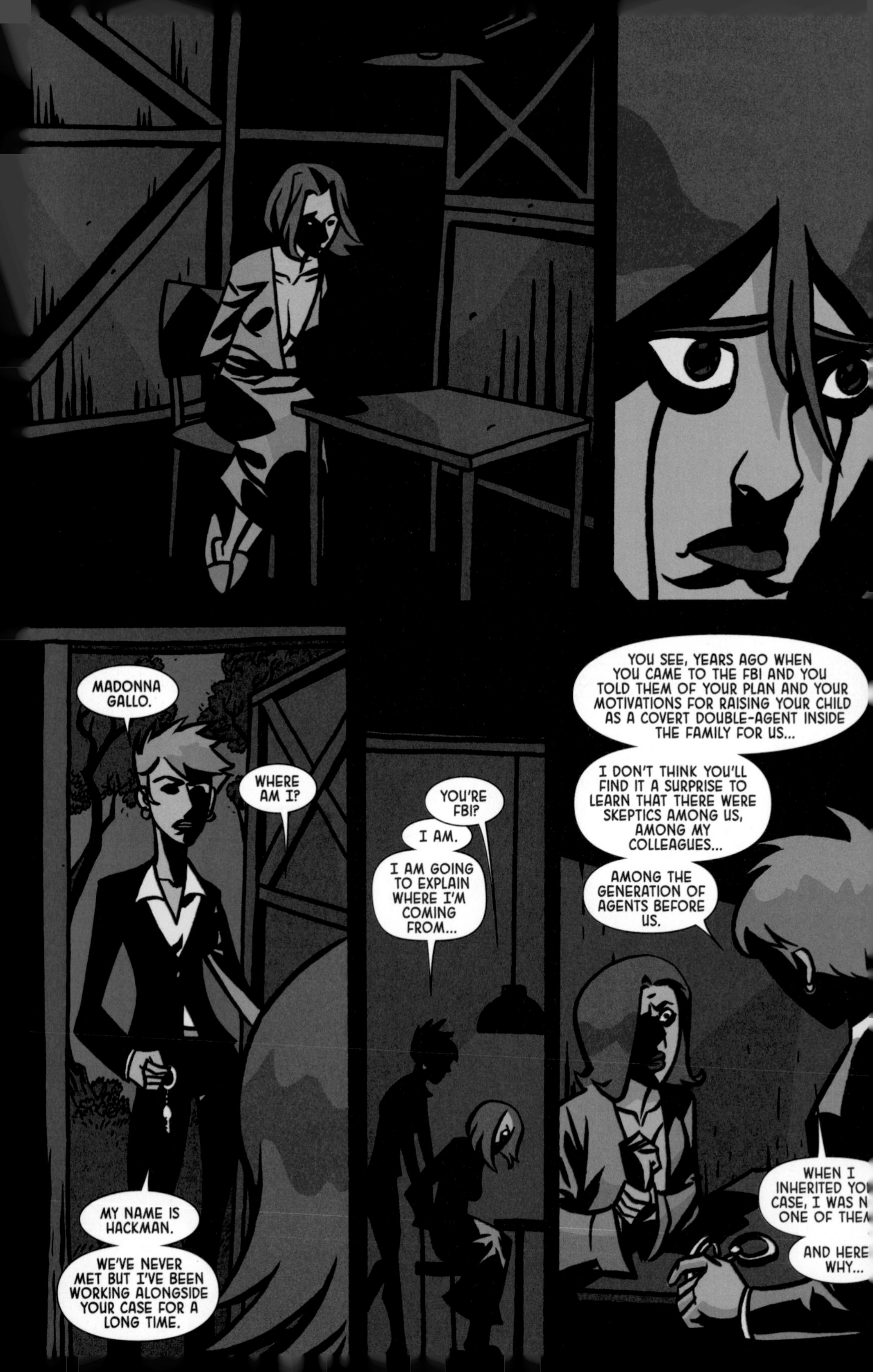
MADONNA GALLO.
WHERE AM I?
MY NAME IS HACKMAN.
WE'VE NEVER MET BUT I'VE BEEN WORKING ALONGSIDE YOUR CASE FOR A LONG TIME.
YOU'RE FBI?
I AM.
I AM GOING TO EXPLAIN WHERE I'M COMING FROM...
YOU SEE, YEARS AGO WHEN YOU CAME TO THE FBI AND YOU TOLD THEM OF YOUR PLAN AND YOUR MOTIVATIONS FOR RAISING YOUR CHILD AS A COVERT DOUBLE-AGENT INSIDE THE FAMILY FOR US...
I DON'T THINK YOU'LL FIND IT A SURPRISE TO LEARN THAT THERE WERE SKEPTICS AMONG US, AMONG MY COLLEAGUES...
AMONG THE GENERATION OF AGENTS BEFORE US.
WHEN I INHERITED YO CASE, I WAS N ONE OF THEM
AND HERE WHY...

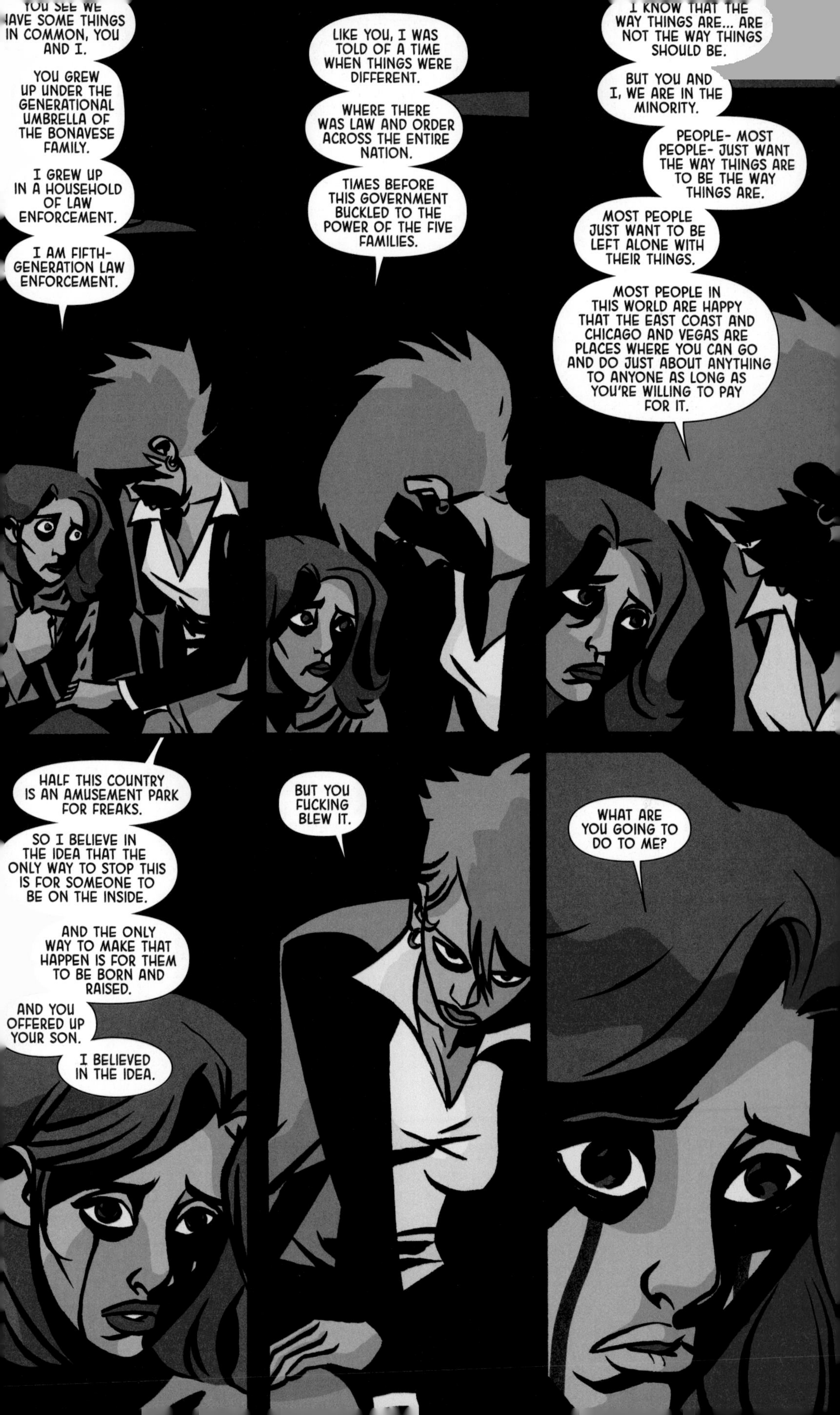
YOU SEE WE HAVE SOME THINGS IN COMMON, YOU AND I.
YOU GREW UP UNDER THE GENERATIONAL UMBRELLA OF THE BONAVESE FAMILY.
I GREW UP IN A HOUSEHOLD OF LAW ENFORCEMENT.
I AM FIFTH-GENERATION LAW ENFORCEMENT.
LIKE YOU, I WAS TOLD OF A TIME WHEN THINGS WERE DIFFERENT.
WHERE THERE WAS LAW AND ORDER ACROSS THE ENTIRE NATION.
TIMES BEFORE THIS GOVERNMENT BUCKLED TO THE POWER OF THE FIVE FAMILIES.
I KNOW THAT THE WAY THINGS ARE... ARE NOT THE WAY THINGS SHOULD BE.
BUT YOU AND I, WE ARE IN THE MINORITY.
PEOPLE- MOST PEOPLE- JUST WANT THE WAY THINGS ARE TO BE THE WAY THINGS ARE.
MOST PEOPLE JUST WANT TO BE LEFT ALONE WITH THEIR THINGS.
MOST PEOPLE IN THIS WORLD ARE HAPPY THAT THE EAST COAST AND CHICAGO AND VEGAS ARE PLACES WHERE YOU CAN GO AND DO JUST ABOUT ANYTHING TO ANYONE AS LONG AS YOU'RE WILLING TO PAY FOR IT.
HALF THIS COUNTRY IS AN AMUSEMENT PARK FOR FREAKS.
SO I BELIEVE IN THE IDEA THAT THE ONLY WAY TO STOP THIS IS FOR SOMEONE TO BE ON THE INSIDE.
AND THE ONLY WAY TO MAKE THAT HAPPEN IS FOR THEM TO BE BORN AND RAISED.
AND YOU OFFERED UP YOUR SON.
I BELIEVED IN THE IDEA.
BUT YOU FUCKING BLEW IT.
WHAT ARE YOU GOING TO DO TO ME?

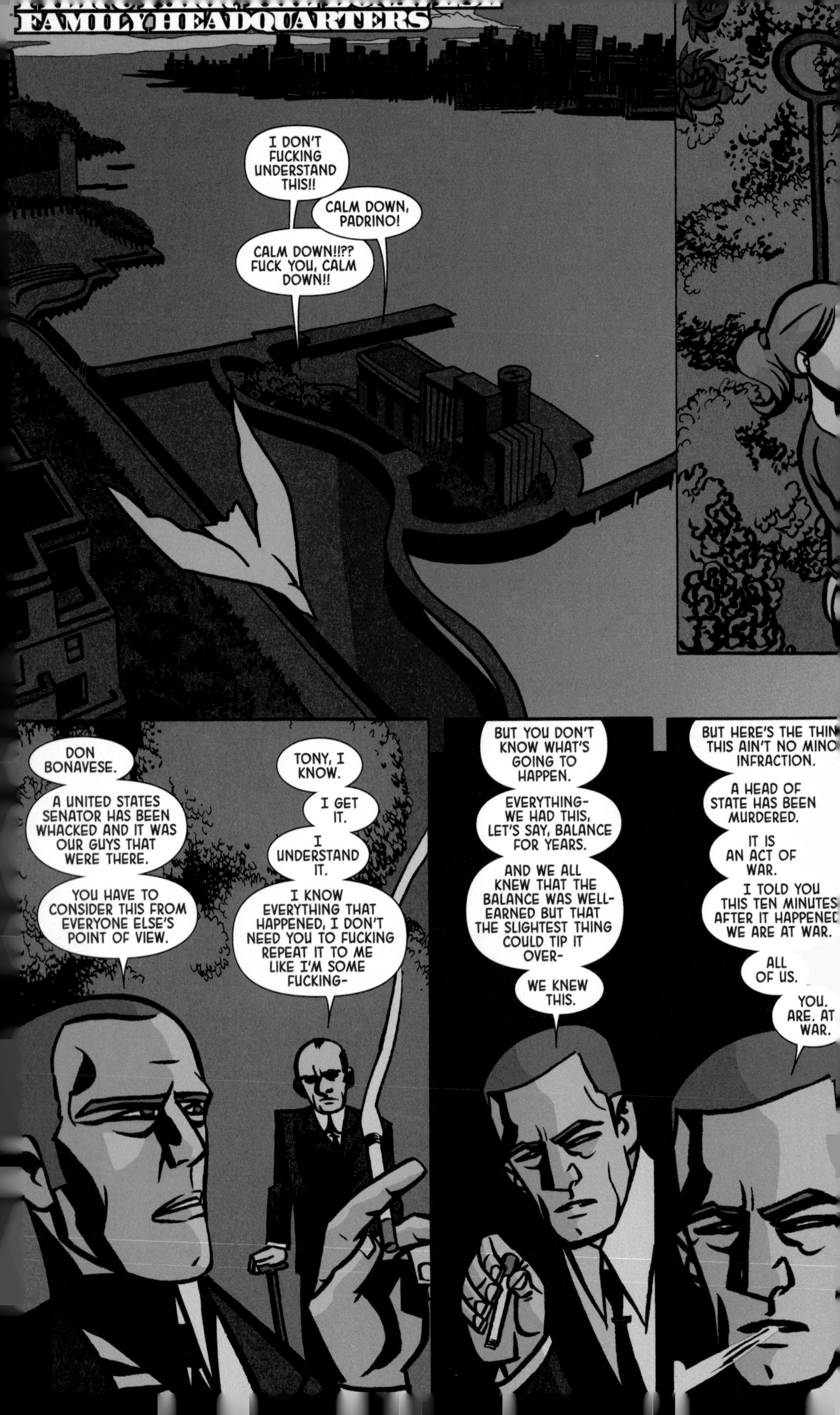

FAMILY HEADQUARTERS
I DON'T FUCKING UNDERSTAND THIS!!
CALM DOWN, PADRINO!
CALM DOWN!!?? FUCK YOU, CALM DOWN!!
DON BONAVESE.
A UNITED STATES SENATOR HAS BEEN WHACKED AND IT WAS OUR GUYS THAT WERE THERE.
YOU HAVE TO CONSIDER THIS FROM EVERYONE ELSE'S POINT OF VIEW.
TONY, I KNOW.
I GET IT.
I UNDERSTAND IT.
I KNOW EVERYTHING THAT HAPPENED, I DON'T NEED YOU TO FUCKING REPEAT IT TO ME LIKE I'M SOME FUCKING-
BUT YOU DON'T KNOW WHAT'S GOING TO HAPPEN.
EVERYTHING- WE HAD THIS, LET'S SAY, BALANCE FOR YEARS.
AND WE ALL KNEW THAT THE BALANCE WAS WELL-EARNED BUT THAT THE SLIGHTEST THING COULD TIP IT OVER-
WE KNEW THIS.
BUT HERE'S THE THIN
THIS AIN'T NO MINO
INFRACTION.
A HEAD OF STATE HAS BEEN MURDERED.
IT IS AN ACT OF WAR.
I TOLD YOU THIS TEN MINUTES AFTER IT HAPPENED
WE ARE AT WAR.
ALL OF US.
YOU. ARE. AT WAR.

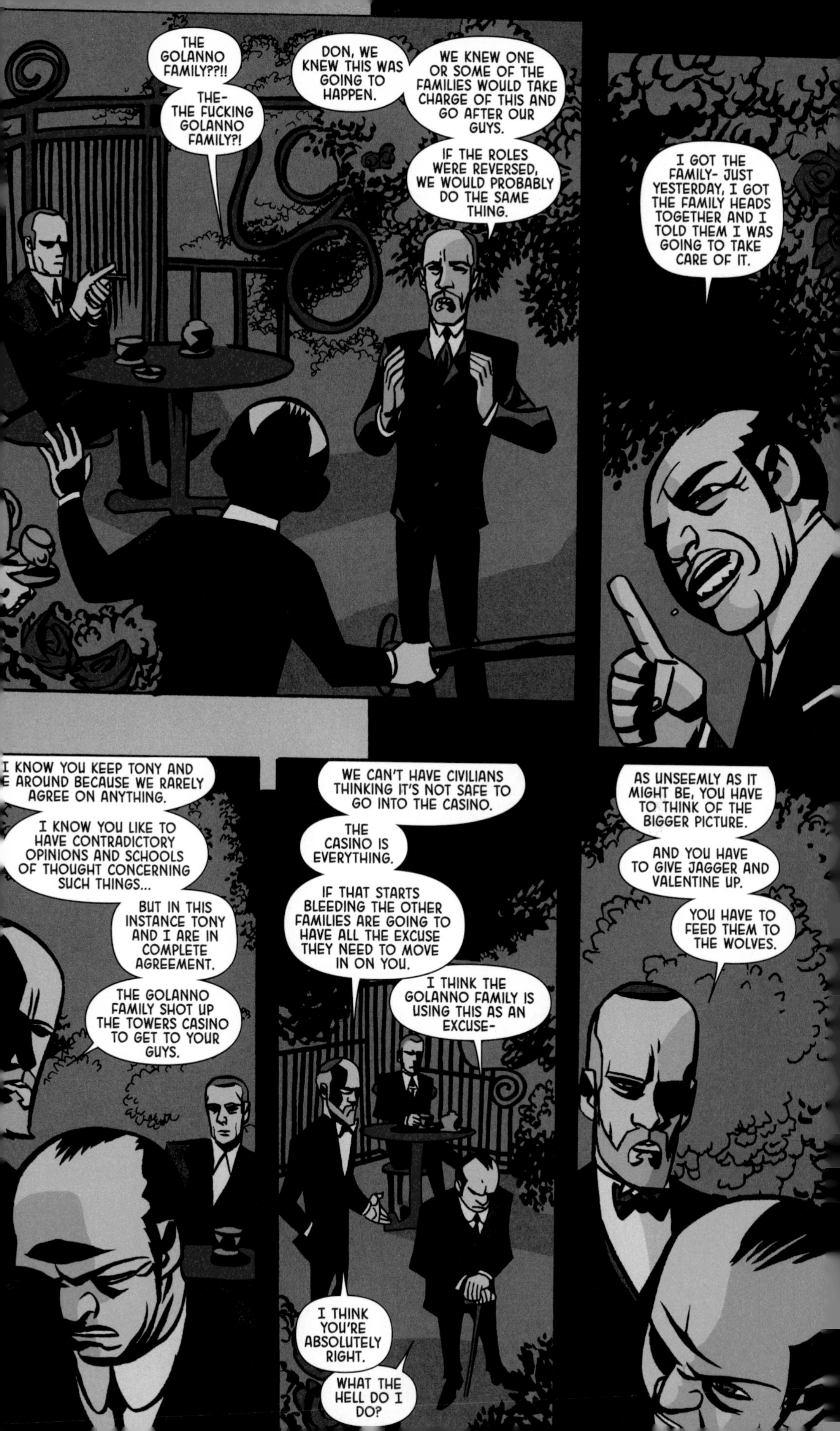
THE GOLANNO FAMILY??!!
THE- THE FUCKING GOLANNO FAMILY?!
DON, WE KNEW THIS WAS GOING TO HAPPEN.
WE KNEW ONE OR SOME OF THE FAMILIES WOULD TAKE CHARGE OF THIS AND GO AFTER OUR GUYS.
IF THE ROLES WERE REVERSED, WE WOULD PROBABLY DO THE SAME THING.
I GOT THE FAMILY- JUST YESTERDAY, I GOT THE FAMILY HEADS TOGETHER AND I TOLD THEM I WAS GOING TO TAKE CARE OF IT.
I KNOW YOU KEEP TONY AND E AROUND BECAUSE WE RARELY AGREE ON ANYTHING.
I KNOW YOU LIKE TO HAVE CONTRADICTORY OPINIONS AND SCHOOLS OF THOUGHT CONCERNING SUCH THINGS...
BUT IN THIS INSTANCE TONY AND I ARE IN COMPLETE AGREEMENT.
THE GOLANNO FAMILY SHOT UP THE TOWERS CASINO TO GET TO YOUR GUYS.
WE CAN'T HAVE CIVILIANS THINKING IT'S NOT SAFE TO GO INTO THE CASINO.
THE CASINO IS EVERYTHING.
IF THAT STARTS BLEEDING THE OTHER FAMILIES ARE GOING TO HAVE ALL THE EXCUSE THEY NEED TO MOVE IN ON YOU.
I THINK THE GOLANNO FAMILY IS USING THIS AS AN EXCUSE-
I THINK YOU'RE ABSOLUTELY RIGHT.
WHAT THE HELL DO I DO?
AS UNSEEMLY AS IT MIGHT BE, YOU HAVE TO THINK OF THE BIGGER PICTURE.
AND YOU HAVE TO GIVE JAGGER AND VALENTINE UP.
YOU HAVE TO FEED THEM TO THE WOLVES.

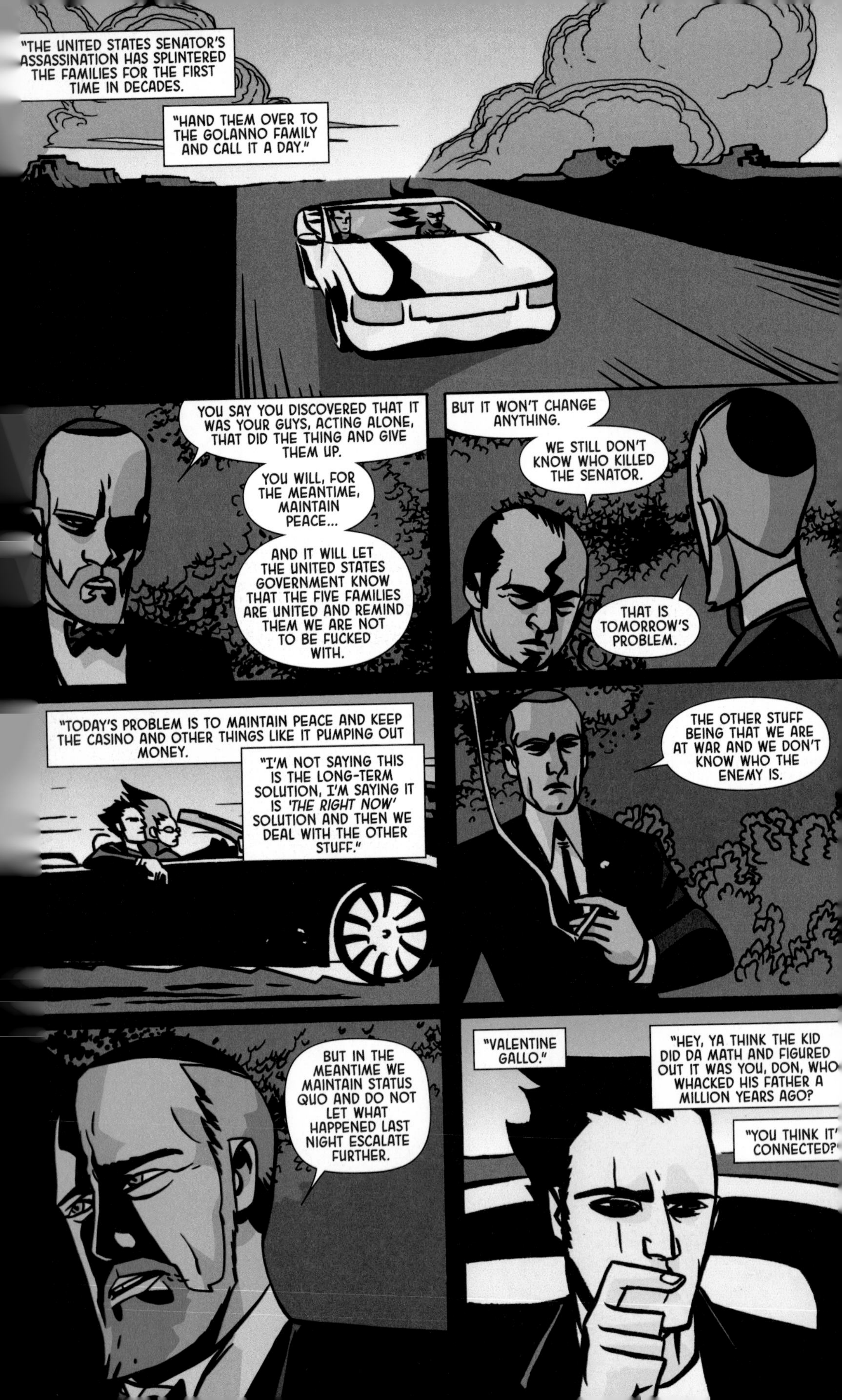
"THE UNITED STATES SENATOR'S ASSASSINATION HAS SPLINTERED THE FAMILIES FOR THE FIRST TIME IN DECADES.
"HAND THEM OVER TO THE GOLANNO FAMILY AND CALL IT A DAY."
YOU SAY YOU DISCOVERED THAT IT WAS YOUR GUYS, ACTING ALONE, THAT DID THE THING AND GIVE THEM UP.
YOU WILL, FOR THE MEANTIME, MAINTAIN PEACE...
AND IT WILL LET THE UNITED STATES GOVERNMENT KNOW THAT THE FIVE FAMILIES ARE UNITED AND REMIND THEM WE ARE NOT TO BE FUCKED WITH.
BUT IT WON'T CHANGE ANYTHING.
WE STILL DON'T KNOW WHO KILLED THE SENATOR.
THAT IS TOMORROW'S PROBLEM.
"TODAY'S PROBLEM IS TO MAINTAIN PEACE AND KEEP THE CASINO AND OTHER THINGS LIKE IT PUMPING OUT MONEY.
"I'M NOT SAYING THIS IS THE LONG-TERM SOLUTION, I'M SAYING IT IS *'THE RIGHT NOW'* SOLUTION AND THEN WE DEAL WITH THE OTHER STUFF."
THE OTHER STUFF BEING THAT WE ARE AT WAR AND WE DON'T KNOW WHO THE ENEMY IS.
BUT IN THE MEANTIME WE MAINTAIN STATUS QUO AND DO NOT LET WHAT HAPPENED LAST NIGHT ESCALATE FURTHER.
"VALENTINE GALLO."
"HEY, YA THINK THE KID DID DA MATH AND FIGURED OUT IT WAS YOU, DON, WHO WHACKED HIS FATHER A MILLION YEARS AGO?
"YOU THINK IT' CONNECTED?

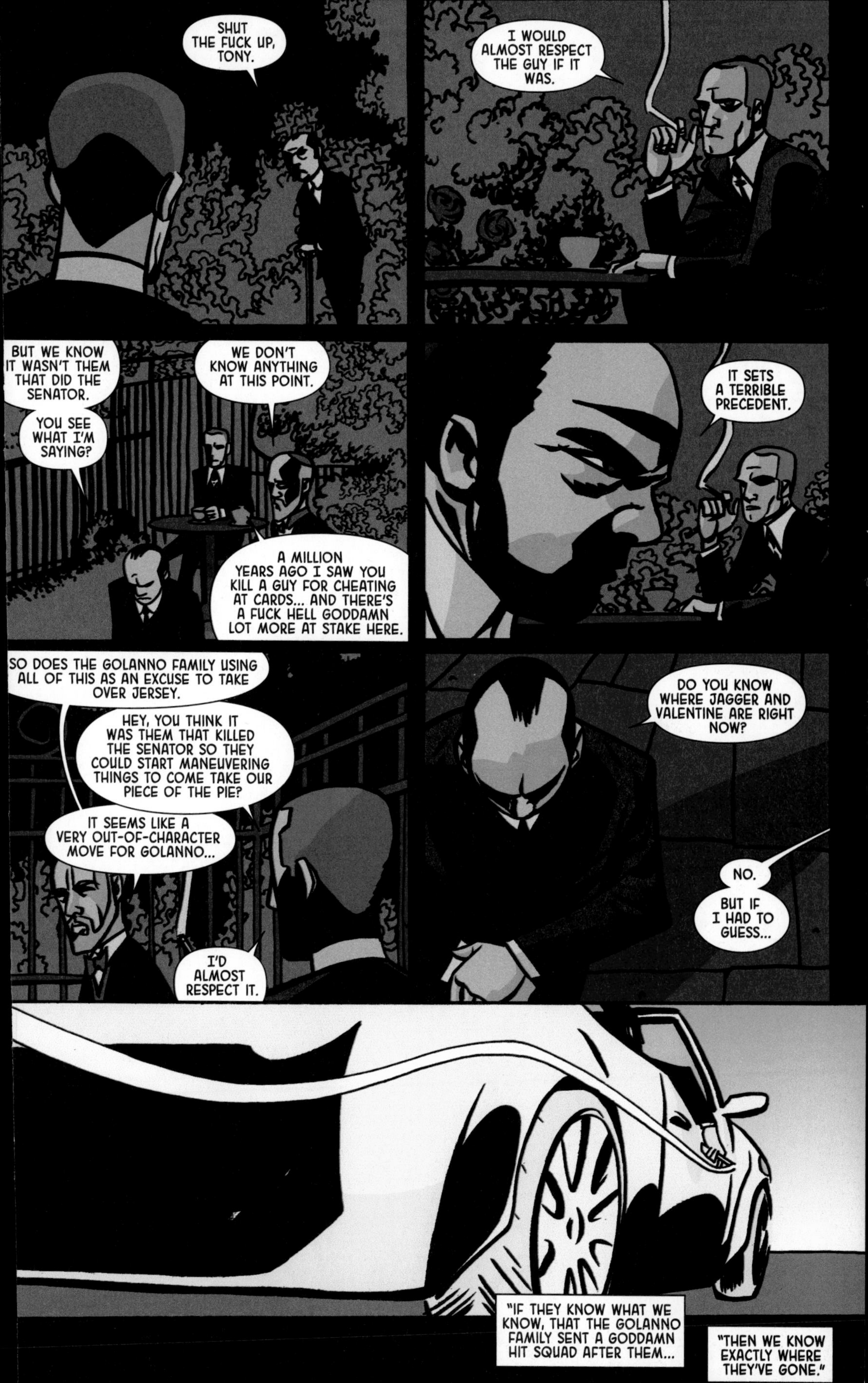
SHUT THE FUCK UP, TONY.
I WOULD ALMOST RESPECT THE GUY IF IT WAS.
BUT WE KNOW IT WASN'T THEM THAT DID THE SENATOR.
YOU SEE WHAT I'M SAYING?
WE DON'T KNOW ANYTHING AT THIS POINT.
A MILLION YEARS AGO I SAW YOU KILL A GUY FOR CHEATING AT CARDS... AND THERE'S A FUCK HELL GODDAMN LOT MORE AT STAKE HERE.
IT SETS A TERRIBLE PRECEDENT.
SO DOES THE GOLANNO FAMILY USING ALL OF THIS AS AN EXCUSE TO TAKE OVER JERSEY.
HEY, YOU THINK IT WAS THEM THAT KILLED THE SENATOR SO THEY COULD START MANEUVERING THINGS TO COME TAKE OUR PIECE OF THE PIE?
IT SEEMS LIKE A VERY OUT-OF-CHARACTER MOVE FOR GOLANNO...
I'D ALMOST RESPECT IT.
DO YOU KNOW WHERE JAGGER AND VALENTINE ARE RIGHT NOW?
NO.
BUT IF I HAD TO GUESS...
"IF THEY KNOW WHAT WE KNOW, THAT THE GOLANNO FAMILY SENT A GODDAMN HIT SQUAD AFTER THEM...
"THEN WE KNOW EXACTLY WHERE THEY'VE GONE."

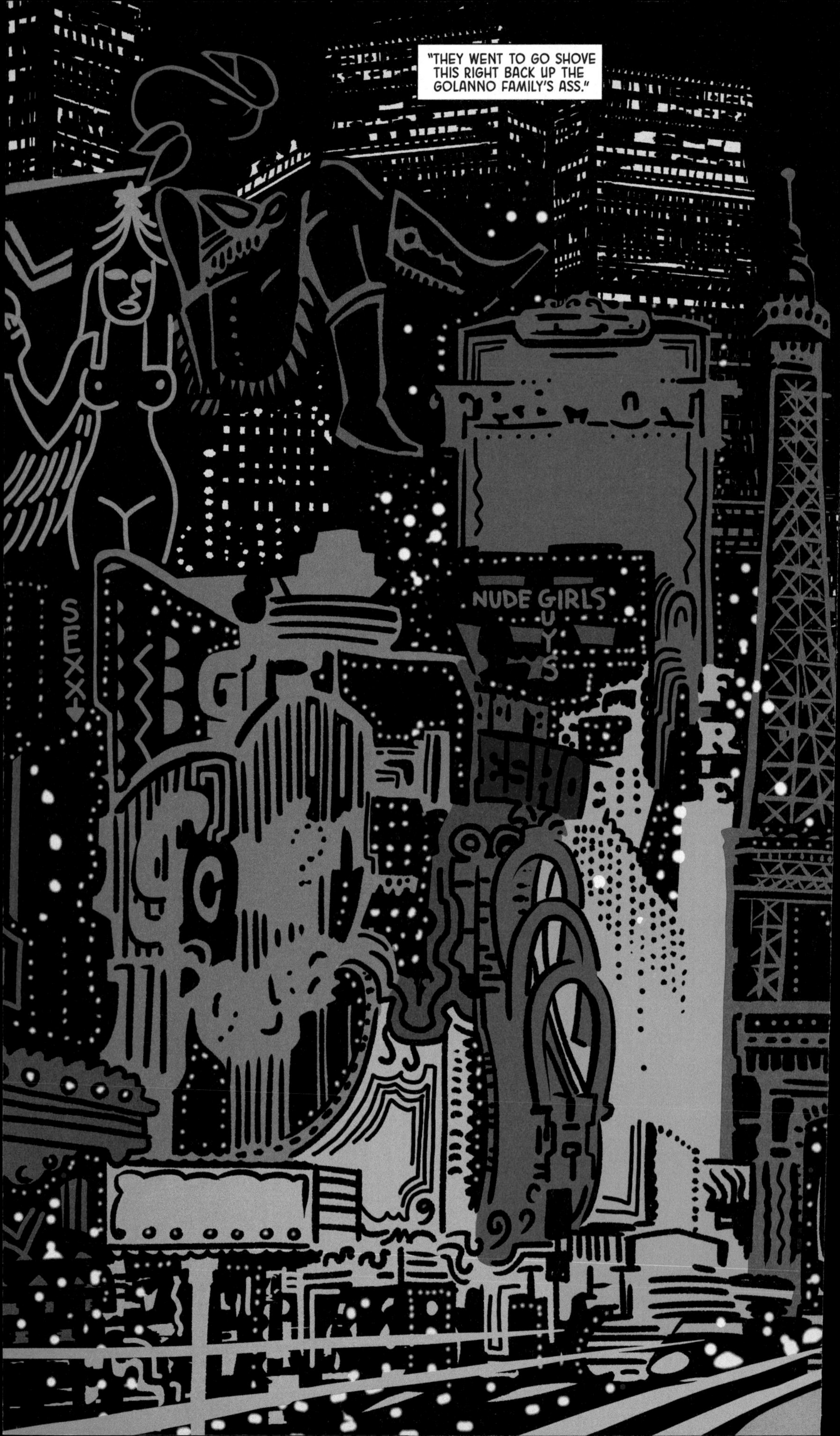
"THEY WENT TO GO SHOVE THIS RIGHT BACK UP THE GOLANNO FAMILY'S ASS."
NUDE GIRLS
GUYS
SEXX

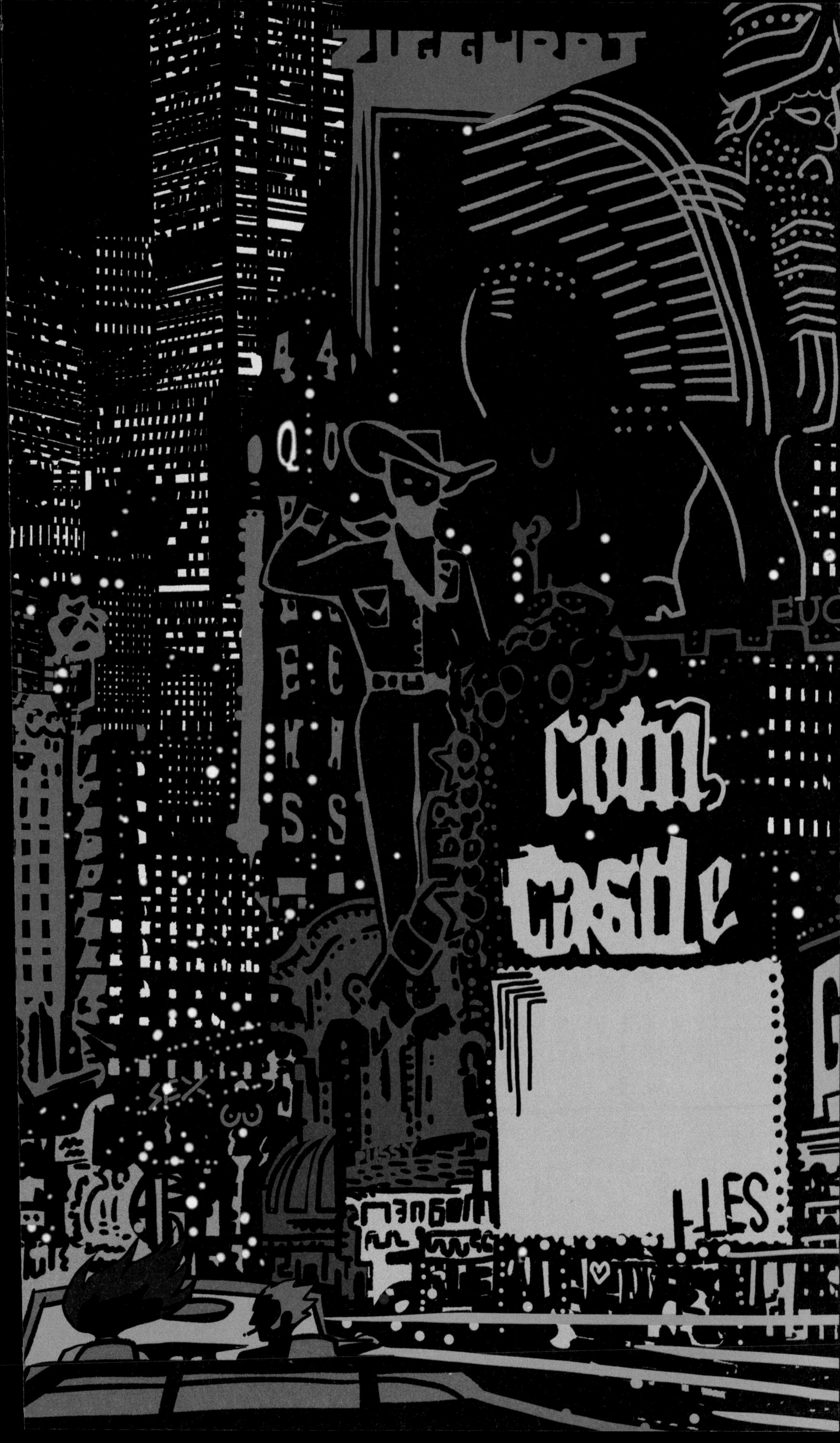

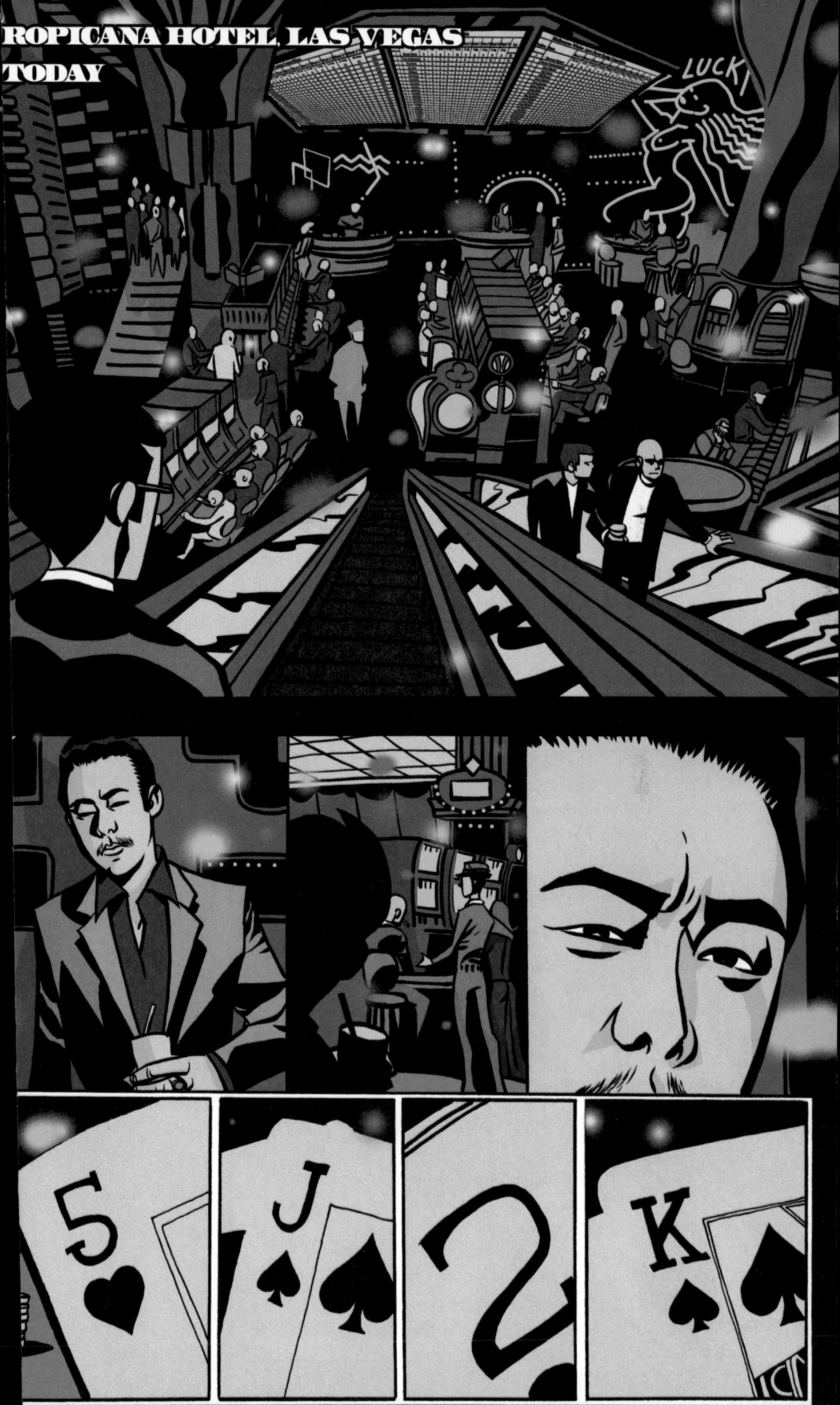
ROPICANA HOTEL, LAS VEGAS
TODAY
LUCKY

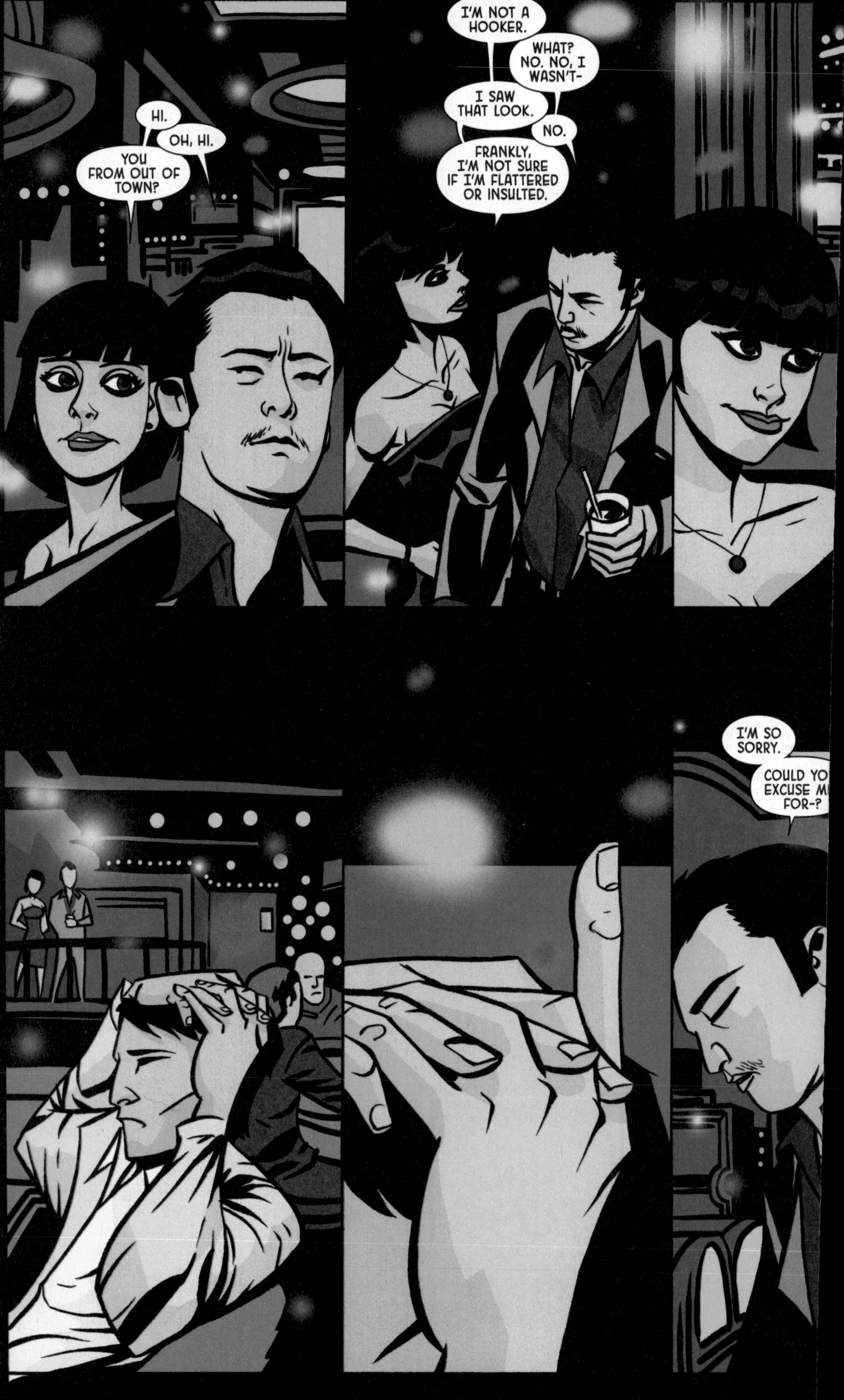
HI.
OH, HI.
YOU FROM OUT OF TOWN?
I'M NOT A HOOKER.
WHAT? NO. NO, I WASN'T-
I SAW THAT LOOK.
NO.
FRANKLY, I'M NOT SURE IF I'M FLATTERED OR INSULTED.
I'M SO SORRY.
COULD YO EXCUSE M FOR-?

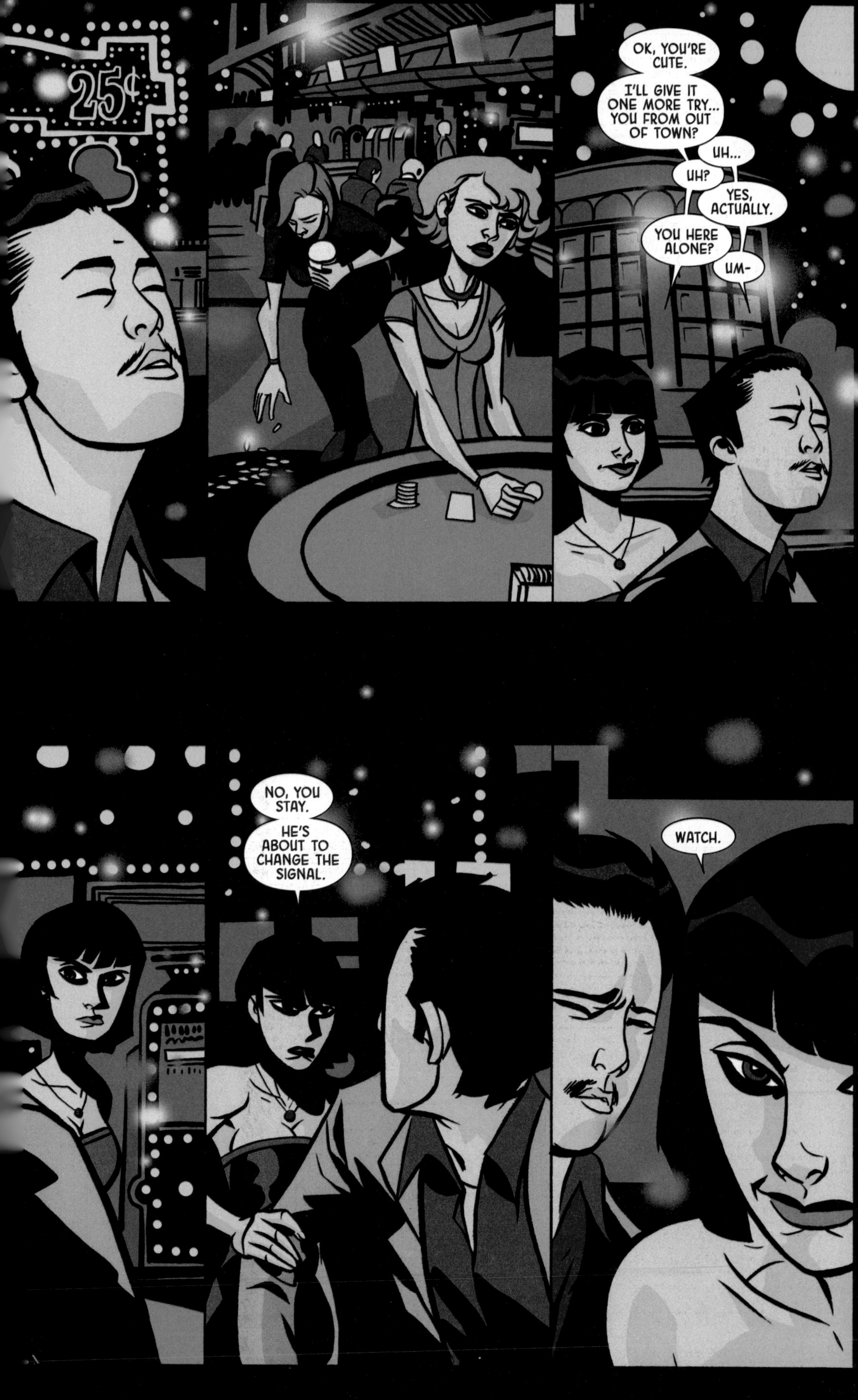
25¢
OK, YOU'RE CUTE.
I'LL GIVE IT ONE MORE TRY... YOU FROM OUT OF TOWN?
UH...
UH?
YES, ACTUALLY.
YOU HERE ALONE?
UM-
NO, YOU STAY.
HE'S ABOUT TO CHANGE THE SIGNAL.
WATCH.

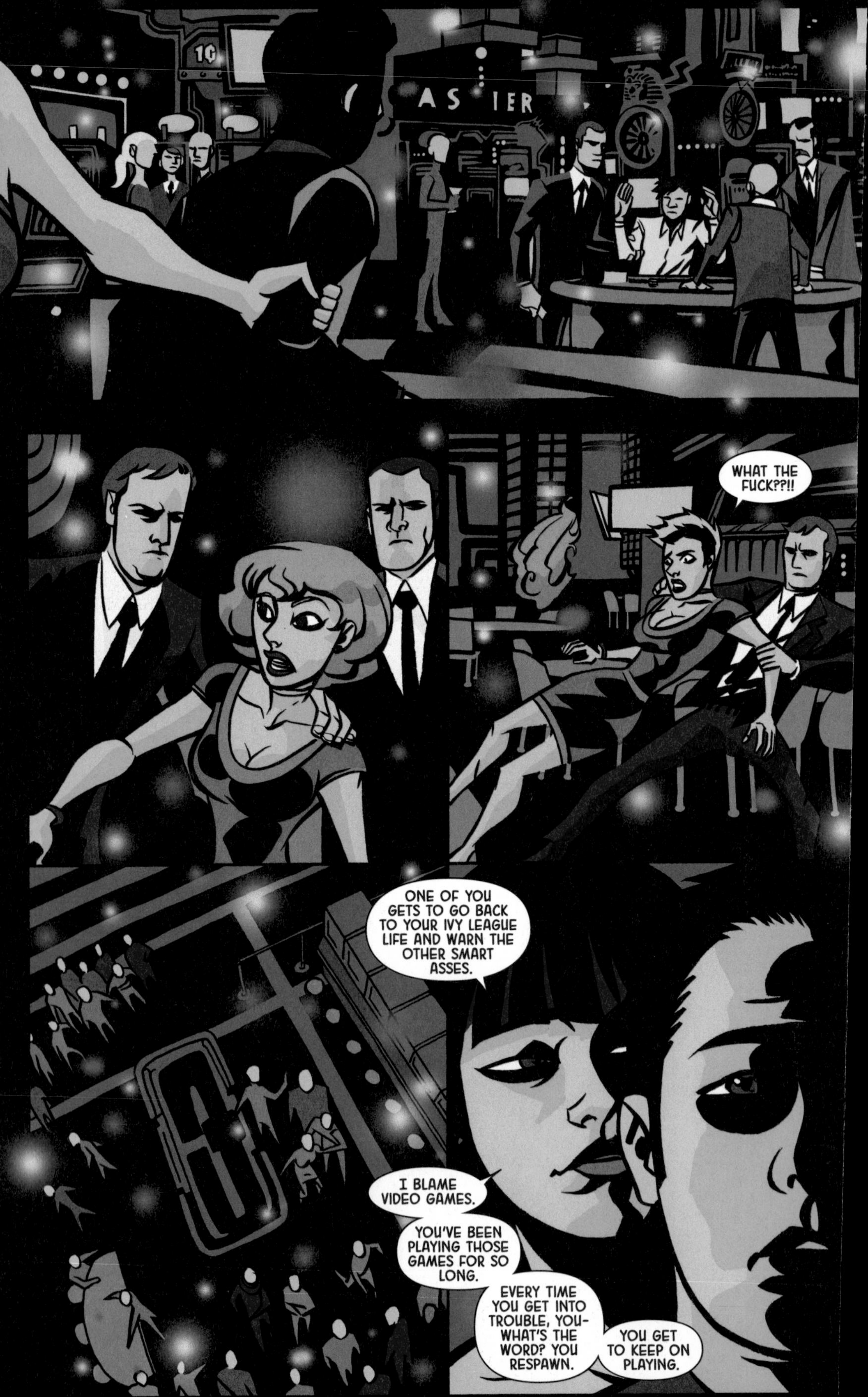
AS IER
WHAT THE FUCK??!!
ONE OF YOU GETS TO GO BACK TO YOUR IVY LEAGUE LIFE AND WARN THE OTHER SMART ASSES.
I BLAME VIDEO GAMES.
YOU'VE BEEN PLAYING THOSE GAMES FOR SO LONG.
EVERY TIME YOU GET INTO TROUBLE, YOU- WHAT'S THE WORD? YOU RESPAWN.
YOU GET TO KEEP ON PLAYING.

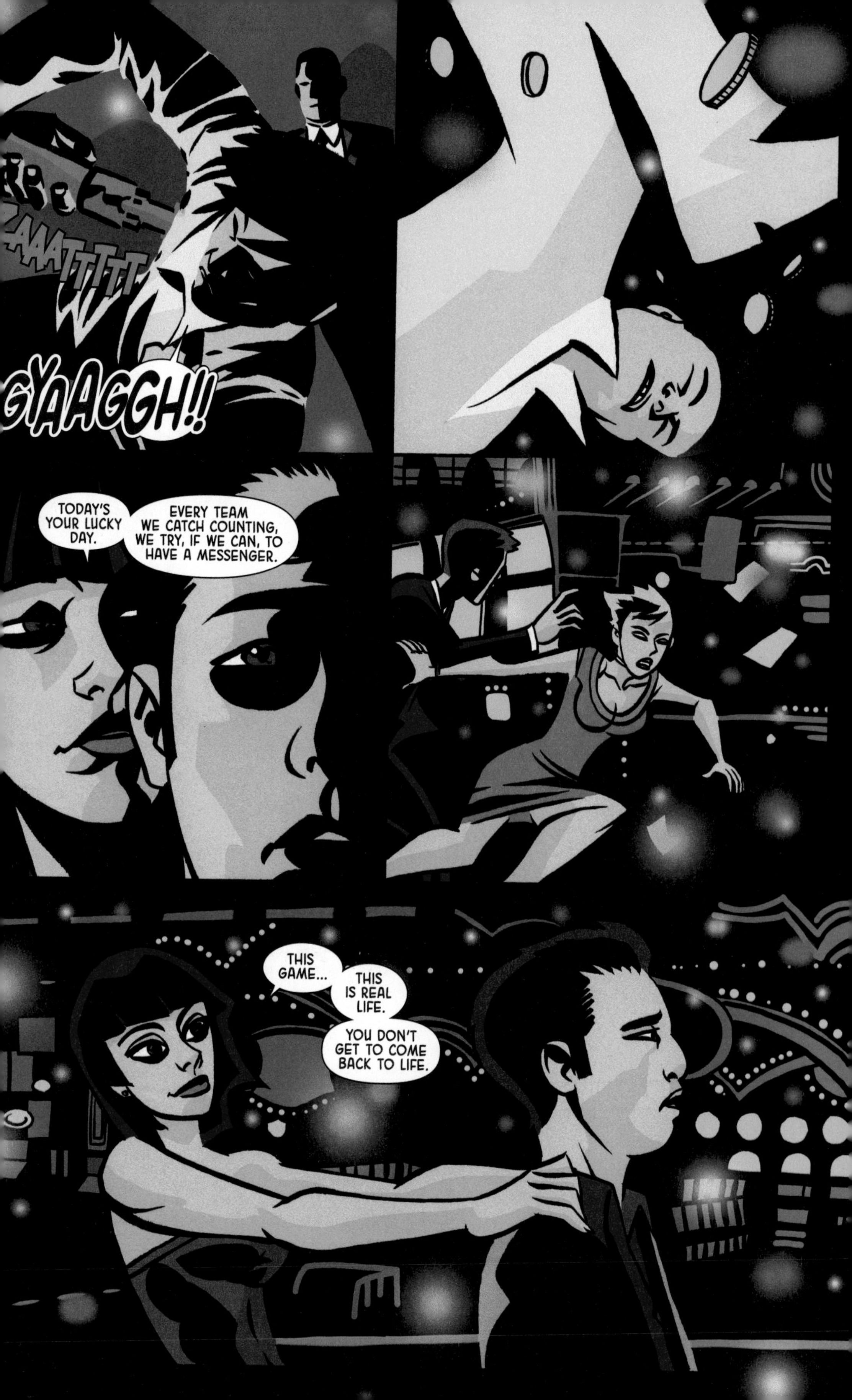

ZAAATTTTTT
GYAAGGH!!
TODAY'S YOUR LUCKY DAY.
EVERY TEAM WE CATCH COUNTING, WE TRY, IF WE CAN, TO HAVE A MESSENGER.
THIS GAME...
THIS IS REAL LIFE.
YOU DON'T GET TO COME BACK TO LIFE.

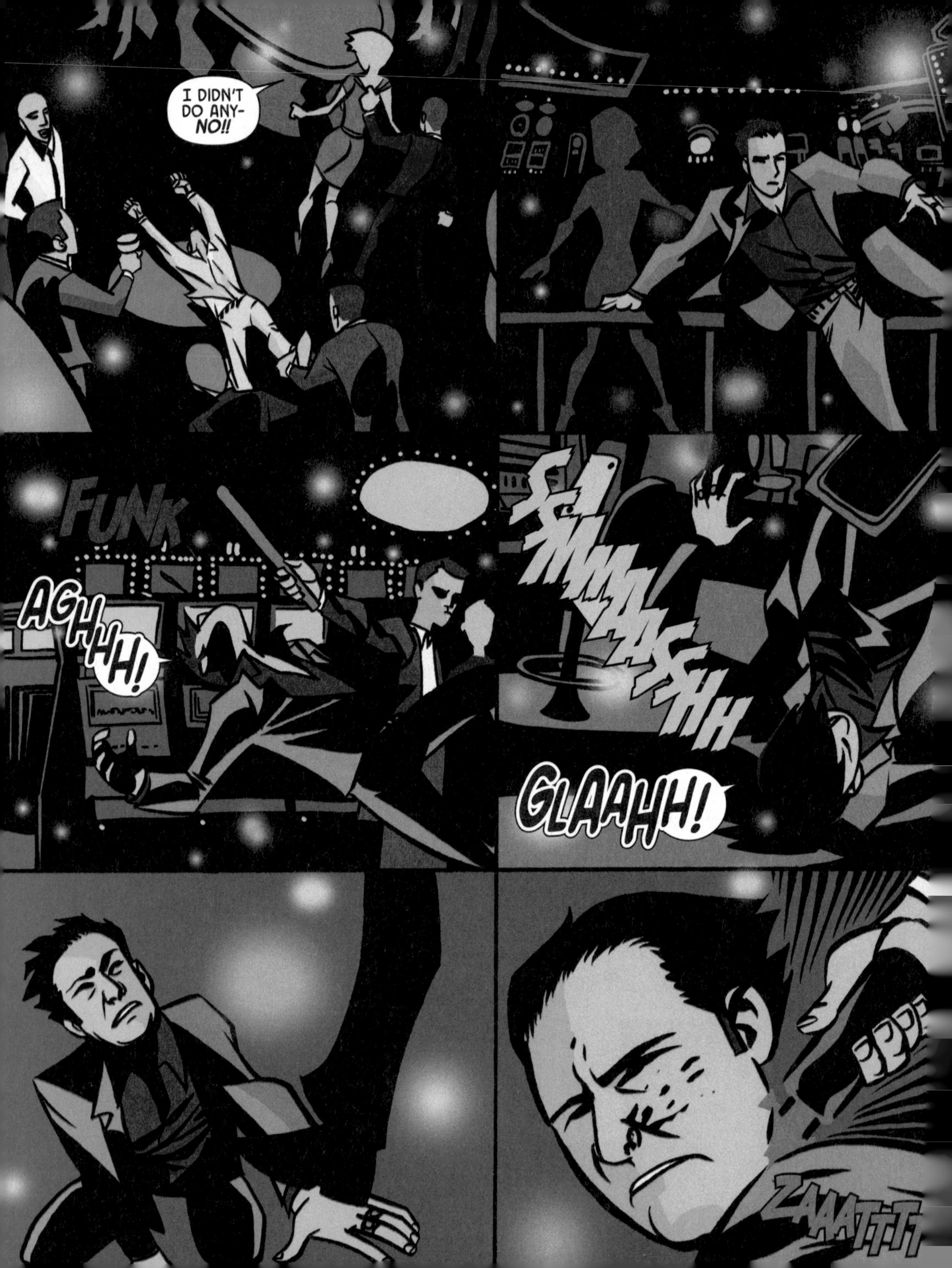
I DIDN'T DO ANY- NO!!
FUNK
AGHHHH!
SMMMASHHH
GLAAHH!
ZAAATTTT

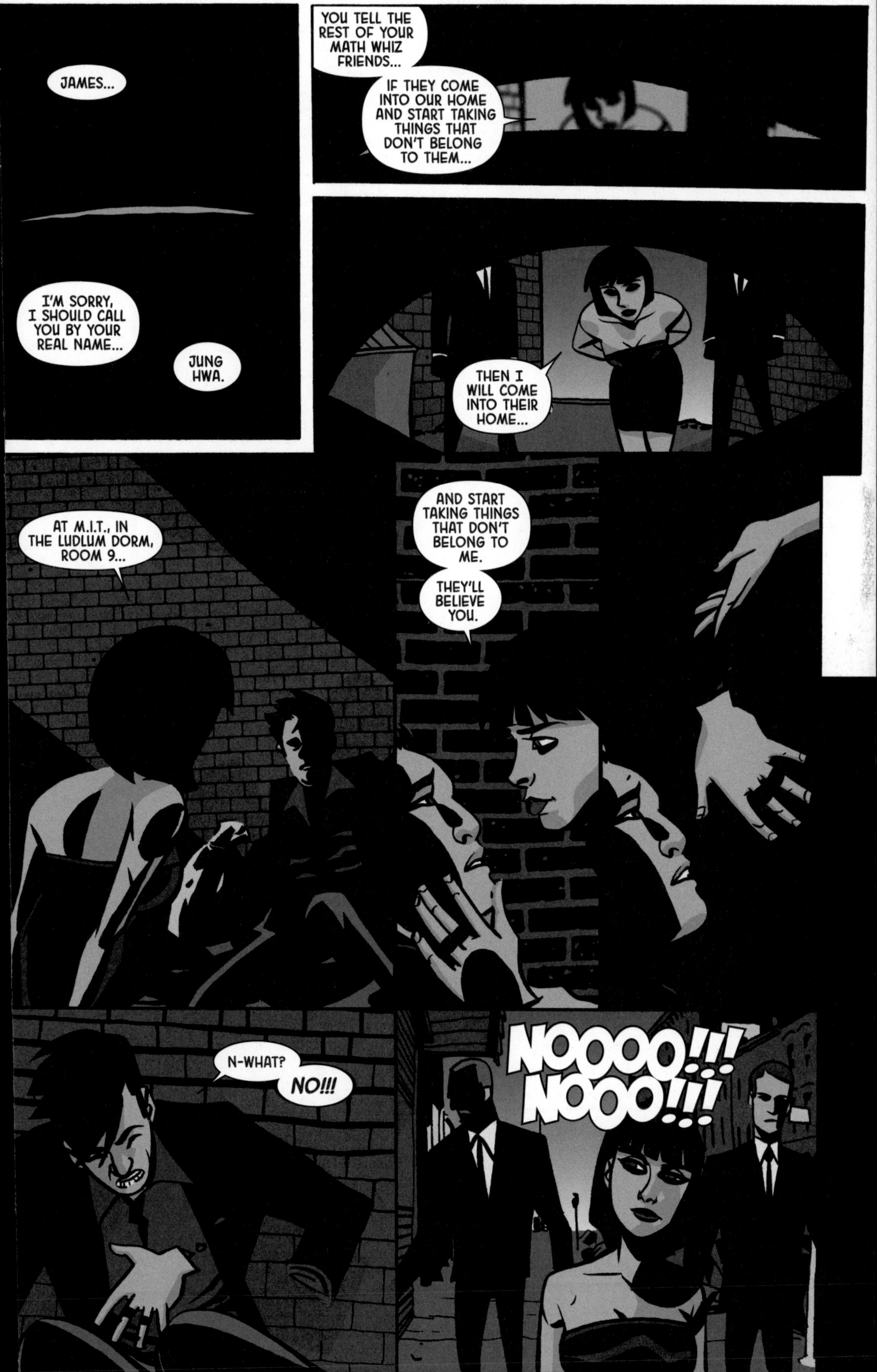
JAMES...
I'M SORRY, I SHOULD CALL YOU BY YOUR REAL NAME...
JUNG HWA.
YOU TELL THE REST OF YOUR MATH WHIZ FRIENDS...
IF THEY COME INTO OUR HOME AND START TAKING THINGS THAT DON'T BELONG TO THEM...
THEN I WILL COME INTO THEIR HOME...
AT M.I.T., IN THE LUDLUM DORM, ROOM 9...
AND START TAKING THINGS THAT DON'T BELONG TO ME.
THEY'LL BELIEVE YOU.
N-WHAT?
NO!!!
NOOOO!!! NOOO!!!

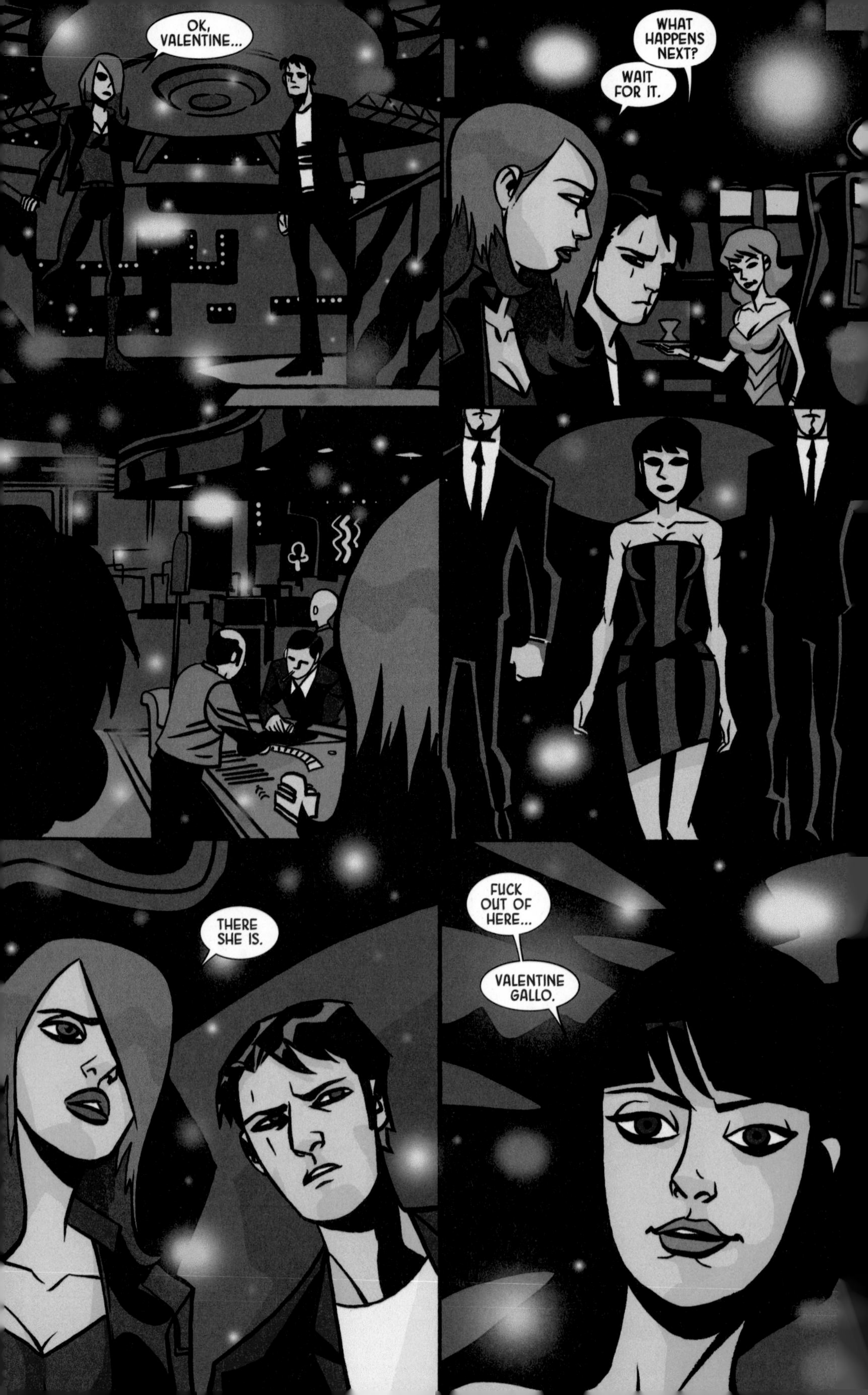
OK, VALENTINE...
WHAT HAPPENS NEXT?
WAIT FOR IT.
THERE SHE IS.
FUCK OUT OF HERE...
VALENTINE GALLO.

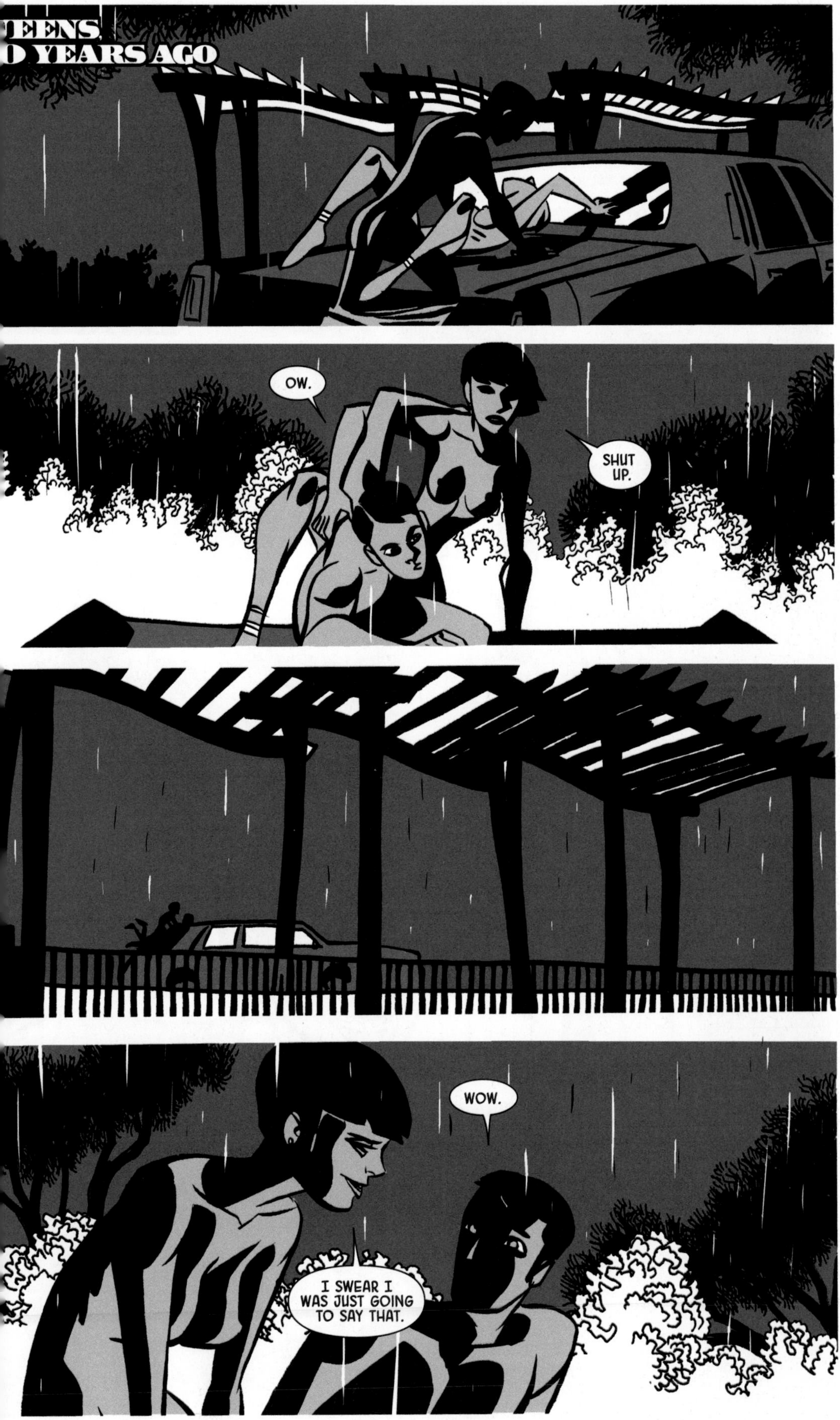
EENS,
YEARS AGO
OW.
SHUT UP.
WOW.
I SWEAR I WAS JUST GOING TO SAY THAT.

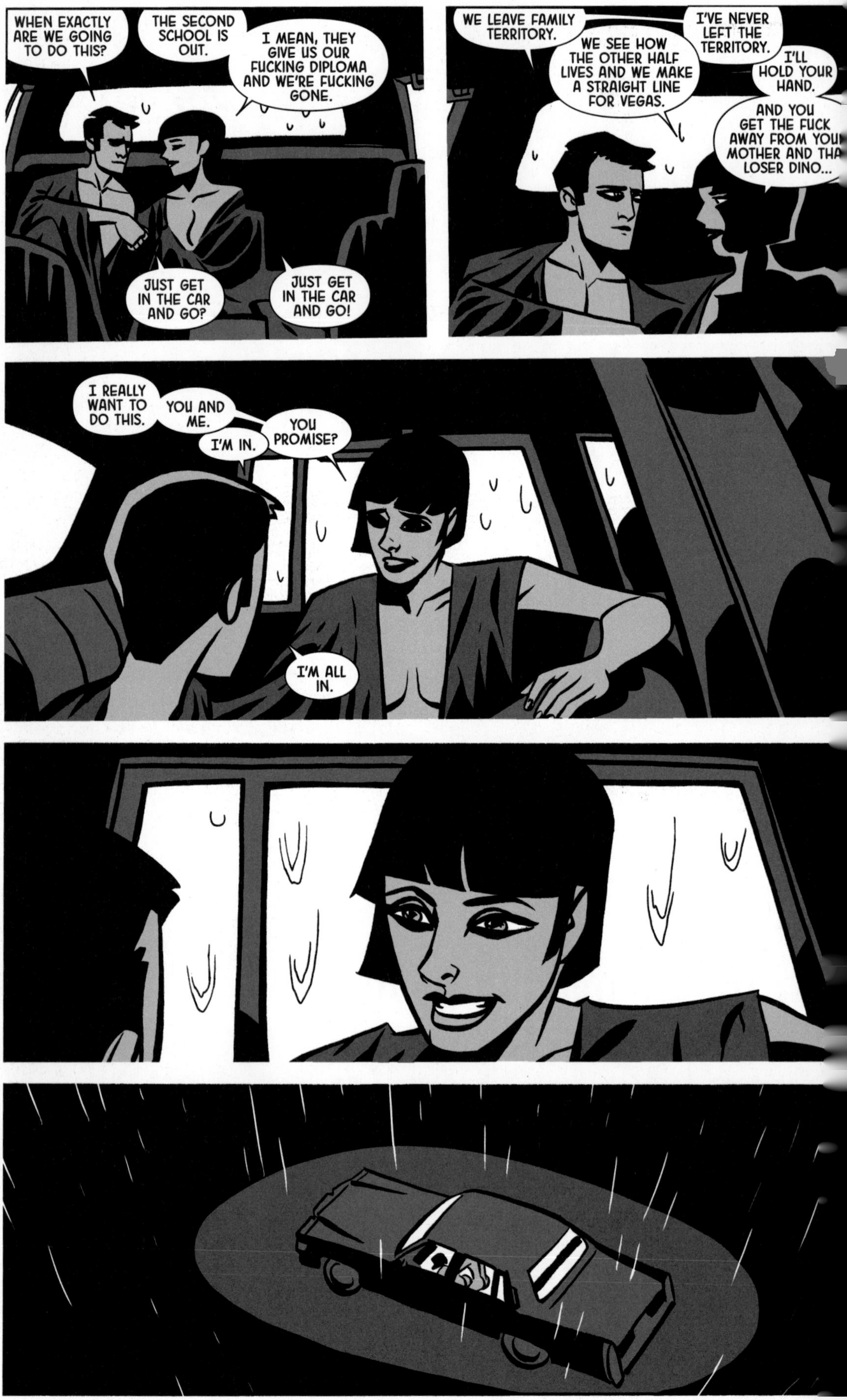

WHEN EXACTLY ARE WE GOING TO DO THIS?
THE SECOND SCHOOL IS OUT.
I MEAN, THEY GIVE US OUR FUCKING DIPLOMA AND WE'RE FUCKING GONE.
JUST GET IN THE CAR AND GO?
JUST GET IN THE CAR AND GO!
WE LEAVE FAMILY TERRITORY.
WE SEE HOW THE OTHER HALF LIVES AND WE MAKE A STRAIGHT LINE FOR VEGAS.
I'VE NEVER LEFT THE TERRITORY.
I'LL HOLD YOUR HAND.
I REALLY WANT TO DO THIS.
YOU AND ME.
I'M IN.
YOU PROMISE?
I'M ALL IN.

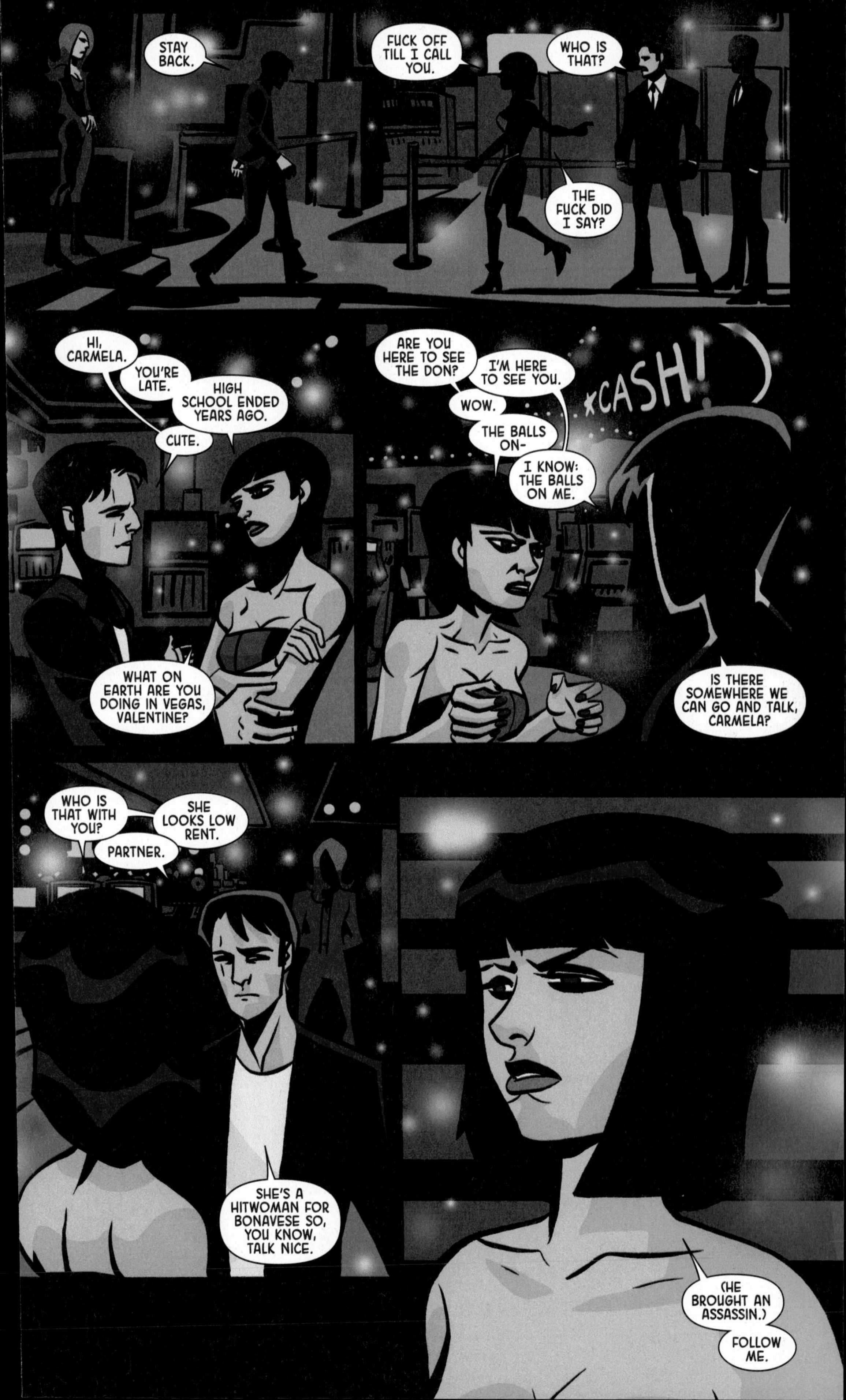
STAY BACK.
FUCK OFF TILL I CALL YOU.
WHO IS THAT?
THE FUCK DID I SAY?
HI, CARMELA.
YOU'RE LATE.
HIGH SCHOOL ENDED YEARS AGO.
CUTE.
WHAT ON EARTH ARE YOU DOING IN VEGAS, VALENTINE?
ARE YOU HERE TO SEE THE DON?
I'M HERE TO SEE YOU.
WOW.
THE BALLS ON-
I KNOW: THE BALLS ON ME.
*CASH!
IS THERE SOMEWHERE WE CAN GO AND TALK, CARMELA?
WHO IS THAT WITH YOU?
SHE LOOKS LOW RENT.
PARTNER.
SHE'S A HITWOMAN FOR BONAVESE SO, YOU KNOW, TALK NICE.
(HE BROUGHT AN ASSASSIN.)
FOLLOW ME.

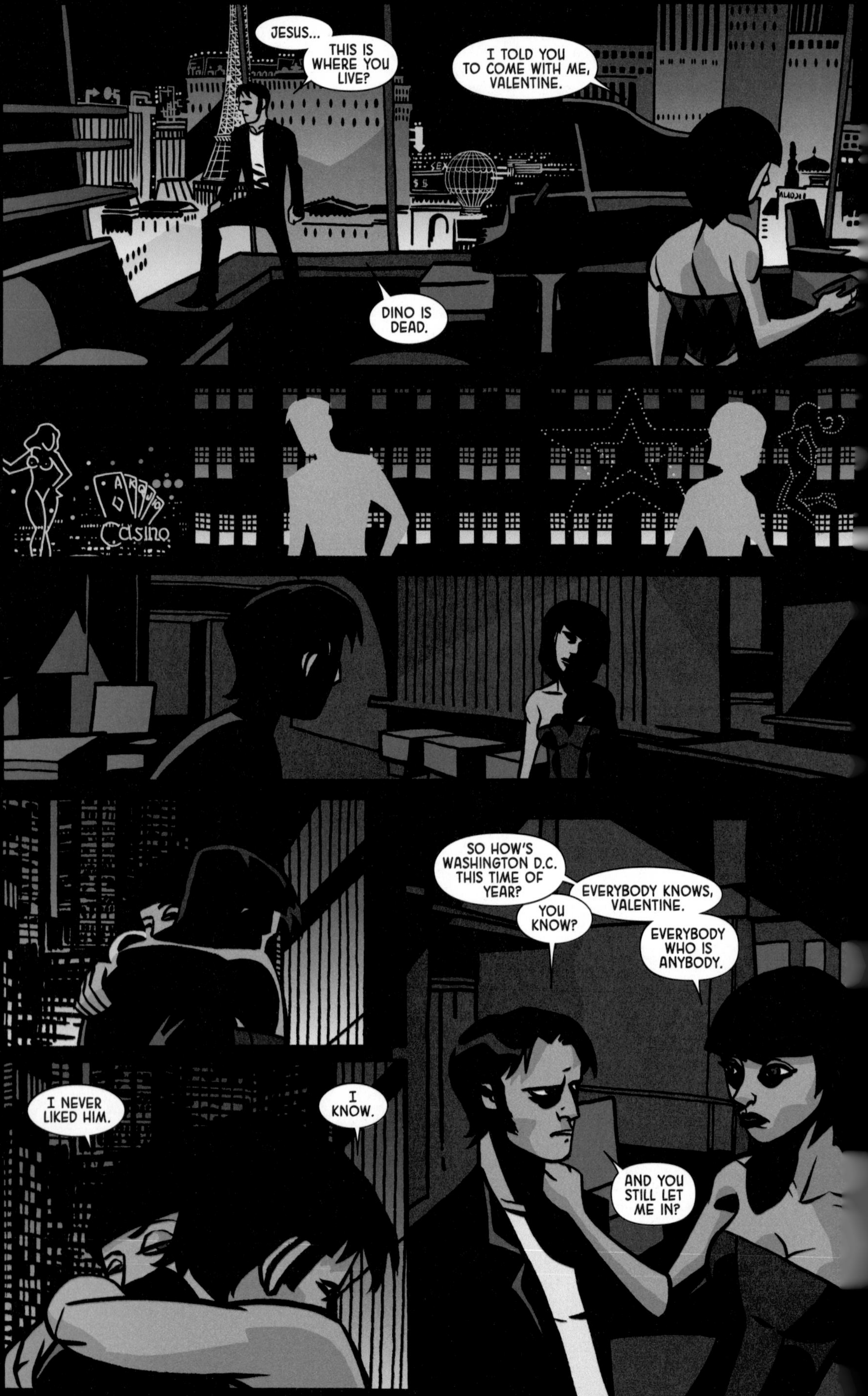

JESUS...
THIS IS WHERE YOU LIVE?
I TOLD YOU TO COME WITH ME, VALENTINE.
DINO IS DEAD.
Casino
SO HOW'S WASHINGTON D.C. THIS TIME OF YEAR?
YOU KNOW?
EVERYBODY KNOWS, VALENTINE.
EVERYBODY WHO IS ANYBODY.
I NEVER LIKED HIM.
I KNOW.
AND YOU STILL LET ME IN?

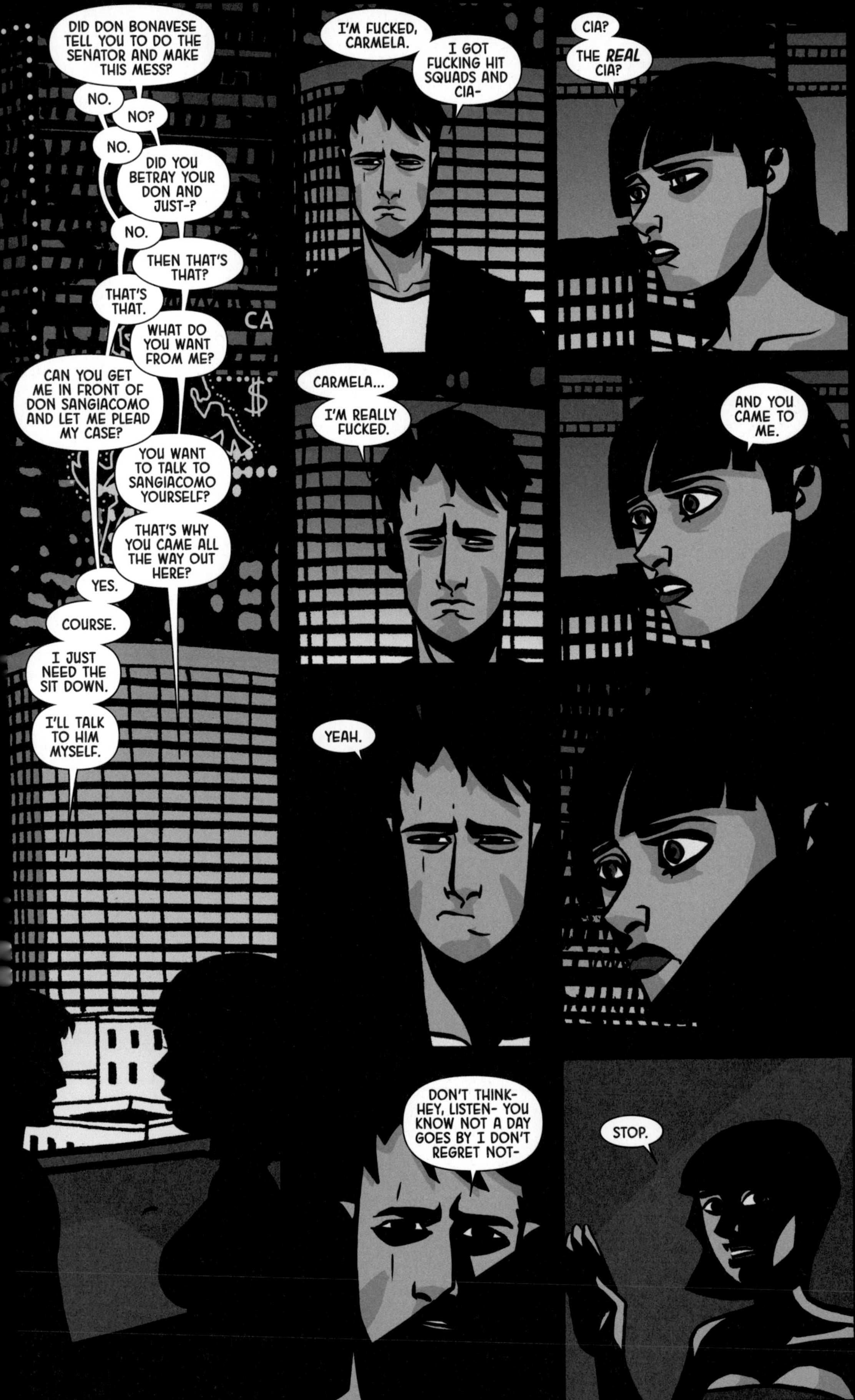

DID DON BONAVESE TELL YOU TO DO THE SENATOR AND MAKE THIS MESS?
NO.
NO?
NO.
DID YOU BETRAY YOUR DON AND JUST-?
NO.
THEN THAT'S THAT?
THAT'S THAT.
WHAT DO YOU WANT FROM ME?
CAN YOU GET ME IN FRONT OF DON SANGIACOMO AND LET ME PLEAD MY CASE?
YOU WANT TO TALK TO SANGIACOMO YOURSELF?
THAT'S WHY YOU CAME ALL THE WAY OUT HERE?
YES.
COURSE.
I JUST NEED THE SIT DOWN.
I'LL TALK TO HIM MYSELF.
I'M FUCKED, CARMELA.
I GOT FUCKING HIT SQUADS AND CIA-
CIA?
THE *REAL* CIA?
CARMELA...
I'M REALLY FUCKED.
AND YOU CAME TO ME.
YEAH.
DON'T THINK- HEY, LISTEN- YOU KNOW NOT A DAY GOES BY I DON'T REGRET NOT-
STOP.

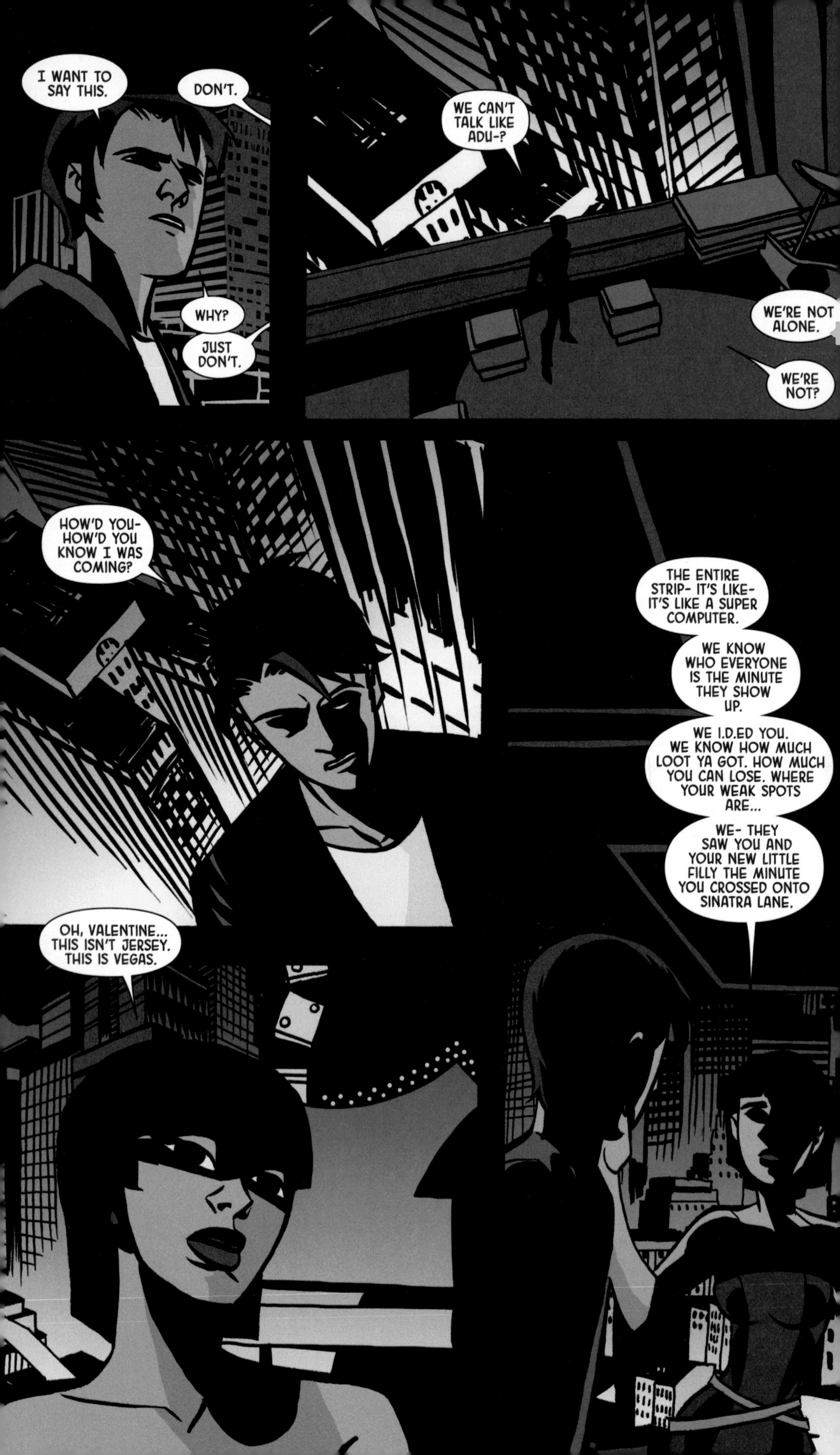
I WANT TO SAY THIS.
DON'T.
WHY?
JUST DON'T.
WE CAN'T TALK LIKE ADU-?
WE'RE NOT ALONE.
WE'RE NOT?
HOW'D YOU- HOW'D YOU KNOW I WAS COMING?
THE ENTIRE STRIP- IT'S LIKE- IT'S LIKE A SUPER COMPUTER.
WE KNOW WHO EVERYONE IS THE MINUTE THEY SHOW UP.
WE I.D.ED YOU. WE KNOW HOW MUCH LOOT YA GOT. HOW MUCH YOU CAN LOSE. WHERE YOUR WEAK SPOTS ARE...
WE- THEY SAW YOU AND YOUR NEW LITTLE FILLY THE MINUTE YOU CROSSED ONTO SINATRA LANE.
OH, VALENTINE... THIS ISN'T JERSEY. THIS IS VEGAS.

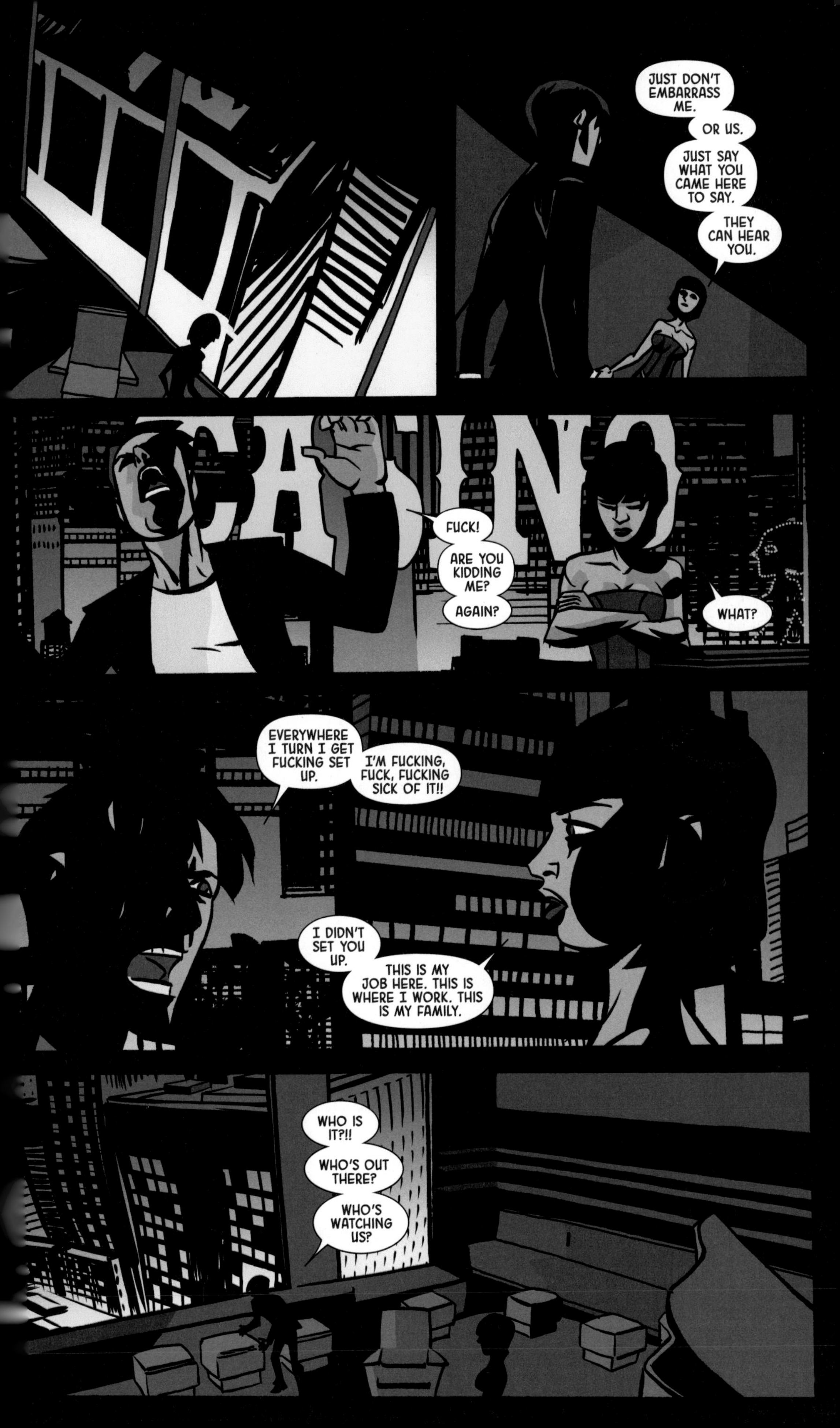
JUST DON'T EMBARRASS ME.
OR US.
JUST SAY WHAT YOU CAME HERE TO SAY.
THEY CAN HEAR YOU.
CASINO
FUCK!
ARE YOU KIDDING ME?
AGAIN?
WHAT?
EVERYWHERE I TURN I GET FUCKING SET UP.
I'M FUCKING, FUCK, FUCKING SICK OF IT!!
I DIDN'T SET YOU UP.
THIS IS MY JOB HERE. THIS IS WHERE I WORK. THIS IS MY FAMILY.
WHO IS IT?!!
WHO'S OUT THERE?
WHO'S WATCHING US?

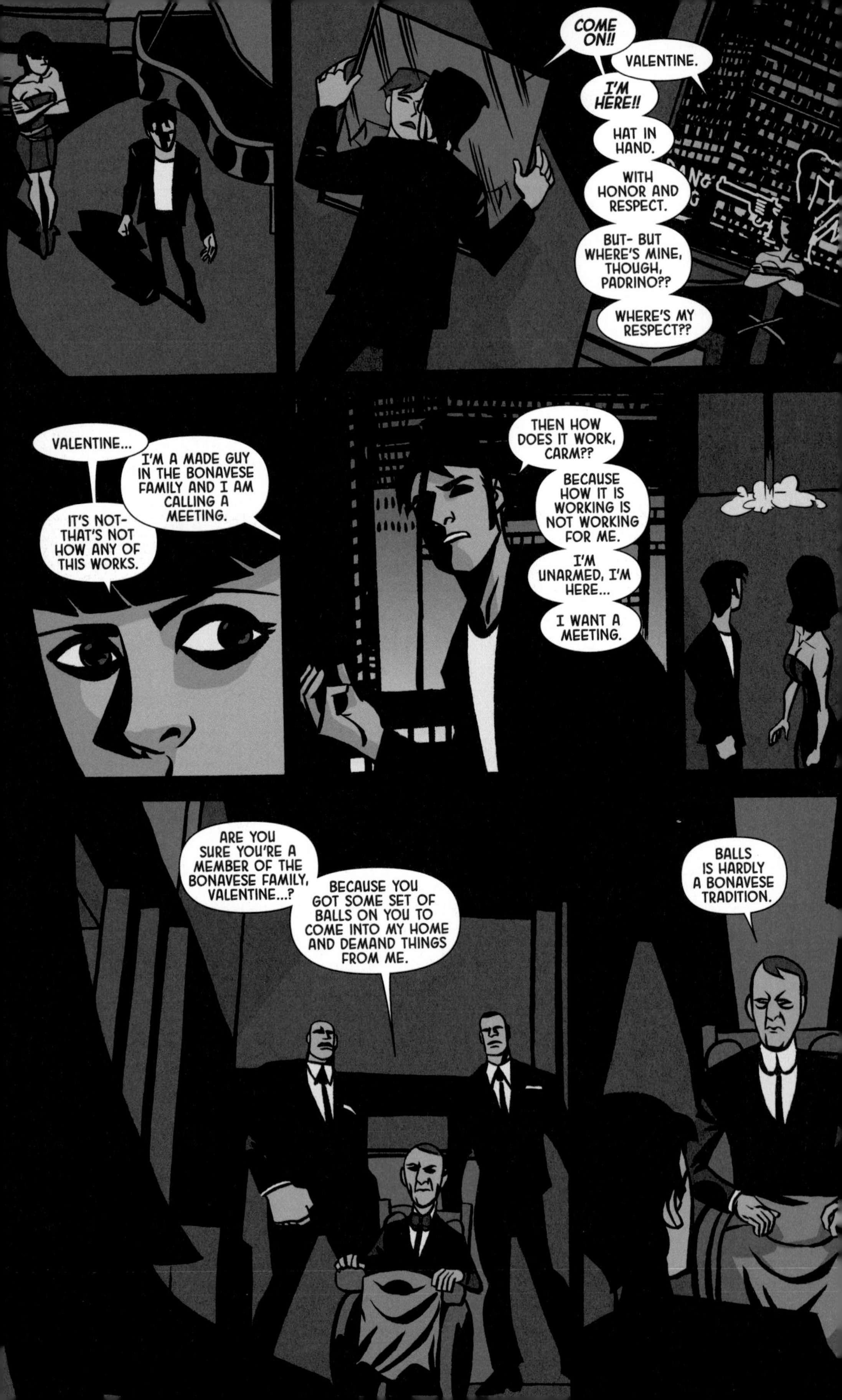

COME ON!!
VALENTINE.
I'M HERE!!
HAT IN HAND.
WITH HONOR AND RESPECT.
BUT- BUT WHERE'S MINE, THOUGH, PADRINO??
WHERE'S MY RESPECT??
VALENTINE...
I'M A MADE GUY IN THE BONAVESE FAMILY AND I AM CALLING A MEETING.
IT'S NOT- THAT'S NOT HOW ANY OF THIS WORKS.
THEN HOW DOES IT WORK, CARM??
BECAUSE HOW IT IS WORKING IS NOT WORKING FOR ME.
I'M UNARMED, I'M HERE...
I WANT A MEETING.
ARE YOU SURE YOU'RE A MEMBER OF THE BONAVESE FAMILY, VALENTINE...?
BECAUSE YOU GOT SOME SET OF BALLS ON YOU TO COME INTO MY HOME AND DEMAND THINGS FROM ME.
BALLS IS HARDLY A BONAVESE TRADITION.

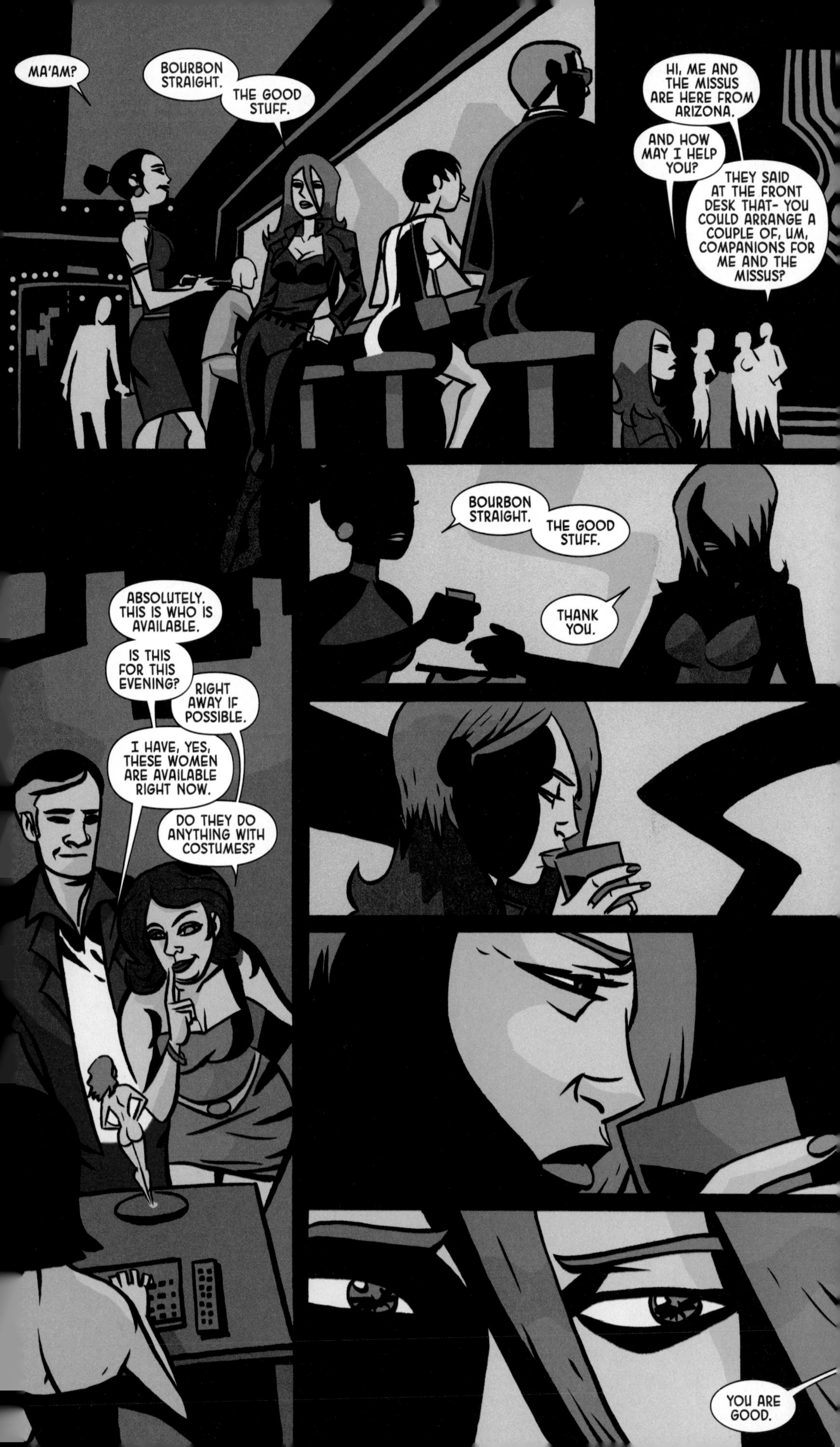
MA'AM?
BOURBON STRAIGHT.
THE GOOD STUFF.
HI, ME AND THE MISSUS ARE HERE FROM ARIZONA.
AND HOW MAY I HELP YOU?
THEY SAID AT THE FRONT DESK THAT- YOU COULD ARRANGE A COUPLE OF, UM, COMPANIONS FOR ME AND THE MISSUS?
BOURBON STRAIGHT.
THE GOOD STUFF.
THANK YOU.
ABSOLUTELY. THIS IS WHO IS AVAILABLE.
IS THIS FOR THIS EVENING?
RIGHT AWAY IF POSSIBLE.
I HAVE, YES, THESE WOMEN ARE AVAILABLE RIGHT NOW.
DO THEY DO ANYTHING WITH COSTUMES?
YOU ARE GOOD.

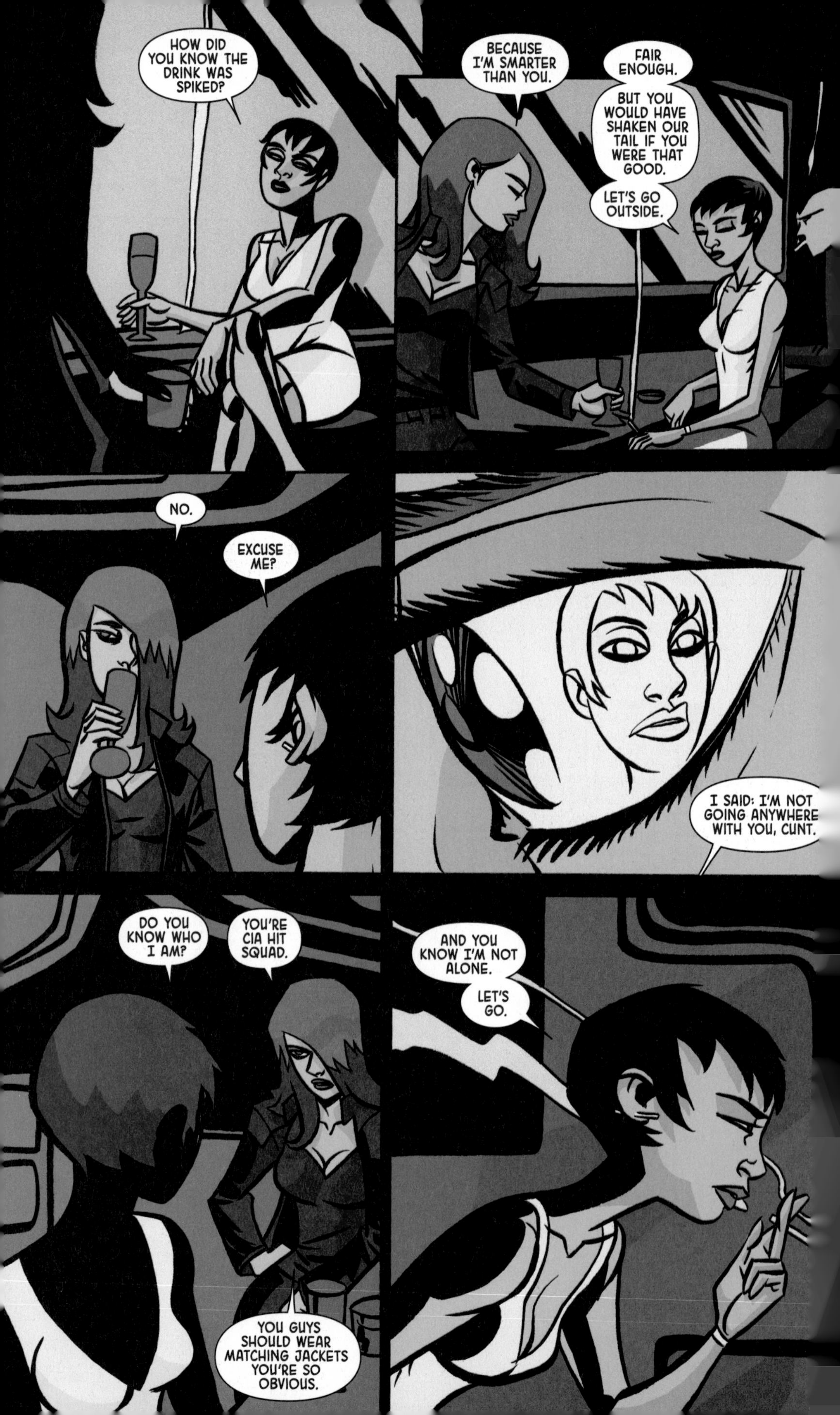
HOW DID YOU KNOW THE DRINK WAS SPIKED?
BECAUSE I'M SMARTER THAN YOU.
FAIR ENOUGH.
BUT YOU WOULD HAVE SHAKEN OUR TAIL IF YOU WERE THAT GOOD.
LET'S GO OUTSIDE.
NO.
EXCUSE ME?
I SAID: I'M NOT GOING ANYWHERE WITH YOU, CUNT.
DO YOU KNOW WHO I AM?
YOU'RE CIA HIT SQUAD.
YOU GUYS SHOULD WEAR MATCHING JACKETS YOU'RE SO OBVIOUS.
AND YOU KNOW I'M NOT ALONE.
LET'S GO.

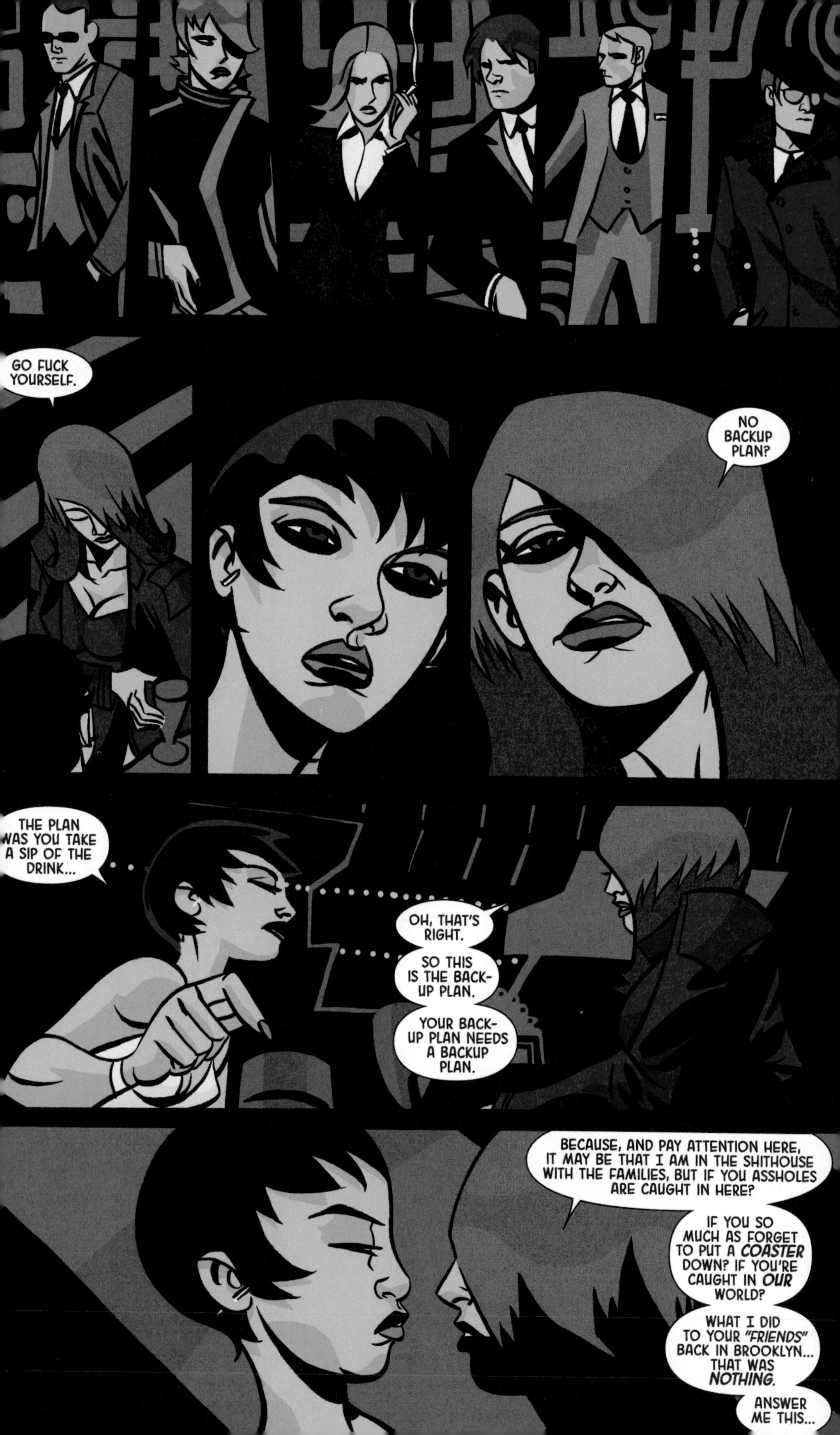
GO FUCK YOURSELF.
NO BACKUP PLAN?
THE PLAN WAS YOU TAKE A SIP OF THE DRINK...
OH, THAT'S RIGHT.
SO THIS IS THE BACK-UP PLAN.
YOUR BACK-UP PLAN NEEDS A BACKUP PLAN.
BECAUSE, AND PAY ATTENTION HERE, IT MAY BE THAT I AM IN THE SHITHOUSE WITH THE FAMILIES, BUT IF YOU ASSHOLES ARE CAUGHT IN HERE?
IF YOU SO MUCH AS FORGET TO PUT A *COASTER* DOWN? IF YOU'RE CAUGHT IN *OUR* WORLD?
WHAT I DID TO YOUR *"FRIENDS"* BACK IN BROOKLYN... THAT WAS *NOTHING*.
ANSWER ME THIS...

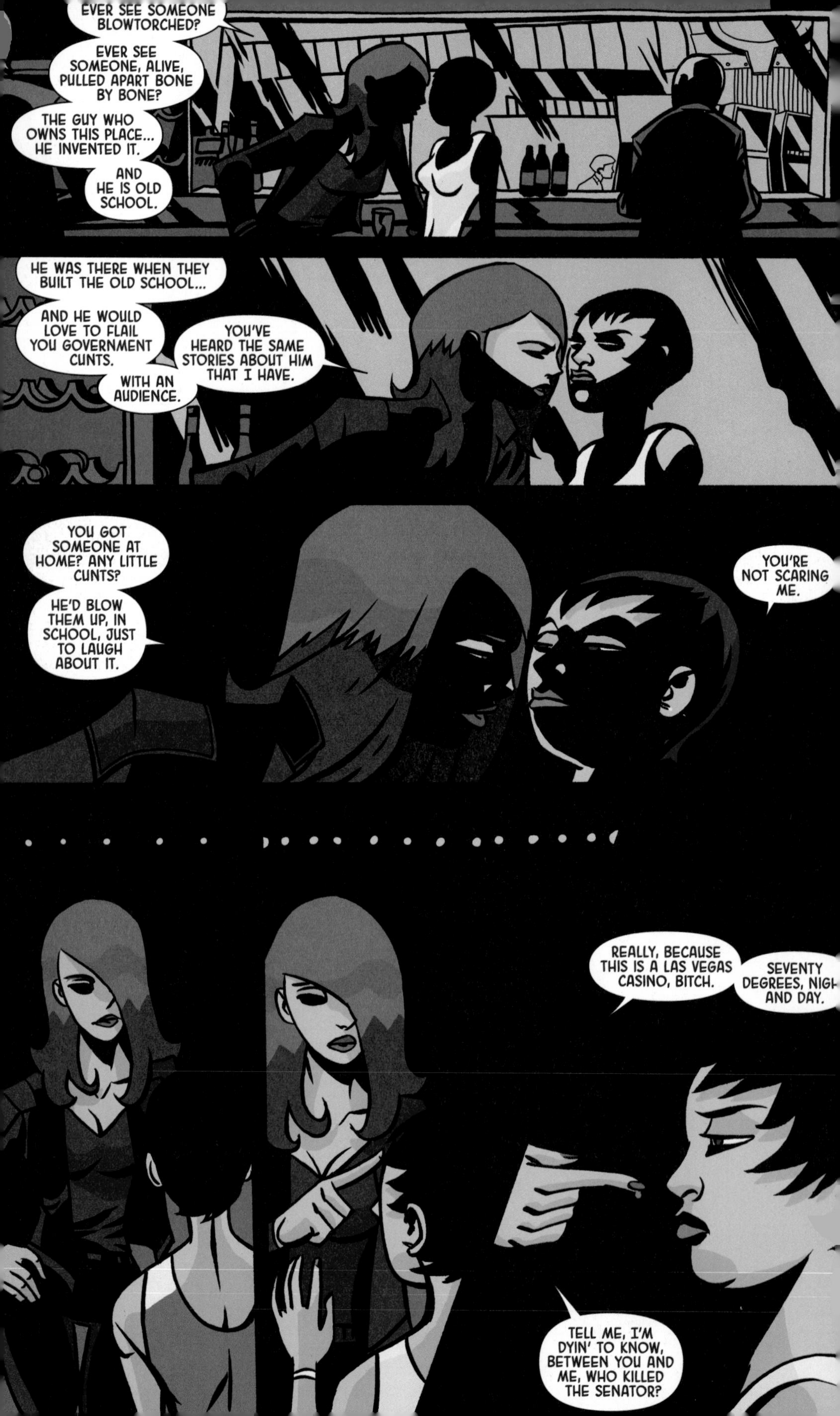
EVER SEE SOMEONE BLOWTORCHED?
EVER SEE SOMEONE, ALIVE, PULLED APART BONE BY BONE?
THE GUY WHO OWNS THIS PLACE... HE INVENTED IT.
AND HE IS OLD SCHOOL.
HE WAS THERE WHEN THEY BUILT THE OLD SCHOOL...
AND HE WOULD LOVE TO FLAIL YOU GOVERNMENT CUNTS.
WITH AN AUDIENCE.
YOU'VE HEARD THE SAME STORIES ABOUT HIM THAT I HAVE.
YOU GOT SOMEONE AT HOME? ANY LITTLE CUNTS?
HE'D BLOW THEM UP, IN SCHOOL, JUST TO LAUGH ABOUT IT.
YOU'RE NOT SCARING ME.
REALLY, BECAUSE THIS IS A LAS VEGAS CASINO, BITCH.
SEVENTY DEGREES, NIGH AND DAY.
TELL ME, I'M DYIN' TO KNOW, BETWEEN YOU AND ME, WHO KILLED THE SENATOR?

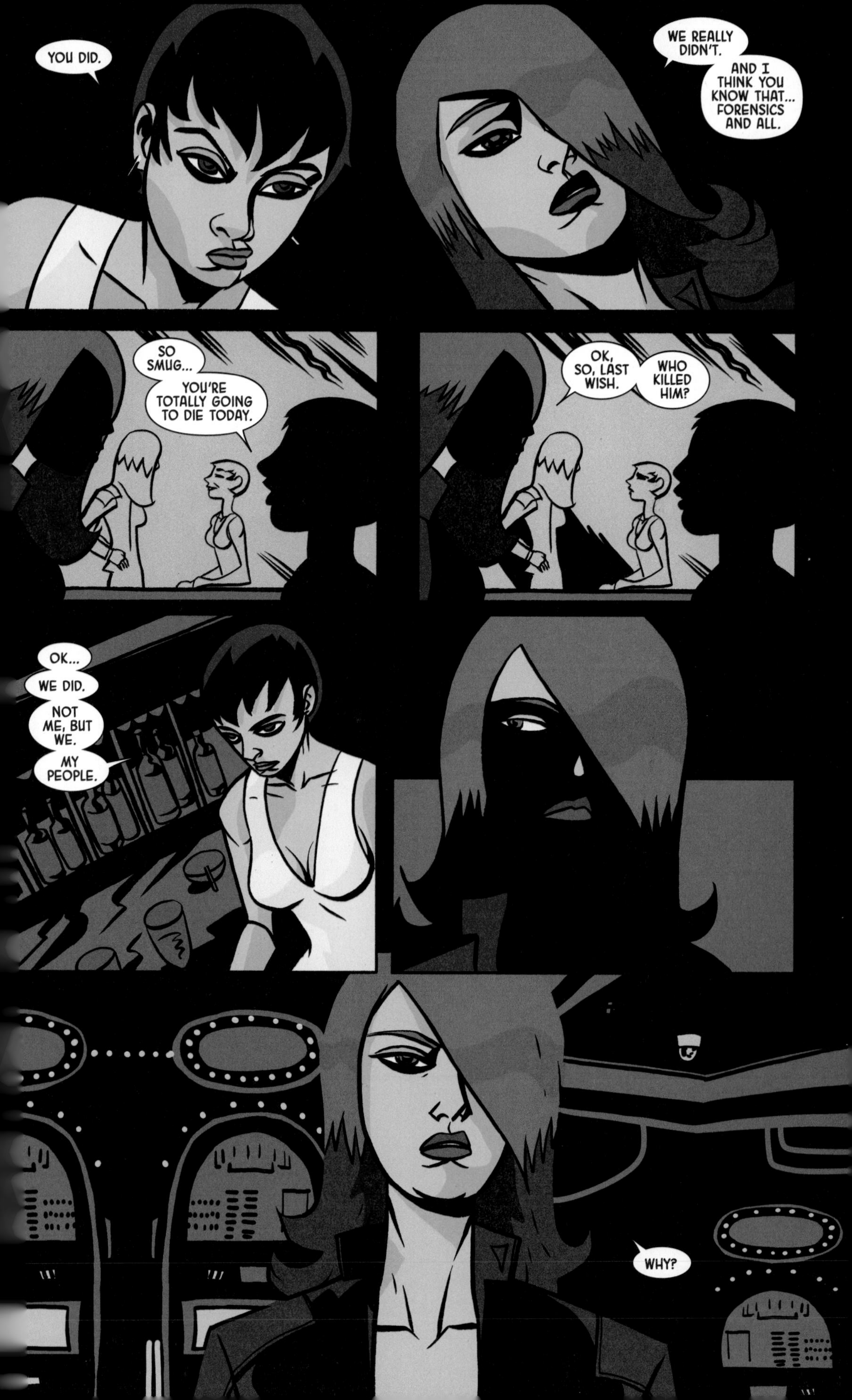
YOU DID.
WE REALLY DIDN'T.
AND I THINK YOU KNOW THAT... FORENSICS AND ALL.
SO SMUG...
YOU'RE TOTALLY GOING TO DIE TODAY.
OK, SO, LAST WISH.
WHO KILLED HIM?
OK...
WE DID.
NOT ME, BUT WE.
MY PEOPLE.
WHY?

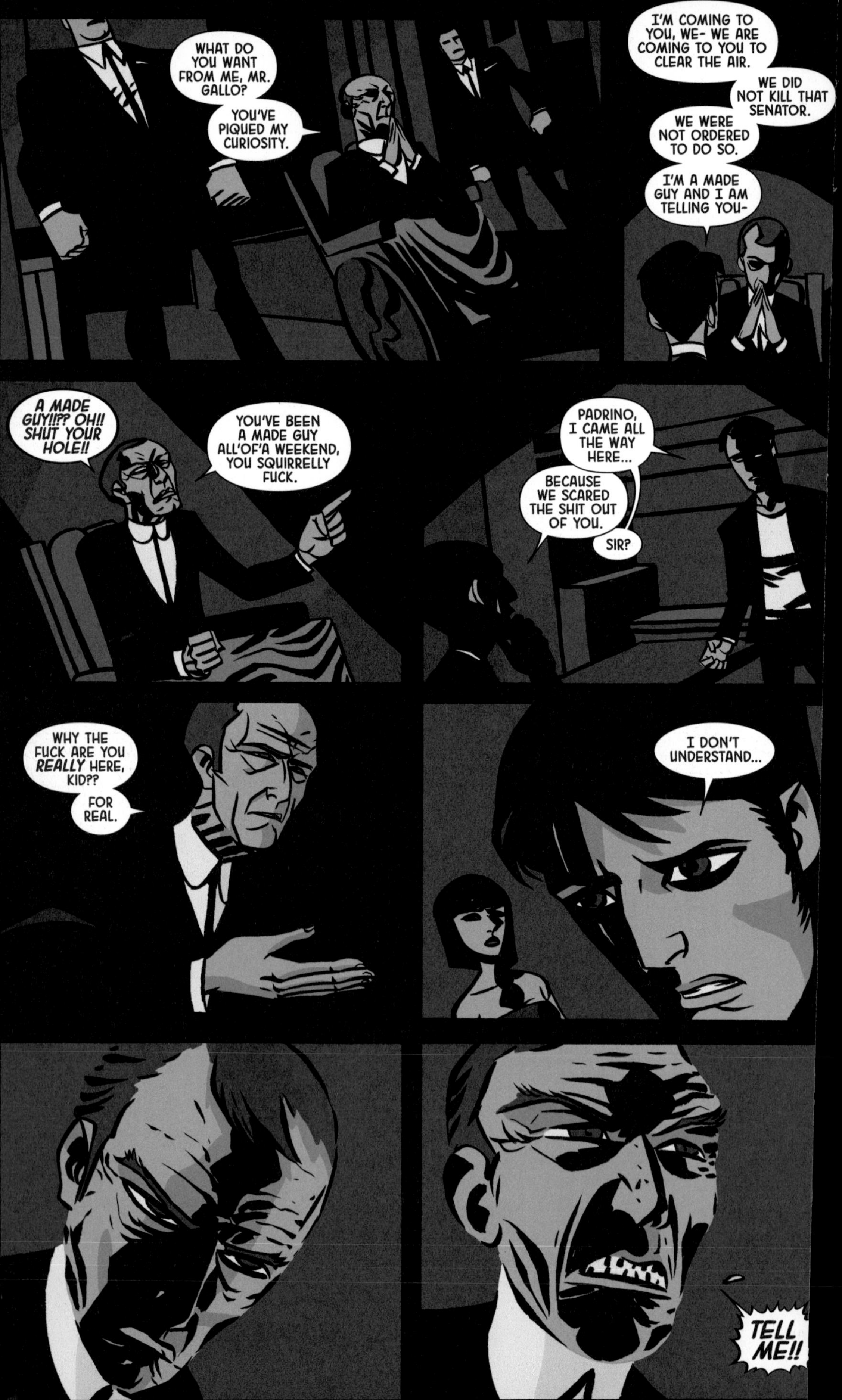
WHAT DO YOU WANT FROM ME, MR. GALLO?
YOU'VE PIQUED MY CURIOSITY.
I'M COMING TO YOU, WE- WE ARE COMING TO YOU TO CLEAR THE AIR.
WE DID NOT KILL THAT SENATOR.
WE WERE NOT ORDERED TO DO SO.
I'M A MADE GUY AND I AM TELLING YOU-
A MADE GUY!!?? OH!! SHUT YOUR HOLE!!
YOU'VE BEEN A MADE GUY ALL'OF'A WEEKEND, YOU SQUIRRELLY FUCK.
PADRINO, I CAME ALL THE WAY HERE...
BECAUSE WE SCARED THE SHIT OUT OF YOU.
SIR?
WHY THE FUCK ARE YOU *REALLY* HERE, KID??
FOR REAL.
I DON'T UNDERSTAND...
TELL ME!!

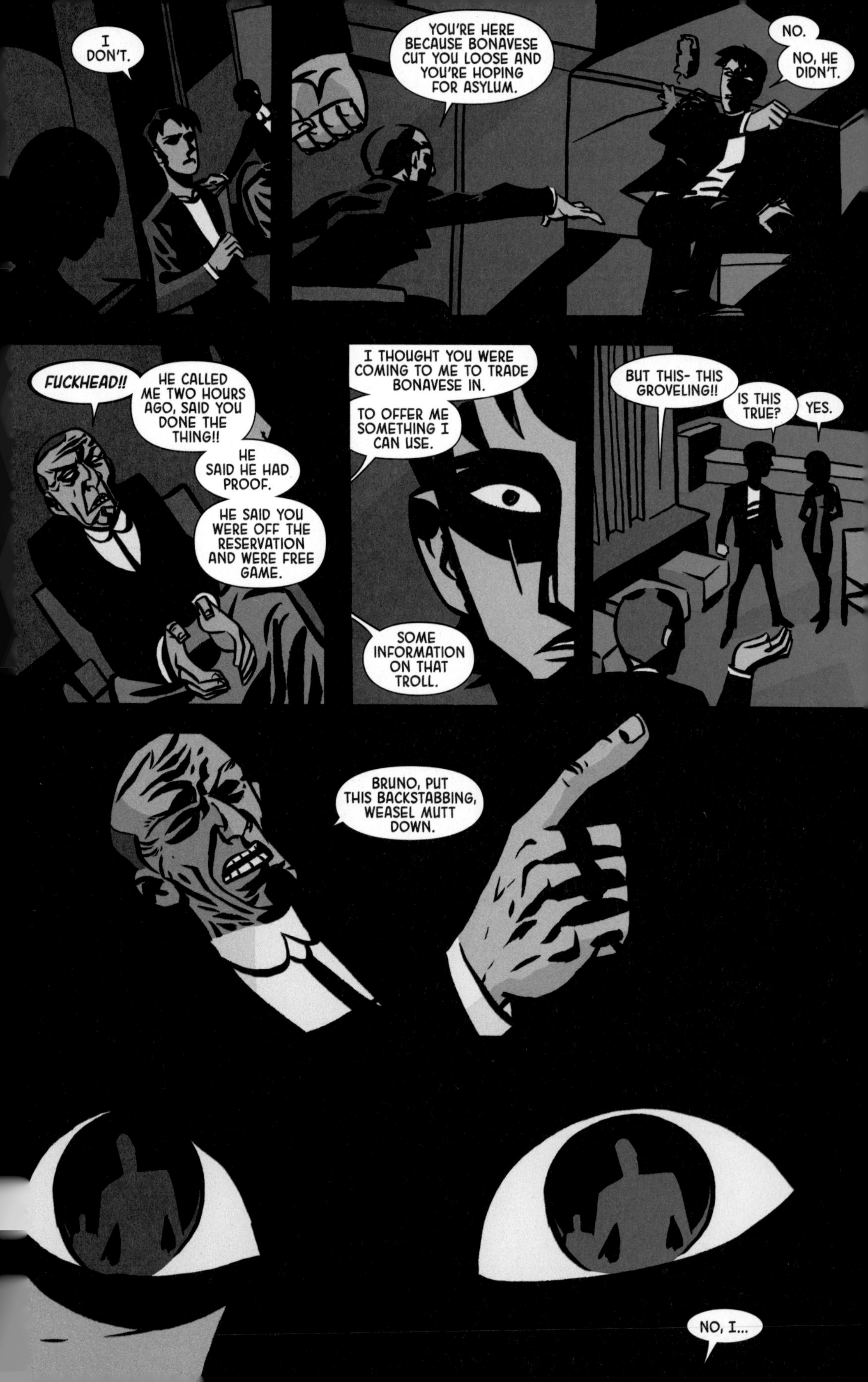
I DON'T.
YOU'RE HERE BECAUSE BONAVESE CUT YOU LOOSE AND YOU'RE HOPING FOR ASYLUM.
NO.
NO, HE DIDN'T.
FUCKHEAD!!
HE CALLED ME TWO HOURS AGO, SAID YOU DONE THE THING!!
HE SAID HE HAD PROOF.
HE SAID YOU WERE OFF THE RESERVATION AND WERE FREE GAME.
I THOUGHT YOU WERE COMING TO ME TO TRADE BONAVESE IN.
TO OFFER ME SOMETHING I CAN USE.
SOME INFORMATION ON THAT TROLL.
BUT THIS- THIS GROVELING!!
IS THIS TRUE?
YES.
BRUNO, PUT THIS BACKSTABBING, WEASEL MUTT DOWN.
NO, I...

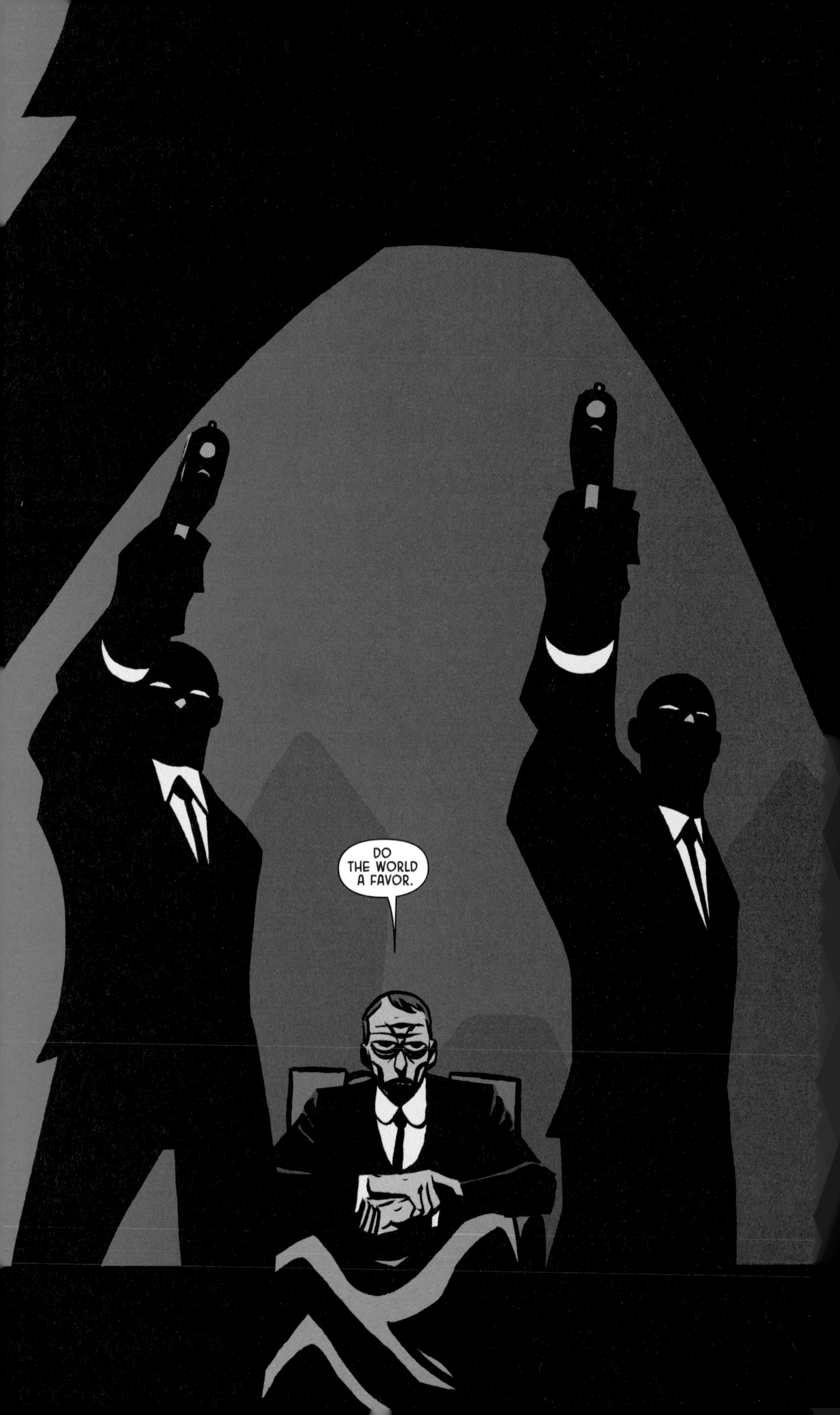
DO THE WORLD A FAVOR.

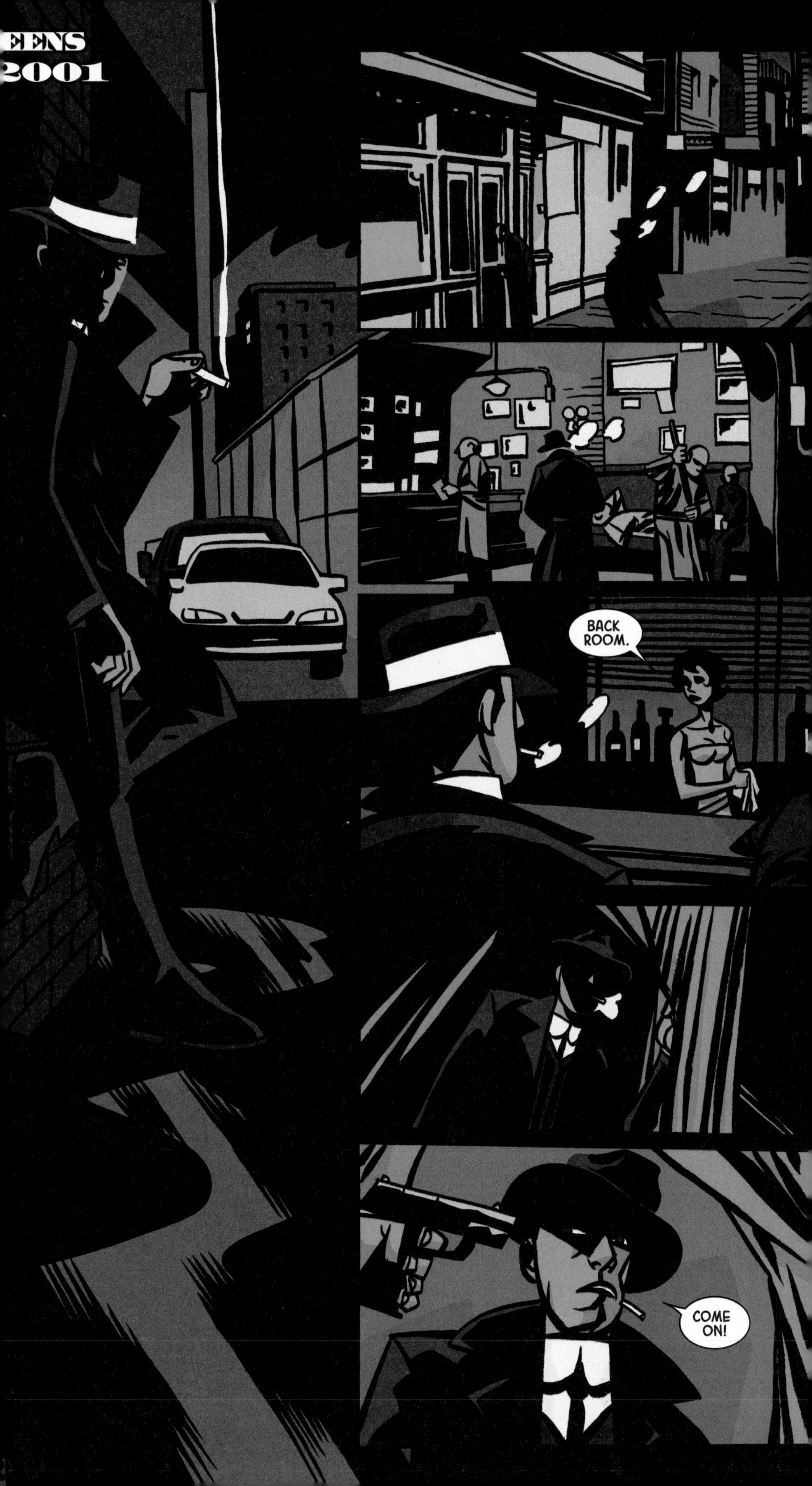
EENS
2001
BACK ROOM.
COME ON!

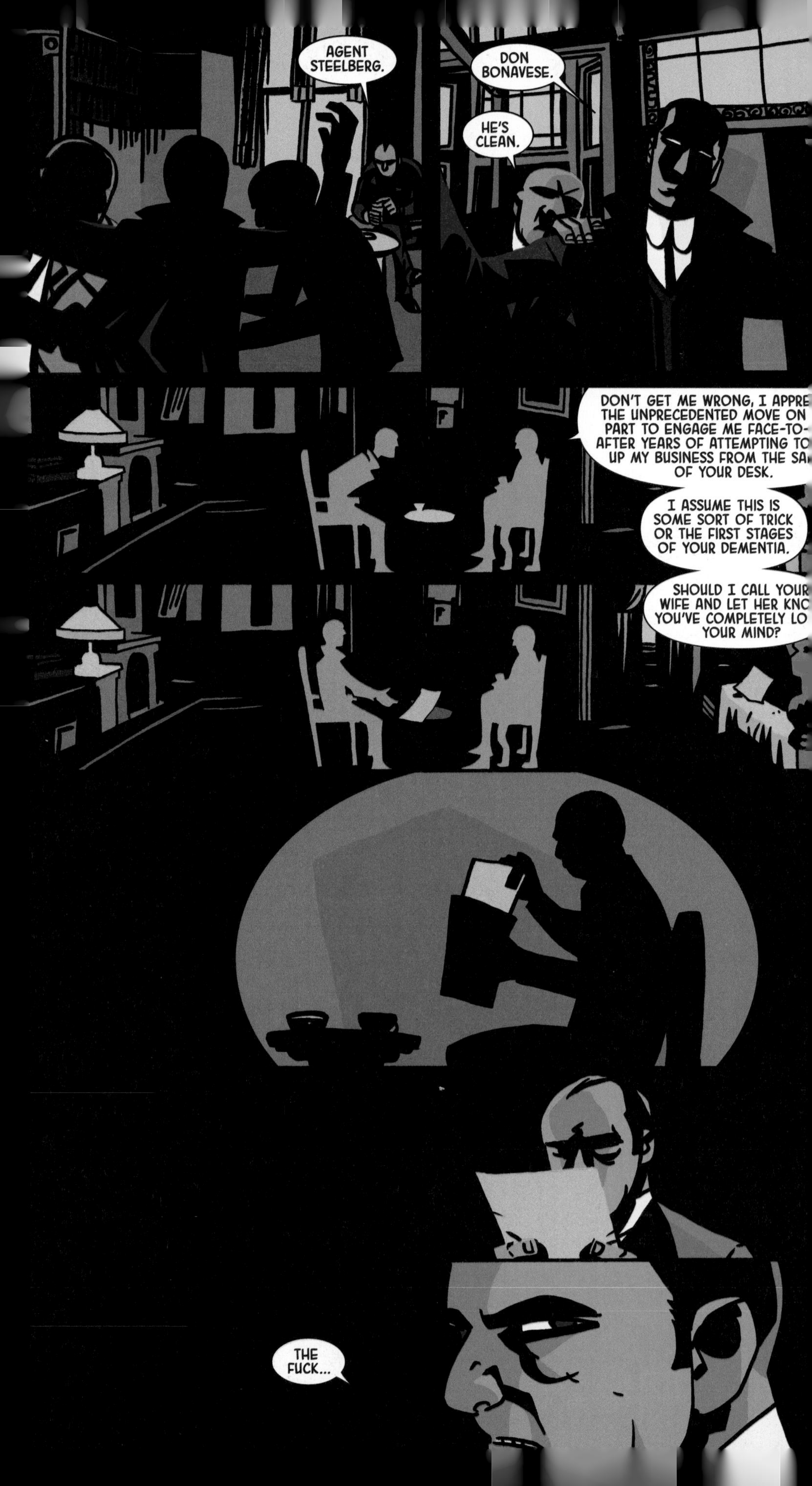
AGENT STEELBERG.
DON BONAVESE.
HE'S CLEAN.
DON'T GET ME WRONG, I APPRE THE UNPRECEDENTED MOVE ON PART TO ENGAGE ME FACE-TO- AFTER YEARS OF ATTEMPTING TO UP MY BUSINESS FROM THE SA OF YOUR DESK.
I ASSUME THIS IS SOME SORT OF TRICK OR THE FIRST STAGES OF YOUR DEMENTIA.
SHOULD I CALL YOUR WIFE AND LET HER KNO YOU'VE COMPLETELY LO YOUR MIND?
THE FUCK...

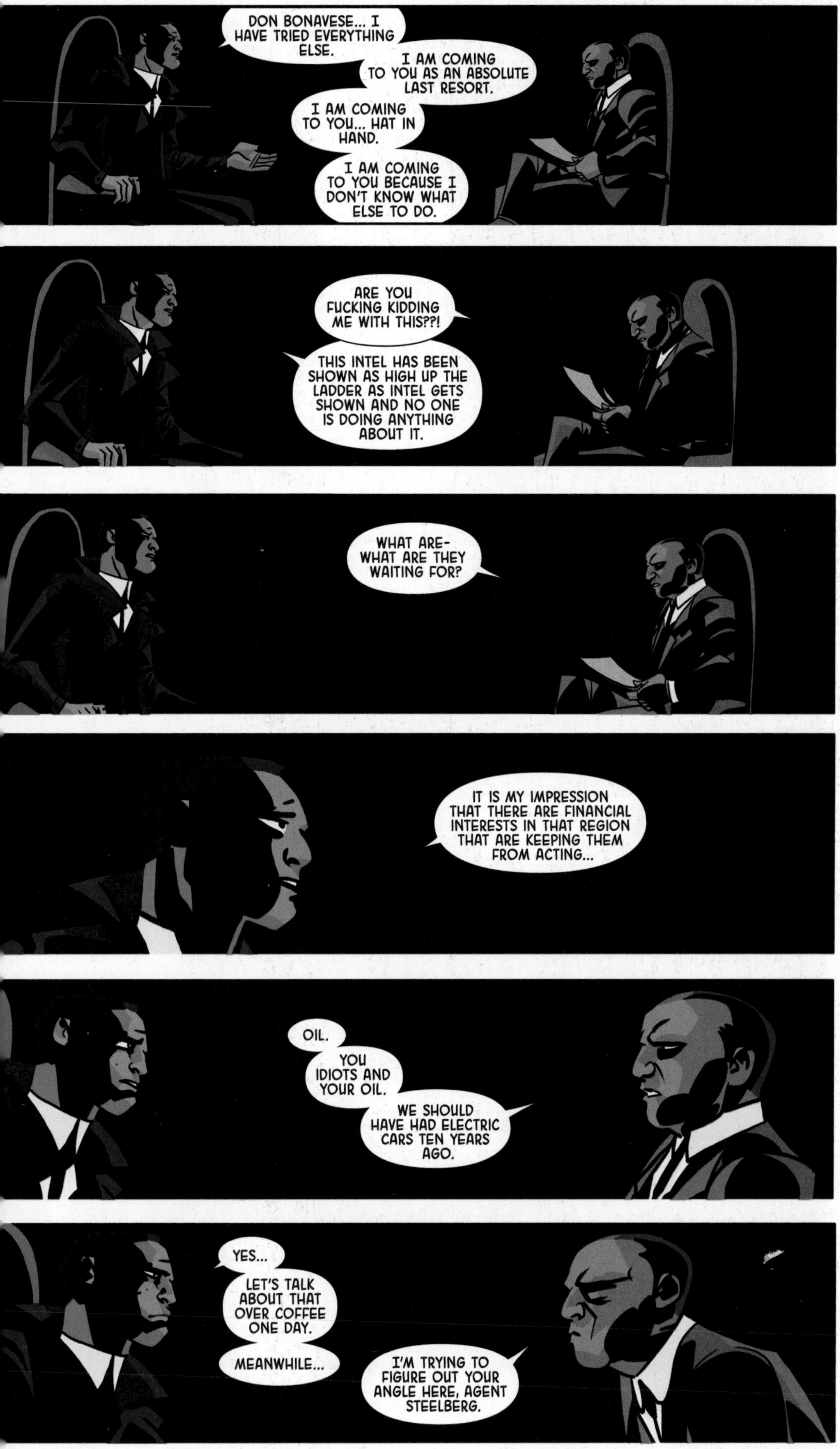
DON BONAVESE... I HAVE TRIED EVERYTHING ELSE.
I AM COMING TO YOU AS AN ABSOLUTE LAST RESORT.
I AM COMING TO YOU... HAT IN HAND.
I AM COMING TO YOU BECAUSE I DON'T KNOW WHAT ELSE TO DO.
ARE YOU FUCKING KIDDING ME WITH THIS??!
THIS INTEL HAS BEEN SHOWN AS HIGH UP THE LADDER AS INTEL GETS SHOWN AND NO ONE IS DOING ANYTHING ABOUT IT.
WHAT ARE- WHAT ARE THEY WAITING FOR?
IT IS MY IMPRESSION THAT THERE ARE FINANCIAL INTERESTS IN THAT REGION THAT ARE KEEPING THEM FROM ACTING...
OIL.
YOU IDIOTS AND YOUR OIL.
WE SHOULD HAVE HAD ELECTRIC CARS TEN YEARS AGO.
YES...
LET'S TALK ABOUT THAT OVER COFFEE ONE DAY.
MEANWHILE...
I'M TRYING TO FIGURE OUT YOUR ANGLE HERE, AGENT STEELBERG.

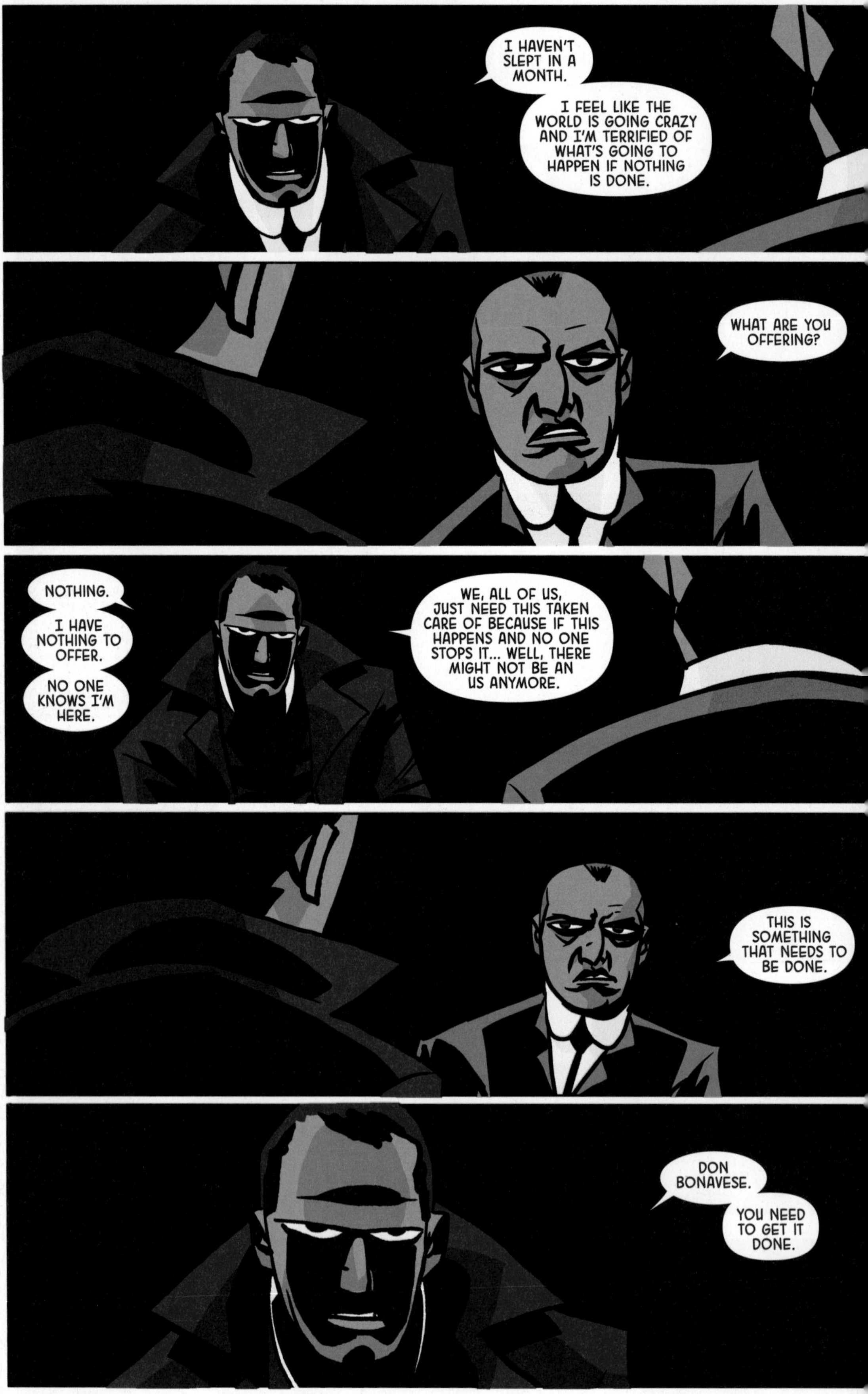
I HAVEN'T SLEPT IN A MONTH.
I FEEL LIKE THE WORLD IS GOING CRAZY AND I'M TERRIFIED OF WHAT'S GOING TO HAPPEN IF NOTHING IS DONE.
WHAT ARE YOU OFFERING?
NOTHING.
I HAVE NOTHING TO OFFER.
NO ONE KNOWS I'M HERE.
WE, ALL OF US, JUST NEED THIS TAKEN CARE OF BECAUSE IF THIS HAPPENS AND NO ONE STOPS IT... WELL, THERE MIGHT NOT BE AN US ANYMORE.
THIS IS SOMETHING THAT NEEDS TO BE DONE.
DON BONAVESE.
YOU NEED TO GET IT DONE.

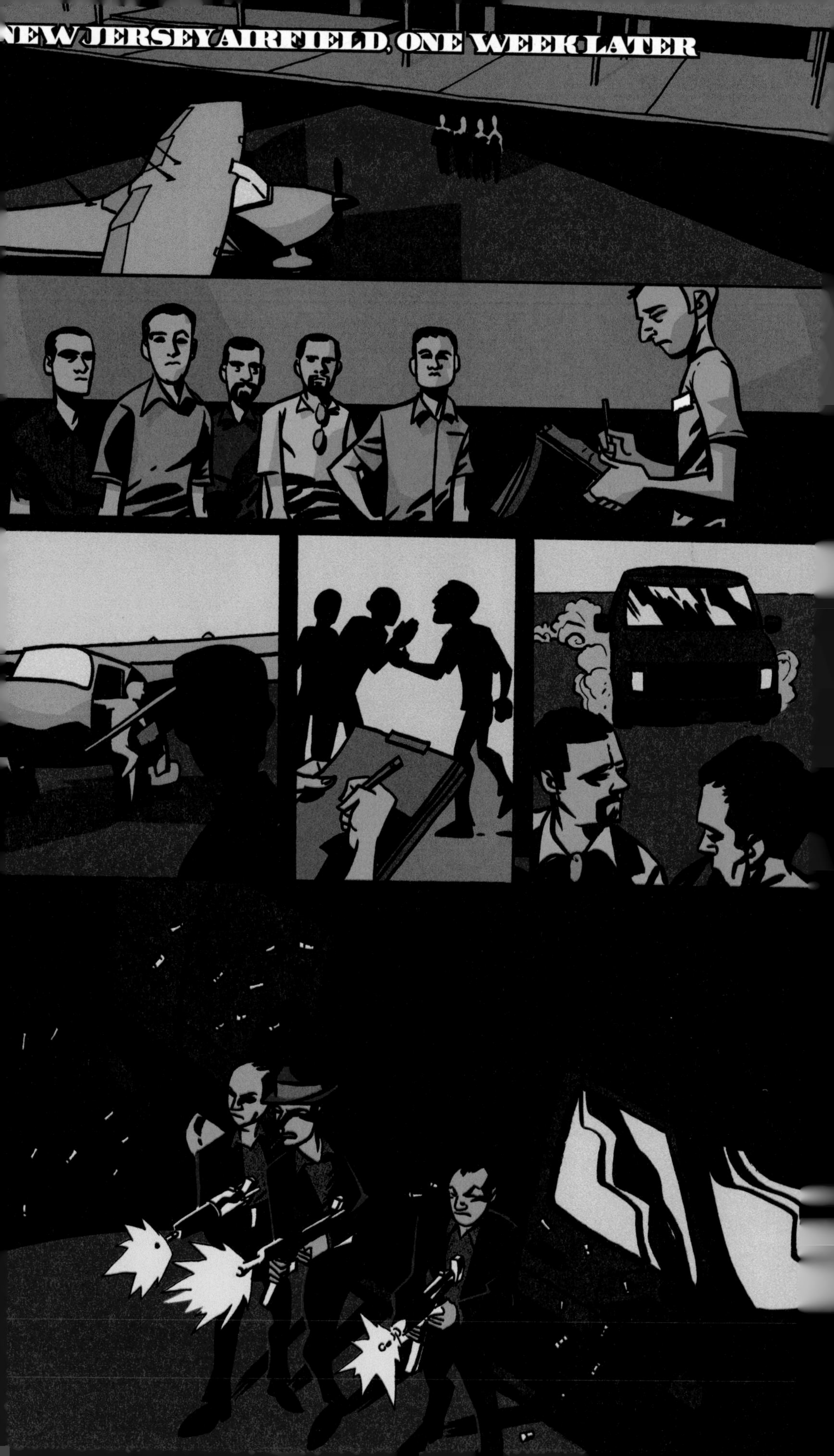
NEW JERSEY AIRFIELD, ONE WEEK LATER

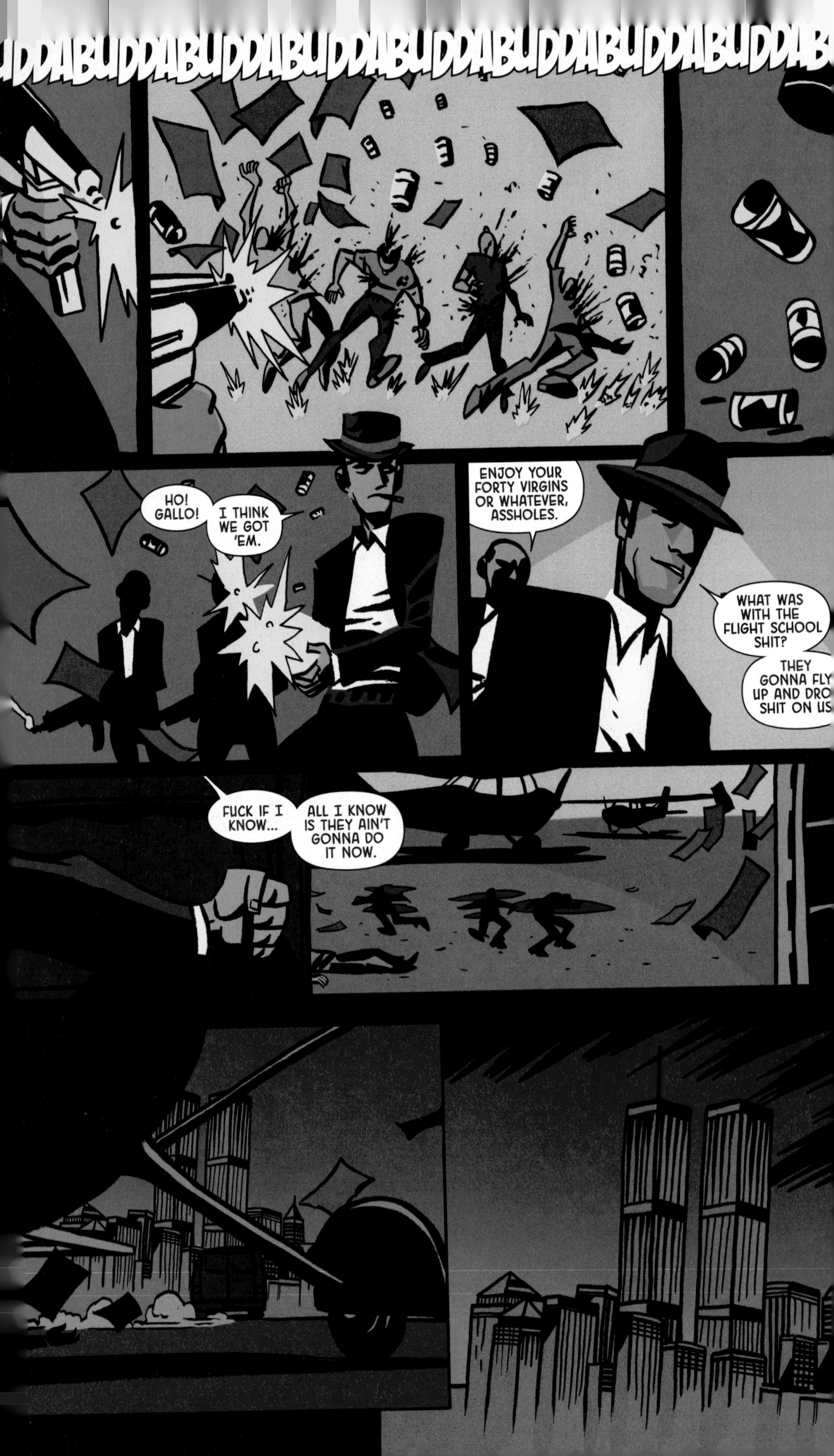

UDDABUDDABUDDABUDDABUDDABUDDABUDDABUDDAB
HO! GALLO!
I THINK WE GOT 'EM.
ENJOY YOUR FORTY VIRGINS OR WHATEVER, ASSHOLES.
WHAT WAS WITH THE FLIGHT SCHOOL SHIT?
THEY GONNA FLY UP AND DRO SHIT ON US
FUCK IF I KNOW...
ALL I KNOW IS THEY AIN'T GONNA DO IT NOW.

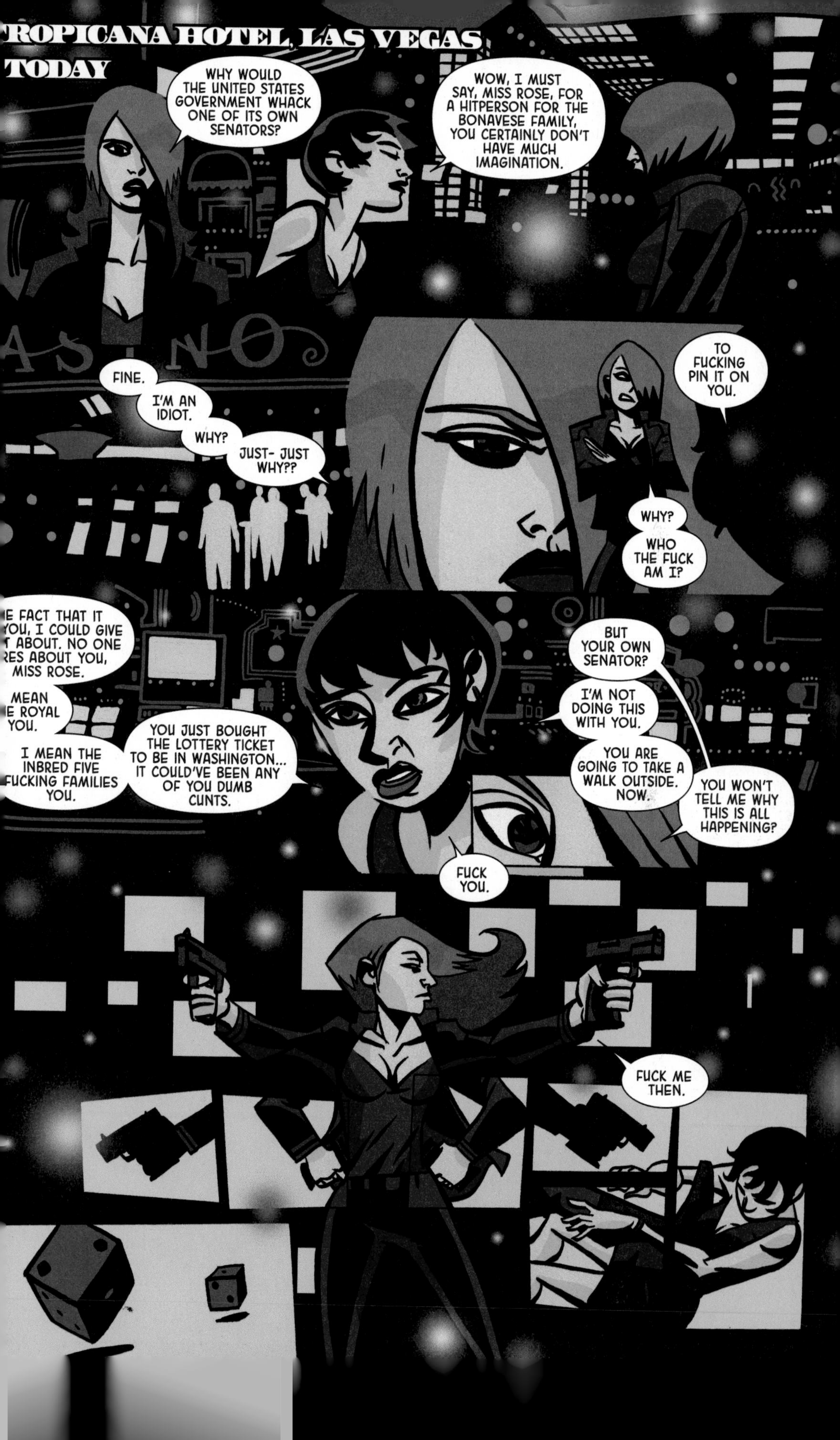
ROPICANA HOTEL, LAS VEGAS
TODAY
WHY WOULD THE UNITED STATES GOVERNMENT WHACK ONE OF ITS OWN SENATORS?
WOW, I MUST SAY, MISS ROSE, FOR A HITPERSON FOR THE BONAVESE FAMILY, YOU CERTAINLY DON'T HAVE MUCH IMAGINATION.
TO FUCKING PIN IT ON YOU.
FINE.
I'M AN IDIOT.
WHY?
JUST- JUST WHY??
WHY?
WHO THE FUCK AM I?
BUT YOUR OWN SENATOR?
E FACT THAT IT YOU, I COULD GIVE T ABOUT. NO ONE RES ABOUT YOU, MISS ROSE.
MEAN E ROYAL YOU.
I MEAN THE INBRED FIVE FUCKING FAMILIES YOU.
YOU JUST BOUGHT THE LOTTERY TICKET TO BE IN WASHINGTON... IT COULD'VE BEEN ANY OF YOU DUMB CUNTS.
I'M NOT DOING THIS WITH YOU.
YOU ARE GOING TO TAKE A WALK OUTSIDE. NOW.
YOU WON'T TELL ME WHY THIS IS ALL HAPPENING?
FUCK YOU.
FUCK ME THEN.

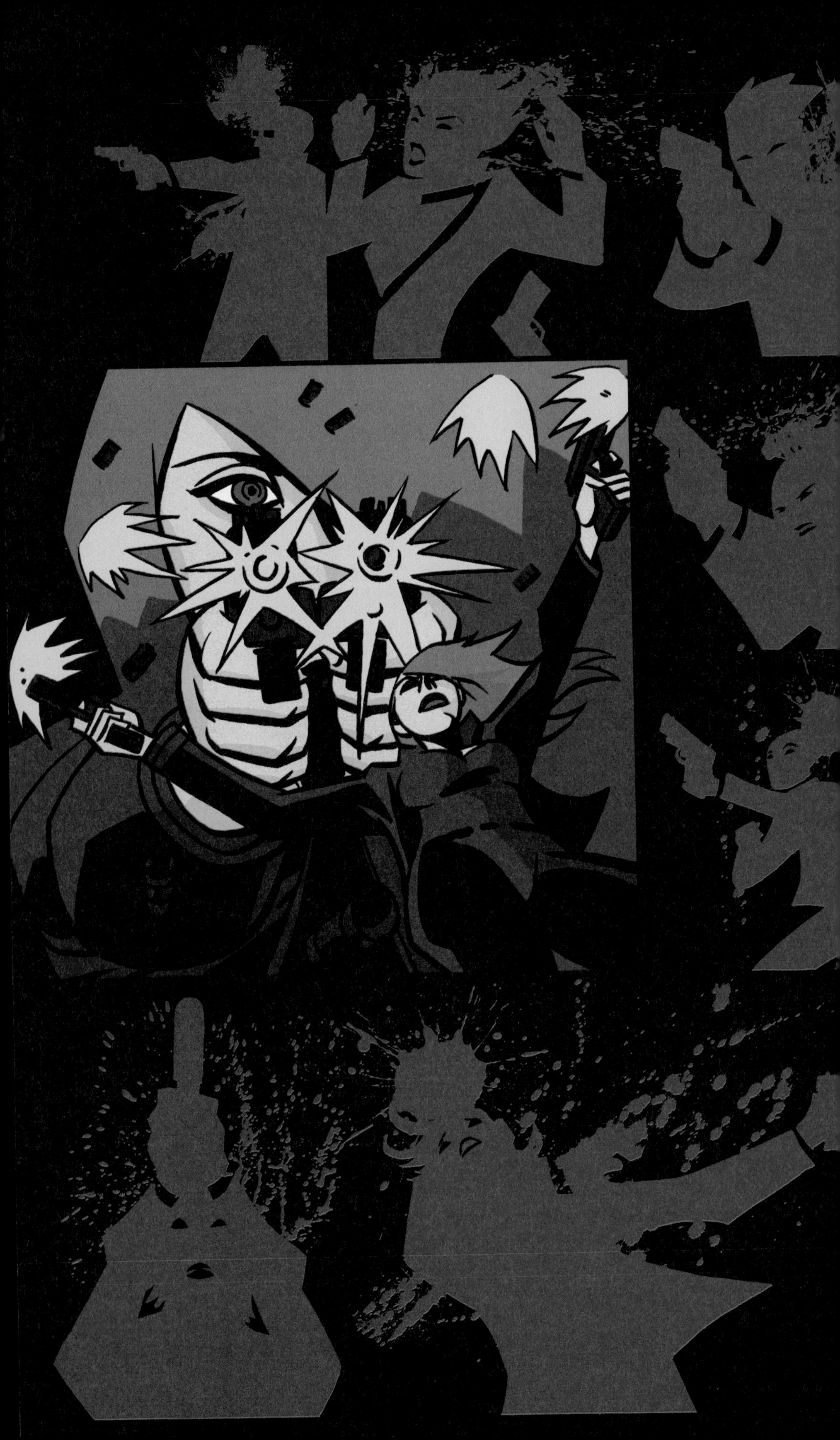

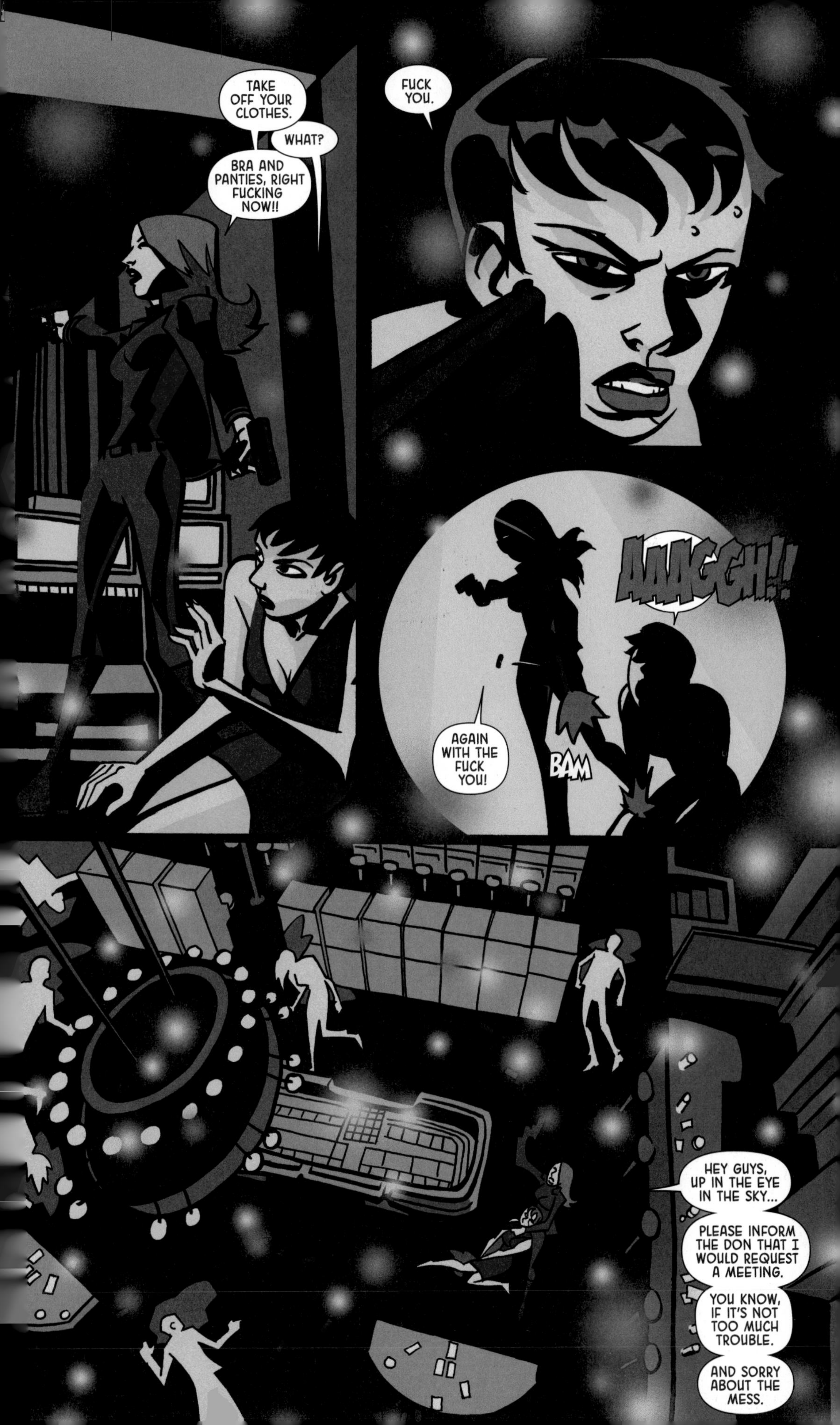
TAKE OFF YOUR CLOTHES.
WHAT?
BRA AND PANTIES, RIGHT FUCKING NOW!!
FUCK YOU.
AAAGGH!!
AGAIN WITH THE FUCK YOU!
BAM
HEY GUYS, UP IN THE EYE IN THE SKY...
PLEASE INFORM THE DON THAT I WOULD REQUEST A MEETING.
YOU KNOW, IF IT'S NOT TOO MUCH TROUBLE.
AND SORRY ABOUT THE MESS.

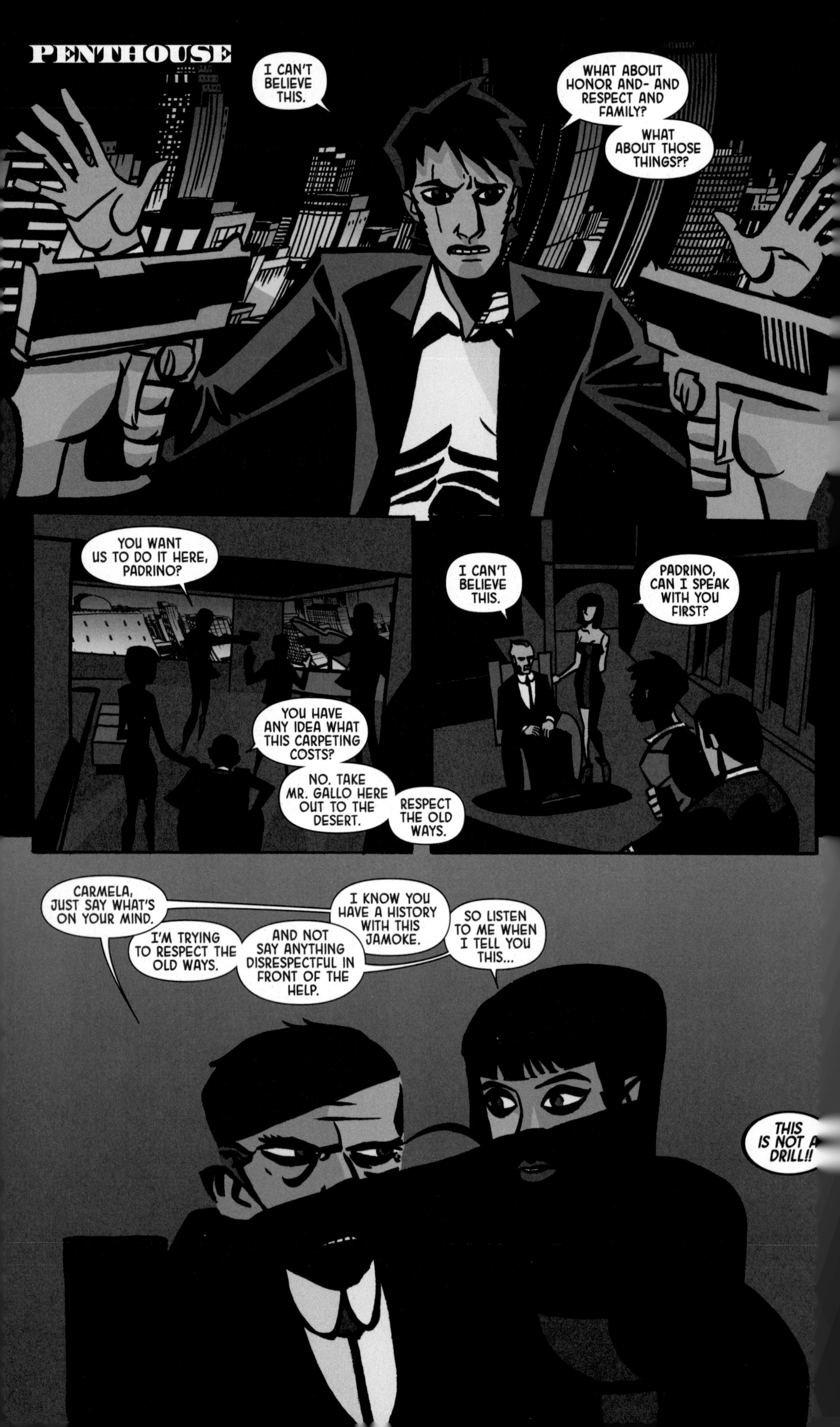
PENTHOUSE
I CAN'T BELIEVE THIS.
WHAT ABOUT HONOR AND- AND RESPECT AND FAMILY?
WHAT ABOUT THOSE THINGS??
YOU WANT US TO DO IT HERE, PADRINO?
YOU HAVE ANY IDEA WHAT THIS CARPETING COSTS?
NO. TAKE MR. GALLO HERE OUT TO THE DESERT.
RESPECT THE OLD WAYS.
I CAN'T BELIEVE THIS.
PADRINO, CAN I SPEAK WITH YOU FIRST?
CARMELA, JUST SAY WHAT'S ON YOUR MIND.
I'M TRYING TO RESPECT THE OLD WAYS.
AND NOT SAY ANYTHING DISRESPECTFUL IN FRONT OF THE HELP.
I KNOW YOU HAVE A HISTORY WITH THIS JAMOKE.
SO LISTEN TO ME WHEN I TELL YOU THIS...
THIS IS NOT A DRILL!!

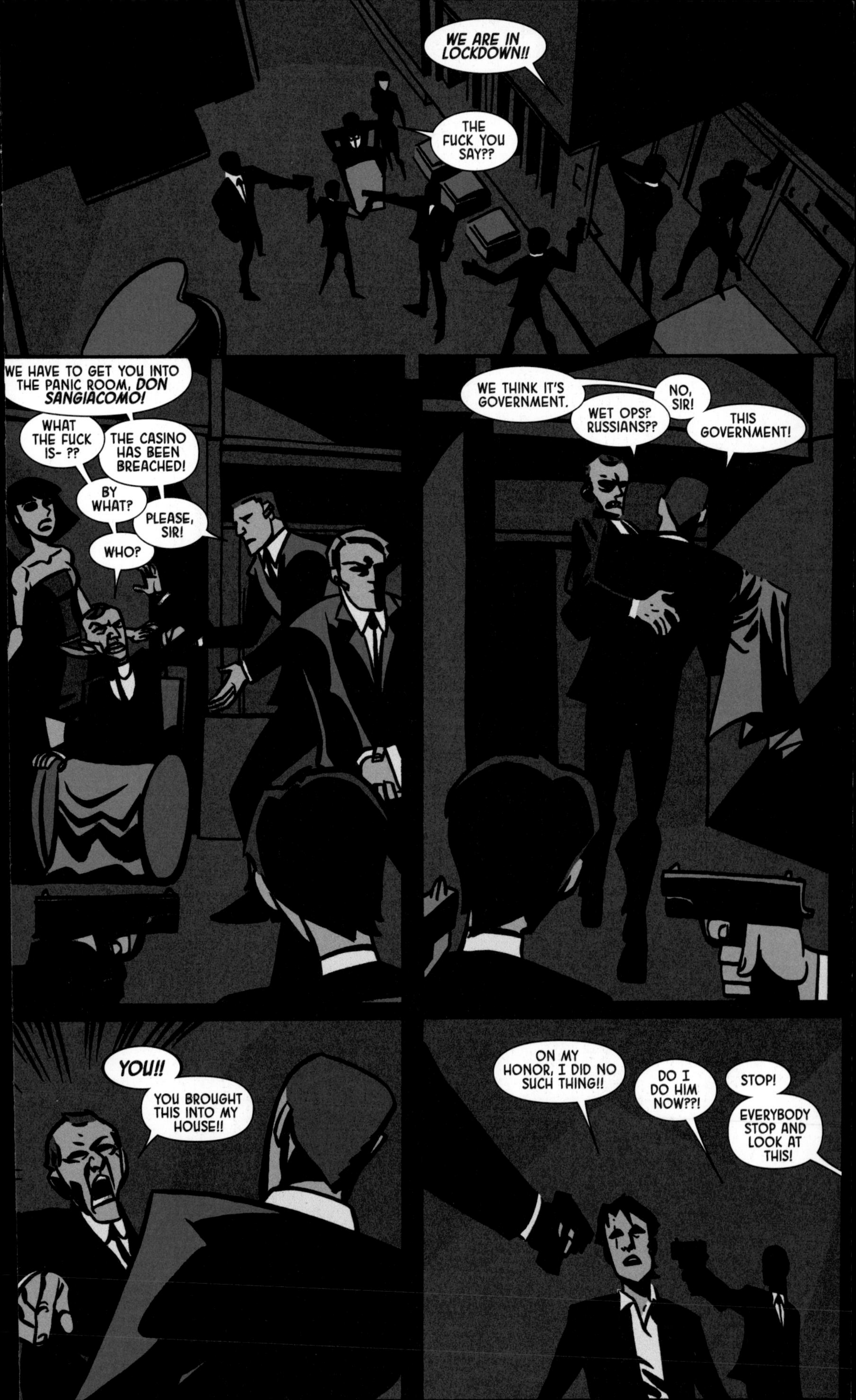
WE ARE IN LOCKDOWN!!
THE FUCK YOU SAY??
WE HAVE TO GET YOU INTO THE PANIC ROOM, DON SANGIACOMO!
WHAT THE FUCK IS- ??
THE CASINO HAS BEEN BREACHED!
BY WHAT?
PLEASE, SIR!
WHO?
WE THINK IT'S GOVERNMENT.
WET OPS? RUSSIANS??
NO, SIR!
THIS GOVERNMENT!
YOU!!
YOU BROUGHT THIS INTO MY HOUSE!!
ON MY HONOR, I DID NO SUCH THING!!
DO I DO HIM NOW??!
STOP!
EVERYBODY STOP AND LOOK AT THIS!

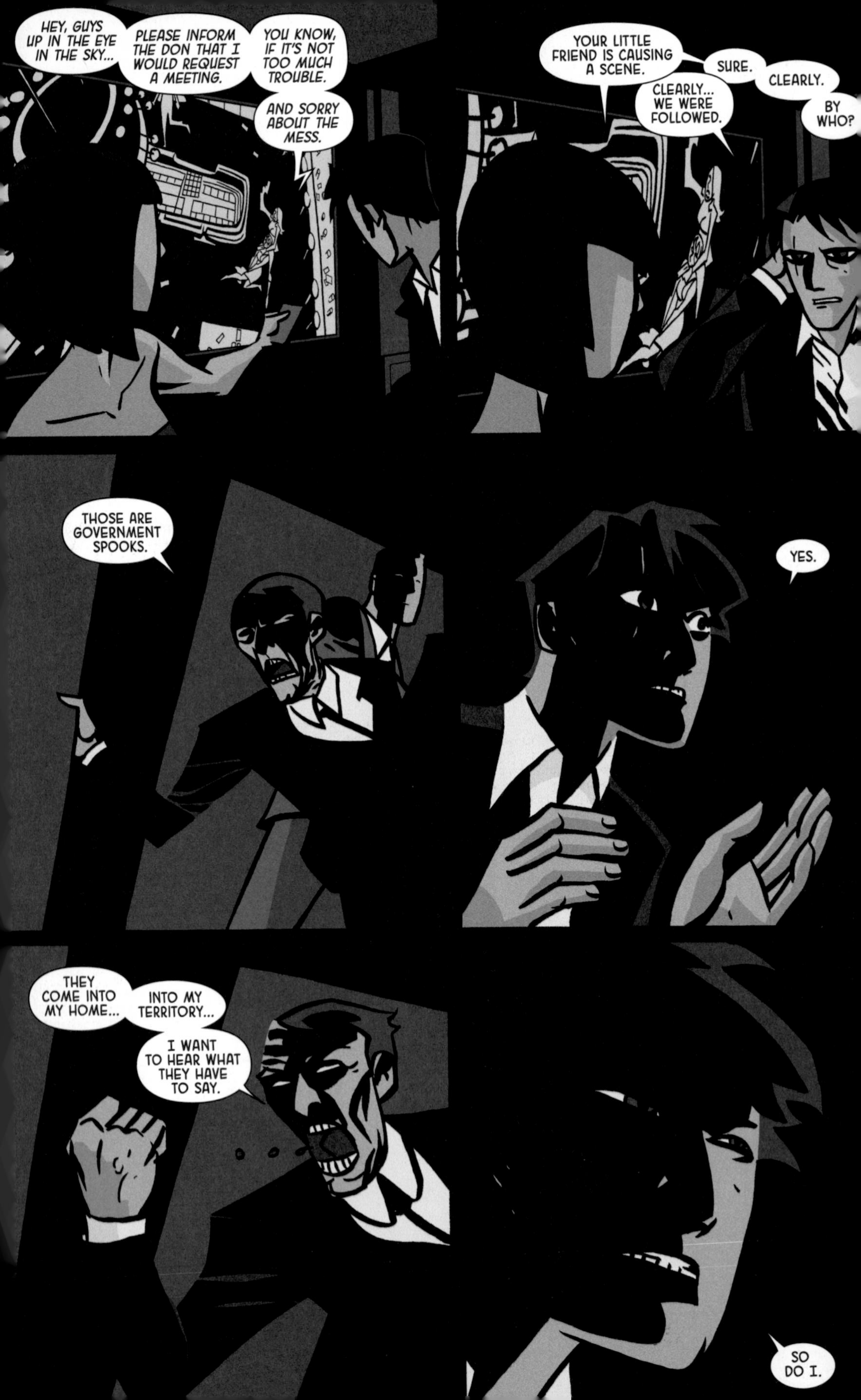
HEY, GUYS UP IN THE EYE IN THE SKY...
PLEASE INFORM THE DON THAT I WOULD REQUEST A MEETING.
YOU KNOW, IF IT'S NOT TOO MUCH TROUBLE.
AND SORRY ABOUT THE MESS.
YOUR LITTLE FRIEND IS CAUSING A SCENE.
SURE.
CLEARLY.
CLEARLY... WE WERE FOLLOWED.
BY WHO?
THOSE ARE GOVERNMENT SPOOKS.
YES.
THEY COME INTO MY HOME...
INTO MY TERRITORY...
I WANT TO HEAR WHAT THEY HAVE TO SAY.
SO DO I.

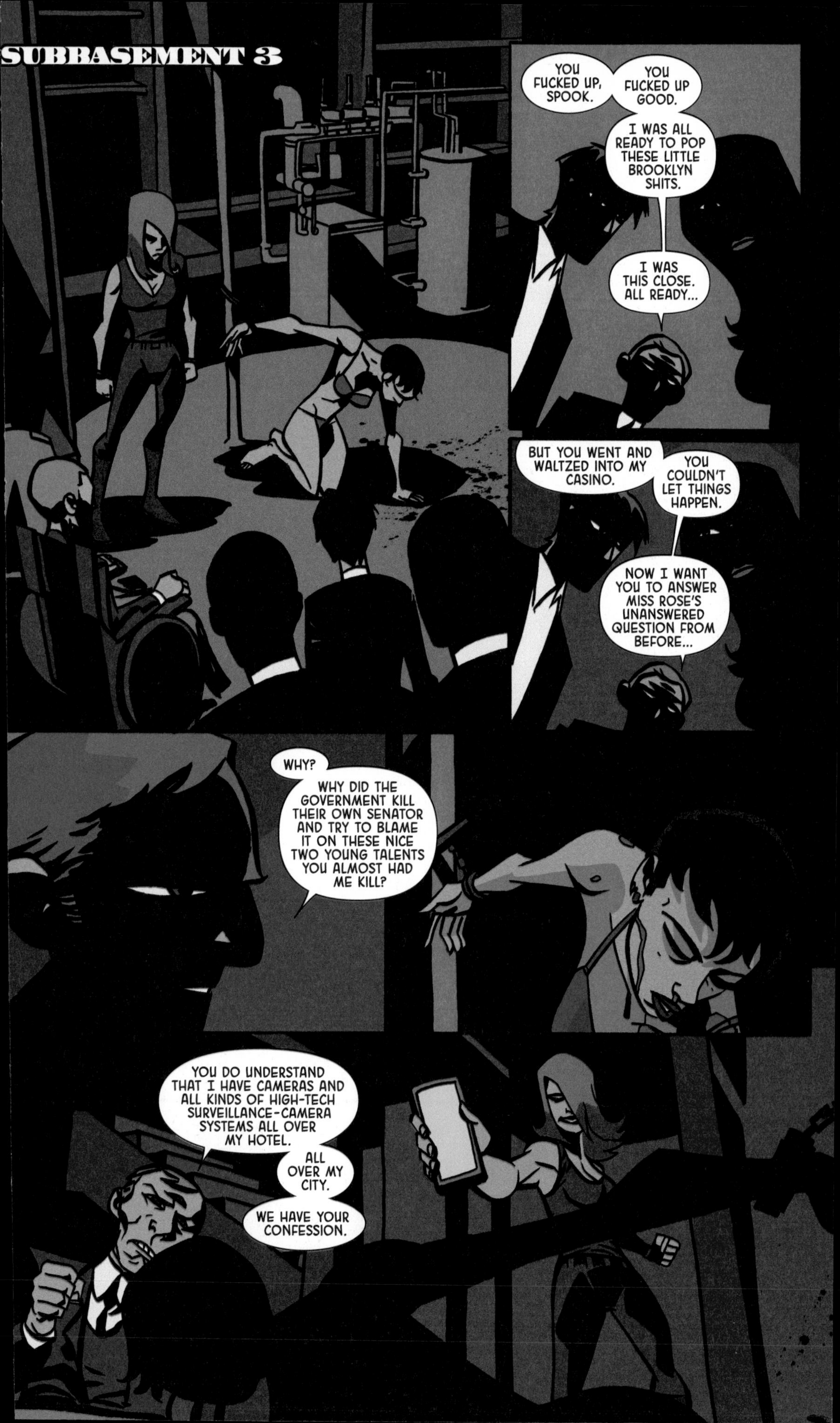
SUBBASEMENT 3
YOU FUCKED UP, SPOOK.
YOU FUCKED UP GOOD.
I WAS ALL READY TO POP THESE LITTLE BROOKLYN SHITS.
I WAS THIS CLOSE. ALL READY...
BUT YOU WENT AND WALTZED INTO MY CASINO.
YOU COULDN'T LET THINGS HAPPEN.
NOW I WANT YOU TO ANSWER MISS ROSE'S UNANSWERED QUESTION FROM BEFORE...
WHY?
WHY DID THE GOVERNMENT KILL THEIR OWN SENATOR AND TRY TO BLAME IT ON THESE NICE TWO YOUNG TALENTS YOU ALMOST HAD ME KILL?
YOU DO UNDERSTAND THAT I HAVE CAMERAS AND ALL KINDS OF HIGH-TECH SURVEILLANCE-CAMERA SYSTEMS ALL OVER MY HOTEL.
ALL OVER MY CITY.
WE HAVE YOUR CONFESSION.

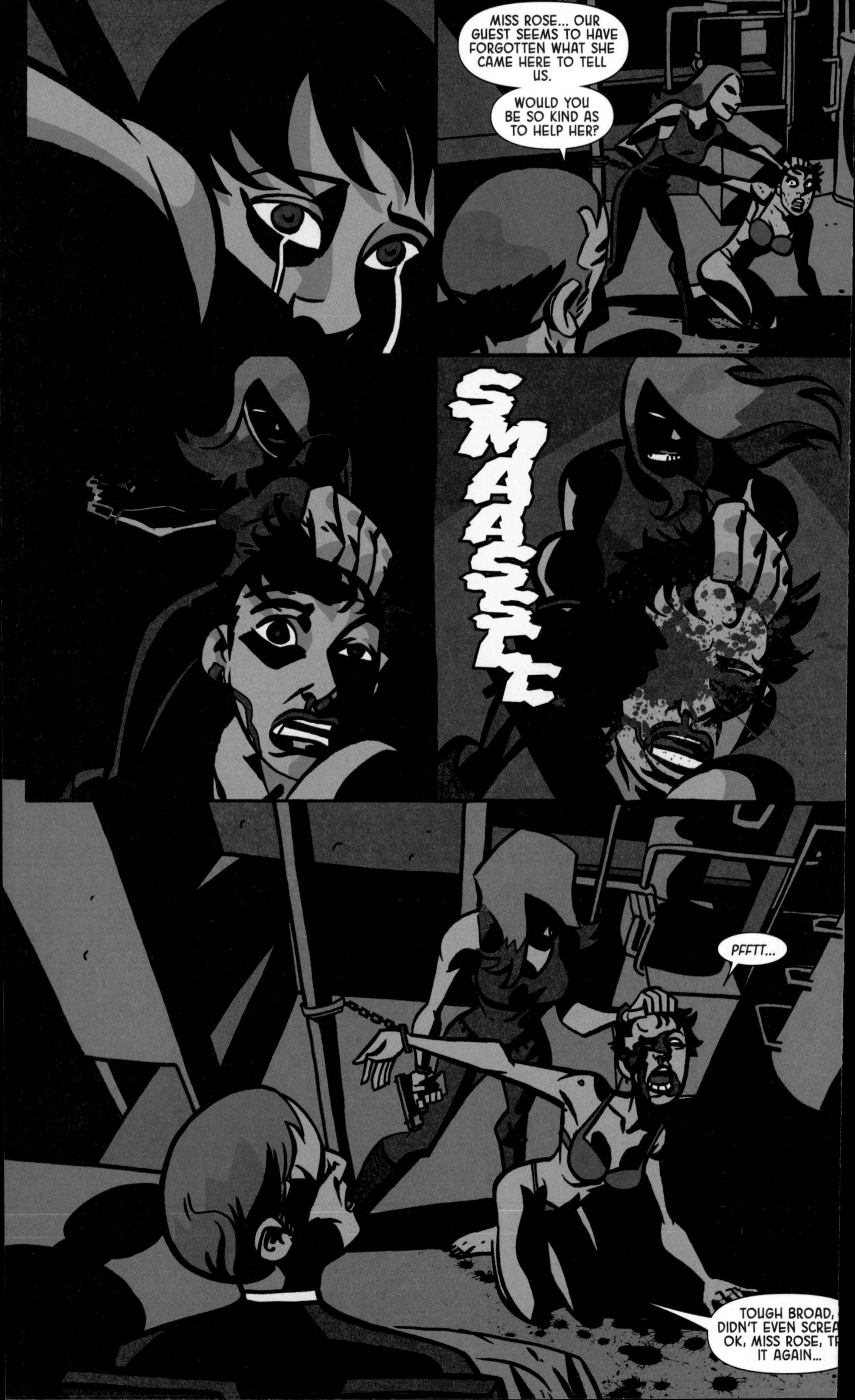
MISS ROSE... OUR GUEST SEEMS TO HAVE FORGOTTEN WHAT SHE CAME HERE TO TELL US.
WOULD YOU BE SO KIND AS TO HELP HER?
SMASSSH
PFFTT...
TOUGH BROAD, DIDN'T EVEN SCREA OK, MISS ROSE, T IT AGAIN...

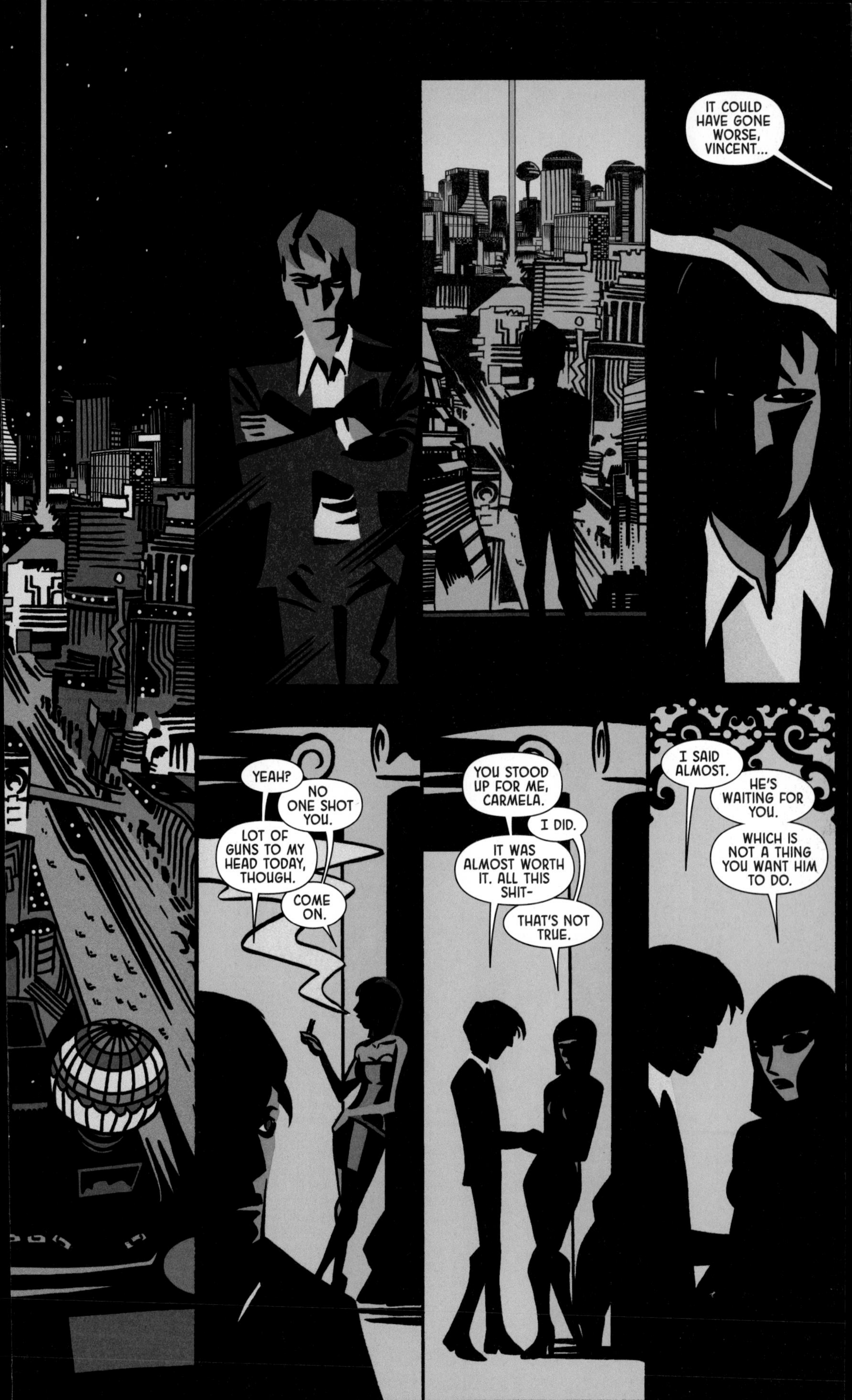
IT COULD HAVE GONE WORSE, VINCENT...
YEAH?
NO ONE SHOT YOU.
LOT OF GUNS TO MY HEAD TODAY, THOUGH.
COME ON.
YOU STOOD UP FOR ME, CARMELA.
I DID.
IT WAS ALMOST WORTH IT. ALL THIS SHIT-
THAT'S NOT TRUE.
I SAID ALMOST.
HE'S WAITING FOR YOU.
WHICH IS NOT A THING YOU WANT HIM TO DO.

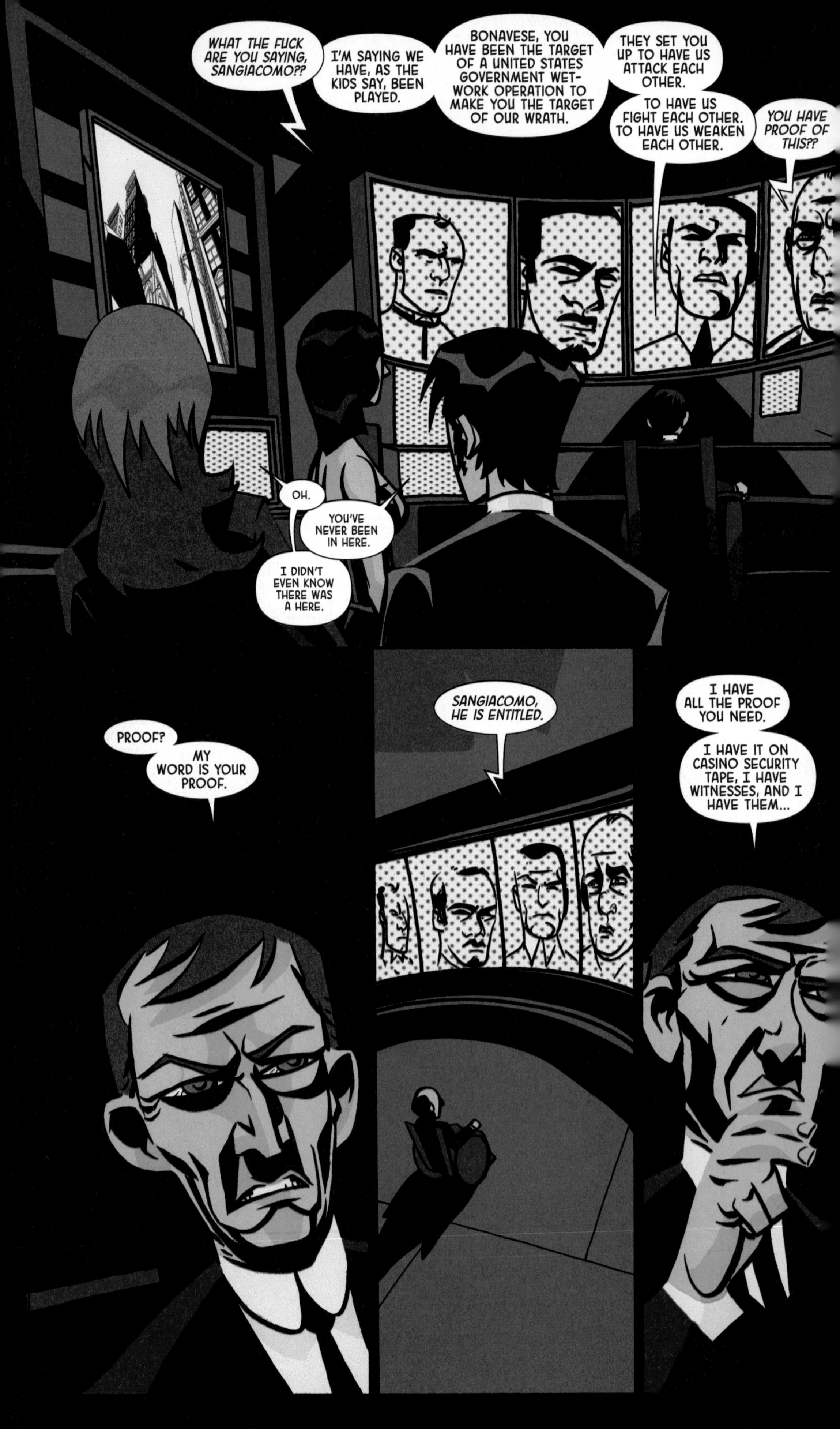
WHAT THE FUCK ARE YOU SAYING, SANGIACOMO??
I'M SAYING WE HAVE, AS THE KIDS SAY, BEEN PLAYED.
BONAVESE, YOU HAVE BEEN THE TARGET OF A UNITED STATES GOVERNMENT WET-WORK OPERATION TO MAKE YOU THE TARGET OF OUR WRATH.
THEY SET YOU UP TO HAVE US ATTACK EACH OTHER.
TO HAVE US FIGHT EACH OTHER. TO HAVE US WEAKEN EACH OTHER.
YOU HAVE PROOF OF THIS??
OH.
YOU'VE NEVER BEEN IN HERE.
I DIDN'T EVEN KNOW THERE WAS A HERE.
PROOF?
MY WORD IS YOUR PROOF.
SANGIACOMO, HE IS ENTITLED.
I HAVE ALL THE PROOF YOU NEED.
I HAVE IT ON CASINO SECURITY TAPE, I HAVE WITNESSES, AND I HAVE THEM...

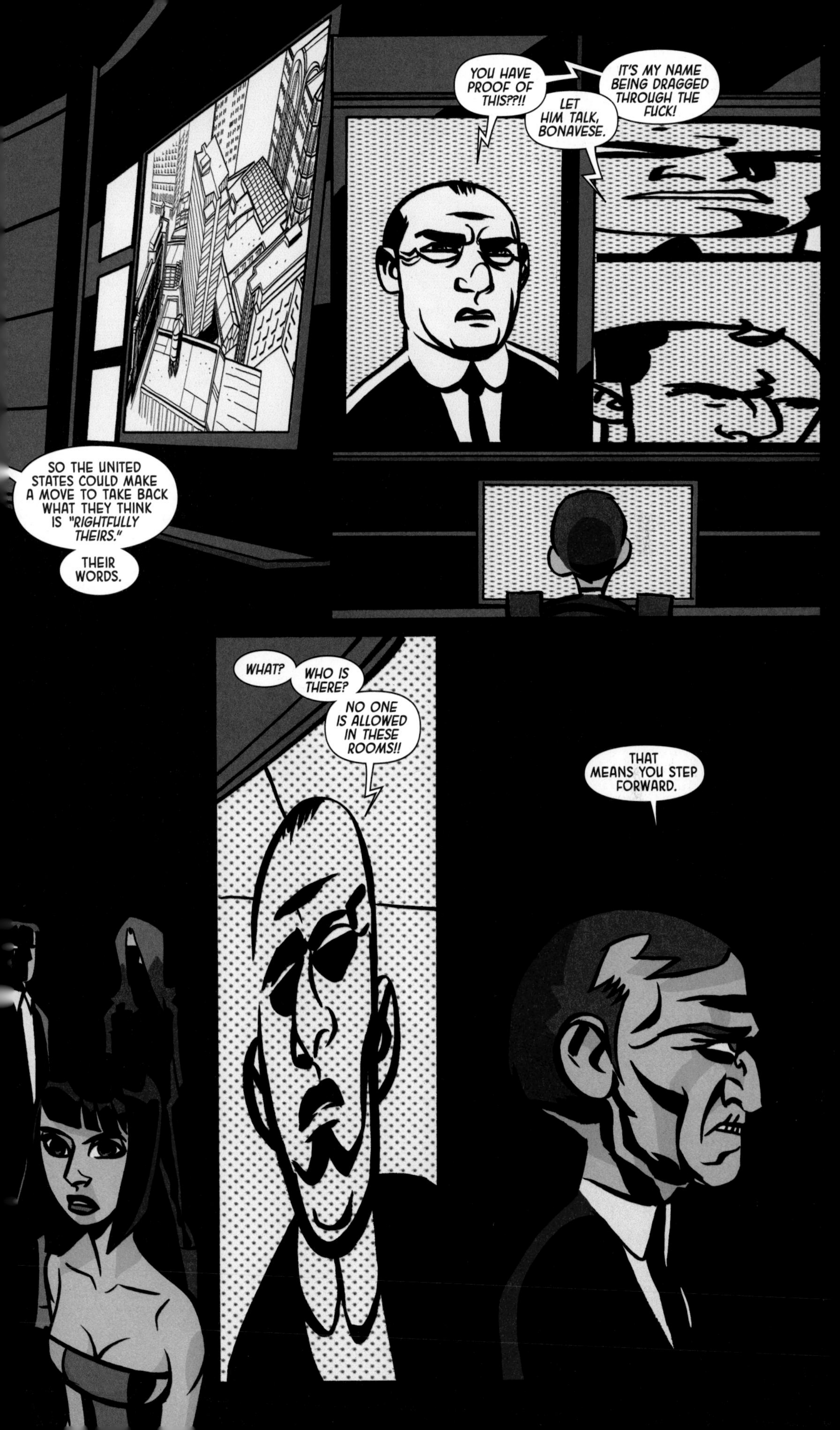
YOU HAVE PROOF OF THIS??!!
LET HIM TALK, BONAVESE.
IT'S MY NAME BEING DRAGGED THROUGH THE FUCK!
SO THE UNITED STATES COULD MAKE A MOVE TO TAKE BACK WHAT THEY THINK IS "RIGHTFULLY THEIRS."
THEIR WORDS.
WHAT?
WHO IS THERE?
NO ONE IS ALLOWED IN THESE ROOMS!!
THAT MEANS YOU STEP FORWARD.

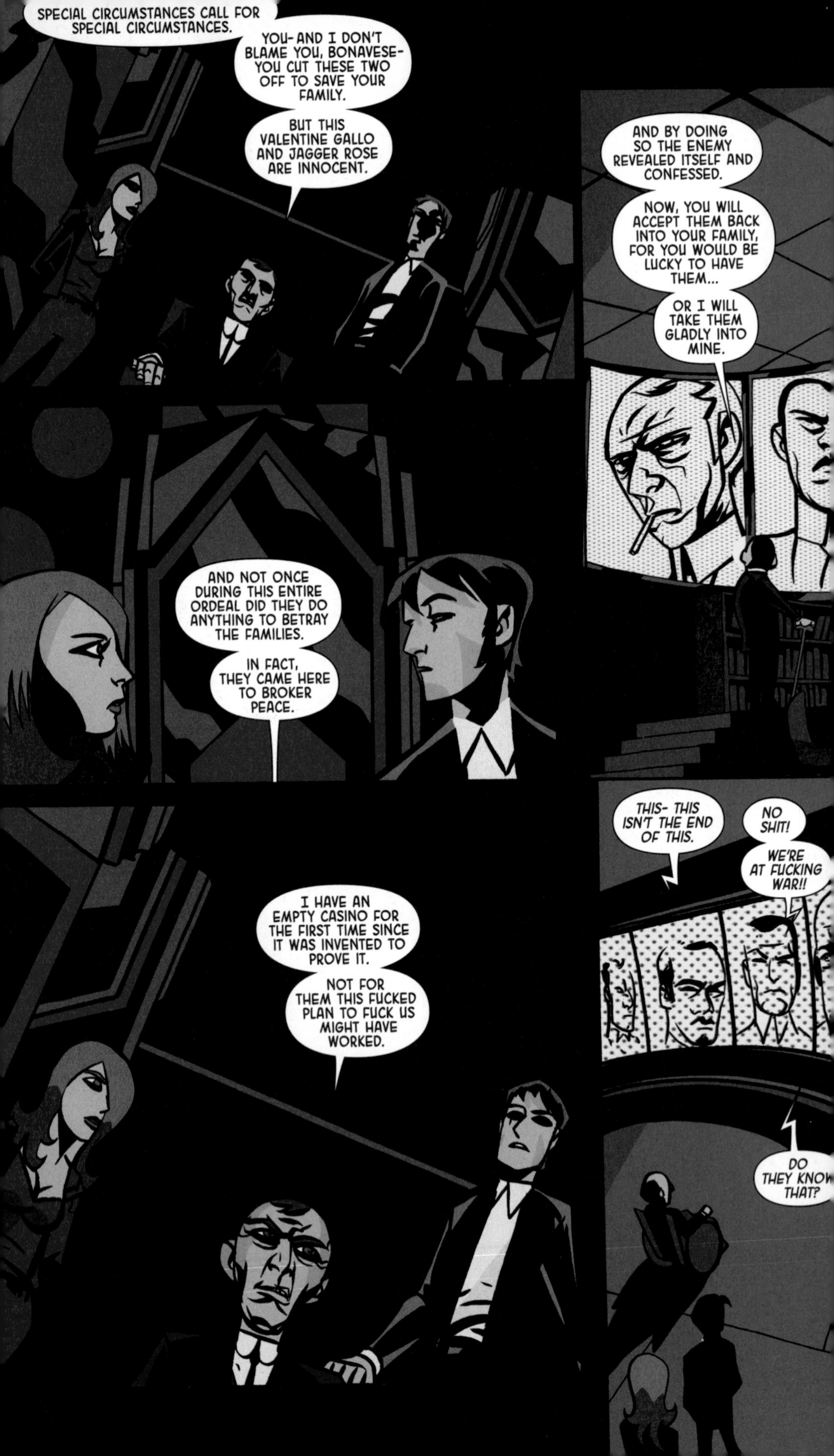
SPECIAL CIRCUMSTANCES CALL FOR SPECIAL CIRCUMSTANCES.
YOU- AND I DON'T BLAME YOU, BONAVESE- YOU CUT THESE TWO OFF TO SAVE YOUR FAMILY.
BUT THIS VALENTINE GALLO AND JAGGER ROSE ARE INNOCENT.
AND BY DOING SO THE ENEMY REVEALED ITSELF AND CONFESSED.
NOW, YOU WILL ACCEPT THEM BACK INTO YOUR FAMILY, FOR YOU WOULD BE LUCKY TO HAVE THEM...
OR I WILL TAKE THEM GLADLY INTO MINE.
AND NOT ONCE DURING THIS ENTIRE ORDEAL DID THEY DO ANYTHING TO BETRAY THE FAMILIES.
IN FACT, THEY CAME HERE TO BROKER PEACE.
I HAVE AN EMPTY CASINO FOR THE FIRST TIME SINCE IT WAS INVENTED TO PROVE IT.
NOT FOR THEM THIS FUCKED PLAN TO FUCK US MIGHT HAVE WORKED.
THIS- THIS ISN'T THE END OF THIS.
NO SHIT!
WE'RE AT FUCKING WAR!!
DO THEY KNOW THAT?

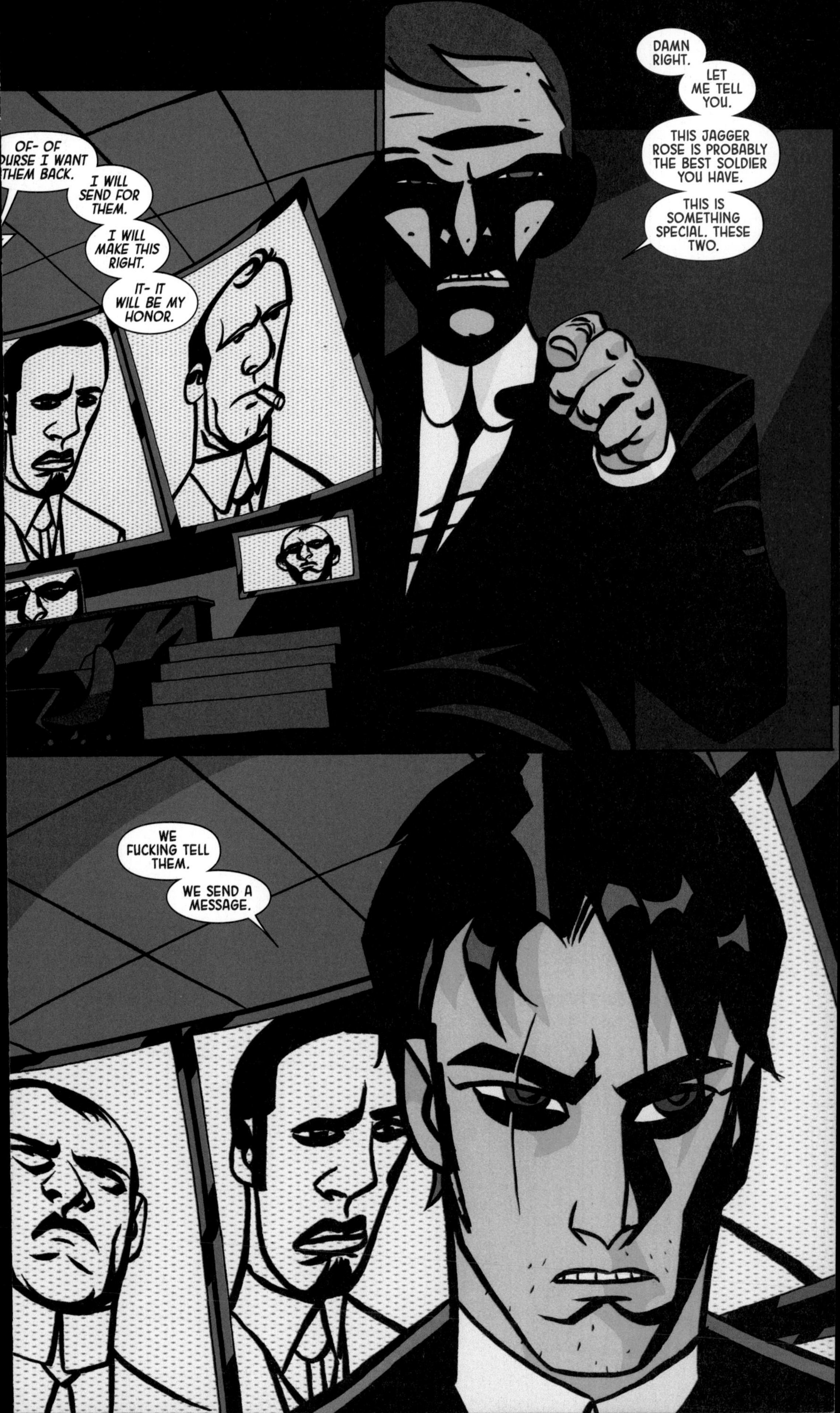
OF- OF
OURSE I WANT THEM BACK.
I WILL SEND FOR THEM.
I WILL MAKE THIS RIGHT.
IT- IT WILL BE MY HONOR.
DAMN RIGHT.
LET ME TELL YOU.
THIS JAGGER ROSE IS PROBABLY THE BEST SOLDIER YOU HAVE.
THIS IS SOMETHING SPECIAL. THESE TWO.
WE FUCKING TELL THEM.
WE SEND A MESSAGE.

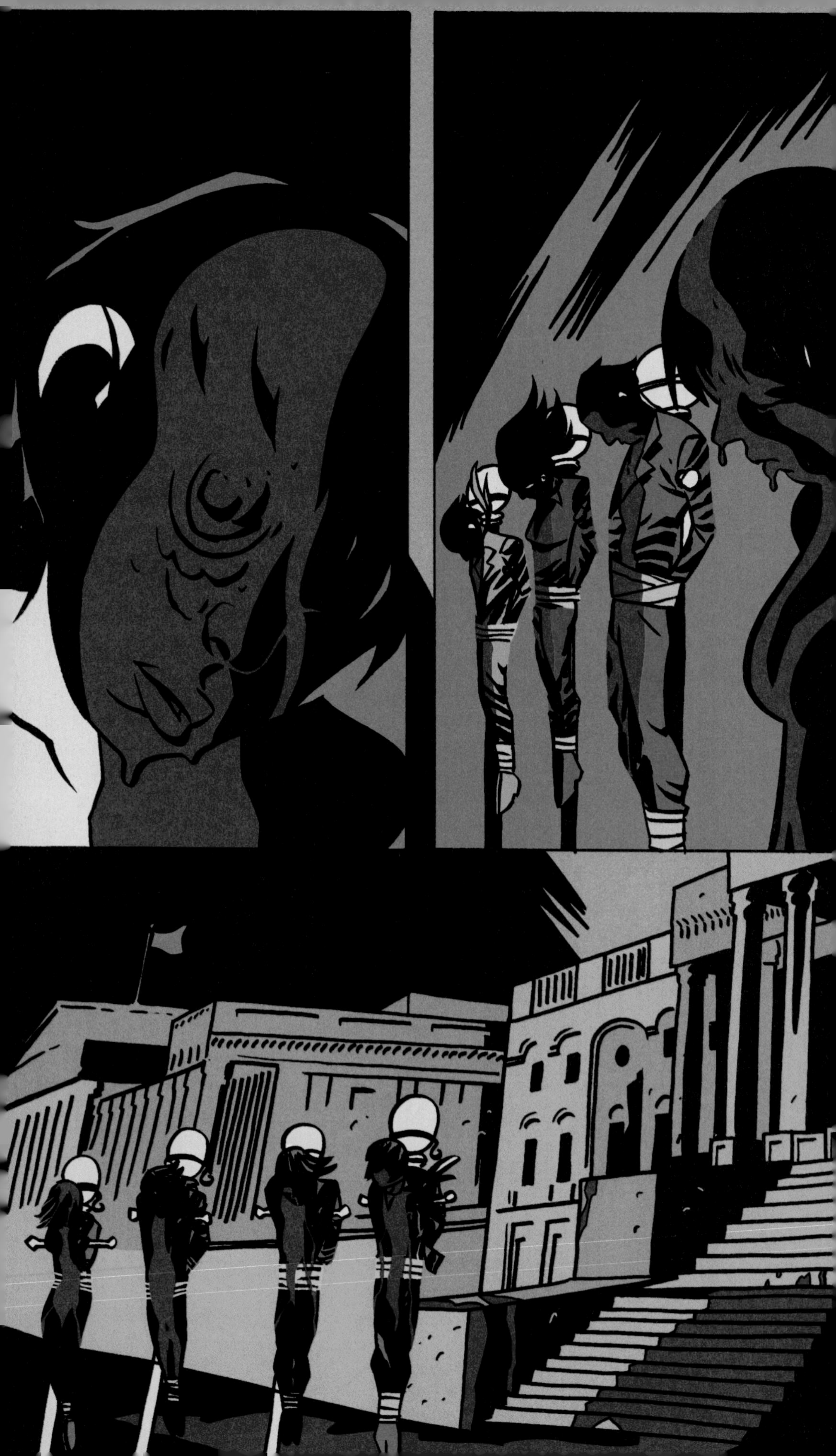

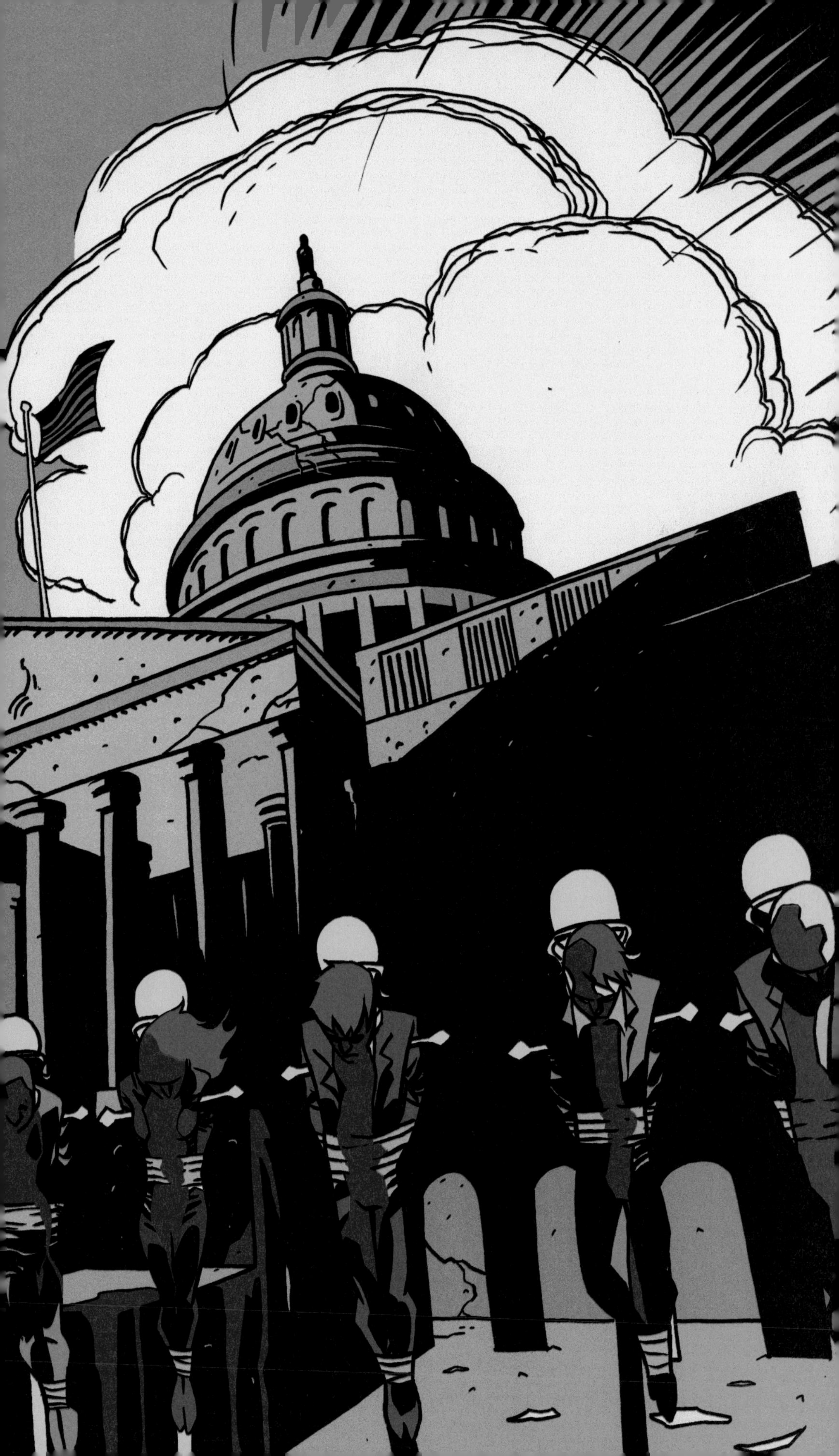

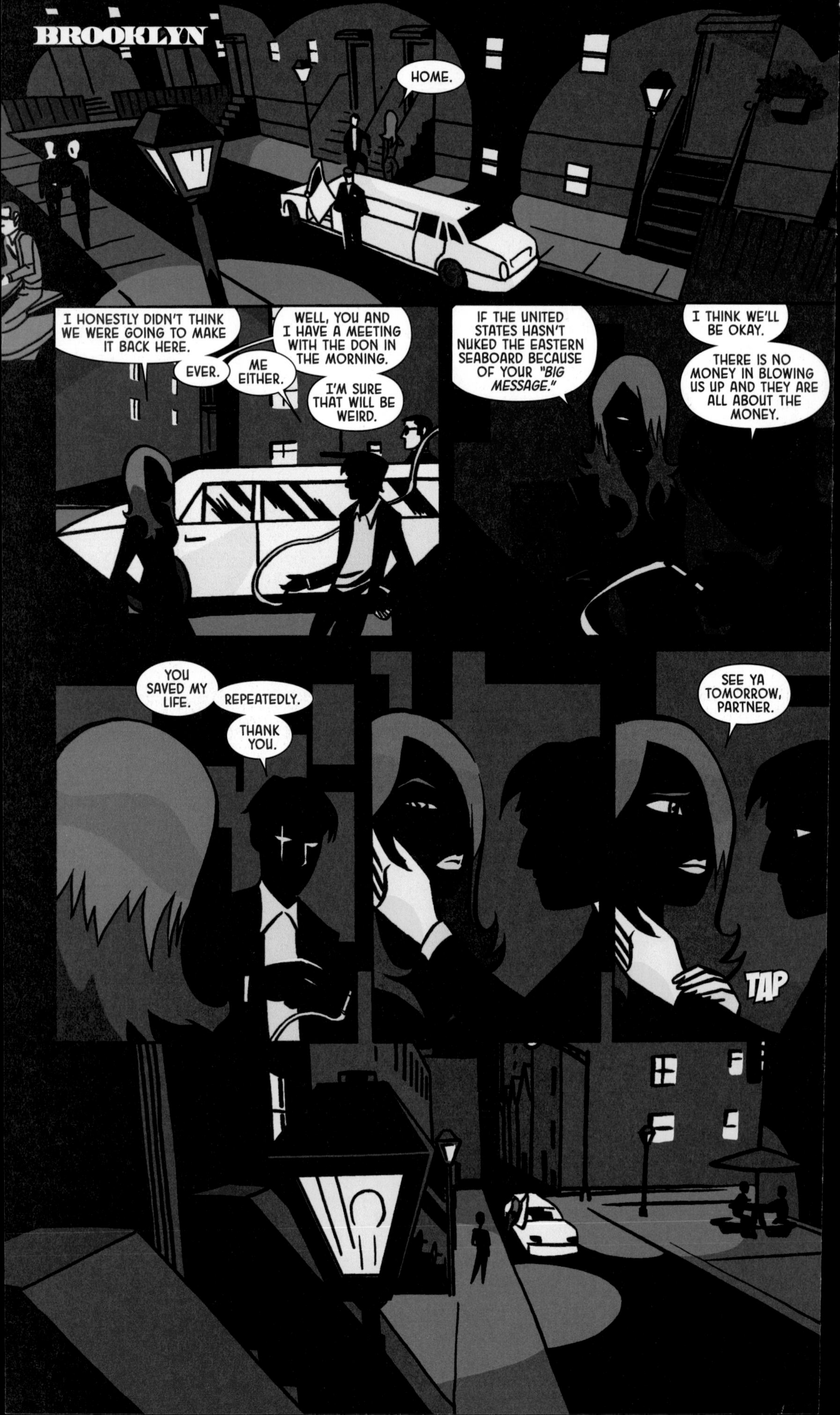
BROOKLYN
HOME.
I HONESTLY DIDN'T THINK WE WERE GOING TO MAKE IT BACK HERE.
EVER.
ME EITHER.
WELL, YOU AND I HAVE A MEETING WITH THE DON IN THE MORNING.
I'M SURE THAT WILL BE WEIRD.
IF THE UNITED STATES HASN'T NUKED THE EASTERN SEABOARD BECAUSE OF YOUR "BIG MESSAGE."
I THINK WE'LL BE OKAY.
THERE IS NO MONEY IN BLOWING US UP AND THEY ARE ALL ABOUT THE MONEY.
YOU SAVED MY LIFE.
REPEATEDLY.
THANK YOU.
SEE YA TOMORROW, PARTNER.
TAP

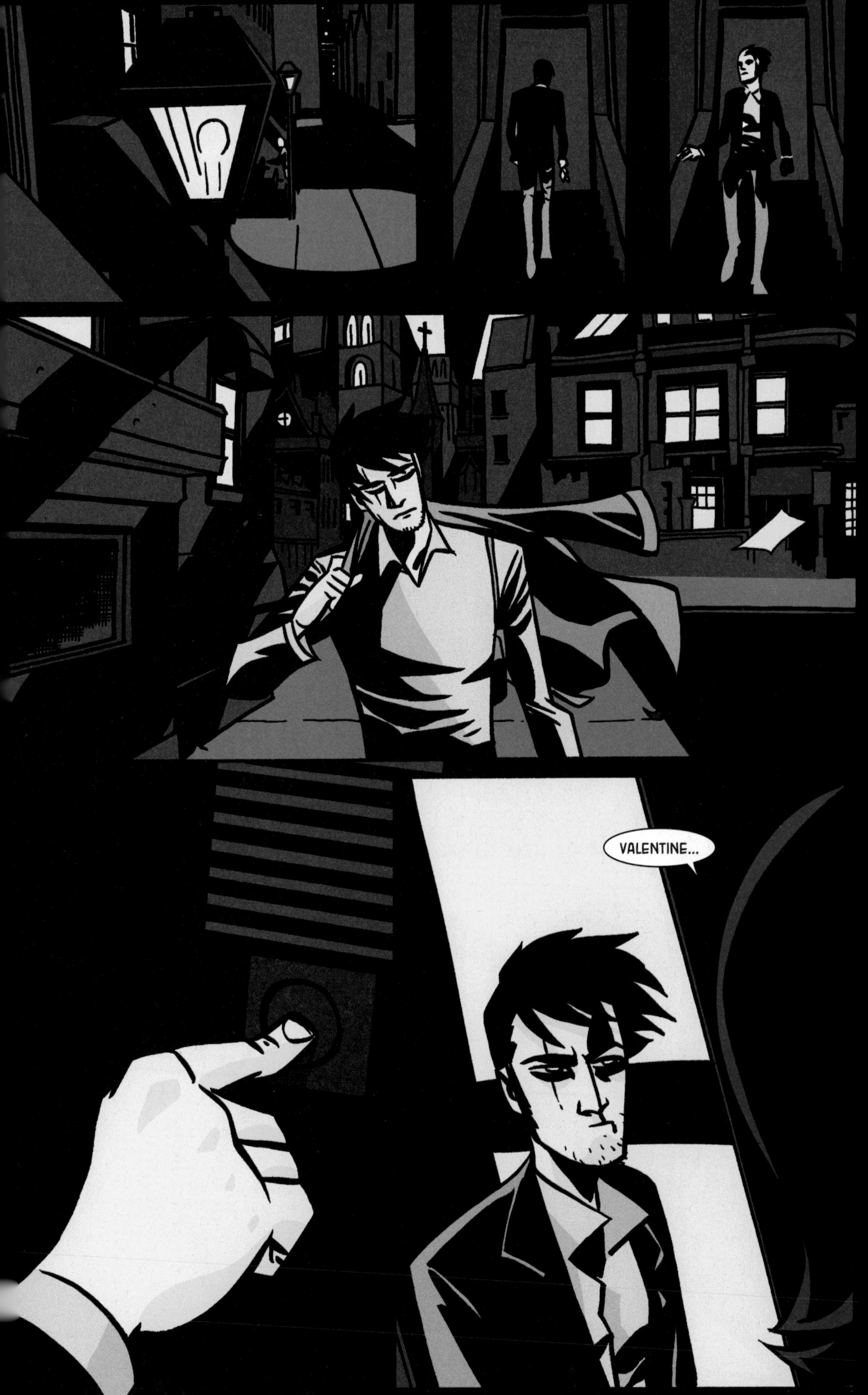
VALENTINE...

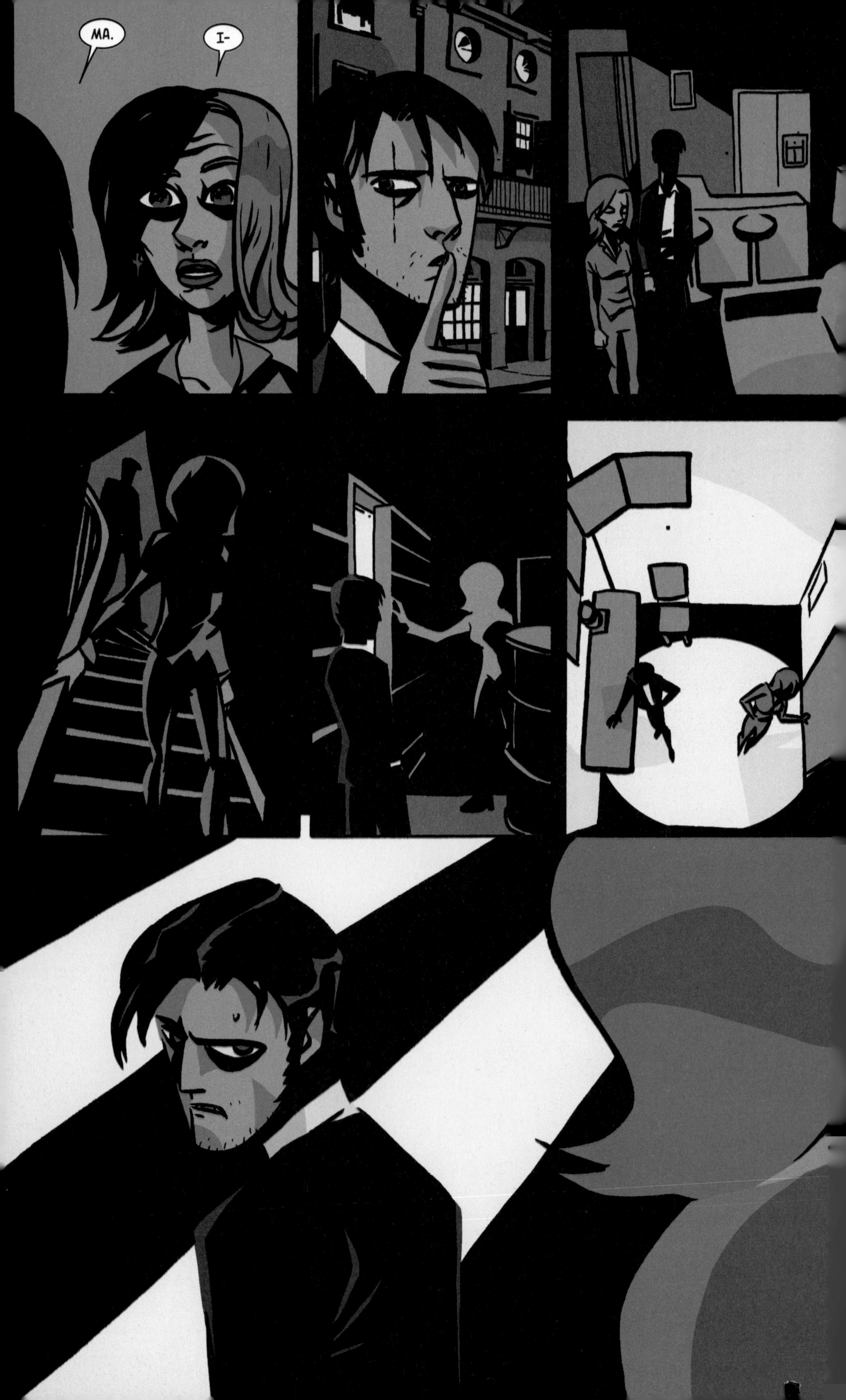
MA.
I-

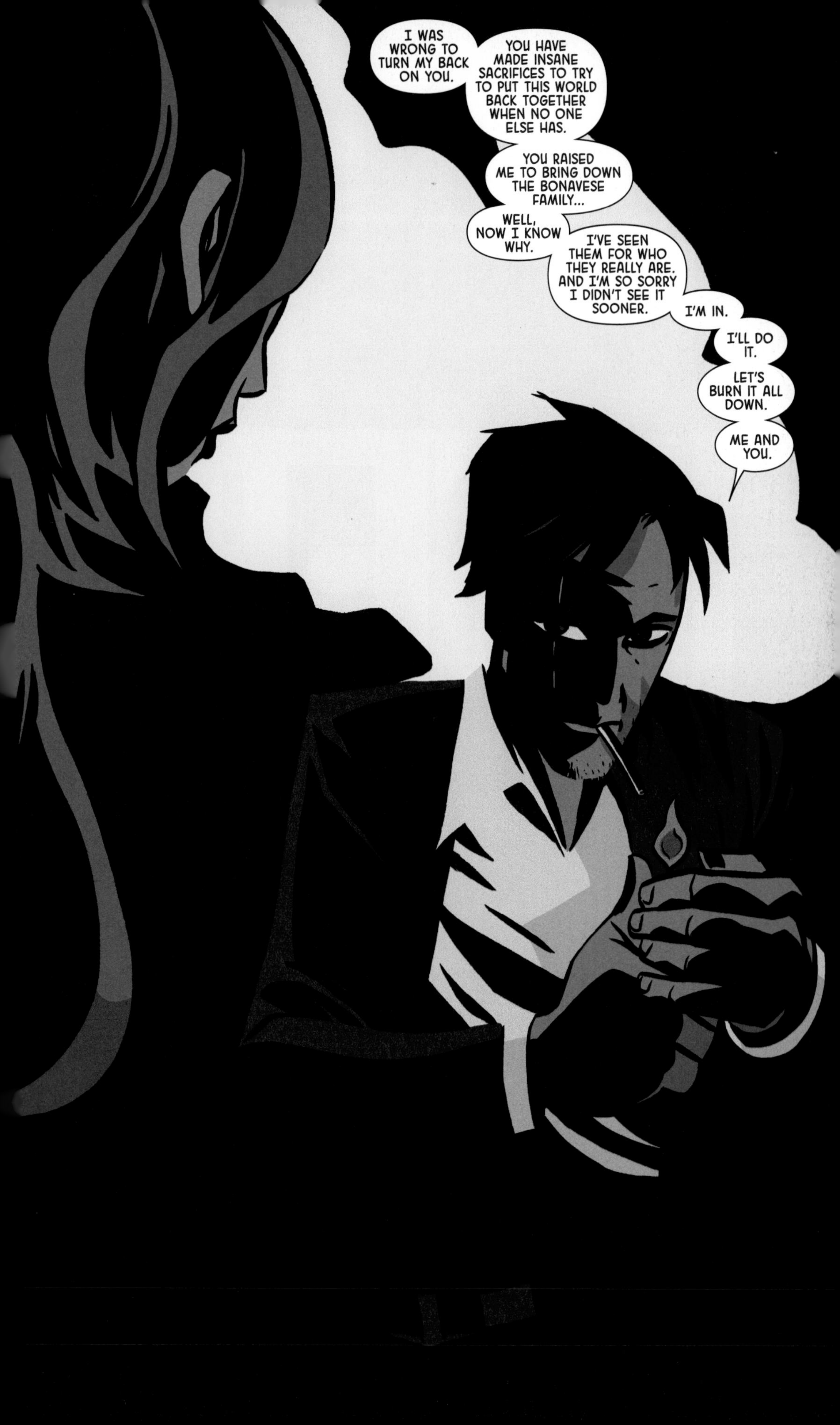
I WAS WRONG TO TURN MY BACK ON YOU.
YOU HAVE MADE INSANE SACRIFICES TO TRY TO PUT THIS WORLD BACK TOGETHER WHEN NO ONE ELSE HAS.
YOU RAISED ME TO BRING DOWN THE BONAVESE FAMILY...
WELL, NOW I KNOW WHY.
I'VE SEEN THEM FOR WHO THEY REALLY ARE. AND I'M SO SORRY I DIDN'T SEE IT SOONER.
I'M IN.
I'LL DO IT.
LET'S BURN IT ALL DOWN.
ME AND YOU.

INTERM

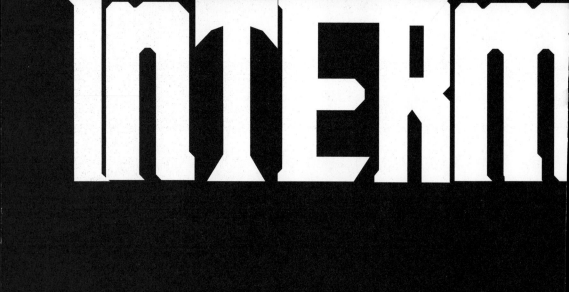

SSION

TO BE CONTINUED...
IN BOOK 2:
THE UNITED STATES
VS. MURDER INC

THE UNITED STATES OF
MURDER INC
COVER GALLERY

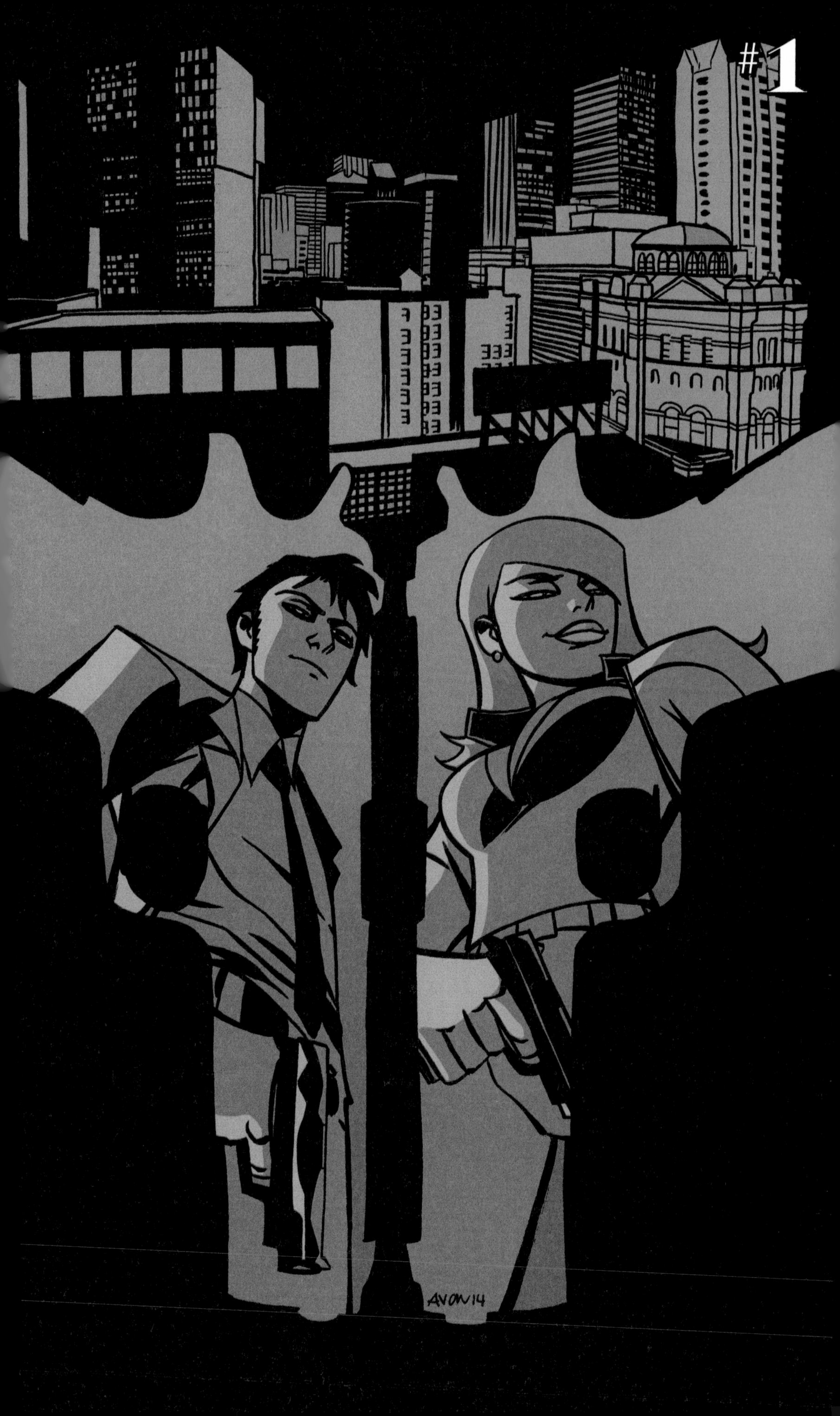
#1
AVON14

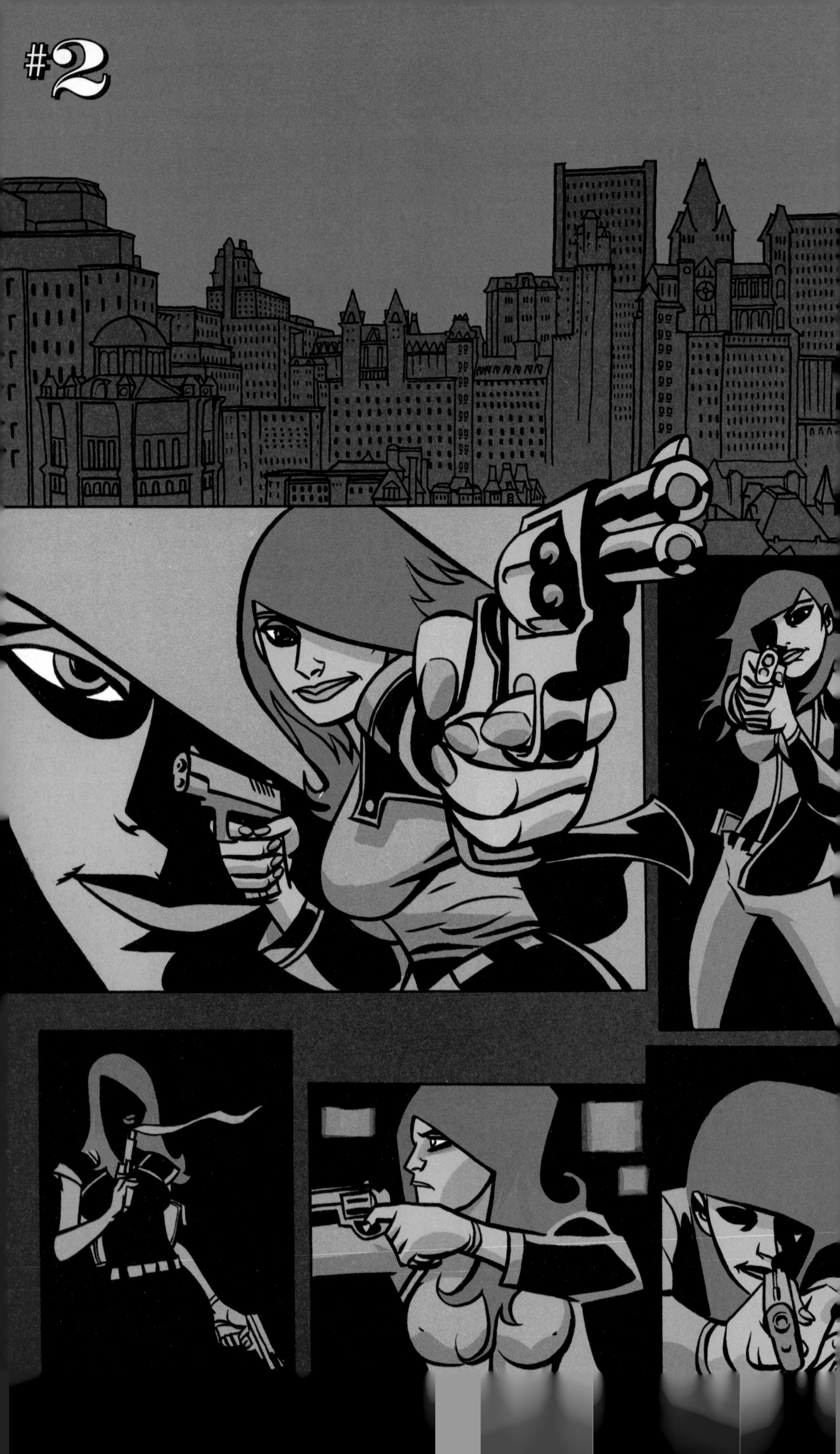
#2

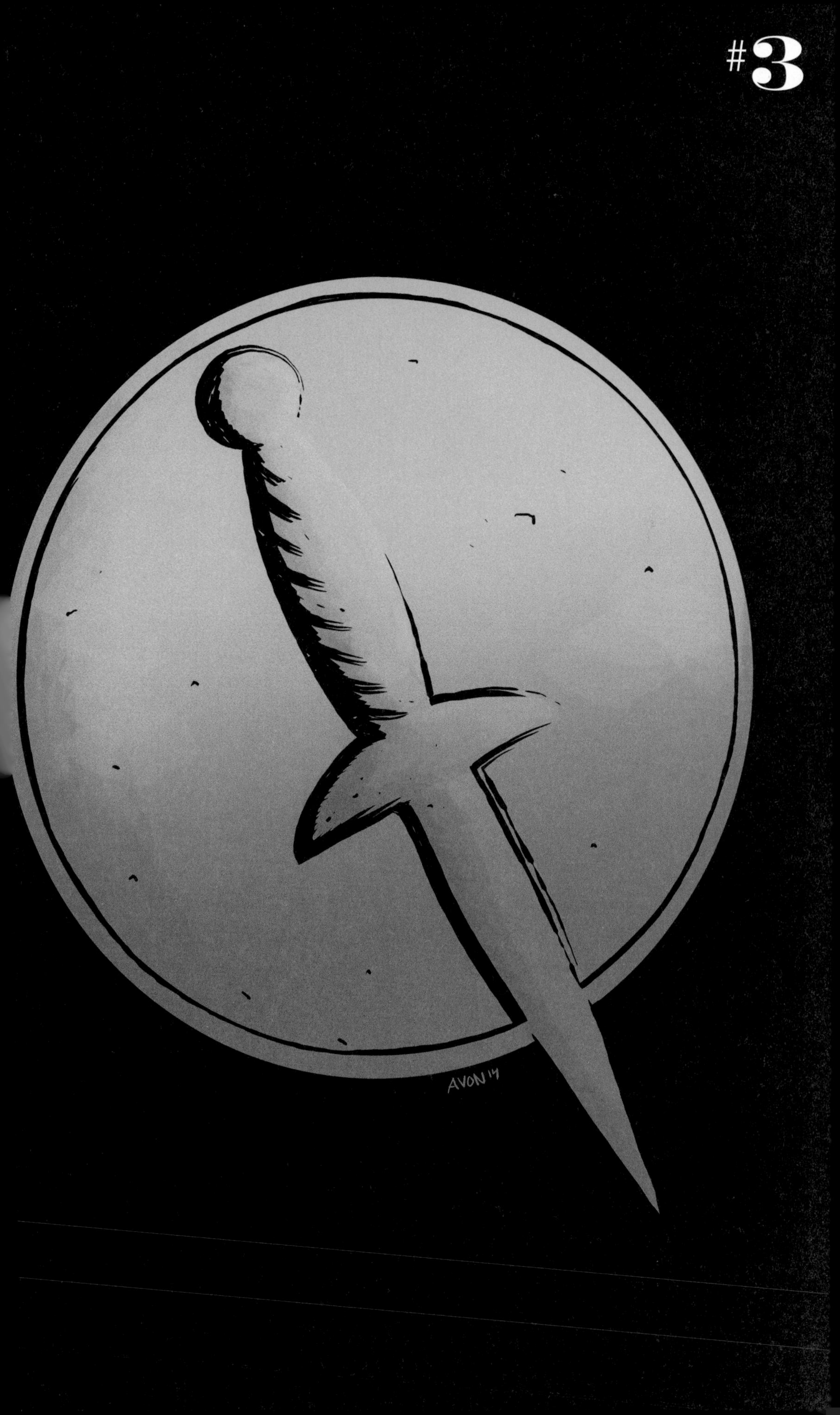
#3
AVON'14

#4

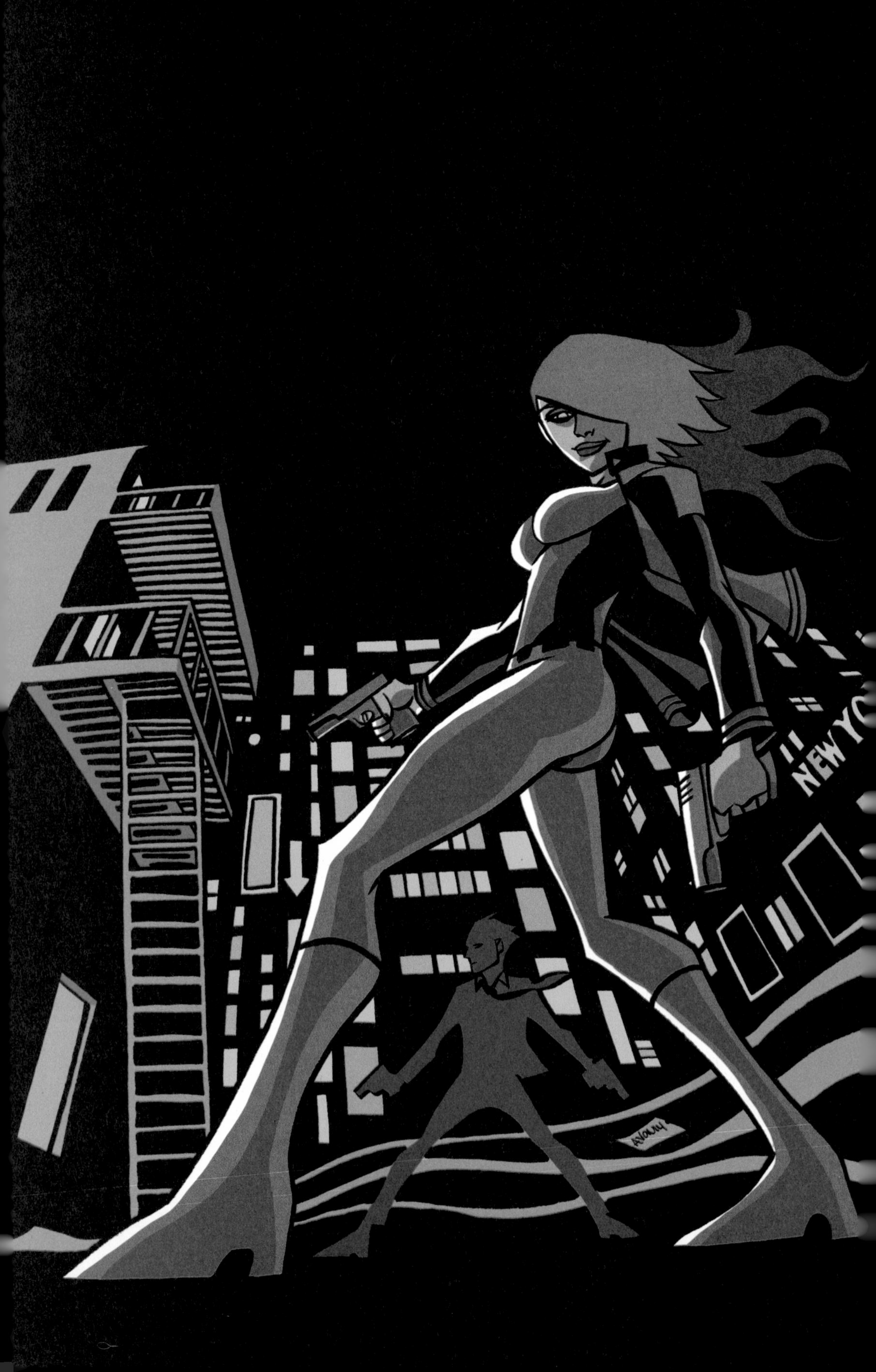
NEW

#5

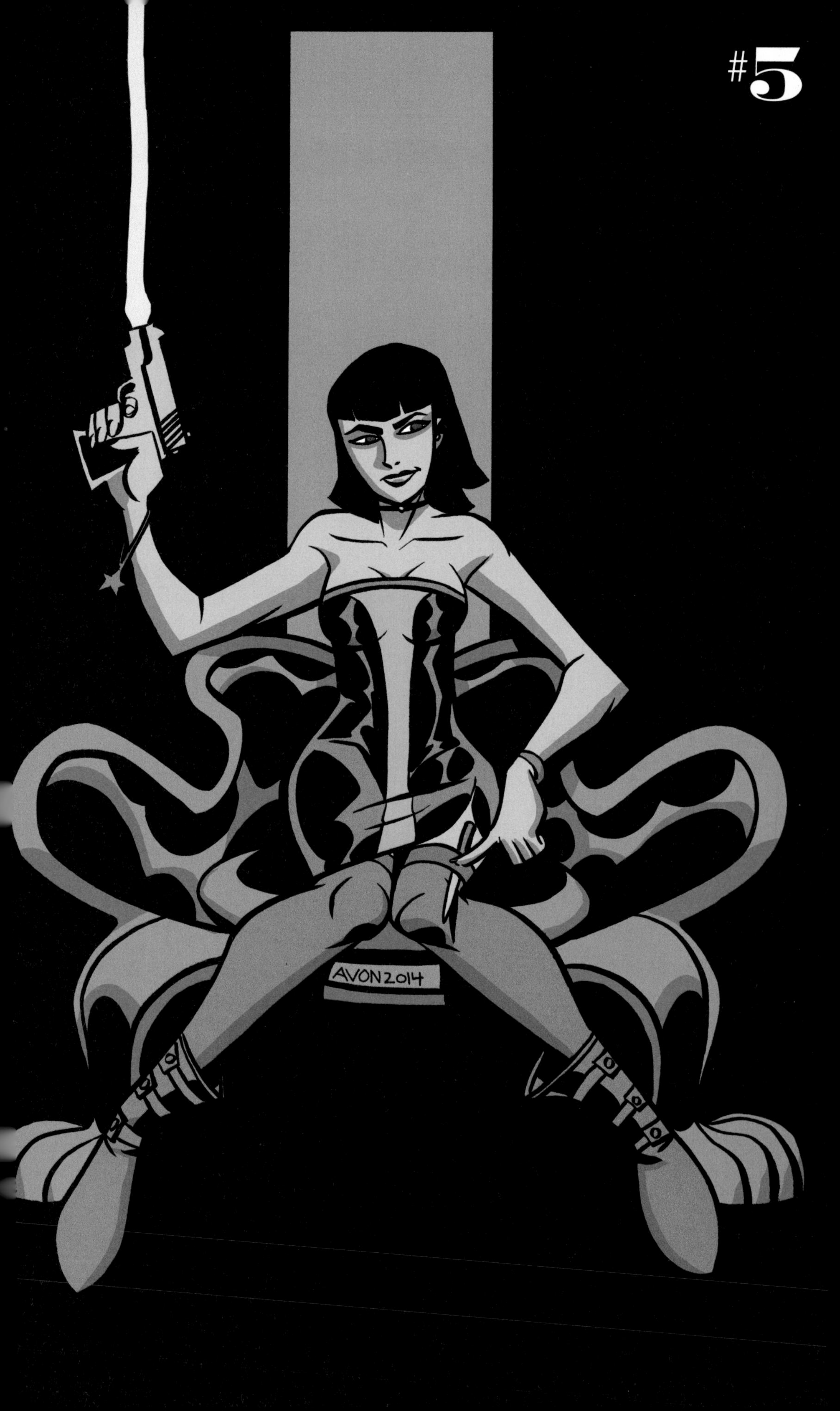
AVON2014

#6

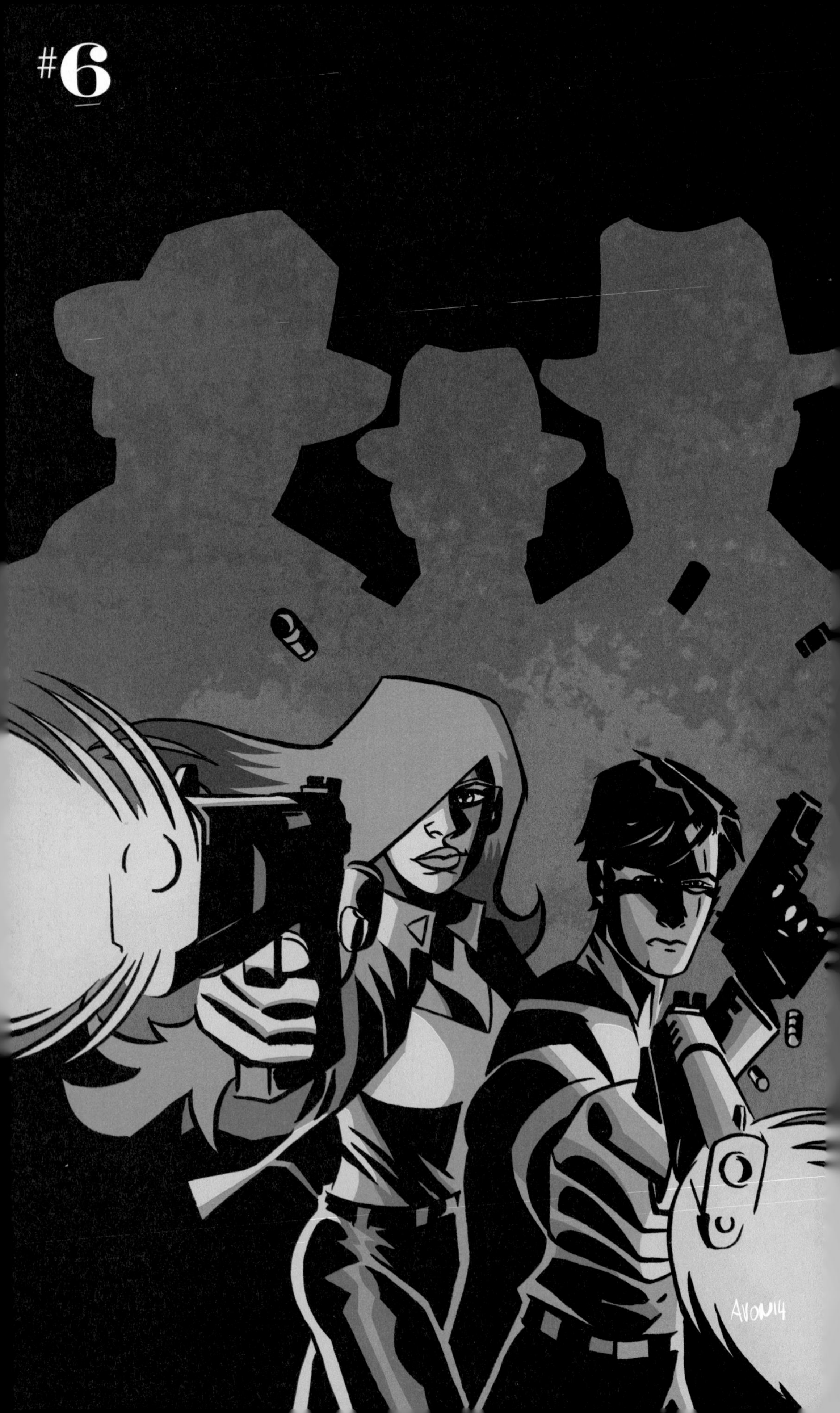
AVON14

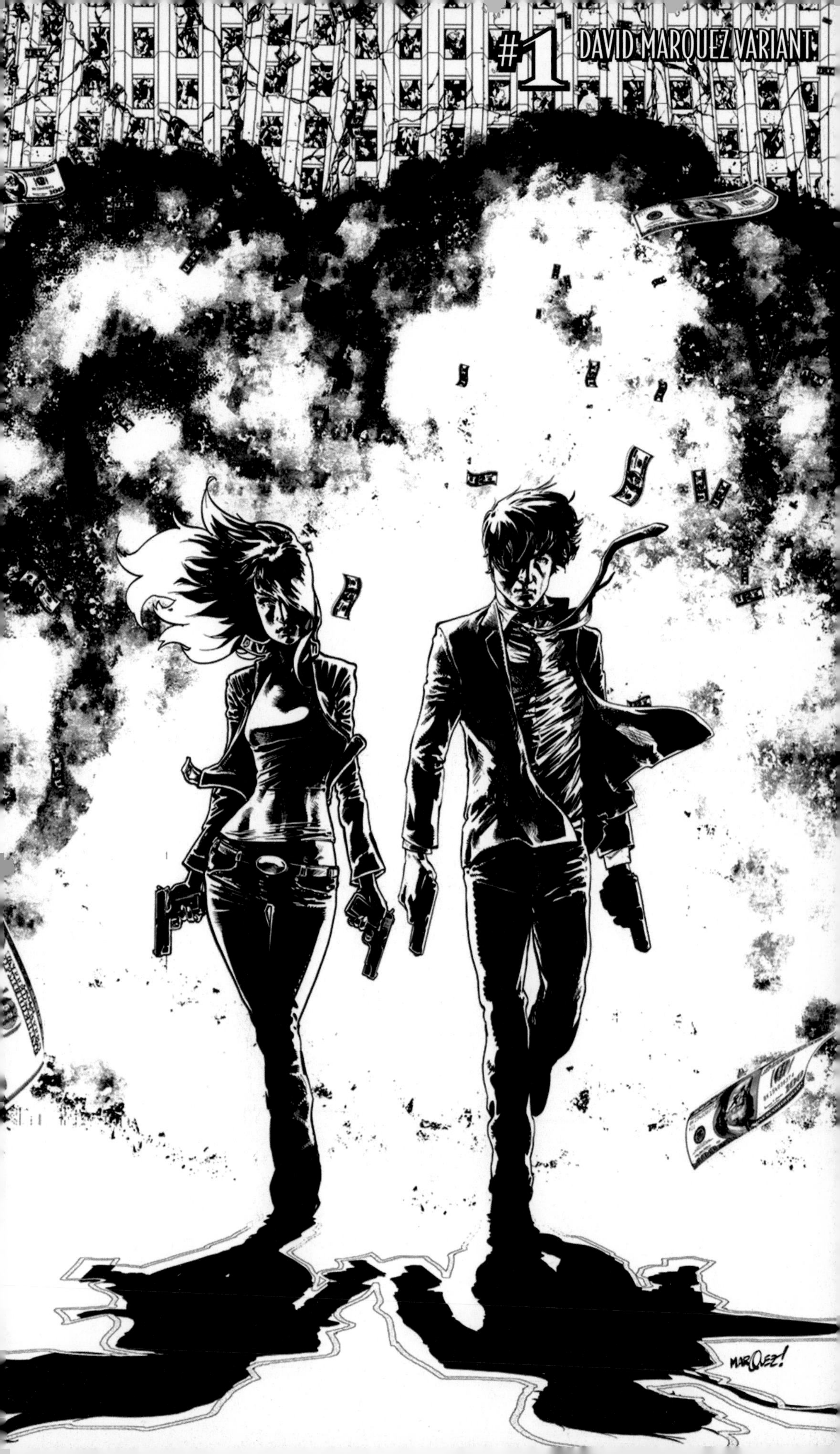
#1
DAVID MARQUEZ VARIANT
MARQUEZ!

#1 BRIAN MICHAEL BENDIS VARIANT

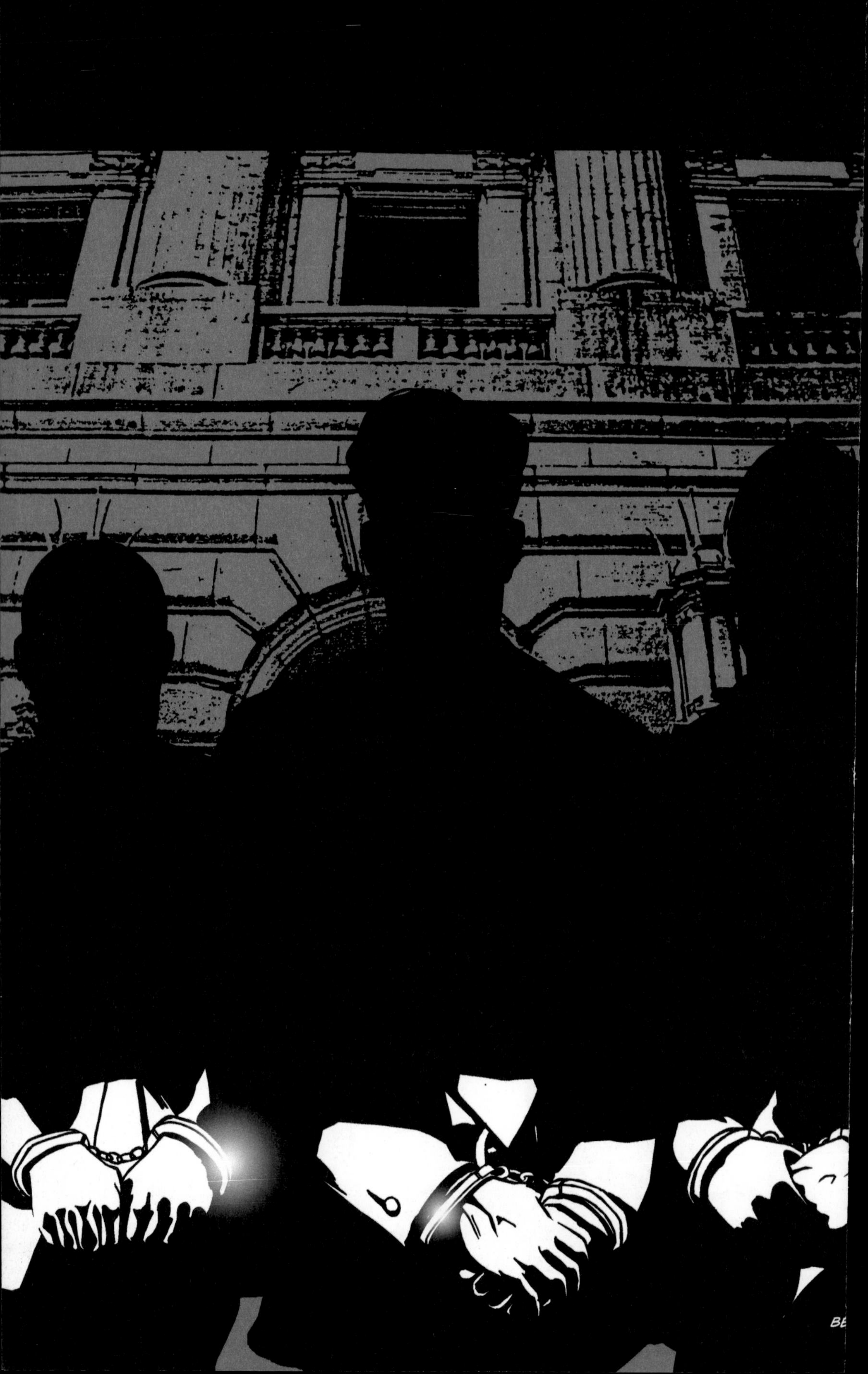

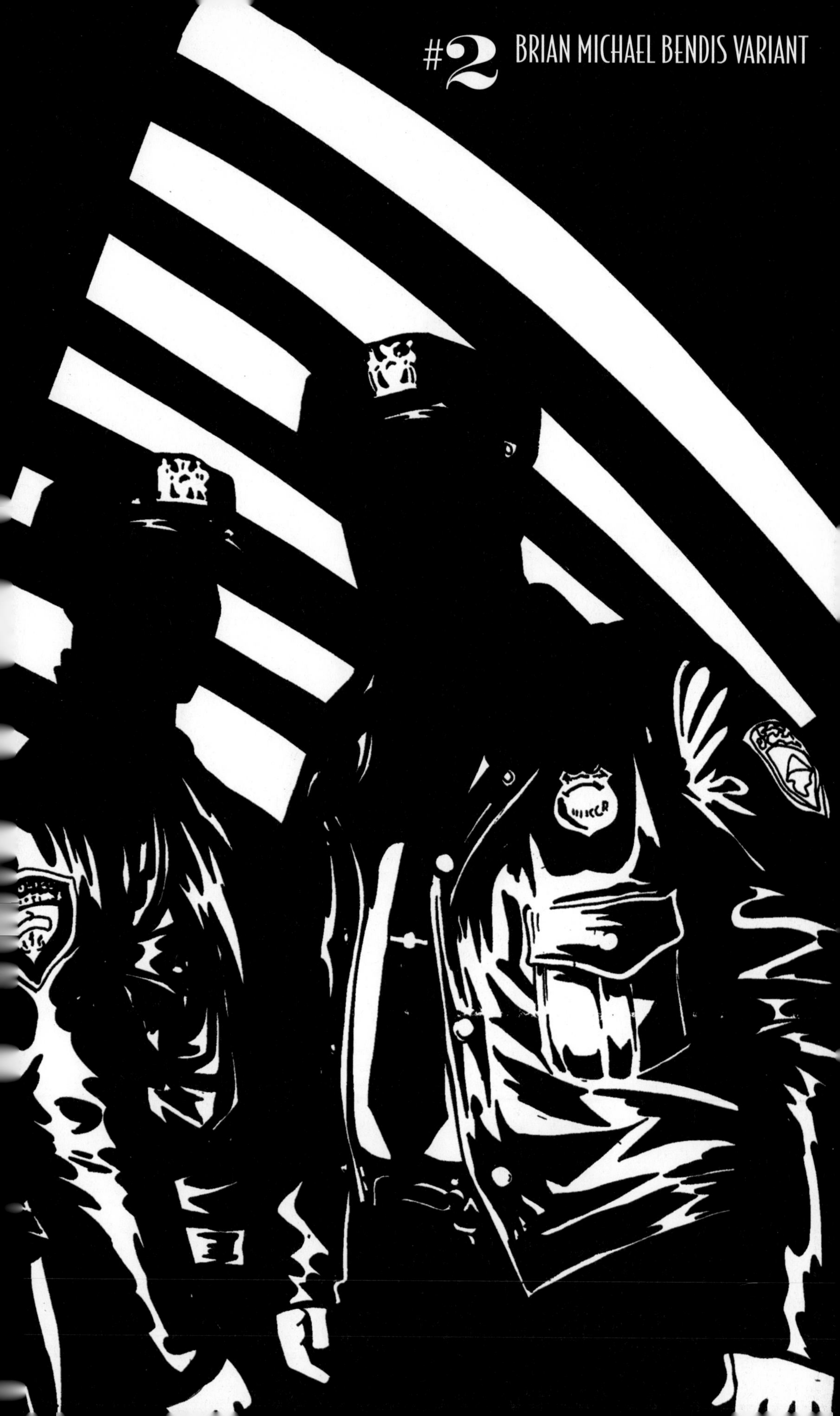
#2 BRIAN MICHAEL BENDIS VARIANT

#3 BRIAN MICHAEL BENDIS VARIANT

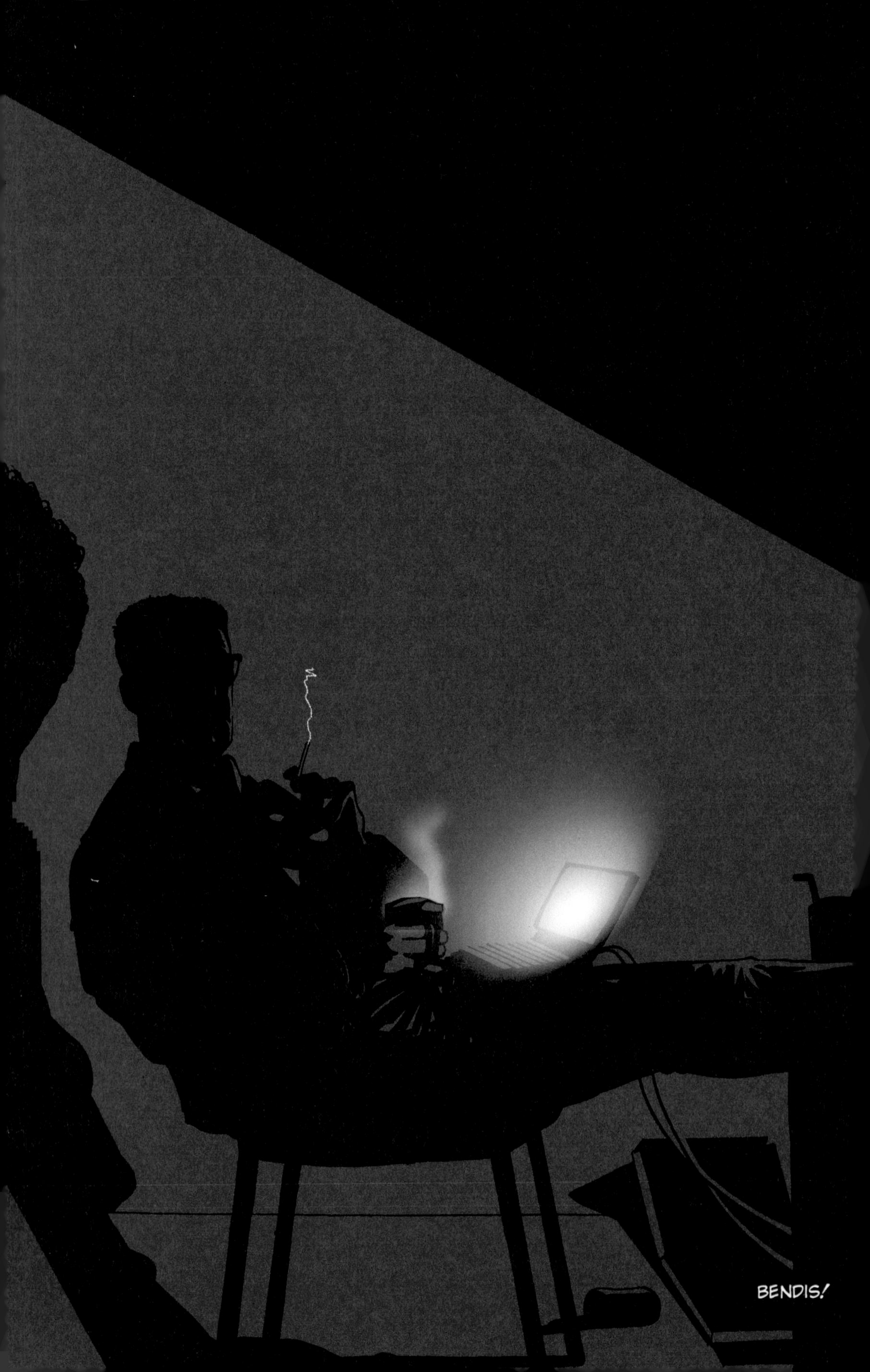
BENDIS!

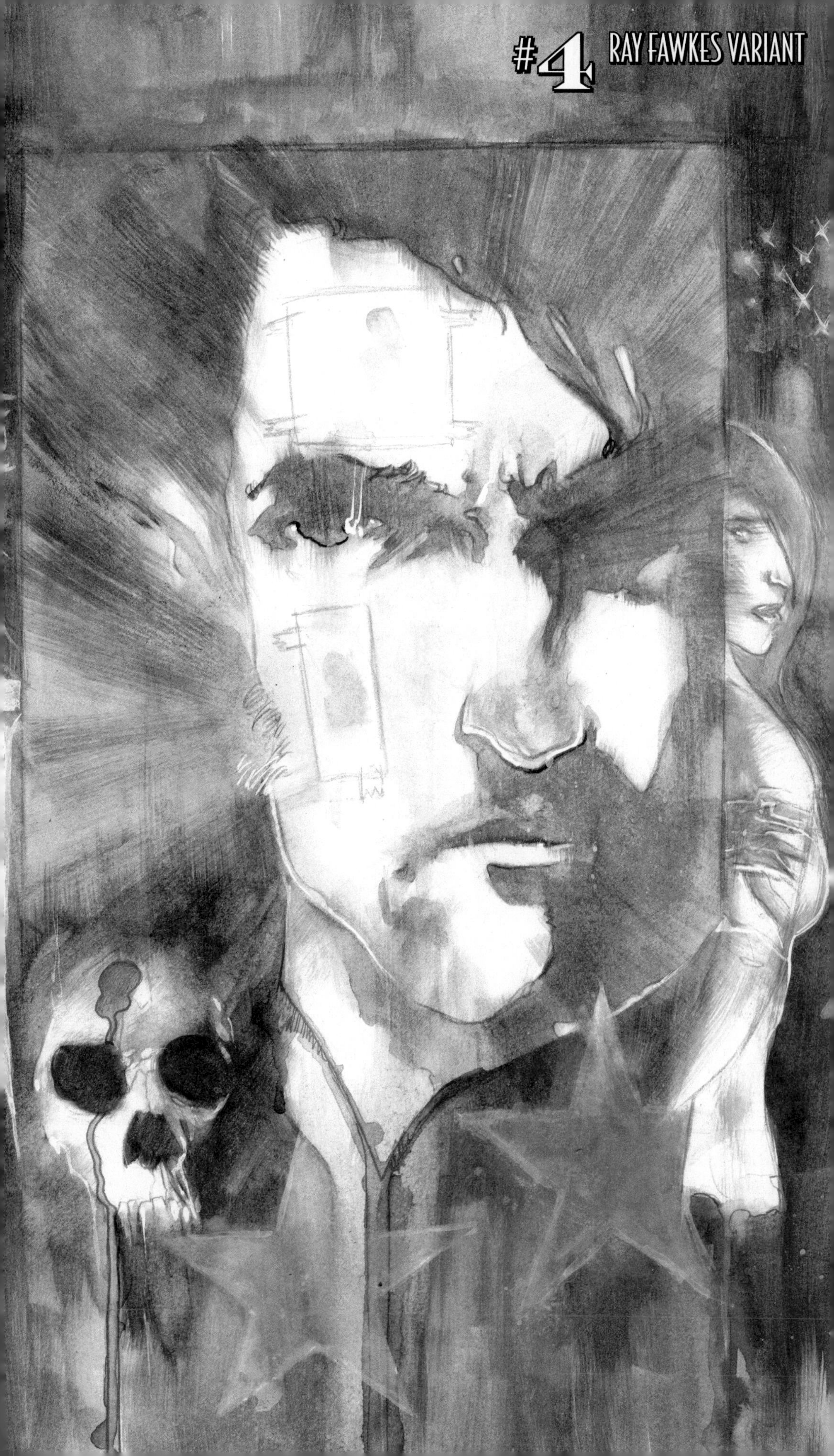

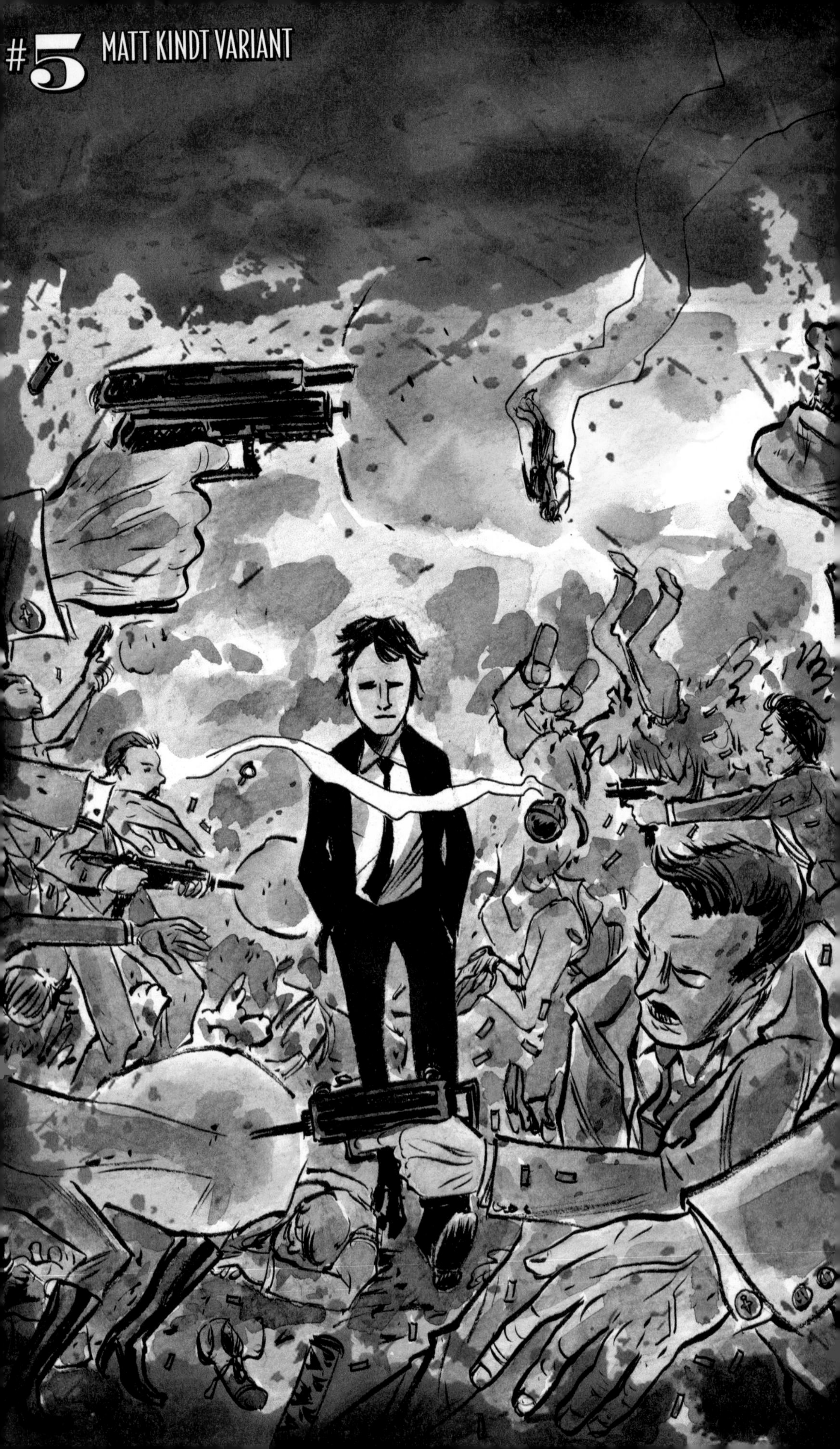
#5 MATT KINDT VARIANT

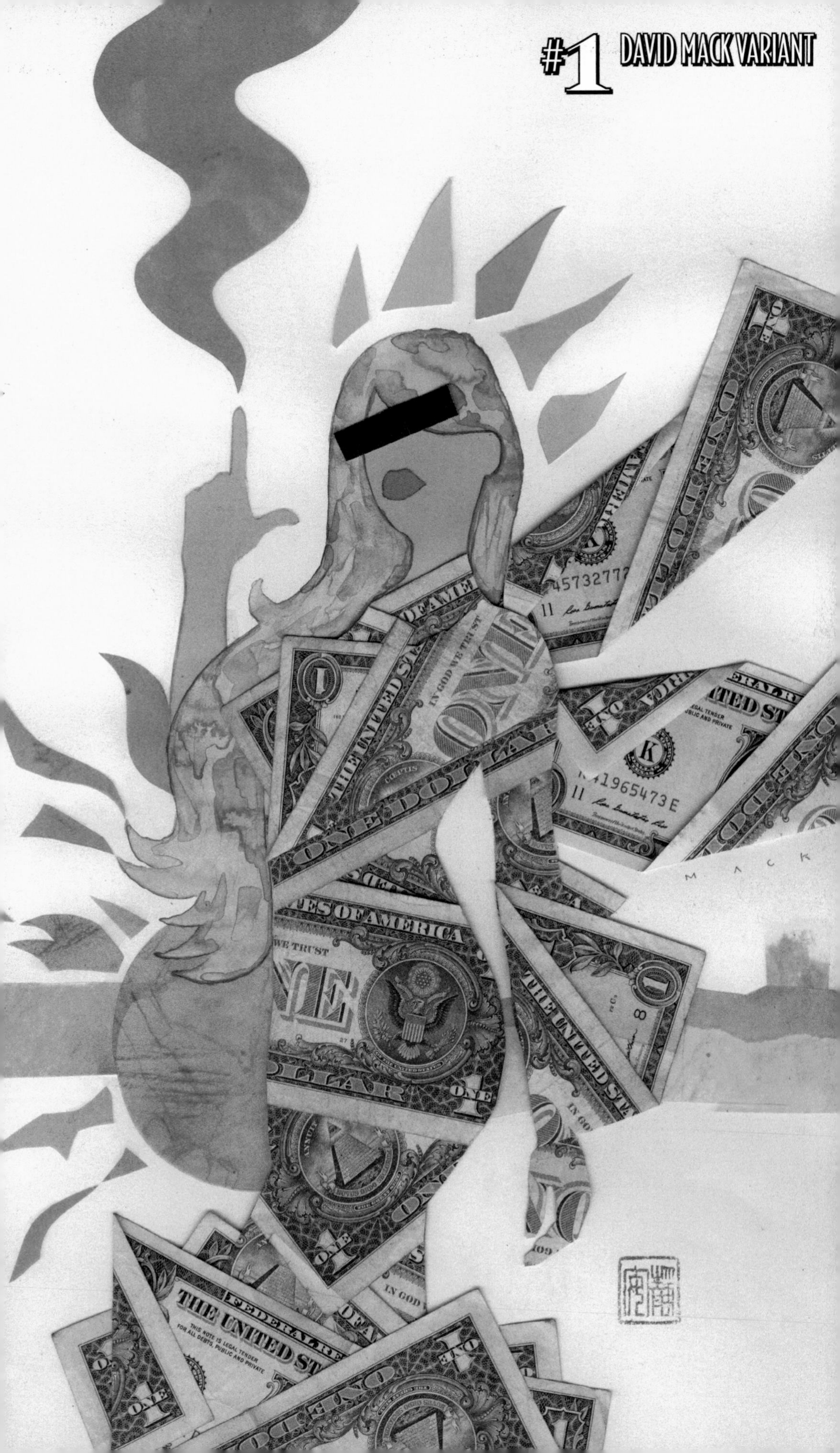
#1 DAVID MACK VARIANT
MACK

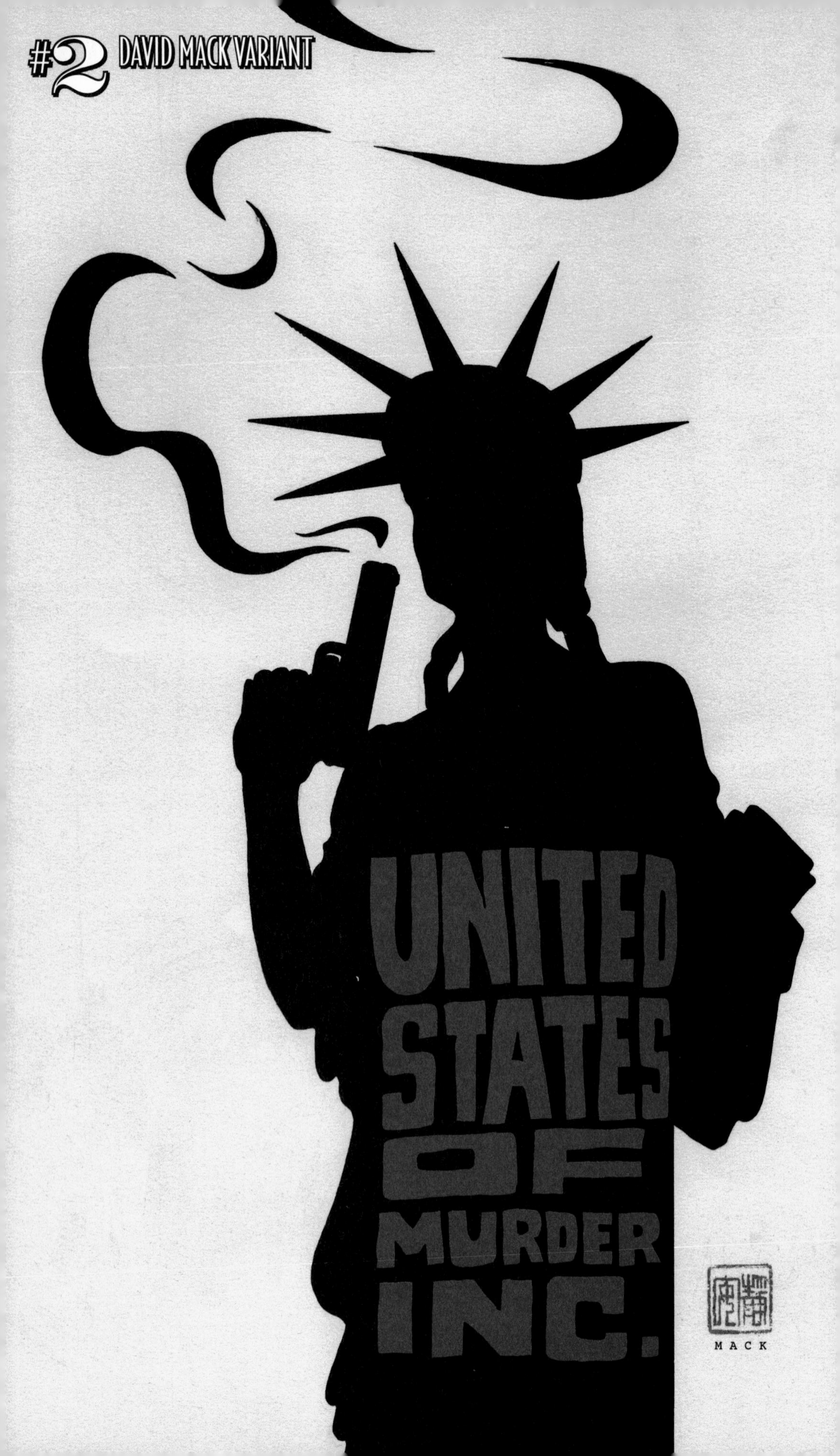
#2 DAVID MACK VARIANT
UNITED
STATES
OF
MURDER
INC.
MACK

#3 DAVID MACK VARIANT

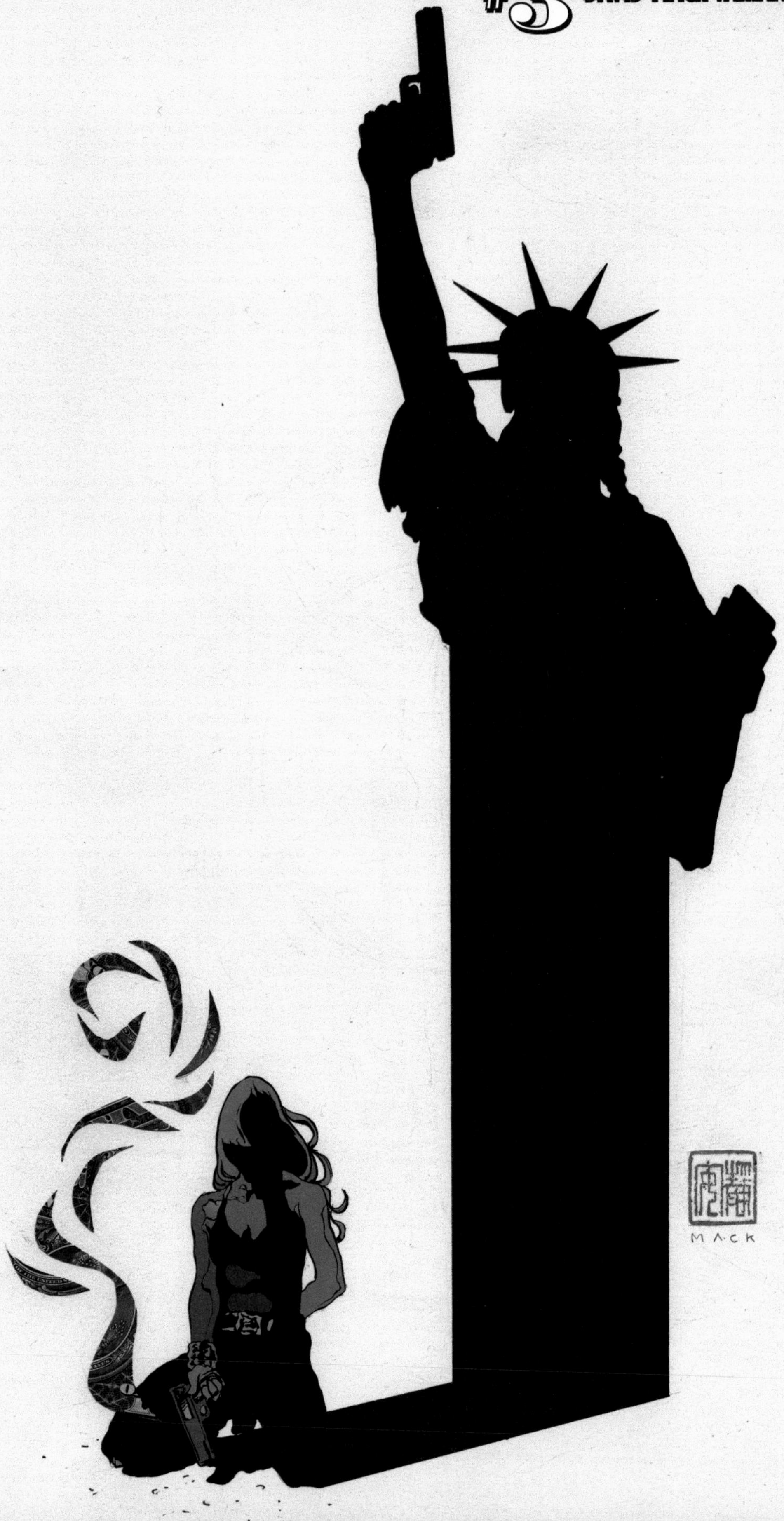
MACK

#4 DAVID MACK VARIANT

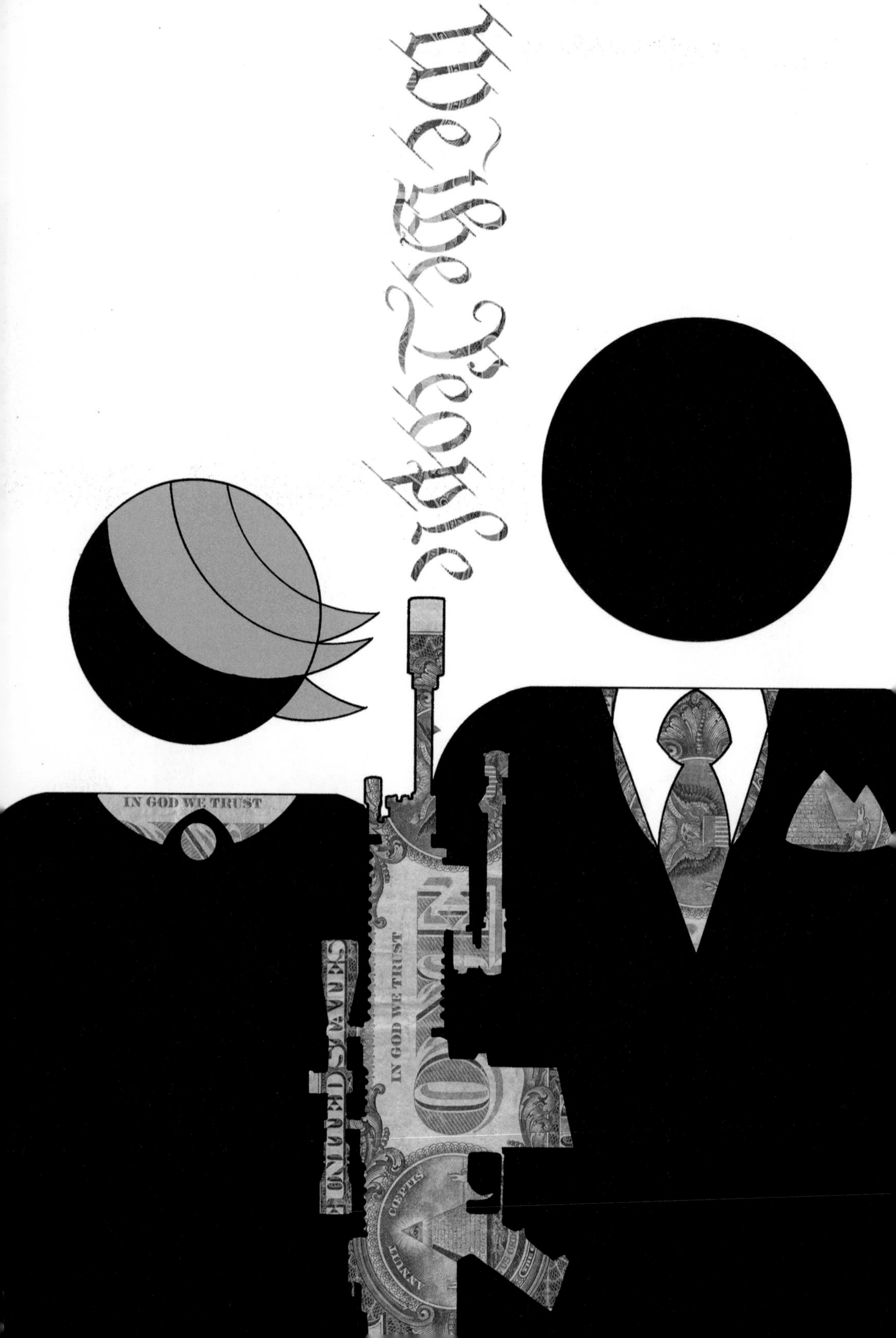
We the People
IN GOD WE TRUST
IN GOD WE TRUST

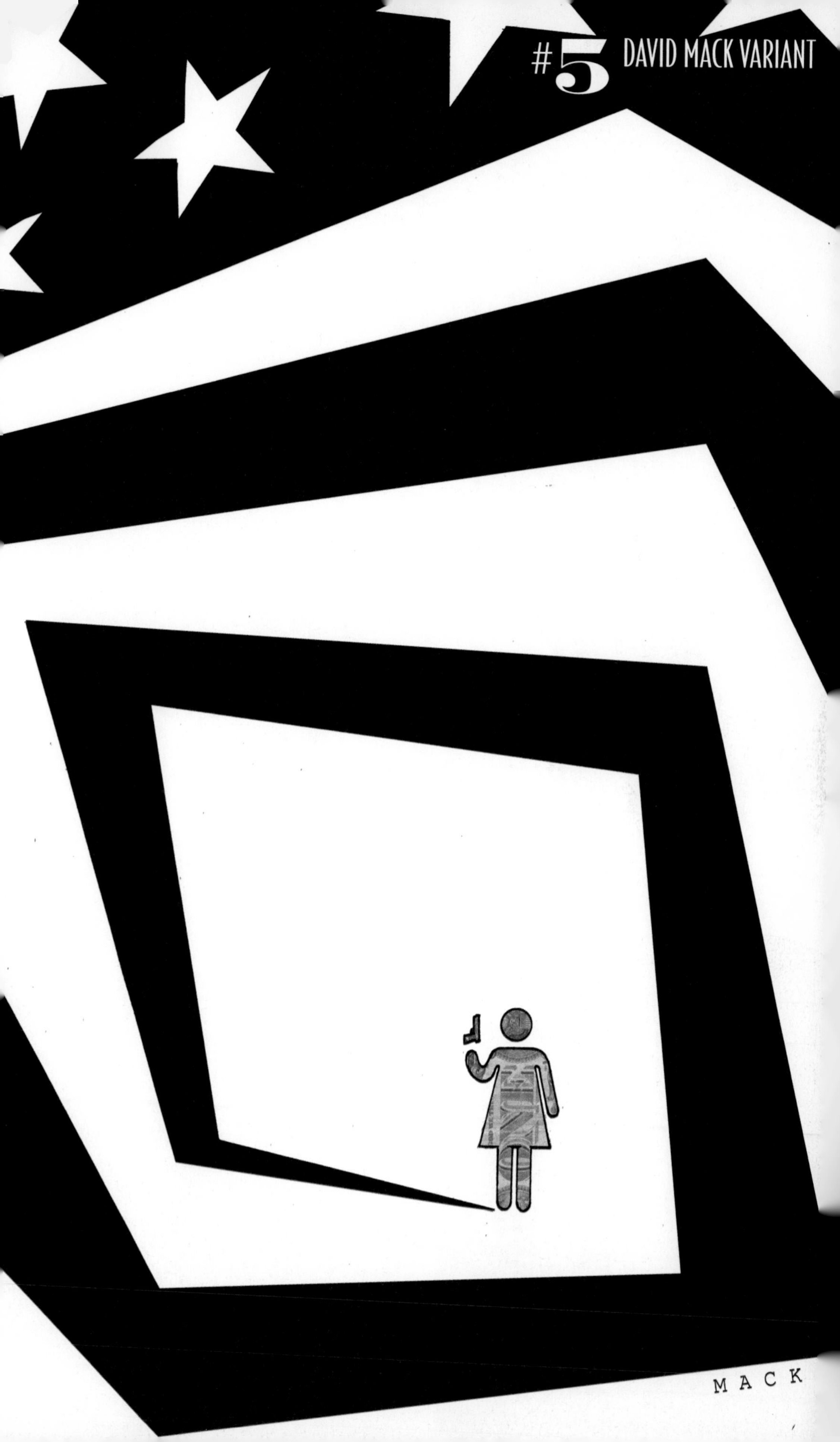
#5 DAVID MACK VARIANT
MACK

#6 DAVID MACK VARIANT

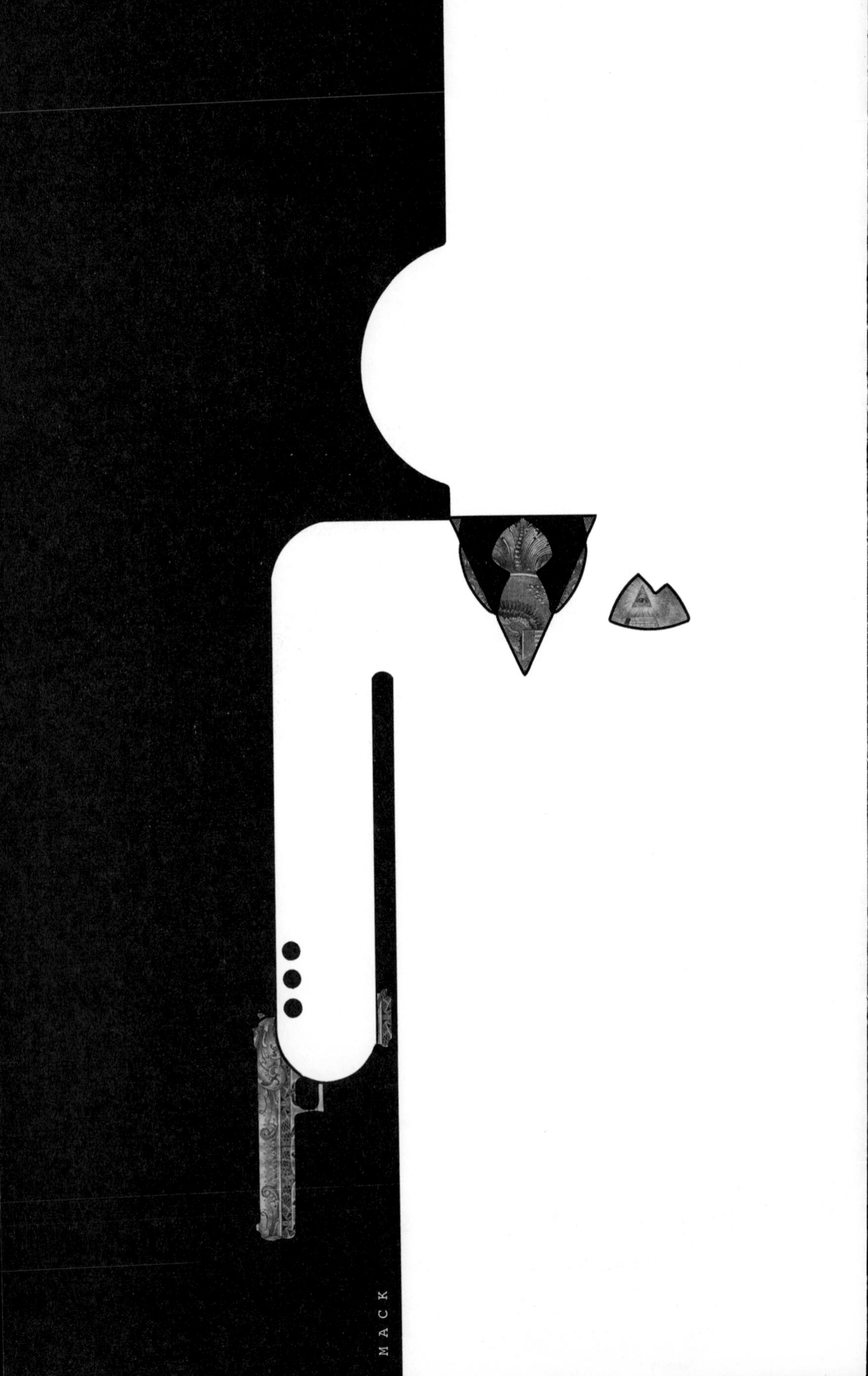
MACK

THE UNITED STATES OF MURDER INC.

Issue #1 - Script and Sketches
by Brian Michael Bendis and Michael Avon Oeming

PAGE 1

1–Int. Party room/backstage—night

Our hero, Valentine, is looking right at us with a quizzical look as a woman off-panel adjusts the tie on his very nice suit.

VALENTINE

Mom.

2–Over Valentine's shoulder, we see his mother, Madonna, almost tearing up, with glassy eyes. Not tears but very emotional eyes.

She has these huge eyes and these killer dimples. A woman who still keeps herself together. You can tell that back in the day she was quite something.

You can also tell from her big eyes that she has seen a lot of pain and death. A lot of things that have changed her. A lot of secrets that she keeps inside.

Even from her son. Her son being the thing in her life she is most proud of.

MADONNA

Shut up.

VALENTINE

Are you gonna cry?

MADONNA

You wanna slap?

3–She adjusts the lapel on his suit. She is so proud of him. All dimples. She holds it together. He looks down at her and can't help but be amazed. Truly.

Behind them, a few silhouettes. Men of means waiting in the wings.

VALENTINE

I've never seen you even come close, Ma.

I'm allowed to declare this an historic event.

MADONNA

Shut your fuckin' mouth.

4–Valentine feels her unconditional love. She knows it's time to let go. The wheels are in motion and there's nothing she can do to stop what's about to happen.

MADONNA (CONT'D)

M'not gonna kiss you because I don't want to get any make up or nothin' on ya.

VALENTINE

Go sit, ma.

You're freakin' me out.

5—Valentine watches as his mother walks away into the shadows.

OLD MAN (OFF-PANEL)

You ready, Mr. Gallo?

6—Valentine is peeking behind the curtain to the stage. Nothing too obvious just a slab of light giving him a look at his future.

Behind Valentine, a rotund old man, Bonavese, with a walking cane. Standing behind him ominously. Think Bob Hoskins.

BONAVESE

Valentine, you ready?

VALENTINE

Am I, Padrino?

BONAVESE

Follow me.

PAGE 2

1–Large panel. Over Valentine's shoulder, many men armed with guns, in light suits, are standing around a table. In the center of the table there is a human skull sitting on top of a piece of paper and a knife.

The shadows are so thick behind this ceremony that we can't tell where we are or who else is in the room.

2–Low looking up, Valentine approaches and looks down at...

3–Valentine's p.o.v. The human skull sitting on top of a piece of paper and a very ornate knife.

On the piece of paper is the image of a saint.

4–Bonavese picks up the knife and looks at it.

BONAVESE (CONT'D)

In my day, this ceremony went a little differently.

It was done in a backroom. Away from the world.

And you had to earn it with a lifetime of service.

You had to be more than just blood.

You had to prove your worth and loyalty.

5–Bonavese holds the knife up to Valentine. Showing it to him. Engraved. Old school. Like four-hundred-years-old old school.

BONAVESE (CONT'D)

But your father, and his father before him...they were truly honorable men.

In many ways they were the backbone of this organization, this family...

I would make an exception for you, Valentine, even if our ways had never changed.

Take the knife.

6–Valentine holds the knife.

BONAVESE (CONT'D)

Who we are is who you are.

Do you agree?

VALENTINE

Yes, sir.

BONAVESE

Show us.

PAGE 3

1–Valentine holds it to his lower lip. He is getting ready to cut himself.

2–Valentine jabs the knife into the inside of his lower lip.

3–The knife has blood on it.

4–Profile. Valentine leans forward and the blood from the wound drips/pours onto the skull.

BONAVESE (CONT'D)

You honor your father and your father's father with
this blood oath to the family.

5–The blood pours down the front of the skull's face.

6–Bonavese takes the knife himself

7–Bonavese cuts Valentine's finger.

8–Bonavese takes Valentine's hand and smears Valentine's finger blood on the image of the saint.

PAGE 4-5

Double-page spread

1–From behind Bonavese, Valentine looks to the Godfather and wipes his bloody lip. Not sure what is going to happen next.

2–Bonavese picks up the bloody image of the saint. Another man hands him a long match already lit.

3–Bonavese lights the image of the saint on fire.

4–The paper is burning quickly as Bonavese hands it to Valentine.

BONAVESE (CONT'D)

If you betray your family...

Your flesh will burn like this saint.

5–Valentine looks at the burning paper in his hand. The saint is burning.

6–The burning paper is almost gone and about to burn Valentine's fingers.

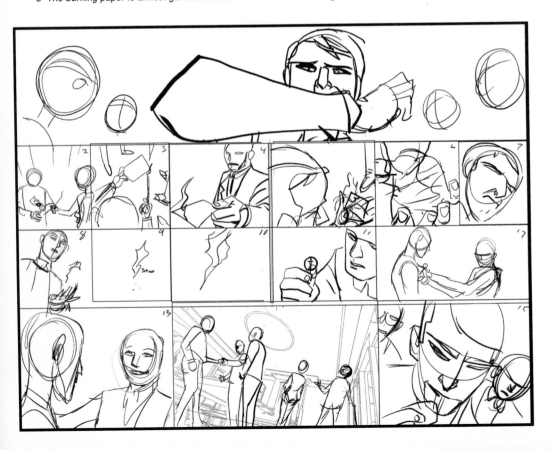

7–Valentine winces as it clearly hurts. A test of endurance.

8–Valentine opens his fingers and the piece of burning paper floats into the air. Embers.

VALENTINE

Ah!

9–The piece of burning paper disappears as it burns itself out.

10–The piece of paper is gone. Just a tiny swirl of smoke.

11–Bonavese pulls out a small gold pin. A circular pin with a symbol on it. A dagger pointed down.

12–Bonavese puts the pin on Valentine's lapel.

13–Valentine turns to see the boss smiling. The serious part is over.

BONAVESE

And that's that.

14–All the men are smiling and parting ways...some shaking his bloody hand. Bonavese claps his hands and yells out.

BONAVESE (CONT'D)

Let's eat!!

15–Valentine takes all the goodwill from his fellow soldiers. His lip still bleeding. A spotlight on him as he looks out and sees...

PAGE 6-7

Double-page spread

Wide of the party room.

We now see the entire Bonavese family is there. Hundreds of tables of people of all shapes and sizes. Dozens of good families. Mothers, fathers, wives, husbands, children and grandmothers and grandfathers...cousins.

In the old days, the days before things went differently, this ceremony was done in secret in a secret back room, but now that the families are an established part of society, this ceremony is done in public, in front of the people, like a bar mitzvah or a wedding.

The ceremony part is over and the catering is about to begin. There will be eating and drinking and dancing.

This was Valentine's ceremony. He is a made man.

2–On the bottom of the spread we see that table number one features his mother, Madonna, clapping, still with glassy eyes but no tears.

Other members of his family that really won't play any part of this story.

Except for another guy his same age. His cousin Dino. Thick, strong, curly haired, multi cultural. We imagine his dad was a made guy and his mother was a hooker who had Dino out of wedlock to many's embarrassment. Good guy, good friend, but he is a point of gossip and pity.

Dino is so happy. Applauding. Yelling. This is the best day of their lives.

DINO

Oh my god!!

Fuck yeah!!

MADONNA

Be quiet, Dino.

DINO

This is CRAZY!!

He did so good!!

PAGE 8

1–Ext. Hoboken, New Jersey

2–Ext. Street

3–Ext. Pier C park

The Bonavese family headquarters is actually built on the Pier C park structure. Instead of being a park it is a family business compound.

Instead of the compound being hidden away, it is what anyone would see as the real estate crown jewel of New Jersey.

This subtle difference shows the family business is done out in the open in opulence. It says everything about what's different about our world.

This isn't a sci-fi flying car alternate reality. This is basically our reality with the subtle differences that the mob is doing things out in the open—everything from timeless rituals to how and where they live.

A stunning mansion is built on this pier. A small fleet of yachts.

4–From behind a man's hand holding a tomato drink that may or may not have alcohol in it...Valentine is walking across the pier to the opening of the guarded gate.

It is not guarded like a mob compound but like the way the White House is guarded.

Valentine looks good.

5–From behind Valentine, Myer Bloom, a handsome Jewish mob lawyer, is enjoying his drink and coming up to shake Valentine's hand.

MYER BLOOM

Mr. Gallo.

VALENTINE

Mr. Bloom.

MYER BLOOM

First time at the pier?

VALENTINE

Yes sir.

MYER BLOOM

Hell of a party last night.

VALENTINE

Thank you for that.

Really.

6–They shake hands. All this is new to Valentine. This is his first meeting this high up the food chain.

He doesn't know what to expect and everyone's friendly faces and politeness are blowing his mind.

MYER BLOOM

Don't thank me.

I just do what the big guy says.

How did the rest of your night go?

PAGE 9

1–Int. Hotel room—night

Flashback! Valentine is riding the hell out of a busty hooker while another is behind him. We imagine she is shoving her pinky, or something else, right up his ass.

The room is trashed. A champagne bottle is open on the bed and soaking the sheet as the three ride each other feverishly.

He is shocked at the experience. This is not every day.

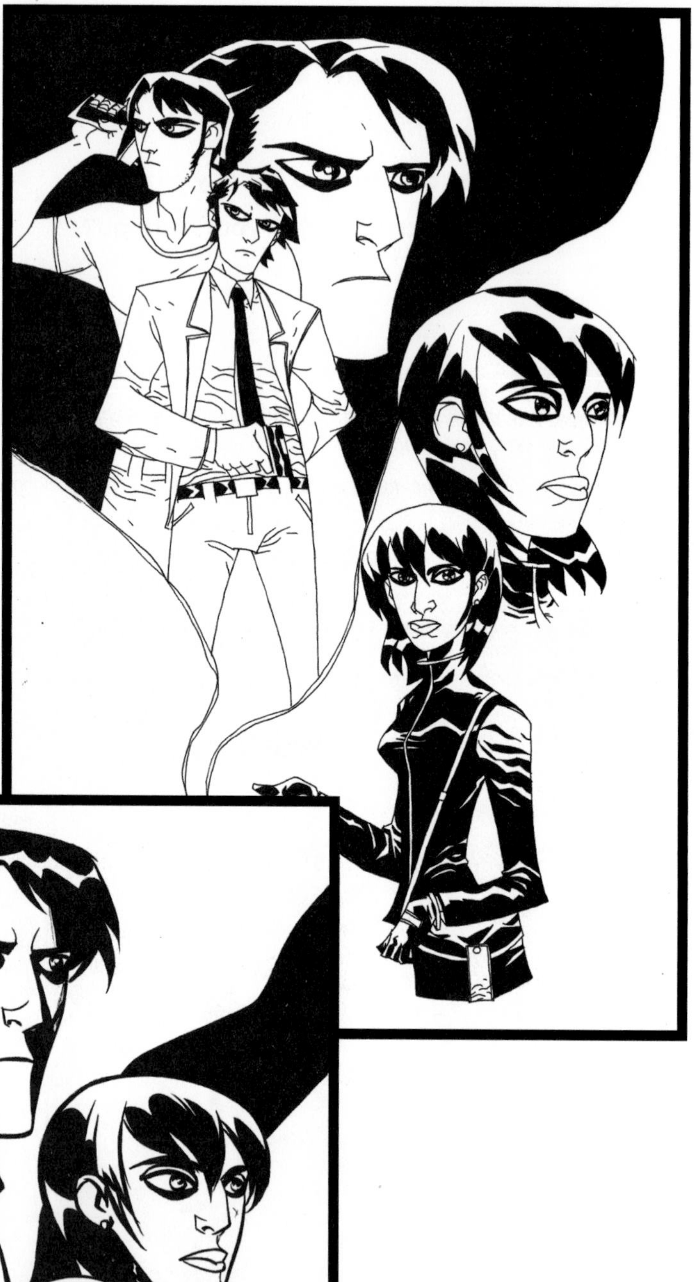

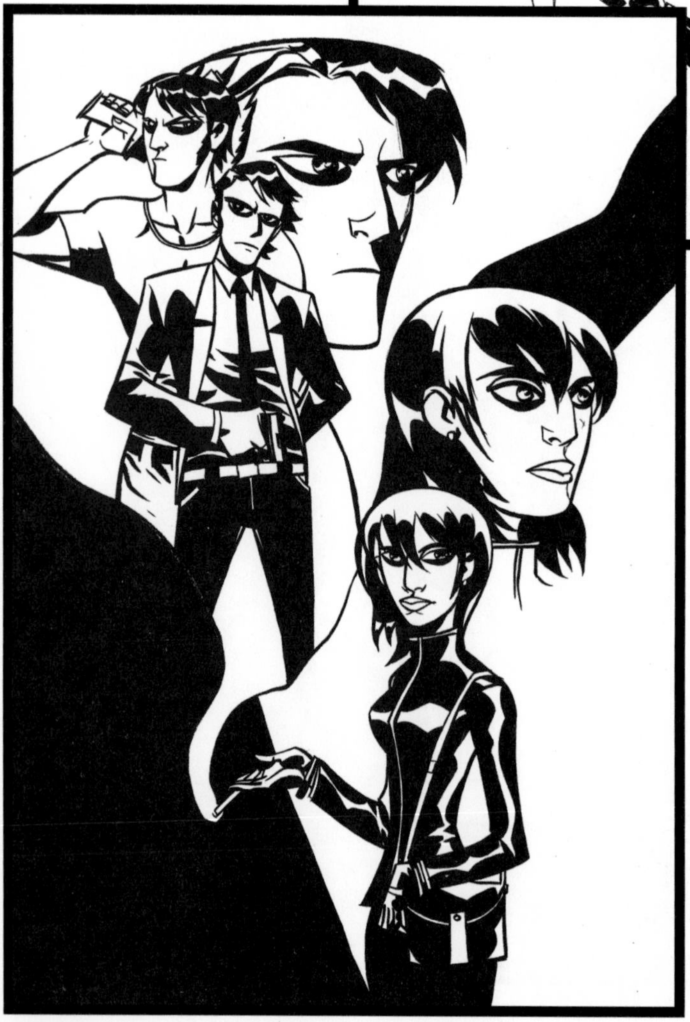

2–Ext. Pier C park

Resume! Valentine and Myer are walking toward us.

VALENTINE

All right.

MYER BLOOM

You can thank him for that too.

He's waiting for you.

3–Valentine is escorted through a lovely, well-kept garden. Bonavese is in a cobblestone garden. A couple of garden style fancy tables and chairs. The place is perfect.

Bonavese is being served tea by a gorgeous Korean woman.

Another sharp dressed but relaxed older man, fit, is greeting Valentine. His name is Tony Tuzzo. The underboss.

TONY TUZZO

Valentine.

VALENTINE

Mr. Tuzzo.

4–Valentine sits at a small table with Tony. Mr. Bonavese is sipping his tea at another table with a tablet and a newspaper and his tea.

TONY TUZZO

So, you ready to get down to it?

VALENTINE

'Course.

TONY TUZZO

You understand you won't be working the poker games in town anymore.

VALENTINE

I actually DIDN'T know that.

TONY TUZZO

You're a made guy now.

You don't need to be wipin' college shitheads' asses anymore.

You're eventually gonna have people doin' that for you.

VALENTINE

So, uh, what WILL I be doing?

5—Tony looks over to Bonavese, Bonavese doesn't even look at them.

BONAVESE

Tell him.

6—Over Valentine's shoulder, Tony pulls out a square metal suitcase, small and oddly shaped, and puts it on the table.

TONY TUZZO

Today you're going on a little trip. As a representative of OURS.

VALENTINE

Oh.

TONY TUZZO

You're gonna go to D.C. and deliver this to a guy.

7—Valentine is shocked because...

VALENTINE

D.C.?

Washington, D.C.?

PAGE 10

1—Tony is laughing at his stupid question. Bonavese isn't even looking at them. He seems to be reading his paper.

TONY TUZZO

Is there another D.C.? This guy!

VALENTINE

Oh, I've, uh, I've never left the territories before.

TONY TUZZO

Yeah, I imagine.

Why the fuck would ya? Nothin' out there.

VALENTINE

So, I, uh...

What do I do exactly?

2—Tony hands him a cash envelope clearly full of cash.

TONY TUZZO

You'll take the train down ta D.C., you'll stay at the Ambassador for the night, deliver this to our guy and you'll come home tomorrow.

VALENTINE

I'm leaving tonight?

TONY TUZZO

Yeah.

VALENTINE

You don't want me to drive?

I can drive.

3—Tony is clearly saying that this is the last time you question an order. Handing him a cash envelope.

TONY TUZZO

You'll take the train down ta D.C., you'll stay at the Ambassador for the night, deliver this to our guy and you'll come home tomorrow.

VALENTINE

Ok.

TONY TUZZO

This is your—let's call it a per diem.

4—Valentine knows not to count the cash in front of them even though he is clearly dying to.

VALENTINE

Who am I meeting?

5—Tony has a small tablet. Showing him a picture of an African-American senator.

TONY TUZZO

Senator Idis Fuller.

VALENTINE

A Senator?

Is he expecting me?

6—*Tony gives him a look that says this is more dangerous than you think.*

TONY TUZZO

No.

But the asshole SHOULD be.

He'll have a lot of questions.

But he'll open the case and then he won't have any more questions.

HE opens it, not you.

7—*Valentine is stunned by all of this but tries to keep it cool. Not sure if he should ask but...*

VALENTINE

Do, I, uh, get a receipt?

PAGE 11

1—*Over Valentine's shoulder, Tony belly laughs.*

TONY TUZZO

What the fuck are you talking about?

2—*Valentine does not like being laughed at or talked down to. He feels embarrassed in front of the Godfather.*

VALENTINE

Am I—I don't think these questions are stupid.

I've never done nothin' like this before.

I should walk out of here not knowin' what the fuck I'm doing?

3—*Tony rolls his eyes and calms himself. He sees the kid is pissed even though he doesn't care. No disrespect was meant.*

TONY TUZZO

Nah uh. No.

You don't get a receipt.

You come back here you say: package delivered.

4—*Over Tony's shoulder, Valentine is looking over to the Godfather. Not sure if he's taking this too far.*

VALENTINE

Can I bring someone?

TONY TUZZO

No.

VALENTINE

I've—I've never left the territories before. I'd like to bring someone.

5–Over Valentine's shoulder, Bonavese finally looks at him. Did Valentine just insult him even though he didn't mean to. Bonavese doesn't take his eyes off the newspaper.

BONAVESE

Your shmuck of a cousin?

VALENTINE

He's not a—with all due respect.

BONAVESE

His father was a whore-mongering shmuck and HE is a shmuck.

6–Over Tony's shoulders, Valentine on the left, and the Godfather on the right, Valentine isn't sure if he should keep this going but...

VALENTINE

I can vouch for him.

TONY TUZZO

Jesus!

BONAVESE

No you can't.

But you're one of us. It's your call.

And it's on YOUR tab.

I'm not payin' out for that half a whore.

7–Valentine holds the envelope in one hand and touches the case with the other. Basically downloading all of this information. Making sure he is clear.

VALENTINE

Yes, sir.

8–Bonavese looks at him for the first time. Completely annoyed.

BONAVESE

Valentine...

Go away.

Double-page spread

1–Ext. Bullet train to Washington, D.C.

Thin panel across both pages.

DINO

Fuck me.

2–Int. Train

First-class cabin.

Valentine and Dino are taking their seats in the first-class cabin. They sit on the opposite end of the cabin from a handful of slimy young Wall Street assholes that are gathered around the first-class open bar.

They are chasing the Asian lady bartender out of the cabin with their obnoxious behavior. They are drunk and coked up and headed to some Georgetown party they think is going to kick ass but probably won't.

One guy in particular looks like a young John Turturro. He is named Eddie.

Valentine has the case and is calm and cool. Dino is looking out the window like a puppy. A little under dressed but so excited.

WALL STREET ASSHOLE

Oh come on, baby, if I wanted that look I'd'a stayed at home.

WALL STREET ASSHOLE 2

Good one.

VALENTINE

Be cool, Dino.

DINO

We're leavin' the territory. This is crazy!

VALENTINE

Are you bein' cool?

2–Two shot. Dino sits in the same couch-like seat as Valentine. Looking at him with love. Valentine feels his look and ignores it.

3–Same.

DINO

You vouched for me.

VALENTINE

I need a human shield.

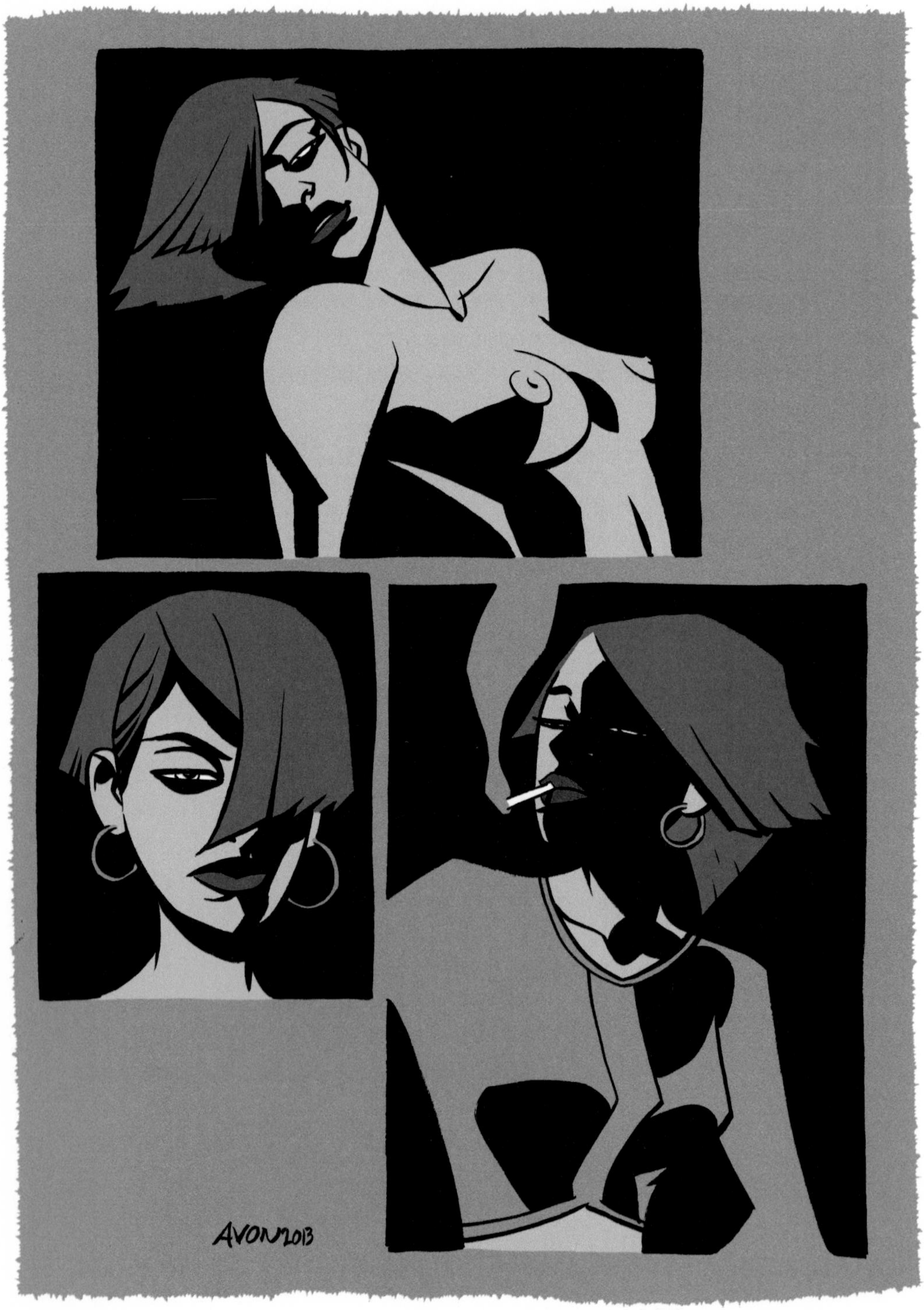
AVON2013

DINO

You love me.

4–Dino and Valentine watch the Wall Street assholes trip over themselves to run the Asian bartender out of the cabin.

WALL STREET ASSHOLE

I mean I want ACTUAL sex on an ACTUAL beach!!

WALL STREET ASSHOLE 2

Oh!!

VALENTINE

Look at all these Wall Street shmucks. One day to get away from them and there they are.

DINO

Hey, fuck 'em.

They pay up just like the rest of us.

VALENTINE

Assholes.

5–Dino and Valentine watch as Eddie is tripping over himself and spilling his drink. Laughing at whatever he just did or said. Spilling a drink.

DINO

For real.

VALENTINE

I know that one guy.

DINO

Yeah?

VALENTINE

What's HE leavin' the territory for?

6–Dino and Valentine. Dino looks to the left. Valentine staring at the Wall Streeters on the right.

DINO

He's allowed to.

Hey, where'd the redhead from the platform go?

Back in steerage.

7—Over Dino and Valentine's shoulder, Eddie stands up and drunkenly points at Valentine. Just recognizing him through his drunken haze.

EDDIE

Hey, I know you.

You deal the cards down at you-know-where!

VALENTINE

Go siddown, Eddie.

8—From behind Valentine, Eddie, drunk and stumbling, looks like he is looking for a fight.

EDDIE

The fuck you say to me??

VALENTINE

I said go sit down.

Asshole.

9—Low looking up. Eddie, drunk, about to punch Valentine right in the nose but stops.

10—Eddie's p.o.v. The pin.

11—Same as nine. Eddie stops himself because he knows what the pin means.

12—Valentine looks at him with a cocked eyebrow that says: yeah, go sit the fuck down.

PAGE 14-15

Double-page spread

1—Big panel. Dino is up on his feet and clocks Eddie right in the jaw. Hard. No one fucks with his friend.

SPX: WHACK

2—"Camera" on the floor. Eddie hits the floor. His nose blood sprays. Dino is already kicking him.

SPX: FUMP

EDDIE

Oh!

3—Eddie's p.o.v. Low looking up and wide. Eddie's Wall Street friends are stunned. Looking down shocked.

4—Same. Eddie's Wall Street friends all point and burst out and laugh at him.

WALL STREET ASSHOLE

Aaaaahahahahahaha!!

WALL STREET ASSHOLE 2

Douchebag!!

5—Dino sits down. Valentine is annoyed but at the same time grateful.

VALENTINE

He WAS backing off.

DINO

I already had my arm cocked.

I couldn't stop.

VALENTINE

And the kick.

DINO

It's my signature move.

6—Eddie shaking, crawls to his drunk asshole friends. They laugh at him and throw dollar bills. They make it rain on him.

WALL STREET ASSHOLE

Tough guy!!

WALL STREET ASSHOLE (CONT'D)

Come on, honey, give me a lap dance.

WALL STREET ASSHOLE 2

That doesn't even make any sense!

7—Dino and Valentine. Valentine concedes a thank you. Dino, looking off panel to the left, is already deciding to go find the red head.

VALENTINE

Thank you.

DINO

I'm gonna go find the red head.

VALENTINE

I said thank you.

8—From over Valentine's head, Dino leaves the car as a woman enters. In the shadows we can just tell a woman is coming in. Pink and purple hair.

DINO

Yeah yeah...

9—Valentine cocks an eyebrow as he sees...

PAGE 16

1–Page tall. Enter our female lead. Our femme fatale. JAGGER ROSE. She looks amazing. She enters first class and surveys all that she sees. She oozes sex and violence.

She owns the room by walking in. Nothing slutty, just smoldering. A practiced perfected move.

2–Valentine watches her as Jagger moves over to the bar and the Wall Street idiots. Eddie plugging his nose with tissues as she steps over him.

His drunk friends are very taken with her. All eyes on her and she knows it.

3–The drunk Wall Streeters watch Jagger slide behind the bar, drop her coat and start making a mixed drink. She looks amazing. Nonplussed.

4–Eddie drops on the bar and snarls at her.

EDDIE

A whiskey.

5–Jagger continues making her drink. Ignoring him.

6–Eddie has had enough shit for one day.

EDDIE (CONT'D)

Which part of WHISKEY do you not under—?

PAGE 17

1–From behind Eddie, Jagger takes the bottle she's holding and smashes it over his head. Hard.

2–Valentine watches, surprised, as Eddie hits the ground and his friends point in her face to protect him and protest her.

WALL STREET ASSHOLE

You DUMB BITCH!!

WALL STREET ASSHOLE 2

I'm gonna have your JOB, Sally!

3–Jagger pulls a gun on them. Really nonplussed.

JAGGER ROSE

Name's not Sally.

Get off the train.

4–The Wall Street guys are shocked. Some laughing.

WALL STREET ASSHOLE 2

The fuck you say to—??

5–Jagger casually SHOOTS HER GUN as she takes a sip of her drink.

SPX: BAM

Double-page spread

1—The Wall Streeters freak the fuck out. She grazed one of their arms but she certainly changed the mood of the conversation.

WALL STREET ASSHOLE

What the FUCK!??

2—Jagger is enjoying her drink. Smoking gun up.

Who's next?

3—From behind Jagger who pours another drink, gun still up, the Wall Streeters stumble out past Valentine. Eddie on the floor. Out cold and bleeding.

WALL STREET ASSHOLE

Fucking goddamn!

WALL STREET ASSHOLE (CONT'D)

What fucking kind of train?

WALL STREET ASSHOLE (CONT'D)

Let's just GO!!

I'm bleeding!!

Shot me!!

4—Valentine calmly watches as Jagger steps over Eddie's body with the two drinks. Heading toward him.

VALENTINE

How much are they paying YOU to bartend?

I think I can get you something better in the city...

JAGGER ROSE

I'm not the bartender, you ass.

5—Jagger offers him a drink and sits in Dino's seat.

Here we get a sense of their chemistry. They are very different from Walker and Deena.

Although she is a fierce opponent and feisty broad, she is steely-eyed and in control, while Deena is wild nervous energy.

Valentine is young, a few years younger than her, and very into her. He is trying to be cool but years away from being able to pull it off. But still charming.

VALENTINE

Thank you.

Who ARE you?

JAGGER ROSE

A girl comes onto your train, shows a gun, shoots a guy, and you just sit here?

VALENTINE

Well, I don't like to judge.

JAGGER ROSE

No, I'm serious.

How do you know that I'm not here to take the briefcase from you?

6–He sips his drink. He somehow never considered it but maybe he should have. But he still doesn't think it is an issue.

She is sipping her drink and rolling her eyes.

VALENTINE

Huh.

Dunno.

JAGGER ROSE

Sexist.

VALENTINE

No.

JAGGER ROSE

If I was a guy—

VALENTINE

You'd look terrible in that outfit.

7–She looks at him. Smolder. He puts his foot on the briefcase as to half block it.

JAGGER ROSE

You know exactly what I mean.

VALENTINE

You don't know what's in the briefcase.

JAGGER ROSE

No.

YOU don't know what's in it.

8–Same. She sips. He thinks to himself.

JAGGER ROSE (CONT'D)

You don't fucking RECOGNIZE me, do you?

VALENTINE

Um...

JAGGER ROSE

Really.

VALENTINE

Did we—?

9–Flashback! To the sex party last night. He's trying to think if she was one of the call girls. She wasn't. It might be funny to use a stat of the same panel from previously.

10–Same as 8. He decides she wasn't there but he's not a hundred percent. She rolls her eyes to the sky.

VALENTINE (CONT'D)

No, that wasn't you...

JAGGER ROSE

Jesus help me.

11–Same. Valentine holds out his hand to handshake she doesn't accept. Back to sip her drink.

VALENTINE

Hi, I'm—

JAGGER ROSE

Valentine. I KNOW.

I went to school with your sister.

12–Same. He is stunned. She is subtly annoyed.

VALENTINE

We did? You did?

JAGGER ROSE

Yes. I've slept over at your house.

VALENTINE

Shit, I'm sorry.

You're—um—you're—

13—Same. She drinks. Muttering to herself.

> ### JAGGER ROSE
>
> Jagger—Jagger Rose.
>
> God damn it.

> ### VALENTINE
>
> Ok.

> ### JAGGER ROSE
>
> Fuck you.

> ### VALENTINE
>
> How many colors was your hair back then?

14—Same.

> ### JAGGER ROSE
>
> Put the pin away.

> ### VALENTINE
>
> What?

> ### JAGGER ROSE
>
> The coronation pin.
>
> Put it away.

15—Angle on his made man pin on his lapel.

PAGE 20

1—Jagger takes the pin and puts it under his lapel. He still wears it but not so anyone can see. He is a little put off.

> ### JAGGER ROSE (CONT'D)
>
> We're clearing Baltimore which means that little pin
> just became an ARREST ME pin.

> ### VALENTINE
>
> Hey.

> ### JAGGER ROSE
>
> You are out of the territory and you are out here
> without a net.

2–Jagger goes back to her drink. Valentine is genuinely stunned.

VALENTINE

Who are you?

JAGGER ROSE

Don Bonavese sent me.

VALENTINE

HE sent you?

To do what?

3–Jagger looks him over. He is trying not to look at her cleavage.

JAGGER ROSE

Keep an eye on you.

VALENTINE

He didn't say anything about you.

JAGGER ROSE

I know. He finds it funny.

VALENTINE

You're here to escort me?

4–Jagger sits back and watches him try not to stare at her boobs.

JAGGER ROSE

I'm not an escort.

I'm here to protect you.

VALENTINE

What?

JAGGER ROSE

Deal with it.

VALENTINE

I gotta guy.

JAGGER ROSE

Yeah? Where is he?

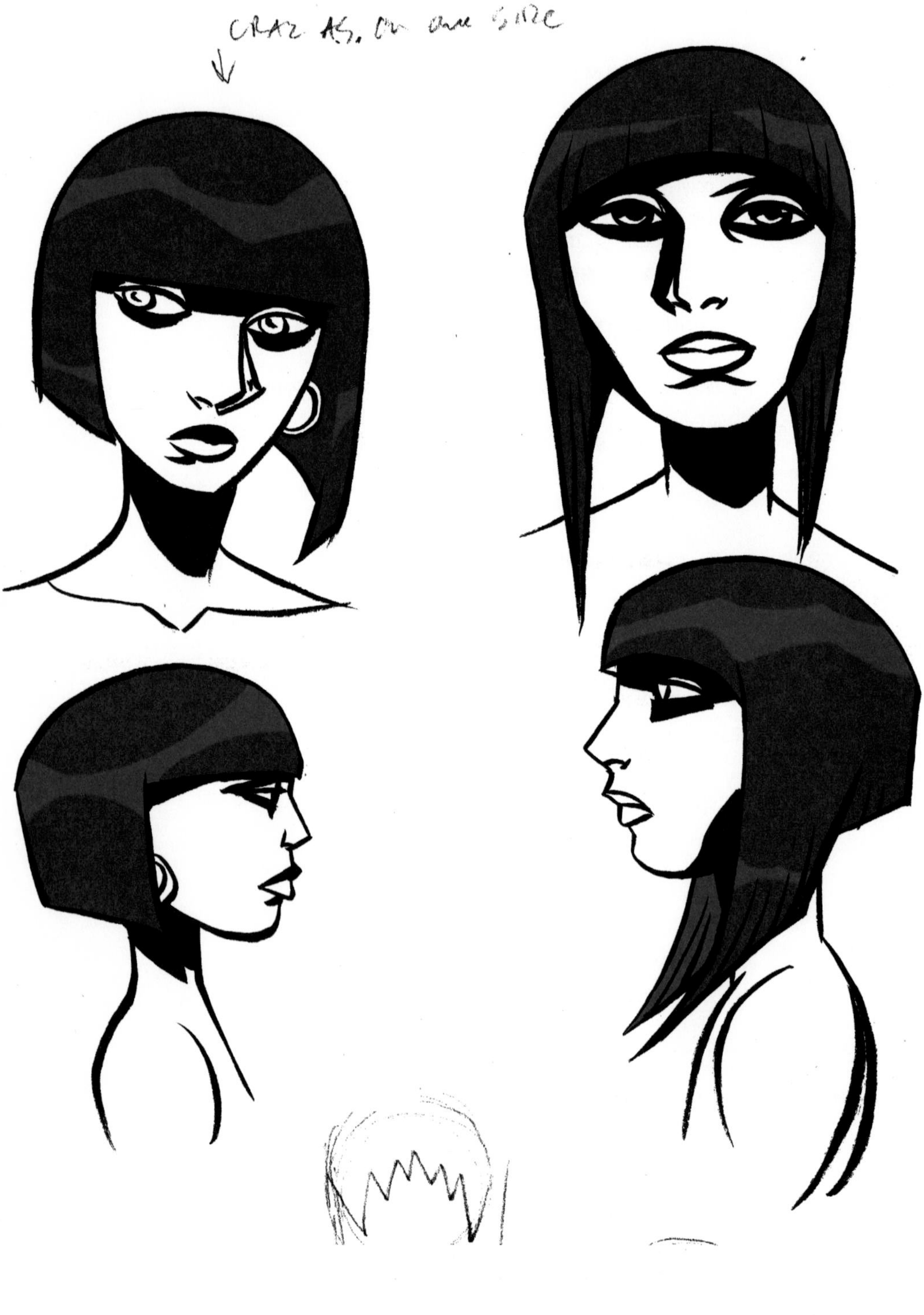

VALENTINE

Good point.

5–From behind Jagger and Valentine, a couple of guys from train security who look just like us come in and see the crazy mess.

TRAIN SECURITY

What the—

What the fuck is going on in here?

PAGE 21

1–Jagger pulls out a couple of folded hundreds and smoothly hands them to him.

JAGGER ROSE

Excuse us.

We're on a date.

2–The security guy takes the cash. His partner eyeballing his half over his shoulder.

TRAIN SECURITY

Yeah, uh, ok.

JAGGER ROSE

Thanks.

3–Jagger leans back and takes a drink. No big deal. He stares at her. In awe now more than any leering.
4–Same. She doesn't even look at him.

JAGGER ROSE (CONT'D)

It'll never happen.

VALENTINE

What?

JAGGER ROSE

I will never sleep with you.

5–Same. Valentine is uncomfortable. Jagger is a rock. Enjoying her beverage.

VALENTINE

Excuse me.

JAGGER ROSE

Your penis will NEVER be in my vagina.

It'll never happen.

VALENTINE

Yeah, well...Never say never.

JAGGER ROSE

It'll NEVER happen.

6–Same. He leans forward. Uncomfortable. Eyeing her out of the side of his eye. Jagger knows it.

7–Same.

JAGGER ROSE (CONT'D)

Touch my boob.

VALENTINE

What?

PAGE 22

1–Valentine sits up and looks at her. She has not budged. Sitting back with her drink.

JAGGER ROSE

Touch my boob.

All guys think about when they see boobs is how much they want to touch them.

We have work to do.

Touch my boob, right now, demystify them, get it out of your system...and you can focus.

2–Same.

VALENTINE

No.

JAGGER ROSE

Last chance.

3–Same. Valentine can't believe her. She sips her drink.

4–Same. Valentine thinks about it. He wants to...

5–Same. Valentine reaches out and almost touches her boob. She doesn't flinch.

6–Same. Valentine decides against it. She doesn't budge.

VALENTINE

No.

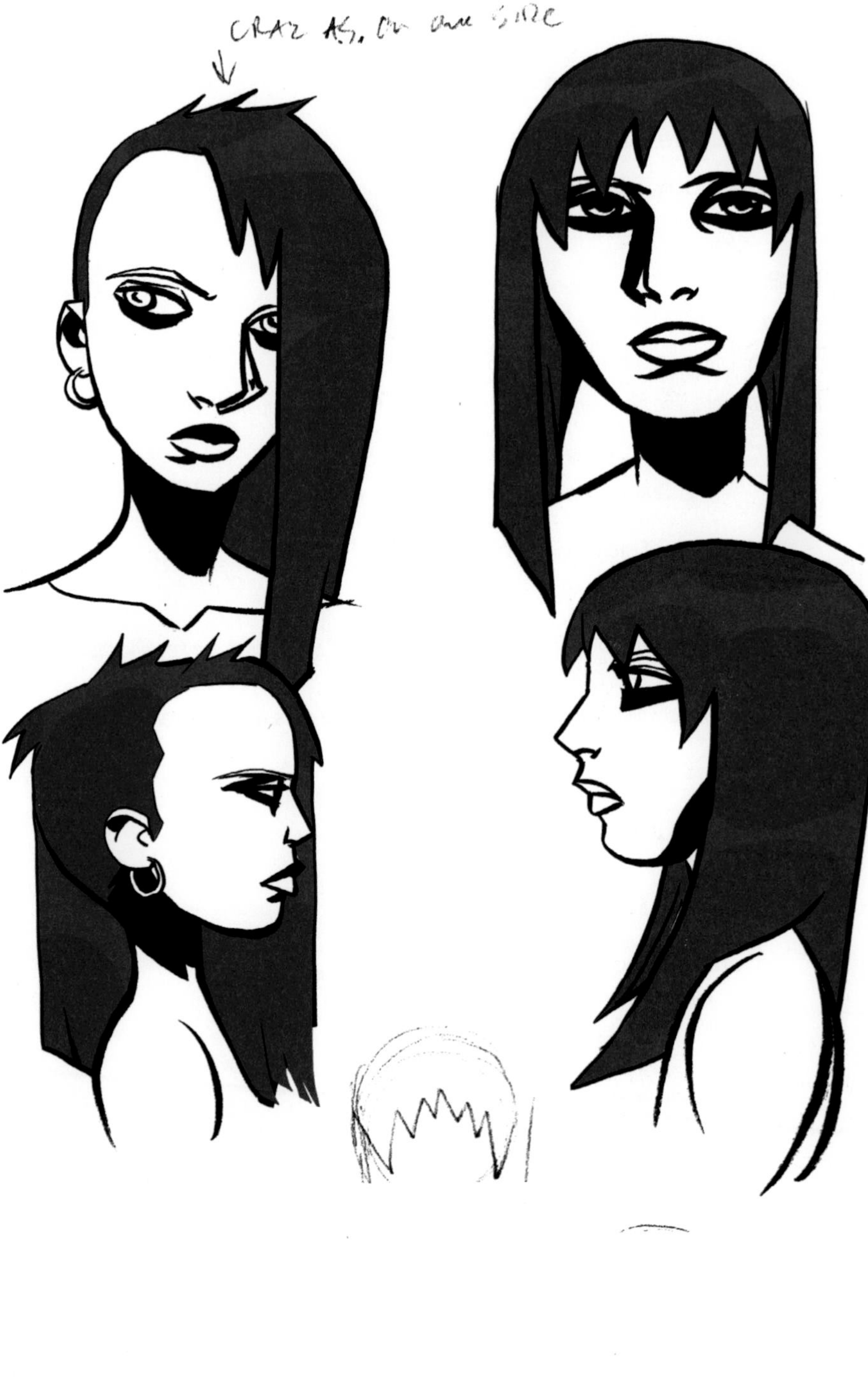
CRAZ AS. ON ONE SIDE

JAGGER ROSE

Ok.

Offer rescinded.

We understand each other?

VALENTINE

You're nuts.

JAGGER ROSE

Then we understand each other.

Hey look...

PAGE 23

1–Ext. Washington, D.C.

The train is pulling into the beautiful Washington, D.C. Iconic.

But it is not that opulent. The air is terrible. Sickly. As if something has happened where the air is actually cleaner in the territory than it is in the rest of the world.

JAGGER ROSE NARRATION

We're in THEIR nation's capital.

2–Int. Train station

Dino, Val and Jagger are walking through the train station. The Wall Street guys are keeping their distance. Others mill about.

Tons of uniform angry cops walking around or standing tall. The first cops we have seen.

VALENTINE

Strike out?

DINO

Couldn't find her. Who is SHE?

VALENTINE

Says she went to school with my sister.

DINO

SHE—OH DAMN. She did.

Hey BRACES.

3–Jagger turns around and looks at him as if to say: Do you think that's really how this is going to go. He holds up his hands in surrender. He meant no disrespect.

DINO (CONT'D)

You—hey, oh ok. You look much better.

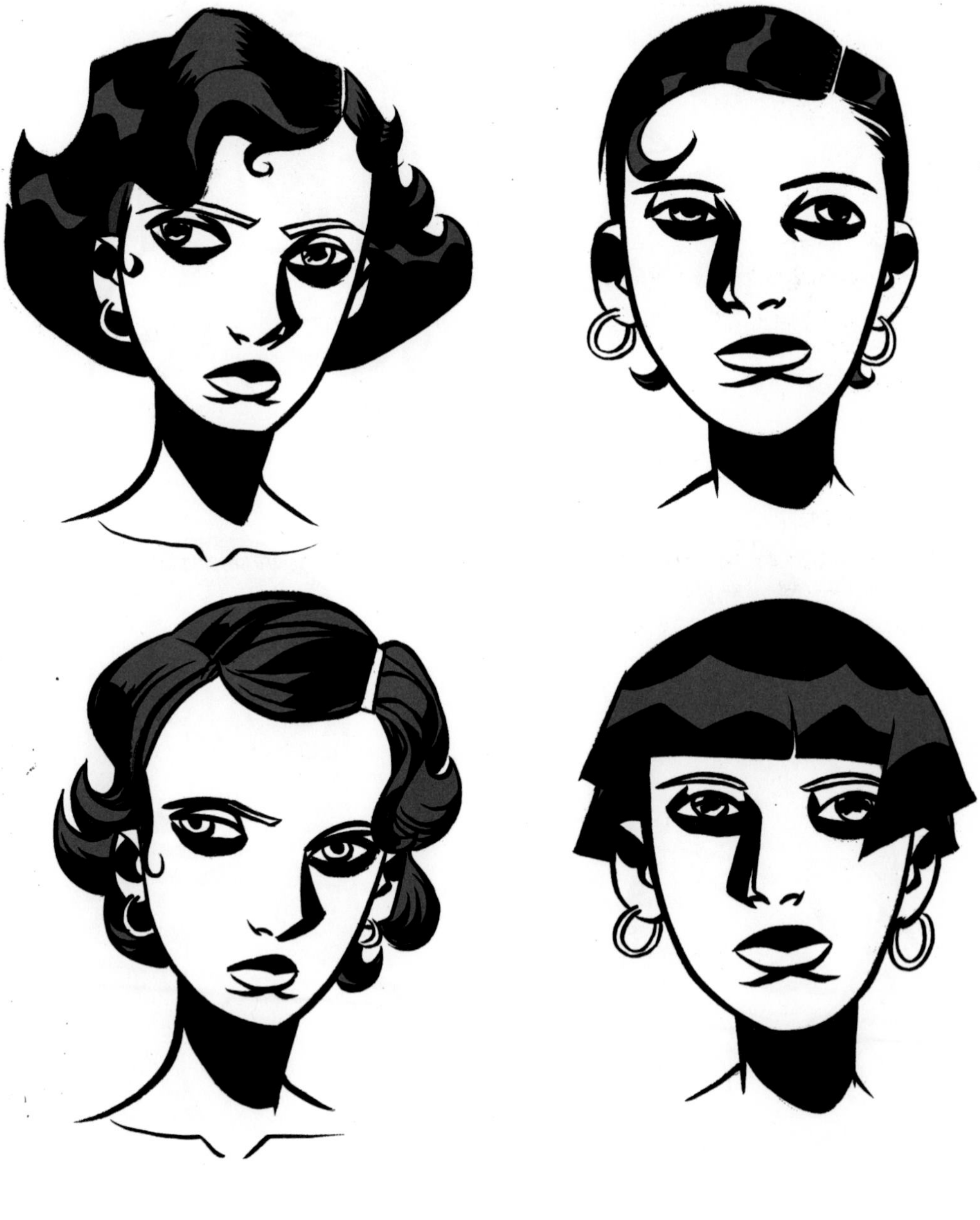

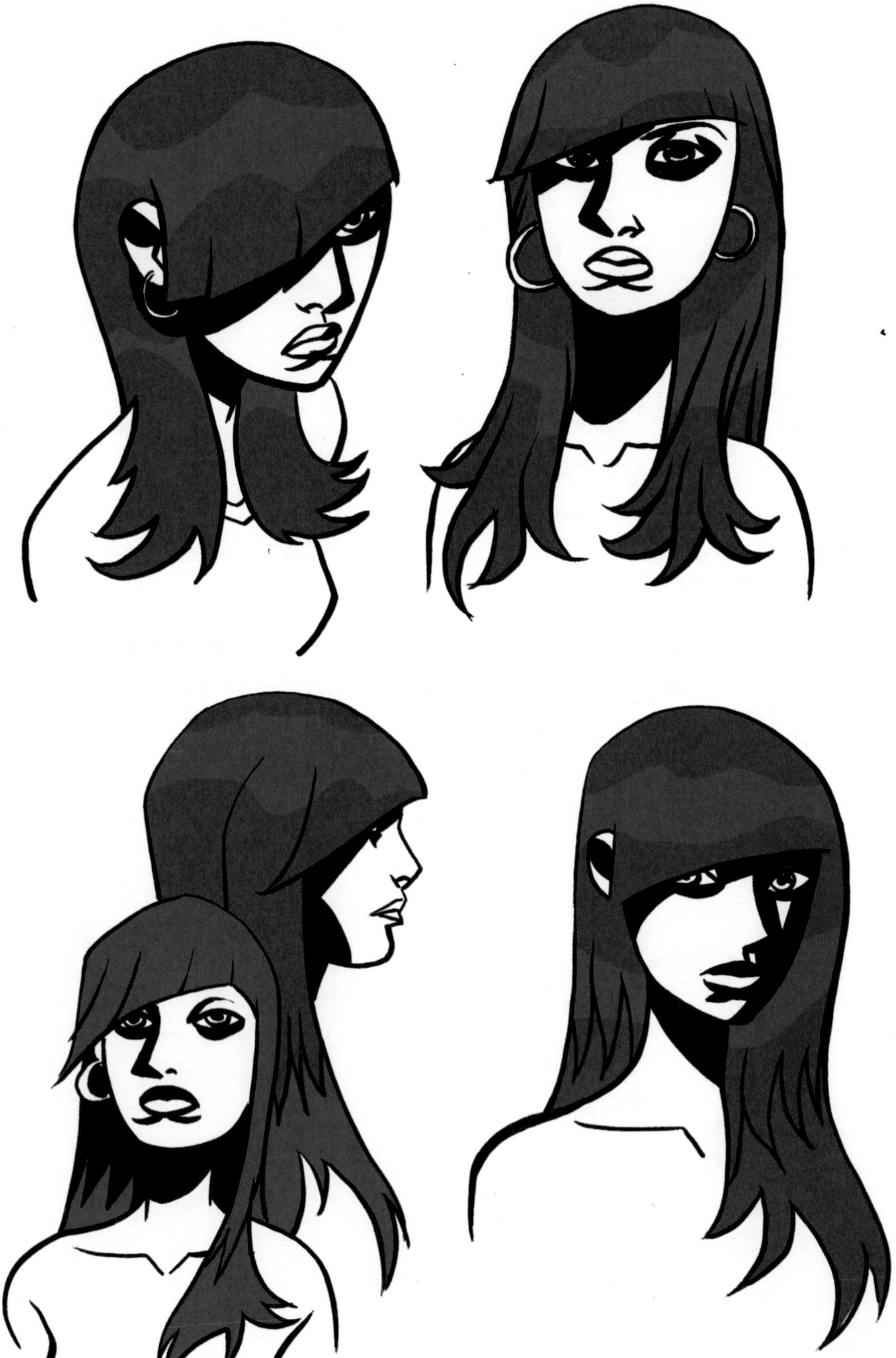

JAGGER ROSE

I know.

THANK you.

4—From behind Val, Val stops at the newsstand and sees the one that catches his eye.

The book: The United States of Murder Incorporated.
How the United States Government Gave up the East Coast to the Mob. *By Shecky Finklestien.*

Other books include: Mice Templar—*NOW A MAJOR MOTION PICTURE,* Takio *the YA novel by Olivia, etc.*

5—Jagger Rose sees what Valentine is looking at. Dino is staring at one of the cops like he is an alien from outer space.

JAGGER ROSE (CONT'D)

That's a funny one.

An oral history and no one is sayin' nothin'.

PAGE 24-25

Double-page spread

1—Ext. Washington, D.C./private club—day

A secret club. A members-only club. Something very skull and bones. A type of club for very wealthy and powerful people.

2—Ext. Street

Across the street, Jagger, Valentine and Dino are watching. Dino still underdressed. Already bored.

Behind them a cobble stone half wall and a black spiked fence separating them from a small city park.

JAGGER ROSE (CONT'D)

The Senator is in there.

It's one of those fancy boys only, members-only, circle jerks for the elite and powerful.

Don't get any on you.

VALENTINE

Let's go.

JAGGER ROSE

It's on you.

3—Valentine looks at Jagger as she gestures to him like a game show hostess. People mill about. The sidewalk is crowded.

JAGGER ROSE (CONT'D)

The Don said this was on you and that is a boys only club.

Put the pin on.

VALENTINE

You told me to take it off.

4–Jagger puts it back where she originally unpinned it from. Dino doesn't like her.

JAGGER ROSE

And now I'm telling you to put it on.

There are places out here in the wild where you want to wear that pin.

This is one of them.

5–Int. Club
From behind the guard/host at the opulent dark wood, low-light front desk. Valentine walks into the club with the case. Backlit to the front door light.

DESK MANAGER

May I help you?

VALENTINE

I have a package for Senator Fuller.

6–The man at the desk is about to shoo him away but...
7–The desk clerk's p.o.v. He sees the pin.
8–The host picks up the phone and at the same time points Valentine down the dark wood hall full of paintings and trophies.

DESK MANAGER

Down the hall.

Third room on your right.

The Dupont Club, may I help you?

9–Doorway—Valentine enters a doorway and looks down at...

PAGE 26

1–Over Valentine's shoulder. The Senator is a very tall African American. 60.

VALENTINE

Senator Fuller?

2–The Senator looks up from his paper with a politician's shit phony smile.
3–Small panel. Angle on the pin.
4–Same as 2. His smile drops. He knows what this is.

SENATOR

How the fuck did you even get in—nevermind.

5–Valentine hands over the case. The Senator looks at it.

SENATOR (CONT'D)

And am I supposed to open this now?

VALENTINE

That's completely up to you.

SENATOR

I don't understand you people.

6—Low looking up, Fuller is genuinely pissed.

SENATOR (CONT'D)

You have everything you said you wanted.

You have an entire chunk of the country to do that which you may.

And STILL it is not enough.

You're too young to remember what things were like before—this...

THIS is insane.

7—The Senator opens up the case and looks inside.

PAGE 27

1—Over the Senator's shoulder, it is a foam molded case. Two compartments. On the left, a beautifully stacked large pile of thousand dollar bills in a perfectly cased foam setting.

Right next to it is a dead, bloody bird. Bloody. Also encased.

2—The Senator looks at him with complete contempt.

SENATOR (CONT'D)

Message received.

Thank you.

3—Valentine is not sure what he is supposed to do now. Should he leave.

4—The Senator wants him to leave.

SENATOR (CONT'D)

Is there a singing telegram portion of this message?

No?

Then good-bye.

5—Ext. Club

Valentine walks out of the club into the sunny crowded street.

6—Int. Club

The Senator is so angry. Looking in the case.

7—Ext. Street

Over Valentine's shoulder, Jagger, across the street eating a street dog, is about to throw it away when...

8—Int. Club

The Senator slams down the case in anger.

PAGE 28-29

Double-page spread

Boom. The entire front of the building explodes. The street erupts into chaos.

People and cars get hurt. Fire. Blood.

Valentine goes flying into a metal gate across the street. He really took a hit.

PAGE 30

1—Jagger picks herself up. Head ringing. She is scraped and injured.

2—Jagger dives and puts the fire out on a stunned and struggling Valentine's shoulder.

3—Valentine looks up. Dazed. Head bleeding. Confused.

4—Over Valentine's shoulder, Dino is dead. As are many others.

Dino is impaled on the thick black fence that was separating the sidewalk from the small city park.

5—Valentine, horrified, dirty, sooty, stares at us. He's in shock. He didn't know what to expect from all of this but he certainly didn't expect any of this.

PAGE 31

1—Ext. Funeral home/back room—night

Dino lies in the closed casket. The casket is in perspective toward us. At the end of it, Valentine is still in shock. His head is bandaged.

Clearly they have gotten themselves and Dino out of Washington and back to New York.

2—Over Valentine's shoulder, on the other side of this long, cluttered funeral home back room full of coffin parts and wreaths and other things.

Jagger is having a heated conversation with Tony and Myer. Clearly something went wrong. Something is wrong. Whatever it is Jagger was not in on it. That is for sure.

The mobsters look panicked but are keeping it together. Trying to figure out what happened.

JAGGER ROSE

(muffled)

Didn't even tell him I was coming and the fucking case was rigged??!!

TONY TUZZO

(muffled) It wasn't!

JAGGER ROSE

(muffled)

Are you fucking kidding me!??

3—Valentine squints. Mistrusting. Bloodshot eyes. Unshaven. Did they send him there to die? Did they send him there on a suicide mission without telling him?

4—Over Valentine's shoulder, Myer has had enough of Jagger's accusatory shit. Tony is walking up to Valentine with purpose.

MYER BLOOM

(muffled)

Enough!! Ok??!! Enough!!

Everyone is fucking upset, goddamn it!!

TONY TUZZO

I want to hear it from you.

You talked to the guy? The Senator?

5—Tony is right in Valentine's face. Reading his face. Looking for clues of a lie. Valentine is bubbling with rage.

VALENTINE

I walked into the club, I handed him the briefcase.

TONY TUZZO

He opened it in front of you?

VALENTINE

Yeah.

TONY TUZZO

You saw what was inside?

VALENTINE

Yeah.

TONY TUZZO

What did he say?

6—Valentine squints. Bloodshot eyes. Unshaven.

VALENTINE

He said you were greedy fucking assholes and told me to fuck off.

7—Valentine's p.o.v. Tony and Myer look at him. Not sure if the insult is coming from him or from the dead Senator. Jagger pacing behind them.

PAGE 32

10 equal size panels. All tight. Suspense.

1—Tony is trying to put this together.

TONY TUZZO

That's exactly what he said?

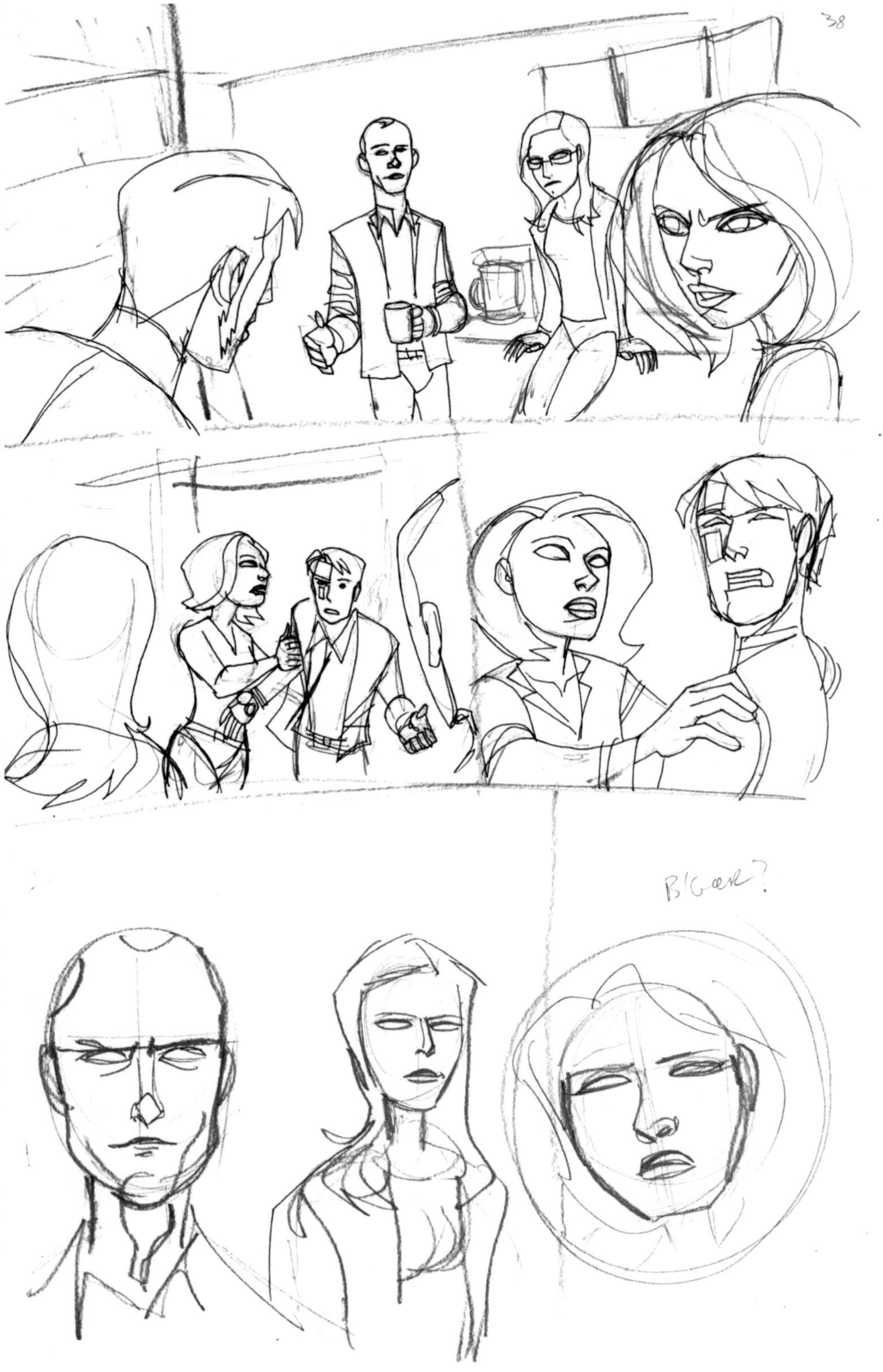
B'GGER?

2–*Valentine is exhausted.*

VALENTINE

I'm paraphrasing, but yeah.

3–*Same as 1.*

TONY TUZZO

Did he close the case in front of you?

4–*Same as 2.*

VALENTINE

I don't—I don't know.

5–*Same as 1.*

TONY TUZZO

It's important.

6–*Valentine has no idea what he is thinking.*

VALENTINE

Why?

7–*Tony doesn't understand how Valentine doesn't understand...*

TONY TUZZO

Because we're trying to determine if it was the briefcase that did the job.

8–*Valentine is confused.*

VALENTINE

Of COURSE it was.

9–*Myer leans in...trying to get this in his head. Sincere. Sweating.*

MYER BLOOM

Valentine listen to me...

We wouldn't do that to you.

10–*Valentine doesn't know this to be true.*

VALENTINE

Why not?

PAGE 33

10 equal size panels. All tight. Suspense.

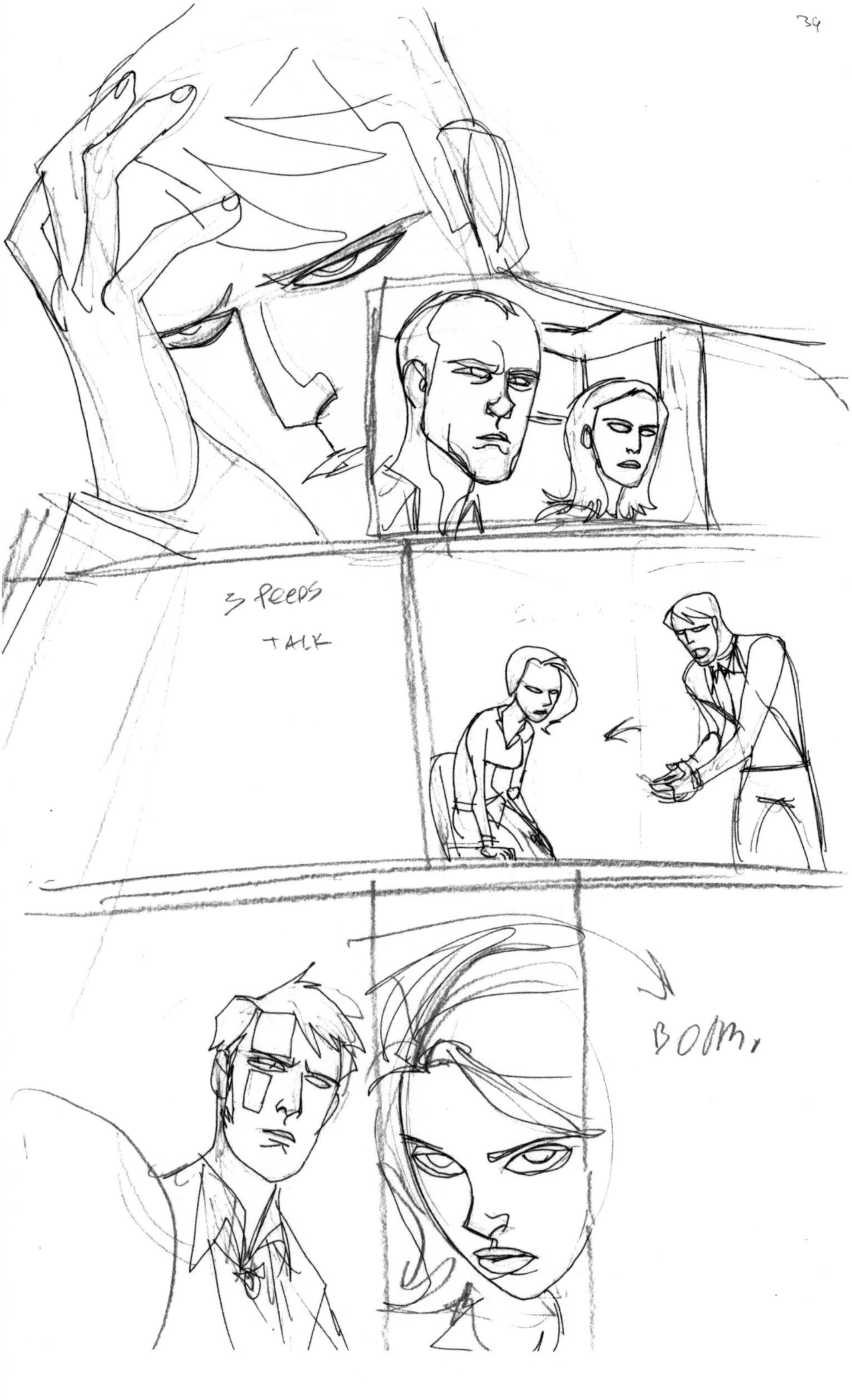
3 PEEPS
TALK
BOOM.

1–Same as 9, last page.

MYER BLOOM

You're one of us.

2–Valentine is bubbling with rage.

VALENTINE

My friend is DEAD.

3–Tony points at us. Totally sincere.

TONY TUZZO

Hey, that's on YOU!

We told you not to bring him.

4–Same as 2.

VALENTINE

You're saying YOU didn't do this.

5–Tony holds up his hand. Sincere.

TONY TUZZO

I swear on Christ Almighty.

6–Same as 4.

VALENTINE

I want to hear it from him.

I want to hear it from Don Bonavese.

7–Myer holds up his hands. There's nothing to discuss.

MYER BLOOM

That can't happen at the moment.

8–Valentine doesn't trust any of this.

VALENTINE

Why not?

9–Same as 7.

MYER BLOOM

He's not here.

He left for the old country.

10–Valentine clearly doesn't believe them.

Double-page spread

1—On the other side of the room, Jagger is pacing. She is clearly shaken as well. She may be on Val's side more than he thinks.

Three men in the background.

TONY TUZZO

Maybe you should go home—sleep it off.

VALENTINE

SLEEP IT OFF?

TONY TUZZO

Don't worry about your boy.

We'll take care of the arrangements.

2—Over Valentine's shoulder, Myer sees Valentine doesn't believe them and understands.

MYER BLOOM

This is bad business, Val. This is not what we do.

We don't send our soldiers on suicide missions.

We'd HAVE no soldiers.

You see that, right?

3—Valentine sees the logic but...Val's phone rings.

SPX: GLEE GLEE

4—Valentine looks at his iPhone. It's his mom. The mobsters argue behind him.
Reads: Mom

TONY TUZZO

Someone got to the case.

MYER BLOOM

It wasn't THE CASE!!

TONY TUZZO

It wasn't the case?? The case just happens to be—

5—Valentine puts a finger to his ear and turns away from them and answers.

VALENTINE

Hello? Ma.

Ma, I'm ok.

What? No.

No reason.

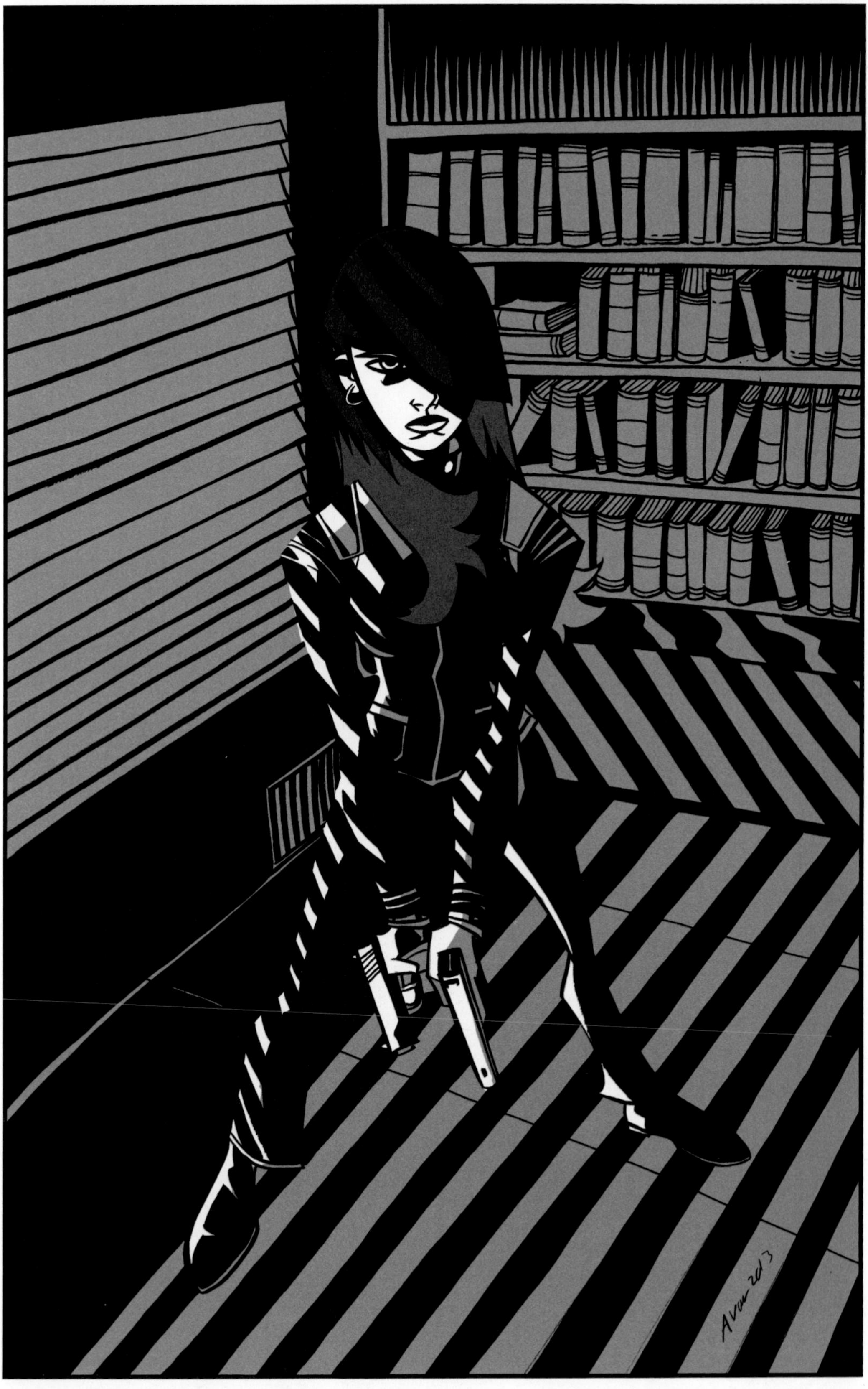

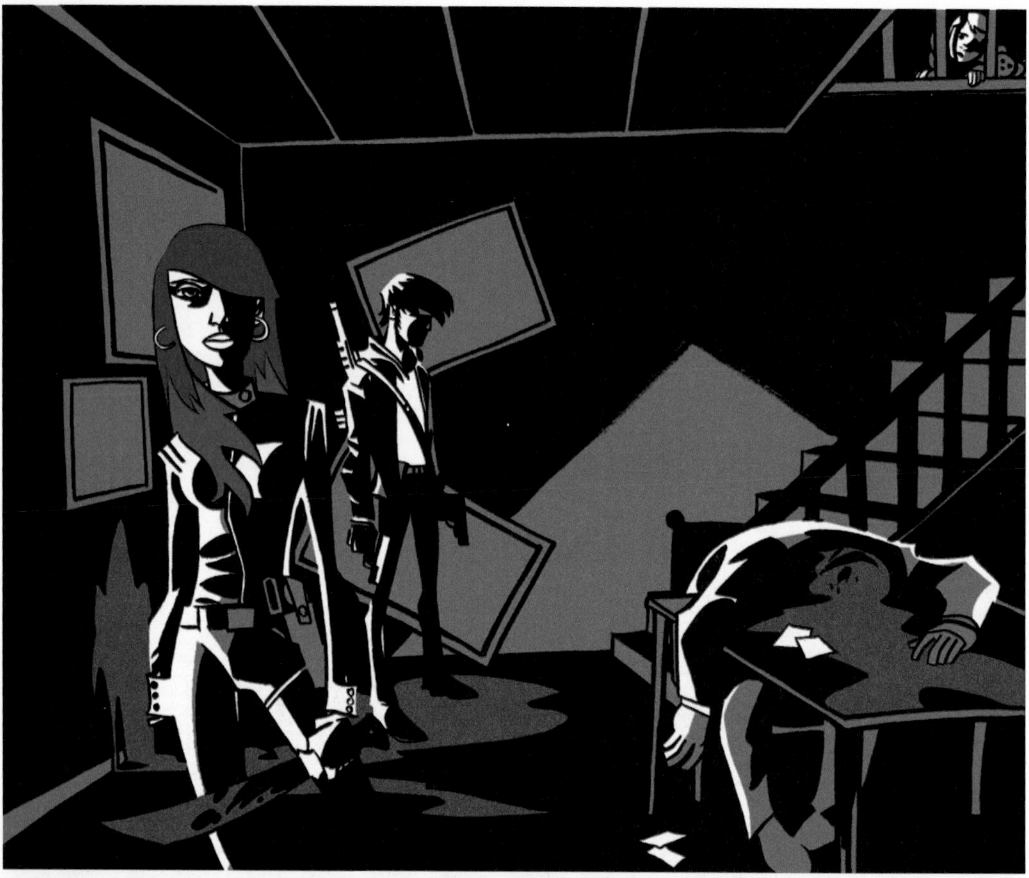

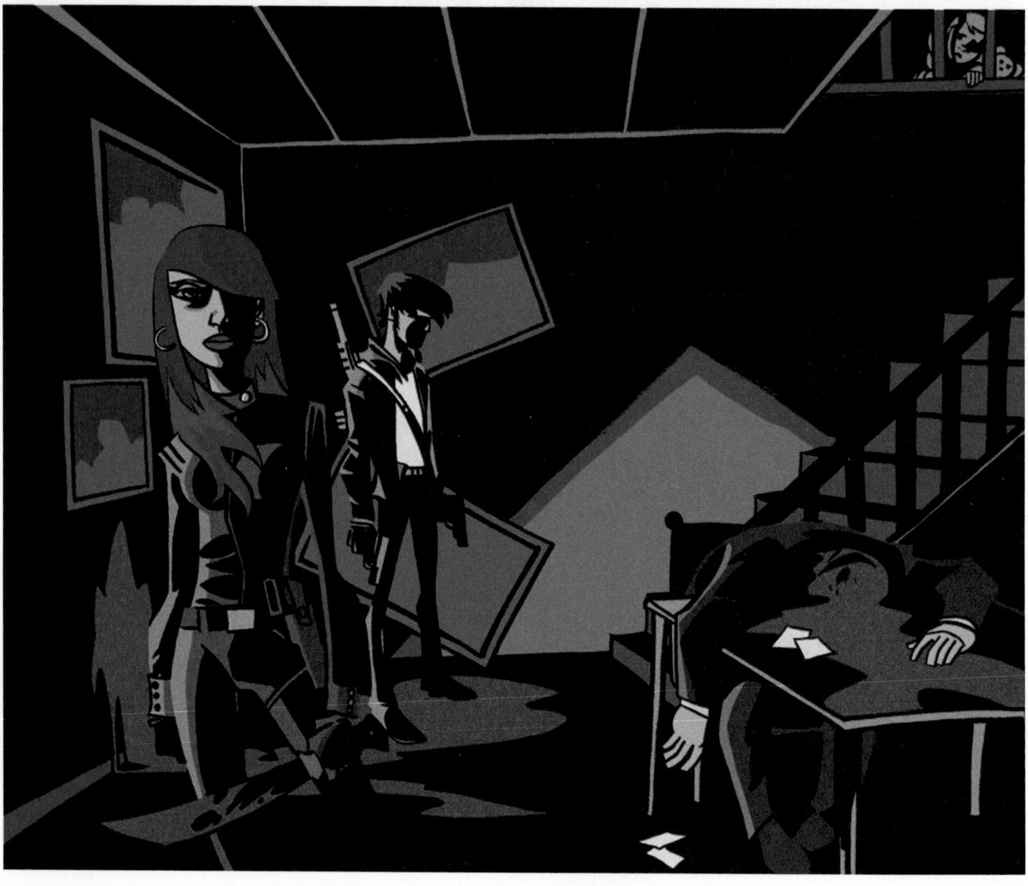

6–Valentine is walking away from the gangsters as he talks to his mom. Finger to his ear. Annoyed.

VALENTINE (CONT'D)

No. I'm ok.

Right now?

Maybe now ain't a good time, Ma.

No, I'm just tired—yeah, I can be there in 20 minutes.

Yeah, yeah, ok...

7–Valentine, without breaking his stride, hangs up and keeps walking toward us and away from the mobsters.

VALENTINE (CONT'D)

I gotta go.

TONY TUZZO

Best you not say nothin' to no one till we know what the score is.

MYER BLOOM

We'll get to the bottom of this, Valentine.

We always do.

TONY TUZZO

We always do.

8–Valentine is most of the silhouette foreground. Walking away from them. All we can see past him is Jagger hugging herself.

PAGE 36-37

Double-page spread

1–Ext. Brooklyn street

Valentine, lost in dark thought and despair, walks through the streets of Brooklyn. Colorful and alive. These people feel protected. These people are very used to a very specific way of life.

The families have protected this area for so long that they don't know any other way of life.

2–Valentine comes to the steps of his mother's nice brownstone. She's dressed smart and already at the door atop the small staircase.

MADONNA

What the hell happened to your head?

3–Valentine has climbed the steps. She is looking at his bandage and isn't happy.

VALENTINE

Nothin'.

MADONNA

My ass.

VALENTINE

It's nothing.

MADONNA

A made guy three days and already someone bashed your fucking head in.

VALENTINE

Ma.

MADONNA

Get in here.

4–Int. Mom's brownstone

Inside her very average, very well-kept apartment. Not exactly an old-school Italian apartment...something more modern.

A classy, smart, modern woman who has had the place herself for a while. She is doing something nice with it. We imagine that Valentine has made sure that she hasn't ever needed money.

She is walking him toward us.

VALENTINE

What was so important?

MADONNA

I want you to keep an open mind.

I want you to keep your mouth shut.

VALENTINE

What?

MADONNA

I'm serious.

I will never be more serious.

5–Int. Basement steps

They are walking into the basement. Bending not to bang his head. One single lightbulb behind them.

VALENTINE

You want me to move something?

6–Madonna goes to the back wall of typical, cluttered basement shelves. She is reaching into them.

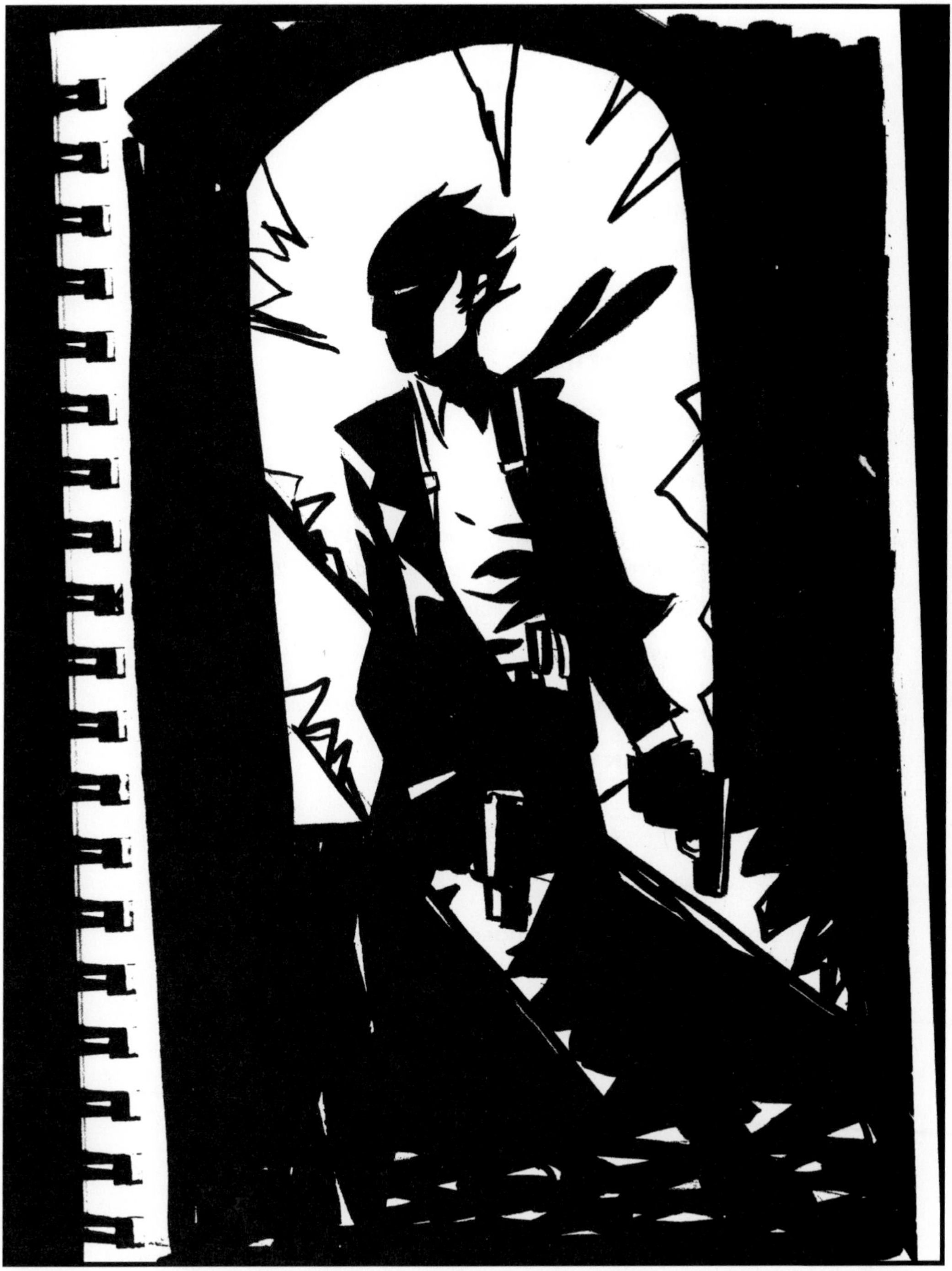

7—*Valentine squints. What is this?*

8—*Madonna has grabbed the hidden clasp on the back wall.*

9—*She pulls the clasp and reveals that the shelf wall is actually a door that opens. It reveals itself to be a door.*

10—*A door to another room that Valentine, although he's lived here his entire life, did not know was there.*

VALENTINE (CONT'D)

Since when is this a door?

I lived in this house eighteen years…

MADONNA

It was your father's panic room.

A safe room. In case something happened.

11—*Before they go inside, the light coming from inside the mystery room, she turns around and says to him.*

VALENTINE

Ma, you're freakin' me out.

MADONNA

I would never put you in this position if I didn't think you were ready.

And I meant what I said: listen. Don't talk.

Do you trust me?

12—*Same but tighter. He has no idea what is going on. She wants his full attention.*

VALENTINE

What—the—fuck, Ma?

MADONNA

Don't make me slap those terrible words out of your mouth.

VALENTINE

Seriously, what is going on?

13—*Over Valentine's shoulder she gives him one last look as she is about to open the door.*

PAGE 38

1—*Big panel. She opens the door and a handsome man and woman in cheap suits with coffee are just standing to greet him. Clearly they are FBI. Their names are AGENT GLASS and AGENT BELL.*

It is a very well-lit, clean, white room. With a table and a couple of chairs. And some coffee. That is it.

In the corner we can see there is a monitor that may have been hooked up to some kind of panic room system that has long been outdated.

AGENT GLASS

Valentine Gallo, it is a pleasure to meet you.

2–Valentine cautiously enters the room at his mother's gesture as she closes the door. There is something very odd and alien about this white, well-lit, clean room.

VALENTINE

The fuck is this?

Do you live in this room?

AGENT GLASS

This is a place where we can talk and be sure that no one is listening.

VALENTINE

Who would be listening in our kitchen?

3–Valentine looks at his mom and can't for the life of him figure out what this is about. She is trying to keep him calm but with a mother's stern strong demeanor.

MADONNA

Did I say just sit down and listen?

I said to sit down and listen!

VALENTINE

I'll sit down when you tell me what the hell this is.

4–Over Valentine's shoulder, the agents both know that what they are saying are words that have never been spoken aloud. And once they are said out loud...they can never be taken back.

AGENT GLASS

We're federal agents, Mr. Gallo.

AGENT BELL

From outside the territories.

AGENT GLASS

Obviously.

5–Valentine looks at his mother like she is announcing she is an alien from outer space.

MADONNA

And so am I.

1–The agents lean in and don't give him a second to digest that whopper.

AGENT BELL

The families have had their run of things on the East Coast for so many years...

I'm not sure you even know there was a time when what they do was considered illegal.

2–Valentine steps back without even realizing he's doing it as the agents and his mother talk amongst themselves. His back is almost to the closed door.

MADONNA

He's not stupid.

AGENT BELL

It's just people his age—

MADONNA

How old are YOU?

This is the way it's been since before ALL OF US was born...shut the fuck up.

VALENTINE

Ma?

3–Over Valentine's shoulder, his mother sits down and we can feel like a huge weight is being lifted off of her as she says these words she has been dying to say to him for so many years.

MADONNA

This isn't how it's supposed to be, Val.

Ok?

The families, the territories...

They—it ain't right.

VALENTINE

It's—it's the way it is.

MADONNA

But that don't make it right.

4–Valentine is appropriately frustrated.

VALENTINE

What the fuck are you talking about??!!

You just went to my ceremony!! I'm sworn in by blood!!

5—Madonna looks right at him and says her ultimate truth.

MADONNA

And you were BORN an undercover federal agent.

6—Slightly low looking up, Valentine knows that his mother is not joking.

PAGE 40

1—Over Valentine's shoulder, she is looking right at him and telling him how it is.

MADONNA (CONT'D)

I birthed you into this world for this purpose.

No outsider could ever infiltrate the families.

It had to be blood.

It had to be one of us.

2—Same but tighter. She explains it as clearly as she can.

MADONNA (CONT'D)

They killed your father and your father's father.

They killed them, Val.

No one pays. No one goes to jail.

They just get richer and richer.

So I BIRTHED you into this.

3—Valentine is open mouthed shocked. This is fucking real??

MADONNA (CONT'D)

All the while praying that this day would never need to come.

That somehow the world would right itself.

But that day never came.

And here we are.

4—Madonna looks at him and says it with complete confidence

MADONNA (CONT'D)

You're going to pull this all apart, Val.

All of it.

Every single brick. From the inside.

And they'll never even see it coming.

5—The agents are very excited but trying to keep their composure.

AGENT BELL

Do you know what the families did to take control
of this part of the country?

AGENT GLASS

Does he know who his great-grandfather was?

6—Madonna stops talking. She looks right at her son. She means business. But this secret will floor him.

MADONNA

No.

7—Valentine looks back at her. He is scared to ask??

PAGE 41

Full-page spread

Ext. The East Coast—sunset

The sun sets across the eastern seaboard.

The sun sets across The United States of Murder Incorporated.

Small white typewriter text across the middle of the spread reads: The United States of Murder Incorporated.

TO BE CONTINUED